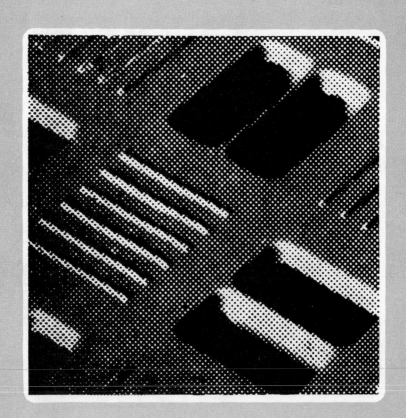

Multivariate Analysis in Marketing
SECOND EDITION

David A. Aaker, UNIVERSITY OF CALIFORNIA AT BERKELEY

The Scientific Press, 670 GILMAN STREET, PALO ALTO, CA 94301, (415) 322 - 5221

MULTIVARIATE ANALYSIS
IN MARKETING
2nd edition
David A. Aaker

Copyright © 1981 by The Scientific Press

Published by The Scientific Press

ISBN 0-89426-029-4

Cover design and illustrations by Rogondino & Associates
Typography by The Scientific Press
Printed in the USA.

Debra Jones Ringold

To my parents

Preface

This book is intended as a supplementary text for a market research course, a marketing models course, or a second statistics course. The objective is to introduce and illustrate the use of multivariate analysis techniques and to provide some understanding of their limitations as well as their power. The only background assumed is that of a first course in statistics. The book is also designed for the professional researcher who wants to update and expand his or her knowledge or to review these techniques in a systematic manner.

The book follows the outline and thrust of its predecessor volume (published in 1971 by Wadsworth Publishing Company). Of course, much has happened in multivariate analysis since 1971 and these advances are reflected in this book. An overview of the book is presented in the introduction which follows.

Each of the selections is followed by a set of discussion questions and is designed to test the reader's understanding and ability to apply concepts. These discussion questions should make the book richer and more useful.

I owe a great debt of gratitude to the many marketing researchers and practitioners who have over the years pioneered in the use of multivariate analysis is marketing, especially those whose work is represented in this volume. In this spirit a special acknowledgment is due to Paul E. Green, whose energy, competence and imagination continue to spark the development and application of multivariate analysis in marketing. I would like to thank Paul Kelly and his publishing company, The Scientific Press, who have developed the unique capability to publish specialized books for our discipline quickly and economically.

David A. Aaker

About the Author

David A. Aaker, a Professor in the School of Business Administration at the University of California at Berkeley, received a B.S. degree at MIT and M.S. and Ph.D. degrees at Stanford. He has authored or co-authored seven books including *Marketing Research* (with George S. Day; Wiley), *Advertising Management* (with John G. Myers; Prentice-Hall) and *Consumerism* (with George S. Day; The Free Press) and numerous articles on multivariate analysis, advertising decision making, R & D management, data analysis, consumerism and planning. He is an editorial review board member of *Management Science* and *Journal of Marketing* and an Advisory Editor of John Wiley. An active consultant, speaker and researcher in both the United States and Japan, he was named one of the top thirty thought leaders in marketing.

Contents

PART 2: THE ANALYSIS OF INTERDEPENDENCE

Multivariate Analysis in Marketing

David A. Aaker

Only two decades ago the use of multivariate methods in marketing was something of a novelty. During the intervening years enormous progress has been made in the application and acceptance of these tools. Some of the early techniques like factor analysis, regression analysis, and the experimental design models are now used routinely by researchers and practitioners. Others, such as cluster analysis, AID, and discriminant analysis, are proving to be extremely helpful in the right context. More recently, we have seen the dramatic introduction, dissemination, and use of multidimensional scaling and conjoint analysis (or trade-off analysis). Clearly, the length of introductory and growth stage of multivariate techniques has been extremely short. Additional approaches are now being introduced, many of which build on existing ones and show considerable potential. One of the new growth areas for marketing may be in the area of simultaneous equations, where the consideration of recursive systems and the use of unobservable variables both seem very promising.

There are several reasons why multivariate analysis has made the impact that it has. First, schools of business and management have for some time been training undergraduate, MBA and Ph.D. students in the use of quantitative methods in general and in statistics in particular. Thus, there are now many people who are capable of advancing the field by pioneering new applications rather than the handful who existed in the 1960s. Further, a considerable number of organizations now have operating managers who are knowledgeable about and comfortable with multivariate analysis, rather than just a few staff specialists.

A second reason is that there simply are important marketing problems that are inherently multidimensional and which therefore lend themselves naturally to multivariate analysis — problems such as segmentation, positioning, and the refinement of new products and services.

A third reason is the continuing development of the power and flexibility of the computer. Analysis is now feasible that would have been prohibitively expensive only a few years ago and would not even have been possible two decades ago. Further, the interactive capability of the computer has had a dramatic impact upon data collection and analysis, and this is still evolving.

A fourth reason is the need to manage, interpret, and use the great masses of data that have emerged, partly because of computer capabilities and partly because of the growing need for information to support decisions being made in dynamic and uncertain environments.

A fifth reason is the theoretical development of models and algorithms that have come out of mathematics, statistics, econometrics, psychology, sociology, and elsewhere. These theoretical advances have served to both create and improve techniques.

Multivariate analysis can naturally be divided into two areas: the analysis of dependence and the analysis of interdependence. In the former, a variable or group of variables is the focus of the analysis. This variable(s) is called the dependent variable and is explained or predicted by the remaining ones, which are termed independent or explanatory variables. The analysis of dependence is usually oriented toward prediction or toward gaining an understanding of the relationship between the dependent variable(s) and the independent variables. In contrast, in the analysis of interdependence there is no one variable or variable subset that is the focus of study that differs in importance from the others. A variable or set of variables is not to be predicted from the others or explained by them. The goal, rather, is to give meaning to a set of variables or objects.

The Analysis of Dependence

The analysis of dependence is concerned either with prediction or with gaining understanding. When prediction is the objective, the dependent variable(s) is to be predicted, given a set of specific values for the independent variables. For example, a model might be desired that would predict sales, given expenditures on advertising, promotion, and direct sales (field salesmen). Such a model might form the basis for conditional sales forecasts — those conditional on marketing inputs. Nearly all management decisions depend upon accurate forecasts of key variables. Of course, if the market environment changes, the analyst must determine if model assumptions have been affected and modifications are needed.

In structural analysis, information is obtained from a knowledge of functional forms and parameter values. For example, we might identify diminishing returns to advertising by determining the relationship of advertising to sales. By studying the parameter values, the variables that are the most effective in predicting the dependent variable might be identified. If promotion seems unrelated to sales, whereas advertising is a significant explanatory variable, the market mix might deserve scrutiny. The objective is to gain understanding of the process being modeled — to test theoretical and conceptual hypotheses. Structural questions often imply a cause-effect relationship. As in correlation analysis, however, any causal judgments must be made very cautiously, for a statistical relationship — even though quite real with respect to a data set — can often have more than one causal explanation.

The different methods that constitute the analysis of dependence can be categorized by the number of dependent variables, the number of equations or relationships, and whether a nominal scale is involved. In a nominal scale,

the numbers merely label or identify objects. The number on a football jersey is an example. One type of nominal variable frequently encountered in the analysis of dependence is the 0-1 binary variable, sometimes called a dummy variable. Suppose we wanted to identify a market group. Those families who are heavy users of a product could be assigned a "1" and all other families a zero. Such a variable could be either a dependent variable or an independent variable.

Figure 1 serves to structure and organize the various multivariate techniques covered in this book. The analysis of dependence techniques are first separated into those which involve only one dependent variable and those involving more than one. They are then again divided on the basis of whether or not the dependent variable is nominally scaled.

In regression analysis, perhaps the most commonly used dependence analysis technique, it is assumed that the single dependent variable and the independent variables are not nominally scaled. This assumption is violated upon occasion, as we shall see, but it still serves to position regression analysis in the structure of Figure 1. Three techniques differ from regression analysis in that the independent variables are assumed to be nominally scaled: AID, conjoint analysis, and experimental design models. AID is an exploratory research tool that attempts to generate groups or segments that differ as much as possible with respect to the dependent variable. Conjoint analysis or

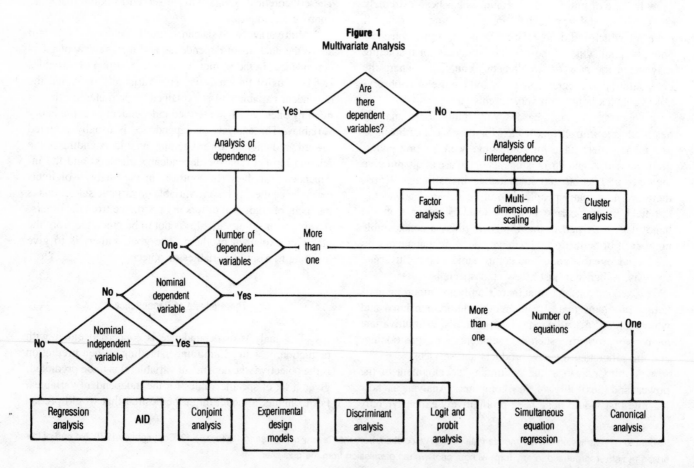

Figure 1
Multivariate Analysis

trade-off analysis involves respondents' making trade-off judgments between product or service features, such as a trade-off between gas mileage and roominess in an automobile-choice situation. In an experimental design model, the independent variable specifies the experimental treatment, such as a high level of advertising or a low level of advertising. When the single dependent variable is nominally scaled, the appropriate techniques are discriminant analysis or logit or probit analysis.

There can be more than one dependent variable involved. In canonical analysis, there is more than one dependent variable but only one equation. In simultaneous equation regression, an equation or model usually appears for each of the dependent variables. The interest, then, is often in the relationship between the dependent variables as well as the relationship between the dependent variables and the independent variables.

The Analysis of Interdependence

As Figure 1 indicates, the analysis of interdependence involves three techniques: factor analysis, multidimensional scaling, and cluster analysis. These techniques are termed the analysis of interdependence techniques because they analyze the interdependence between questions, variables, or objects. The goal is to generate understanding of the underlying structure of questions, variables, or objects and to combine them into new variables. These three techniques can be positioned by the following simple example.

Suppose that we are interested in determining how prospective students select universities. The first step might be to determine how institutions are perceived and evaluated by prospective students. To generate relevant questions, students might be asked to talk informally about schools. More particularly, the students could be asked why one school is preferred or why two are regarded as similar.

The result could be a hundred or more terms such as large, good faculty, expensive, good climate, demanding, bewildering, kind of facilities, athletic programs, social aspects, impersonal, etc. A second step might be to ask a group of prospective students to evaluate the importance to them of each of these attributes. At this point the analysis can get bogged down simply because there are too many attributes or variables. Further, many of these attributes are redundant, really measuring the same construct. To determine which are redundant and what they are measuring, the analyst can turn to factor analysis. One result will be a set of new variables (or factors) created by combining sets of school attributes.

In another phase of the study, groups of students could be identified according to what they are looking for in a college. We might hypothesize that one group is concerned about individual attention; another, low cost; another, proximity to home; and still another, quality education. If such groups exist and can be identified, then it may be possible to isolate several, describe them, and develop a communication program tailored to their interests that would be directed at them. Cluster analysis can be used to identify such groupings. Cluster analysis is used to identify people, objects, or variables that form natural groupings or clusters. A new variable is defined by cluster membership.

Later in the study it might be useful to determine how schools are perceived — which are perceived as similar and which are considered different. Is Stanford more like the University of California at Berkeley because of location and educational quality, or is Stanford perceived as being more similar to Harvard or MIT, two private schools? The general problem of positioning objects such as universities in an interpretable, multidimensional space is termed multidimensional scaling (MDS). The resulting locations or positions upon the relevant perceptual dimensions serve to define new variables.

Part 1

The Analysis of Dependence

Section A
REGRESSION ANALYSIS

2
Sales Effects
of Promotion and Advertising

Don Sunoo

Lynn Y. S. Lin

The advertising industry in general and advertisers in particular have been plagued perennially by the question of measuring the sales effects of promotion and advertising as they have grappled with problems of how to invest advertising dollars for maximum return in product sales. During the past several years, however, management and research professionals in the marketing field have come to a mature understanding of theoretical and practical issues underlying the question. Also, they have reached a high level of sophistication in methods and techniques for testing and measuring the effectiveness of different marketing variables on product sales.

The purpose of this paper is to report on a case study of the use of a standard empirical tool to determine the effect on product sales of two different marketing variables and their interaction when used simultaneously. The particular strategies and their interaction under scrutiny were television advertising and consumer promotion.

This report is based on a research program conducted by a major manufacturer for one of its leading consumer product lines. The product is a frequently used, mature product with a national distribution. It has a healthy market-share position in a declining market for the product category, and it competes with several major brands. The brand has a history of moderate advertising support and of heavy consumer-promotion support. In an annual marketing-strategy meeting, several questions concerning advertising spending were raised. Some of them were: What is the effect of the current advertising spending on sales of the product? What is the effect of current consumer promotion spending on sales of the product? Do advertising and consumer promotion interact to produce an effect on sales?

Data Collection and Analysis

The analyses and discussion presented in this paper are based on data obtained from the ensuing research program, conducted on behalf of the manufacturer, which utilized a field-experiment method made possible by access to a dual-system CATV service. The principle underlying this approach to measuring response to television advertising corresponds to the split-run approach to measuring response to print advertising. CATV-subscribing homes in a single test city are wired to either half of the dual-system distribution cables — panel A and panel B homes. All variables (weather, product distribution, competitive advertising, trade and consumer promotions, etc.) except those being studied were identical for both panels. The two panels, of about 1,000 homes each, were matched on demographics, TV viewing habits, and buying habits for the product category. Panel homes were asked to keep a weekly consumer diary for food, drug, and other purchases. This consumer diary became the major source of data for the analysis of the effect on product sales of television advertising, consumer promotion, and a combination of the two.

In the study, the panel A homes received no advertising exposure to the product while the panel B homes received advertising exposures for a total of 18 four-week periods. A standard multiple regression analysis was applied to the collected data, using sales volume (product purchases) as the dependent variable. The following variables were treated as predictor variables:

X_1 is advertising, presence or absence of advertising exposure. Dummy variable (1 or 0) was applied.

X_2 is consumer promotion, presence or absence of consumer-promotion activities. Dummy variable was applied.

X_3 is an interaction term for X_1 and X_2 (advertising/consumer promotion).

X_4 is a seasonality index based on seasonal sales fluctuations of the product.

X_5 is home panel, A or B; dummy variable was assigned (A = 0, B = 1).

Input data were arranged for each four-week period for both A and B panels. Thus, a total of 36 observations were obtained for each variable. The results of the regression analysis and related data are displayed in Table 1.

Table 1
Results of Multiple Regression

	Regression Coefficients	T Value	Input Means	Correlation Coefficients with Dependent Variable
Dependent Variable* (Sales Volume)	—	—	6.561	—
X_1 (Advertising)	.477	1.71	.388	.33
X_2 (Promotion)	2.928	8.19	1.056	.82
X_3 (Advertising/Promotion)	.593	2.74	.222	.53
X_4 (Seasonal Index)	6.868	3.32	1.000	.61
X_5 (Panel)	−.101	−.27	.500	.01

Constant = −3.665
R^2 = .84

*Sales volume was expressed in terms of average unit purchased per reporting home per four-week period.

With the regression equation solved, the next step was to find the net effect of each of the marketing variables under consideration. This required two phases of computation. The first phase was a 2×2 contingency-type table designed to classify the four different effects (see Table 2):

Table 2

Promotion	Advertising	
	Yes	No
Yes	type 1	type 2
No	type 3	type 4

type 1: gross sales with both advertising and promotion.
type 2: gross sales with promotion only (no advertising).
type 3: gross sales with advertising only (no promotion).
type 4: gross sales with neither advertising nor promotion — i.e., base business.

The second phase of computation was to obtain the net effect of the three variables. This was done as follows:

type 1 − type 4 = net effect of advertising and promotion;
type 2 − type 4 = net effect of promotion only;
type 3 − type 4 = net effect of advertising only;
(type 1 − type 4) − (type 2 − type 4) − (type 3 − type 4) = net effect of interaction of advertising and promotion.

Computational results of the above are displayed in Table 3.

Findings and Discussion

Some key findings obtained from these analyses are:

(1) Consumer promotion was the most important factor affecting product sales. About 80 per cent of the total net effect on sales was accounted for by the consumer promotion variable alone.
(2) The net effect of advertising was a substantial factor, although its magnitude relative to consumer promotion was small — a ratio of 1:6. Only 13 per cent of the total net effect was accounted for by the television advertising variable alone.
(3) Interaction between television advertising and consumer promotion was a minor effect (8 per cent). Television advertising seemed to enhance consumer promotion *or* consumer promotion to enhance television advertising.
(4) The contribution of the three variables (television advertising alone, consumer promotion alone, and advertising/promotion interaction)

Table 3
Results of Computations for Net Effects

Computation for Gross Effects	Sales Unit (Indexed)	
Type 1: Effect of Both Advertising and Promotion	162	
Type 2: Effect of Promotion Only	149	
Type 3: Effect of Advertising Only	108	
Type 4: Base Business (without Advertising and Promotion)	100	

Computation for Net Effects		Per Cent
Net Effect of Advertising Only: (108 − 100)	8	13
Net Effect of Promotion Only: (149 − 100)	49	79
Net Effect of Advertising/Promotion Interaction: (162 − 100) − (149 − 100) − (108 − 100)	5	8
Net Effect of Both Advertising and Promotion: (162 − 100)	62	100

Recap: Average Sales Unit for Reporting Homes for Four-Week Period

Base Business	100	62
Incremental Sales Due to Advertising Support	8	5
Incremental Sales Due to Promotional Support	49	30
Incremental Sales Due to Advertising/Promotion Interaction	5	3
Total	162	100

accounted for 38 percent of the total product sales, or the product would be expected to maintain as its base business 62 percent of the total product sales achieved — with neither television advertising nor consumer promotion support (this base business would mean a hypothetical withdrawal of advertising and promotion for a short term).

In addition, sales fluctuation of the product by season was computed by utilizing regression equations with the seasonality variable. Figure 1, the graphic presentation of sales levels at each time point, illustrates the magnitude of product sales as a function of base business and the marketing variables with the seasonal pattern.

These findings and results are based on a particular product (brand) in a given time period for a mature product category and its life-cycle stage. In such a context, the findings, especially the magnitude of product sales attributable to each marketing variable, are unique to the brand under study. The

Figure 1
Seasonal Sales Levels as a Function of
Base Business and Marketing Variables

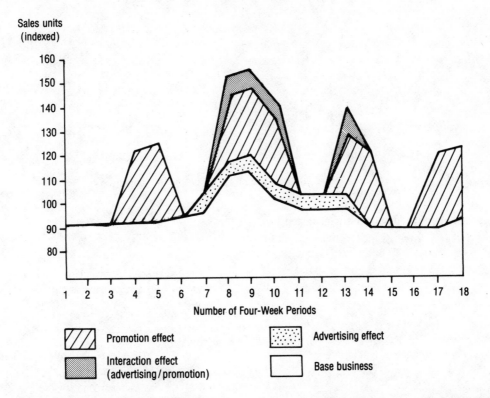

method, however, should have general applicability to other products, other marketing strategies, and most market conditions. The promotion effect accounting for such a large proportion of the total net effect on product sales is plausible for a brand that has been in the market for many years with strong consumer promotion support and moderate advertising support. This finding is viewed as evidence of the applicability of the method.

The findings of this research program, needless to say, provided the product management with useful quantitative guidelines for their understanding and decision making regarding their advertising/promotion investment. Research identified a base business level and defined the relationship between product sales and marketing strategies. This case study demonstrates the efficacy of the regression-analysis application to the solution of such problems in marketing practice.

For Discussion

Consider Table 1. Interpret the regression coefficients. Exactly what does each of them mean? Which independent variable is the most influential? How do the regression coefficient differ in interpretation from the correlation coefficients? Note that dummy variables are used for all the independent variables except X_4. Interpret Table 3 and Figure 1.

Sales Response as a Function of Territorial Potential and Sales Representative Workload

Henry C. Lucas, Jr.
Charles B. Weinberg
Kenneth W. Clowes

Sales management has the responsibility of evaluating sales territories and the sales force. One important step in this evaluation process is to identify variables associated with sales. Although past research has suggested the importance of territory characteristics and workload as predictors of sales [1, 2, 10], the sample sizes have been small and the methodology, in at least one case, questionable. This article presents the results of a study of sales response as a function of potential and workload in a situation offering much better data than have been available in the past.

Review of Problem. The underlying research problem is to study the relationship between sales achieved by a salesperson and variables like territory potential and sales representative workload. Of course, these are not the only variables which are useful in estimating sales results in a territory; such characteristics as type of customers, strength of competition, and company reputation as well as the salesperson's own abilities and experience can be important. However, potential and workload are expected to be the most significant variables related to sales and, for most companies, are the easiest to measure.

Formally, the relationship between sales, potential, and workload to be examined is:

$$(1) \qquad S_i = f(P_i, W_i, X_{1i}, \ldots, X_{ki})$$

where:

$$S_i = \text{sales in territory } i,$$
$$P_i = \text{potential in territory } i,$$
$$W_i = \text{workload in territory } i, \text{ and}$$
$$X_{1i}, X_{2i}, \ldots, X_{ki} = k \text{ other factors pertaining to territory } i \text{ or salesman } i.$$

Past Research. Despite the fact that personal selling expenditures exceed advertising expenditures by a considerable amount, a search of the literature for the past 15 years found only 3 published studies which related data on territory characteristics to sales [2, 6, 10]. Similarly, very few analytic approaches have been published for resolving sales force allocation problems. Some notable approaches are a method for designing sales territories [5], procedures for allocating sales representatives over customers [7] and products [9], and several articles dealing with sales force compensation [3, 4, 12].

Although Semlow's study [10] is widely quoted, Weinberg and Lucas [11] have shown that Semlow's results are based on a spurious relationship. The major problem with [10] is that the independent or predictor variable, P_i, appears in the denominator of the dependent or criterion variable, S_i/P_i.

The study reported in [1, 2] is an attempt to find a linear or nonlinear relationship between a salesman's sales and eight independent variables, including market potential and number of accounts a salesman calls on. Unfortunately only 25 observations were available so that the ratio of variables to observations is too high for the results to be meaningful. The third published study [6] is not directly relevant here because sales are measured not by salesman, but by sales districts which contain up to eight salesmen. (The results show that sales volume is closely related to number of salesmen in a district.)

In summary, the problem of relating salesperson performance to territory characteristics, notably potential and workload, has been little studied despite its importance. The studies which have been reported are based on small samples and, in at least one case, are methodologically questionable.

Research Design

Introduction. The study reported in this article was conducted in one division of a major national ready-to-wear apparel company.[1] Equations relating sales by salesperson to the independent variables of territorial potential, salesperson's workload, and account quality were estimated. It was hypothesized that sales are positively related to potential and account quality and negatively related to workload measures. High potential and high quality accounts mean that the sales representative has greater opportunity and should have higher sales. A high workload on the other hand means that a salesperson either has to call on more customers or spend more time traveling, so lower sales are expected.

Definition of Variables. The variables in the present study are shown in Table 1. The *sales* variable is bookings by the sales representative during the 1972 selling season, a figure obtained from company computer records. *Potential* is usually defined as the capacity of a market to absorb a product over a given time period. There are a number of possible ways to measure potential, though actual industry sales are most frequently used as an approximation to market potential [2].

The company studied here had recently acquired a set of data which included sales of retail clothing by sex and age grouping for each county in the continental United States. Potential in the study is taken from these data and is defined to be the total retail sales of clothing to men and boys by county for the United States in 1972. When there was more than one salesperson for the company in the county, each salesperson was assigned the percentage of potential in that county represented by his or her percentage of company sales in the county.[2] This potential measure is probably the best one available to this company. These potential data were *not* available when the sales representatives were assigned to territories.

Account quality is a difficult variable to measure. In this study, company history indicated that the number of buying entities is a good indicator of account quality [8]. A buying entity is the lowest level that can place an order, for example, the sportswear section of the men's department. Better accounts tend to have more buying entities; for any given account, very little added time or effort is involved in selling to multiple buying entities. Thus, it is expected that the number of buying entities will be positively related to sales representative workload.

---

[1] The company desires to remain anonymous and certain details have been disguised to maintain confidentiality.

[2] Other methods for assigning potential to sales representatives were considered when there was more than one person in a county. For example, those counties could have been ommitted but in this case salespersons would have to be represented by fractions. The approach described in the text was chosen since it results in "many sales representaives." The effect of this procedure on the results reported is minor.

Table 1
Variables in the Study

Symbol	Variable Name	Description
S_i	Sales	Bookings by salesperson during 1972 season
P_i	Potential	Total men's and boy's retail sales in 1972 in salesperson's territory apportioned according to percentage of sales in the county
Q_i	Number of buying entities	Number of locations (e.g., sportswear section of men's department) capable of placing an order
W_{1i}	Number of counties	Number of counties in which salesperson has accounts
W_{2i}	Number of accounts	Number of accounts in salesperson's territory

An ideal workload measure should reflect differences among territories like the number of customers who must be seen, the difficulty of making the sale, travel, and overhead items like reporting, or trip planning. In this study, there are two workload measures, number of counties and number of accounts, and both are expected to be negatively related to sales. The number of counties reflects aspects of the workload such as travel time and trip planning. A large number of accounts in this company also indicated a high workload because there are more clients to see.

National and Regional Sales. Historically, the company's first marketing efforts were on the East Coast and gradually spread across the country. It was recognized within the company that there were regional variations in sales. Hence, it was decided to analyze the data on a regional as well as a national basis. The regions — named East, Central, and West — were based on historical analysis of the company's marketing program and natural geographic boundaries. In Table 2, selected characteristics of each territory are presented. These data show that the company is strongest in terms of average sales per salesperson in the East and weakest in the West. The mean and standard deviation of potential, number of counties, number of accounts, and number of buying entities all increase as one goes from East to Central to West.

Models. Two multivariate models were postulated — a linear model and a multiplicative power function:

$$S_i = a_{11} + b_{11}P_i + b_{12}Q_i + b_{13}W_{1i} + b_{14}W_{2i} \qquad (2)$$

$$S_i = a_{21} P_i{}^{b_{21}} Q_i^{b_{22}} W_{1i}^{b_{23}} W_{2i}^{b_{24}}. \qquad (3)$$

The variables are those defined in Table 1 (the first subscript of the coefficients in (2) and (3) distinguishes the linear model from the power function). Equation (3) was chosen to present a model of decreasing returns to scale for increased potential and account quality and decreased workload. This multiplicative form allows for interaction effects and the coefficients can be interpreted as elasticities.

Analysis. In order to provide the strongest evidence for the validity of the results, especially because of the methodological problems of past studies, the sample of 248 observa-

Table 2
Territory Characteristics

	Characteristics	East	Central	West
n	Number of salespersons	83	65	100
$\bar{S}_i$	Average sales (000)	745(265)[a]	680(270)	650(325)
$\bar{P}_i$	Average potential (000)	15,900(8200)	27,700(19,700)	61,000(37,800)
$\bar{Q}_i$	Average number of buying entities	240(80)	345(100)	355(135)
$\bar{W}_{1i}$	Average number of counties	9(6)	19(10)	20(14)
$\bar{W}_{2i}$	Average number of accounts	50(25)	62(25)	69(35)

[a] Numbers in parentheses are standard deviations.

tions was divided in half to provide 2 random samples, 1 for estimation and 1 for validation.[3] All equations were first developed using the estimation sample, and the coefficients from the estimation sample were used to predict sales for the validation sample. The R^2 for the validation sample is the square of the Pearson correlation coefficient between these predicted values and the actual sales in the validation sample.

Stepwise multiple regression was used to develop the equations; sales is the dependent or criterion variable and the other variables in Table 1 are predictors of sales. The stepwise algorithm was terminated when an incoming independent variable would no longer be significant at the .05 level with a two-tailed test of significance.

For the curvilinear model (3) a log transformation was used, that is (3) was estimated using (4):

$$(4) \quad \ln S_i = \ln a_{21} + b_{21} \ln P_i + b_{22} \ln Q_i + b_{23} \ln W_{1i}$$
$$+ b_{24} \ln W_{2i}.$$

The R^2 for the curvilinear equation was computed by transforming (4) back into (3). That is, the coefficients of (4) were estimated giving a predicted $\ln S_i$. Antilogs were taken and the predicted sales were correlated with observed sales to yield R^2. Finally, all estimation sample R^2 values for the linear and curvilinear models were adjusted for the appropriate degrees of freedom.

In addition, structural tests were constructed. For (2), coefficients b_{11} and b_{12} should be nonnegative to indicate that increased potential and account quality are associated with increased sales and similarly the workload coefficients b_{13} and b_{14} should be nonpositive. For (3) a similar line of reasoning plus the fact that the logical result is decreasing returns to scale leads to the following anticipated results:

$$(5) \qquad 1 > b_{21} \geqq 0$$
$$1 > b_{22} \geqq 0$$
$$0 \geqq b_{23} > -1$$
$$0 \geqq b_{24} > -1.$$

A linear and curvilinear regression analysis was run for the national sample and for each of the three regions. In total, eight regressions were run on the analysis sample.

Collinearity Analysis. Before presenting the regression results, it is helpful to examine the relationship among the predictor variables for the presence and interpretation of collinearity. In this study, there were two variables which were proxy measures of workload and two variables, potential and number of buying entities, which represent the quality of a sales representative's territory. Some interrelationships among these variables are anticipated. The expectation is that the workload proxies will be related to each other and will be

Table 3
Collinearity Analysis: Simple Correlation Matrix

	Potential	Number of Buying Entities	Number of Counties
National ($n = 129$)[a]			
Number of buying entities	.52[e]		
Number of counties	.28[e]	.64[e]	
Number of accounts	.16	.59[e]	.48[e]
East ($n = 39$)[b]			
Number of buying entities	−.11		
Number of counties	−.22	.71[e]	
Number of accounts	−.29	.75[e]	.61[e]
Central ($n = 33$)[c]			
Number of buying entities	.32		
Number of counties	.32	.38[f]	
Number of accounts	−.27	.30	.20
West ($n = 57$)[d]			
Number of buying entities	.54[e]		
Number of counties	.11	.58[e]	
Number of accounts	.09	.58[e]	.46[e]

[a] Significant Regression Variables:
    Linear: Potential, Counties
    Curvilinear: Accounts, Potential.
[b] Significant Regression Variables:
    Linear: Potential
    Curvilinear: Potential.
[c] Significant Regression Variables:
    Linear: Potential, Buying Entities, Counties
    Curvilinear: Potential, Buying Entities, Counties.
[d] Significant Regression Variables:
    Linear: Potential, Counties
    Curvilinear: Potential, Accounts.
[e] Significant at .01 level, t value varies according to sample size.
[f] Significant at .05 level, t value varies according to sample size.

---

[3] Over 100,000 records of data were summarized to develop the appropriate information for each salesperson. During this processing, several checks were included to insure that the data were complete and accurate. For example, the number of counties in which the sales representative had accounts was compared from two different sources.

statistically independent of the other two variables. Because the variables potential and number of buying entities represent different aspects of quality of a sales representative's territory, the expectation is that they will be independent of each other as well as of the workload variables. In order to examine the interrelationships among the predictor variables, simple correlation matrices (see Table 3) were calculated for the national sample and for each of the three regions.

On a national basis, the data are highly collinear. As shown in Table 3, five of the six possible correlations are positive and significant statistically. These correlations suggest that the national multiple regression analysis results may not be meaningful. Table 2 shows that the means of all four predictor variables increase uniformly from East to West. This reflects different conditions and marketing actions in each of the regions and dominates the expected relationships among the predictor variables themselves. A similar pattern of collinearity does not hold when the analysis is done on a regional basis.

In two out of the three regions, the expected relationships between the two workload variables were found and in the third there was no significant relationship. As discussed below, when used with the stepwise regression procedure, at most one of these two variables entered the regression significantly and at all times with the expected negative sign. This suggests that the two variables number of accounts and number of counties were successful proxies for the workload. Alternative ways of using these two variables as proxies would have been to select arbitrarily one of them as the only variable to use or to construct a new variable which was a linear combination of the other two variables. Neither of these approaches appeared to have any substantial advantage in this application and would have introduced additional arbitrariness into the analysis.

Examination of Table 3 shows that potential is not significantly correlated with either of the workload variables in any of the regions and only once with number of buying entities. This supports the distinction between the potential and workload variables and also the distinction between potential and number of buying entities.

The results for the variable number of buying entities are not as encouraging. In almost all cases, number of buying entities is significantly and positively correlated with the workload measures so that it is doubtful whether number of buying entities, in fact, served as a measure of account quality. Fortunately, this variable entered the stepwise regressions in only one region, the Central, and it was in that region that the least collinearity was manifested.

Overall, the collinearity analysis suggests that the predictor variables represent two major kinds of effects, territorial potential and workload. These effects are distinguishable from each other and, as shown in the next section, are related to sales in a territory.

Results

For the national sample results in Table 4 and the regional subsample results in Table 5,[4] all of the predicted structural conditions are met. Potential and account quality have positive coefficients in the equations, while workload measures have coefficients which are less than zero. For the curvilinear model, the exponent parameters have an absolute value between 0 and 1 indicating decreasing returns to scale as predicted by the relations in (5). In all cases except for the curvilinear model run on the national data, potential is the first variable to enter and has the highest beta weight on the independent variables. In the national curvilinear model, potential was the second variable to enter.

It is interesting to note that there is little difference for the results between the linear and curvilinear models. In the East and Central regions, all of the variables in the linear and curvilinear equations are the same and all entered in the same order. In the West and national analyses, the two workload measures interchange: number of counties is in the linear model and number of accounts in the curvilinear model. The linear and curvilinear forms are probably similar, because for the range of the data, the shape of the sales response curve is close to linear.

The F-values are significant at the .01 level in all cases. The values of the adjusted R^2 are good considering the variables which were not included in the equations such as the strength of competition, transportation available, local fashion and taste variables, and the skill of salesman.[5] The R^2 values of the validation samples compare favorably with the R^2 in the estimation samples, particularly in the East and West.

Comparing the national results to the regional results, it appears that the regional breakdown has improved the explanatory power of the analysis. The value of the R^2 in the regional analysis is never less than the value for the national analysis and the validation R^2 in the regional samples is generally more supportive of the analysis than in the national sample. As discussed earlier in the section on collinearity analysis, in the national P_i, W_{1i}, W_{2i} are significantly positively correlated contrary to expectation. This is not true for the regional analysis.

The results indicate that both potential and workload are important predictors of sales. The only region in which workload measures do not have a significant coefficient is the East. Since this region is the most developed of the three and has the most intense sales force effort (see Table 2), it might be hypothesized that workload is not sufficiently great to be a factor. That is, because of the more intensive coverage in the Eastern region, only potential and not workload per salesman is the binding factor.

---

[4] The subsample regression results might be an artifact because each region has a different penetration. Since penetration is S_i/P_i, the sum of sales divided by potential is constrained in the regression. However, the standard deviation of penetration was the highest in the Eastern Region, next highest in the Central, and lowest in the West. Therefore, it does not appear that a reduction in variance of S_i/P_i is responsible for the findings.

---

[5] All values of R^2 for the estimation sample are adjusted for degrees of degrees of freedom according to the number of variables in the reported results. The R^2 results for the validation samples are not adjusted.

Table 4
National Sample Results

	$N = 129$[a]	$N_v = 119$				

Linear (Sales)				Curvilinear (Ln (Sales))		
$R^2 = .14$[b] $R_v^2 = .09$[c]		$F = 11.04$		$R^2 = .24$ $R_v^2 = .06$		$F = 11.40$
Variable	B	b	t	Variable	B	b	t
Potential	.003	.35	4.12	Ln (Number of accounts)	−.177	−.32	3.88
Number of counties	−6.971	−.29	3.34	Ln (Potential)	.111	.23	2.80
Constant	680.831			Constant	6.020		

[a] N and N_v are sizes of estimation and validation samples respectively.
[b] Adjusted R^2.
[c] R_v^2 is R^2 for validation sample (unadjusted).

Table 5
Regional Subsample Results

EAST

	$N = 39$[a]	$N_v = 44$				

Linear (Sales)				Curvilinear (Ln (Sales))		
$R^2 = .52$[b] $R_v^2 = .57$[c]		$F = 41.28$		$R^2 = .47$ $R_v^2 = .57$		$F = 25.57$
Variable	B	b	t	Variable	B	b	t
Potential	.024	.73	6.43	Ln (Potential)	.479	.64	5.06
Constant	372.980			Constant	1.971		

CENTRAL

	$N = 33$	$N_v = 32$				

Linear (Sales)				Curvilinear (Ln (Sales))		
$R^2 = .40$ $R_v^2 = .23$		$F = 8.24$		$R^2 = .38$ $R_v^2 = .15$		$F = 7.29$
Variable	B	b	t	Variable	B	b	t
Potential	.006	.46	3.13	Ln (Potential)	.241	.43	2.97
Number of buying entities	1.252	.46	3.03	Ln (Number of buying entities)	.608	.46	2.95
Number of counties	−9.279	−.35	2.30	Ln (Number of counties)	−.227	−.39	2.50
Constant	245.237			Constant	1.143		

WEST

	$N = 57$	$N_v = 43$				

Linear (Sales)				Curvilinear (Ln (Sales))		
$R^2 = .24$ $R_v^2 = .39$		$F = 9.74$		$R^2 = .27$ $R_v^2 = .28$		$F = 10.33$
Variable	B	b	t	Variable	B	b	t
Potential	.004	.46	3.92	Ln (Potential)	.272	.43	3.67
Number of counties	−6.593	−.28	2.37	Ln (Number of accounts)	−.180	−.29	2.51
Constant	539.910			Constant	4.168		

[a] N and N_v are sizes of estimation and validation samples respectively.
[b] Adjusted R^2.
[c] R_v^2 is R^2 for validation sample (unadjusted).

Moving from the East to the Central to the West regions, the goodness of fit as measured by R^2 decreases. One possible explanation for this decrease is that the measures of workload (number of accounts and number of counties) are only surrogates for a salesperson's true workload and, as discussed above, workload measures are only relevant in the Central and Western regions. Thus, the lower R^2 values in these two regions may be caused by an inability of surrogate workload measures to reflect completely the true workload.

Overall, the results clearly support the notion that territorial potential and territorial sales are associated for the company in this study. Further, there is evidence to suggest that this association is affected by the salesperson's workload. Analyzing the relationship on a regional basis improved the strength of the association. Unfortunately, no data were availiable which would have allowed an empirical investigation of the reasons for these differences.

Applications

Several applications of the results can be identified. First, sales response functions can be used in setting quotas. A goal which reflects territory characteristics is fairer to the sales representative and more realistic than an arbitrarily developed quota. Second, the results can also be used to set standards for evaluating the sales force as suggested in [2]. However, in contrast, the use of a measure such as quality of the sales representative (for example, from supervisor's ratings) as an independent variable should be avoided; otherwise lower rated sales representatives have a lower standard. Only independent variables unrelated to a sales representative's skill and effort should be used for the purpose of establishing standards. Third, the results can be employed to help determine the sales force size.

Conclusions

This study has shown that territorial potential and sales representative's workload are associated with territorial sales for a company in the retail apparel industry. Linear and curvilinear sales response models both fit the data about equally well. Regional analyses of the sales response functions were more informative than an analysis for the entire nation, possibly reflecting variations across regions which were a result of the past marketing efforts of the company and the competition. The results suggest that territorial potential is a more important determinant of territorial sales than sales representative's workload for this company, but, more generally, that both should be measured in future studies.

There has been a dearth of research on sales force response functions despite the importance of personal selling and the magnitude of money spent on it. Futher research should include replications of the study presented here in other settings. It should also include additional data, if possible, on characteristics of territories or regions to help explain the regional variations that may be observed and data on other marketing and competitive variables which may change differentially across territories. Finally there is a need to try to measure dynamic effects.

References

1. Cravens, David W. and Robert B. Woodruff. "An Approach for Determining Criteria of Sales Performance," *Journal of Applied Psychology*, 57 (June 1973), 242-7.

2. _____, and Joe C. Stamper. "An Analytical Approach for Evaluating Sales Territory Performance," *Journal of Marketing*, 36 (January 1972), 31-7.

3. Davis, Otto A. and John U. Farley. "Allocating Sales Force Effort With Commissions and Quotas," *Management Science*, 18, Part II (December 1971), 55-63.

4. Farley, John U. "An Optimal Plan For Salesman's Compensation," *Journal of Marketing Research*, 1 (May 1964), 39-43.

5. Hess, Sidney W. and Stuart A. Samuels. "Experience With a Sales Districting Model: Criteria and Implementation." *Management Science*, 18, Part II (December 1971), 41-54.

6. Lambert, Zarrel V. *Setting the Size For the Sales Force*. State College, Penn.: Pennsylvania State University Press, 1968.

7. Lodish, Leonard M. "Call Plan: Interactive Salesmen Call Planning System," *Management Science*, 18, Part II (December 1971), 24-40.

8. Lucas, Henry C., Jr. "Performance and the Use of An Information System," *Management Science*, forthcoming.

9. Montgomery, David B., Alvin J. Silk, and Carlos E. Zaragosa. "A Multiple Product Sales Allocation Model," *Management Science*, Part II (December 1971), 3-24

10. Semlow, Walter J. "How Many Salesmen Do You Need?" *Harvard Business Review*, 37 (May-June 1959), 126-32.

11. Weinberg, Charles B. and Henry C. Lucas, Jr. "Semlow's Results, are Based on a Spurious Relationship," unpublished manuscript, 1974.

12. Winer, Leon. "The Effect of Product Sales Quotas on Sales Force Productivity," *Journal of Marketing Research*, 10 (May 1973), 180-3.

For Discussion

1. Evaluate the manner in which the variables were operationalized. Can you think of alternatives?

2. What is the difference in parameter interpretation in the multiplicative model? How do the multiplicative model assumptions differ from the linear model assumptions?

3. Why might a "structural test" be performed? Did the model "pass" the test? What was the underlying theory being tested?

4. For a good explanation of regression in general and collinearity in particular, see Wonnacott and Wonnacott, *Introductory Statistics for Business and Economics*, 2nd Edition (New York: John Wiley, 1977). What is collinearity in this context? Did it present a problem?

5. How did the regional results differ from the national results? Why?

6. How could the results be used to determine sales force size?

Fitting Branch Locations, Performance Standards, and Marketing Strategies to Local Conditions

C. Joseph Clawson

There are many situations in which headquarters management desires to make proper allowance for local conditions in selecting new locations, evaluating current performance, and providing marketing support to several geographically separate units. Such units may include, for example, different sales territories, retail stores, banking facilities, and service stations. They could belong to such categories as branch, voluntary chain, or franchise operations.

This article describes how chain marketing managers can more effectively screen new branch locations, set realistic performance standards for different communities, and pinpoint remedial actions through regression models. Examples are given from the savings field.

The Performance Problem in Financial Chains

Consultation with executives of commercial banks and savings and loan associations indicates that they typically regard the long-run attraction of deposits into their local branches as one of the primary limiting factors on their corporate growth and success. By contrast, loan demand of reasonably good quality has in recent years been adequate to make use of the deposits available, particularly in regions of rapid population growth. Indeed, a 1973 Booz, Allen, and Hamilton study has concluded that the primary challenge facing banks in the future will be the acquisition of funds, not the employment of them.[1]

Despite this crucial role of deposit inflows, it is a highly perplexing problem for top executives to set and enforce performance standards, or norms, for their different branches that realistically reflect untapped potentials as well as serious barriers. This is traceable to the wide diversity of populations served and the unusual competitive conditions that the branches face, in varying combinations in different communities. Without such standards, however, it is hard to choose the most promising new locations and decide which existing branches are actually performing above, below, or at par.

Due to these difficulties, many financial managements prefer to deal with site selection and performance control problems in an intuitive way. Others evaluate detailed statistical reports but assign subjective weights to the different influences they perceive. Some simply raise last year's quotas by a certain proportion across the board for all branches. In the absence of better decision-making tools, these methods have some logical justification.

However, the application of stepwise multiple regression models to these tasks is a feasible and more rational alternative. It deserves wider application, not only in financial branch supervision, but in many other organizations where branch managers, franchise operators, salesmen, and others face distinctive local conditions.

The value and feasability of regression analysis for setting sales territorial quotas and evaluating salesmen's performance in manufacturing industries have already been demonstrated elsewhere.[2] This article will take a somewhat different tack, describing a regression approach which has

[1] "Tyros in the Marketing Game," *Business Week* (September 15, 1973), p. 129.

[2] See, for example, David W. Cravens, Robert B. Woodruff, and Joe C. Stamper, "An Analytical Approach for Evaluating Sales Territory Performance," *Journal of Marketing*, Vol. 36 (January 1972), pp. 31–37; and Robert D. Dugan, "Evaluating Territorial Sales Efforts," *Journal of Applied Psychology*, Vol. 44 (April 1960), pp. 107–110.

Reprinted from *Journal of Marketing*, published by the American Marketing Association, Vol. 38 (January 1974), pp. 8–14. No part of this article may be reproduced in any form without prior written permission from the publisher.

been developed for the management of Suburban Financial Corporation (fictitious name). SFC is a holding company for a chain savings and loan association, and desires to apply such analysis to several or all of the following problems:

1. Selecting new branch locations, facilities, and marketing approaches
2. Evaluating merger candidates
3. Setting performance standards for existing branches
4. Identifying problem cases and outstanding examples
5. Relocating dead-end branches
6. Target marketing to special segments within a service area
7. Establishing performance norms as benchmarks to evaluate the effectiveness of new marketing campaigns.

These applications will be discussed in greater detail after the main findings have been presented. The need and potential value of such applications may be substantial for many companies. For instance, SFC's management wishes to gain a better understanding of why its best branch registered an $18,821,000 net savings gain in the same year that its weakest branch showed only a $460,000 net gain. While its average net gain per branch was $3,342,000, the standard deviation around this figure was a disturbing $3,698,000. The stakes, in terms of uncertain profitability on such a wide performance range, were regarded as substantial.

Determinants of Local Savings Performance

Criterion of Savings Performance. The main outcome to be explained in this study was the "net savings gain" of each individual branch of Suburban Financial Corporation during a particular twelve-month period. This consists of total dollar savings deposits received in new and existing accounts during that period from all sources, minus withdrawals, plus that portion of accrued interest that was not withdrawn.

Main Types of Performance Predictors. Figure 1 is a simplified conceptual model showing three general blocks of variables — population, competition, and branch — that should serve as indicators and/or determinants of branch savings performance. These indicators can be quite useful in establishing expected levels of performance.

These three blocks of variables will be discussed in more detail below. At this point, it is essential to emphasize that the variables are highly interactive. For instance, a given branch's characteristics and efforts should tend to reflect (and correlate with) local population size and characteristics. The branch's characteristics and efforts should also affect, and be affected by, the nature and extent of its local competition as well as influence and be influenced by its own net savings gains.

Procedure

Input Data Employed. A representative sample of 26 branches of Suburban Financial Corporation was selected for analysis. Data were gathered on 25 variables for each branch, as listed in Table 1. Included are the criterion variable (X_1) along with 24 predictor variables. These were selected in consul-

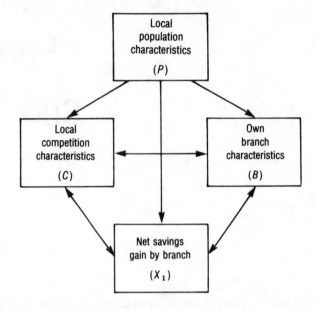

Figure 1
General Correlates of Savings Performance
in a Local Retail Financial Market

tation with management so as to represent each of the major blocks: population (P), competition (C), and branch (B).

All of the data for the population and competition blocks pertain to a circular area with a radius of two miles surrounding each SFC branch. More precise delineation of trading area shapes were regarded as unnecessary, because previous internal studies had indicated that from 60% to 90% of the total savings held in branches of the association belonged to owners residing within two miles of those branches.

Although many of the variables listed in Table 1 are self-explanatory, some may not be. For instance, SFC management desired to ascertain whether its branches were affected favorably or adversely by proximity to the main offices or executive headquarters of other associations (variable 12), by branches of a particular competitor Colossal S&L (variable 13), by branches of large associations in general (variable 14), or by large retail store concentrations (variable 15).

Most of the data were obtained from common sources, such as internal company records, census reports, reports of federal and state regulatory agencies, and field observations. However, unpublished figures on net savings gains and total savings balances of several competitors' branches were supplied on a confidential basis by the competitors, on request. Ratings of exterior attractiveness, interior decor, and parking adequacy for the 26 SFC branches were based on a consensus of executive and researcher judgments. They ranged from a low rating of 1 to a high rating of 5.

Statistical Analysis

A standard computer program was used to carry out stepwise multiple linear regression analysis of the data. This

Table 1
List of Variables Analyzed in Regression Study of 26 Branches

		Units	Mean
Dependent Variable			
X_1	Net savings gain, 12 months, in branch	$000	3,341
Population Block (P)			
X_2	Renter-occupied dwellings	%	50.9
X_3	S&L savings per capita (total savings held in all local S&L facilities, divided by local population)	$	2,645
X_4	Income per capita	$	3,492
X_5	Median value of owner-occupied homes	$	30,247
X_6	Persons age 45–64	%	22.8
X_7	Persons age 65 and over	%	11.1
Competition Block (C)			
X_8	Competing S&L facilities	No.	4.3
X_9	Population per S&L facility	No.	18,361
X_{10}	Commercial bank facilities	No.	10.5
X_{11}	Average net savings gain of local S&L competitors, 12 months	$000	2,970
X_{12}	Share of total local S&L savings held by local main and executive offices of competitors	%	27.2
X_{13}	Branch of Colossal S&L Association nearby	1 or 0	0.27
X_{14}	Total assets of competing S&L associations having local branches	$000,000	2,742
Branch Block (B)			
X_{15}	Retail sales per year within one-half mile radius of SFC branch	$000,000	46.7
X_{16}	Branch inside formal shopping center	1 or 0	0.15
X_{17}	Branch opposite formal center	1 or 0	0.15
X_{18}	Branch approaching formal center	1 or 0	0.04
X_{19}	Branch in central business district	1 or 0	0.50
X_{20}	Branch in free-standing building	1 or 0	0.81
X_{21}	Age of branch	Years	13.1
X_{22}	Exterior attractiveness (rating)	1-5	3.3
X_{23}	Interior decor (rating)	1-5	3.8
X_{24}	Parking adequacy (rating)	1-5	3.6
X_{25}	Branch advertising and promotion cost	$000	23.3

types. In view of the technique's general familiarity to researchers, the methodology will receive limited attention in this article. Primary attention can therefore be directed to the discussion of marketing management applications.

Findings

The data and formulas presented below are actual. However, confidentiality is preserved by using a fictitious name for the savings and loan association and withholding the year and location of the study. Caution should be exercised in generalizing the findings, as such, to other savings and loans or commercial banks, to different geographical areas, or to different years.

The Regression Formula

Table 2 shows that the final equation contains ten distinct indicators, or predictor variables. Each of these variables explains at least 1% of the total variation in net savings gain, as shown by the increases in R^2, ranging from a ratio of .013 to .449. Taken as a group, the ten variables jointly explain 91.5% of the interbranch variation in net savings gains (86.7% when adjusted for degrees of freedom). The F ratio for analysis of variance is 16.11, significant at the .01 level.

The most important single indicator of high SFC branch savings gains is a high average net savings gain by competing facilities within the two-mile area. This variable alone explains 44.9% of the total variation in SFC branch savings gains. Other especially favorable signs are a high percentage of persons age 45 to 64 (the variable explains 14.7%) and highly rated exterior attractiveness of the branch (variable explains 10.6%).

In contrast, branches located in the vicinity of competitors' main or executive offices are shown as suffering a relative disadvantage, as do those located on the approaches to a formal shopping center or surrounded by a large number of renter-occupied dwellings.

From the standpoint of *blocks* of influences, all three blocks contribute materially to the understanding of branch

is a well-developed, widely recognized technique for eliminating weak or duplicative variables, picking the minimum number of strong predictor variables, and measuring the proportionate contribution made by each significant variable to the explanation of performance differentials of many

Table 2
Summary of Major Relationships Revealed in Formula for Net Savings Gain

Variable No.	Description[a]	Block	Regression Coefficient	Initial Increase in R^2	Final t-Value
X_{11}	Average net gain by competitors	C	0.708	.449	3.59
X_6	Age 45–64	P	147.191	.147	1.39
X_{22}	Exterior attractiveness	B	1131.404	.106	3.25
X_4	Income per capita	P	1.142	.053	2.53
X_{25}	Local promotion	B	29.987	.029	2.54
X_{12}	Main and executive offices	C	−35.401	.036	−2.99
X_9	Population per S&L facility	C	0.087	.035	3.16
X_{15}	Retail sales	B	20.531	.028	2.30
X_2	Renters	P	−52.925	.019	−2.23
X_{18}	Approaching center	B	−2505.012	.013	−1.51
—	(Intercept)		−9342.863		

[a] Units are shown in Table 1.

savings intake. Competition variables as a group explain 52.0%, population characteristics explain 21.9%, and branch characteristics and efforts explain a respectable 17.6%. Questions as to whether, when, and how these blocks of variables can be controlled by management action will be discussed shortly.

Excluded Variables

Although 14 of the original 24 predictor variables in Table 1 were statistically eliminated from the final formula in Table 2, this does not mean they were all of no consequence. Several were merely duplicative of stronger variables that were included, and were therefore unnecessary. For instance, simple correlations (not shown) reveal that heavy retail activity near the branches of SFC is often correlated with a large number of competing S&L facilities, large total association assets of these competitors, high S&L savings per capita, and a large percentage of the population age 65 and over. Again, an attractive exterior appearance normally goes with an attractive interior decor. High income per capita tends to accompany high home values and numerous competing S&L branches. A large percentage of renter-occupied dwellings is frequently found where there are many commercial banks and many persons age 65 and over. In all these examples, the simple correlation coefficients were .6 or higher.

Consequently, the excluded characteristics, though hidden in the final equation, still remain in the background and should be thought of as probably present to some degree. This suggests that if data had been unavailable for some of the variables that did enter the formula, some of the excluded variables might very well have survived.

Individual Branch Analysis

Table 3 presents, for Branch 12, an example of the way in which the regression formula aids in estimating the expected net savings gain for each branch. It also helps to explain the estimate, variable by variable.

The data and method for calculating the estimated net savings gain are of primary interest to the researcher and appear in the first four data columns. Marketing managers may find the final right-hand column of greatest interest and use. It shows for any given branch what advantages or disadvantages it has with respect to the average branch.

The main advantages of Branch 12, as shown by high positive figures, are the smaller than average renter population (an advantage of +$992,000) and the complete absence of any main or executive offices of nearby competing associations (an advantage of +$964,000). There are some serious negative indicators, however. One is the poor average net savings gains made by local competitors' branches (a disadvantage of −$1,138,000 for SFC's Branch 12). Another is the branch's very inadequate expenditures on local advertising and promotion (a disadvantage of −$579,000). In general, however, the advantages and disadvantages nearly balance out, with calculated net gain only $141,000 below the all-branch average. The actual net gain was $35,000 below average.

Limitations and Future Directions

The regression formula presented here is basically a demand equation based on a variety of indicators that appear in different combinations. It must be coupled with cost estimates before the most cost-effective alternatives are selected. Moreover, since it is a cross-sectional study, cover-

Table 3

Calculation of Estimated Net Savings Gain for Any Branch
(Illustrated for Branch 12)

No.	Description	Regression Coefficient[a]	Value for Branch 12	Contribution to Estimated Net Savings Gain ($000) Branch 12[b]	All-Branch Average[c]	Difference[d]
X_{11}	Avg. gain of competitors	0.708	$1362	$ 964	$2102	$−1138
X_6	Age 45–64	147.191	25.6%	3768	3360	+ 408
X_{22}	Ext. attractiveness	1131.404	3	3394	3742	− 348
X_4	Income/cap.	1.142	$3667	4187	3986	+ 201
X_{25}	Local prom.	29.987	$ 4	120	699	− 579
X_{12}	Main and exec. offices	−35.401	0	0	− 964	+ 964
X_9	Population per facil.	0.087	13751	1196	1590	− 394
X_{15}	Retail sales	20.531	$ 30	616	959	− 343
X_2	Renters	−52.925	32.2%	−1704	−2696	+ 992
X_{18}	Approaching center	−2505.012	0	0	− 96	+ 96
—	(Intercept)	−9342.863		−9343	−9343	0
	Estimated net savings gain ($000)			$3198	$3339	$− 141
	Actual net savings gain ($000)			3304	3339[e]	− 35
	Residual (actual-estimated)			$ 106	0	+ 106

[a]From Table 2.
[b]Arrived at by multiplying first two columns of this table.
[c]Arrived at by multiplying first column of Table 3 by second column of Table 1.
[d]Difference between Branch 12 contribution and all-branch average contribution: advantage (+), disadvantage (−).
[e]Differs from $3341 in Table 1 due to rounding.

ing a single period of time, it does not show which one of any two correlated variables "causes" the other one, or whether both are the results of a third factor. However, the equation does help in identifying the possible existence of causation. The direction of causation will need to be derived through management judgment; multiperiod, multiequation analysis; or controlled experimentation. Curvilinear relations should also be explored in addition to linear ones. The formula for any given company should also be double-checked against the formulas for its competitors, and against the same company's prior and later experiences, to verify its reliability. Even within the savings and loan industry, the formulas are expected to differ significantly from region to region, year to year, federal- to state-chartered associations, and even among individual institutions. Tailoring and updating are essential.

Summary and Conclusions

This article has described the need, conceptual framework and, in some detail, the expected applications to marketing management of a multiple regression analysis program aimed at evaluating the savings performance of different branches of a chain financial institution.

The study examined the effects of 24 population, competition, and branch indicators on the dollar savings gains of 26 representative branches. The ten best predictors accounted for 91.5% of total interbranch variance, or 86.7% adjusted for degrees of freedom.

A formula of this type, while primarily useful in choosing new branch locations and in monitoring performance of existing branches, is also valuable for other applications, including mergers, problem situations, relocations, target marketing, and branch characteristics.

For Discussion

1. Stepwise regression was used in this study. In stepwise regression, the program selects the single independent variable (X_{11}) that will generate the highest R^2 $(R^2 = .499)$. It then searches for a second variable (X_6) that will provide the highest additional R^2 (.147). It proceeds in this manner as Table 2 suggests until there are no more independent variables left or until the increase in R^2 becomes very small. Evaluate this approach in this context. If a variable is not included, does that mean that it has little influence? Why? What role does theory play in this analysis?

2. How might you reduce the number of independent variables to a more manageable size?

3. How could the model be used to select new branch locations?

Developing Marketing Strategy through Multiple Regression

G. David Hughes

This study focuses on a retailer's problem of increasing sales to his present customers, in this instance college coeds. A solution to this problem was sought by using cross-sectional multiple regression that related the size of dollar purchases of the present customers to their appropriate attitudinal, economic, and sociological variables.

Method

The variables selected after an extensive preliminary investigation included: (1) monthly allowance, in dollars; (2) the number of years in college; (3) attitudes toward the store's price levels, quality, style, selection, and sales service; (4) sorority membership; and (5) the coed's purchases, in dollars, at Willards,[1] a women's clothing store in upstate New York. To disguise the identity of Willards to the respondents, data were collected for four additional stores, but only data for Willards are reported here.

The respondents were a random sample of 70 coeds receiving a monthly allowance who had purchased at Willards during the six months prior to receiving the questionnaire. Thus, the problem investigated was: "How can Willards increase its average sales to its coed customers?"

Measuring the Variables

Data for all variables were collected by mail questionnaire. Although the independence of attitudes and sales reported this way may be questioned, it was the only feasible method for collecting information about cash sales over a six-month period.

The number of years in college (1 through 4) provided a proxy measure of the freedom to purchase that increased with the years away from home. As will be noted below, this variable failed to explain a significant amount of purchase behavior. We do not know, therefore, if the amount of freedom is unimportant, or if the years in college were a poor proxy.

[1] Store names are disguised.

Sorority membership was measured as an attribute, yes or no. A better measurement would have been an estimate of the number of hours per week spent in formal and informal contact with other sorority members. This measurement would enable an estimate of the degree of group influence on buying behavior.

The respective attitudes toward price, quality, style, selection, and sales service of each store were measured on a six-point semantic differential scale, as is illustrated by the following:

	Price					
	High				Low	
Willards	6	5	4	3	2	1
Straights	6	5	4	3	2	1

A scale with only six items has both advantages and disadvantages. Respondent cooperation tends to increase as the number of items (and therefore decisions) decreases. But this fewness of items produces coarse measurements, which in turn lead to estimates of parameters that are extremely sensitive to unit changes in attitude.

Selecting the Form of Regression

Ideally, the structure of the regression should be determined by the theories underlying the relationships among the observable phenomena, but marketing, still in the inductive stage of development, lacks theories and possesses few empirical constants. For precedents we must turn to complementary disciplines.

The linear form was selected first because it was used extensively by economists who have examined the relationship between buying intentions and buying behavior. Much of the work reported by the Survey Research Center, University of Michigan, has included linear regressions.

The second form, the logarithm of the independent variable, was borrowed from psychophysics, the study of the relationships between physical stimuli and human re-

Reprinted from *Journal of Marketing Research,* published by the American Marketing Association, Vol. 3 (November 1966), pp. 412–415. No part of this article may be reproduced in any form without prior written permission from the publisher.

Regressions of Coed Sportswear Purchases on Interdisciplinary Variables

Equation (Standard Error)	Percentage of Variance Explained	Sample Size
Linear Equations		
Sorority and nonsorority members		
(1) $P = -8.341 + 5.082^{*}X_{sl} + .156^{*}X_a + 3.199 X_q$ $\quad\quad\quad (2.500) \quad\quad (.079) \quad\quad (3.496)$ $\quad\quad - 2.480 X_{st} + 1.448 X_{sv} - 1.198 X_y$ $\quad\quad\quad (3.421) \quad\quad (2.333) \quad\quad (2.122)$	$R^2 = .171$†	70
Sorority members		
(2) $P = -48.678 + 12.608$‡$X_{sv} + .196 X_a + 3.933 X_{sl}$ $\quad\quad\quad (5.358) \quad\quad (.117) \quad\quad (4.366)$ $\quad\quad + 3.494 X_y - 2.355 X_q$ $\quad\quad\quad (3.559) \quad\quad (4.247)$	$R^2 = .395$†	29
Nonsorority members		
(3) $P = 6.512 + 5.122^{*}X_{sl} - 1.867 X_y + .066 X_a + 3.286 X_q$ $\quad\quad\quad (2.965) \quad\quad (2.808) \quad (.115) \quad (3.926)$ $\quad\quad - 1.894 X_{sv} - 1.464 X_p$ $\quad\quad\quad (2.662) \quad\quad (3.858)$	$R^2 = .161$	41
Nonlinear Equations		
Sorority members		
(4) $P = 80.559 + 43.258$‡ $\log_e X_{sv} + 13.360 \log_e X_a$ $\quad\quad\quad (22.003) \quad\quad\quad (8.052)$ $\quad\quad - 14.285 \log_e X_p + 3.534 \log_e X_{sl} + 23.108 \log_e X_{st}$ $\quad\quad\quad (15.410) \quad\quad (18.894) \quad\quad (29.231)$ $\quad\quad - 17.621 \log_e X_q + 3.524 \log_e X_y$ $\quad\quad\quad (27.401) \quad\quad (7.901)$	$R^2 = .379$†	29
(5) $\text{Log}_e P = -1.986 + 1.834$‡ $\log_e X_{sv} + .538 \log_e X_a$ $\quad\quad\quad (.794) \quad\quad\quad (.276)$ $\quad\quad + .291 \log_e X_{sl} - 1.271 \log_e X_q + 1.146 \log_e X_{st}$ $\quad\quad\quad (.647) \quad\quad (.923) \quad\quad (.989)$ $\quad\quad + .097 \log_e X_y$ $\quad\quad\quad (.265)$	$R^2 = .476$†	29

* Significant at the .05 level.
† The correlation coefficient standard was at least three times its own standard error.
‡ Significant at the .01 level.
P = Purchases of sportswear, in dollars.
X_{sv} (service), X_{sl} (selection) X_q (quality), X_{st} (style), X_p (price) = Dimensions of store image measured on six-point semantic differential scale with 3.5 equal to the point of indifference.
X_a = Monthly allowance, in dollars.
X_y = Years in college.
Note: Variables are shown in rank order of the amount of variance explained; variables that failed to explain any variance are not shown.

responses. One of the early laws in this field was expressed by Fechner as:

$$R = C \log S$$

where R is the response, C is a constant, and S is an absolute-threshold stimulus, such as weights measured in grams.[2]

Empirical investigators frequently are interested in the percentage change in the dependent variable associated with a one percent change in the independent variable. To an economist this relationship is the coefficient of elasticity.[3] Guilford [1] suggests that this relationship is the general form for psychophysics:

$$Y = aX^b.$$

By transforming the independent and the dependent variables into logarithms, the parameters can be estimated by least-squares linear regression. This transformation yields the third and last of the functions to be considered here. This function was used by Steele [5] when he examined the rela-

[2]Guilford [1, p. 37].

[3]For a discussion of direct estimation elasticity see Johnston [2, pp. 48–9].

tionship between attitudes and milk consumption, and by Reilly [3] when he estimated the squared relationship in his now famous law.

The foregoing brief examination of relevant precedents does not indicate a clear choice of form to apply to the problem of developing marketing strategy. Yet, Shupack's research suggests that results are sensitive to the form of the model. He has concluded that there should be further "investigation of the predictive accuracies of a large number of different models under various circumstances."[4] Because this note is concerned primarily with methodology, and at the risk of appearing to be on a "fishing expedition," we will explore empirically each of the functions noted above.

Findings

The equations, estimated by the least-squares method, are presented in the rank order of the amount of variance explained by each. When a variable failed to explain any variance, it was excluded and is therefore not reported.

Initially the coed market was treated as a single, homogeneous segment and a linear equation was fitted to the entire 70 respondents (Equation 1). The results were not impressive ($R^2 = .171$). After the respondents were divided into sorority members and nonsorority members, a linear equation was fitted to each of these subgroups. The results of the further segmentation were most revealing. The percentage of variance explained by the sorority equation increased to 39.5 percent (Equation 2) while the percentage of variance explained among nonsorority members declined to 16.1 percent (Equation 3). These findings suggest that sorority members tend to be more homogeneous with regard to the variables examined.

Equations (2) and (3) suggest that the merchandising strategy for the sorority group should differ from the strategy for the nonsorority group. In Equation (2), service (X_{sv}) was the most important variable to the sorority members and in Equation (3), selection (X_{sl}) was the most important variable to the nonsorority members. Thus, service should be improved and promoted to the sorority segment and selection should be widened and promoted to the nonsorority segment.

Equation (4) regresses the dollar value of purchases reported by the sorority members on the logarithm of the independent variables. In percentage of variance explained, this function was slightly less desirable because it explained less variance than Equation (2).

Equation (5), the regression of the natural logarithm of purchases on the natural logarithm of the independent variables, explained 47.6 percent of the variance, more than any of the previous equations. This form relates proportional increases in purchases to proportional increases in the independent variables. In this equation, for example, the service parameter (X_{sv}) indicates that a one percent change in re-

spondents' attitudes toward Willards' sales service is associated with a 1.8 percent increase in the same respondents' purchases, an elastic relationship.[5] In the same way, the relationship between purchases at Willards and monthly allowance (.54) is inelastic.

Conclusions

The small experiment described in this note leads to three conclusions about the use of cross-sectional multiple regression. First, the results are encouraging. Marketing strategists should consider the technique as a means of identifying those attitudinal, economic, and sociological variables that are most closely associated with the purchase of particular goods or services. Second, the technique provides a way to identify market segments and those variables within each segment that are closely associated with buying behavior. These variables then become the basis for promotion for each segment.

Finally, the recommendations to management were insensitive to the form of the equation. Equations (2), (4), and (5) yielded the same recommendation: stress service to those coeds who are sorority members. Because of the limited nature of this study we cannot conclude that the recommendations will always be insensitive to the form. Therefore, several forms will usually have to be explored. The availability of computers makes this a rather simple task.

References

1. Joy P. Guilford, *Psychometric Methods*, New York: McGraw-Hill Book Co., Inc., 1954.
2. J. Johnston, *Econometric Methods*, New York: McGraw-Hill Book Co., Inc., 1963.
3. William J. Reilly, *The Law of Retail Gravitation*, New York: Pilsbury Publishers, Inc., 1953.
4. Mark B. Shupack, "The Predictive Accuracy of Empirical Demand Analysis," *Economic Journal*, 72 (September 1962), 550–75.
5. Howard L. Steele, "On the Validity of Projective Questions," *Journal of Marketing Research*, 1 (August 1964), 46–9.

For Discussion

1. Suppose that information on sorority membership was unknown. Would the Equation (1) model be valid? Would it lead to erroneous conclusions?
2. Instead of running Equations (2) and (3), why not just put in a dummy variable for sorority membership?
3. How should you evaluate whether the linear or nonlinear equation is superior? Since the dependent variable differs, can the R^2 values be compared?

---

[4]Shupack [4, p. 575].

---

[5] The term income *sensitivity* is generally used to describe the relationship between *dollar* purchases and income, while income *elasticity* is used to describe the relationship between the *quantity* purchased and income. This distinction is important to long-run analyses because of price changes. The term elasticity was used throughout this article because it is more widely understood and because the analysis examined purchases in the short run.

6

Dynamic Effects
of Short Duration Price Differentials
on Retail Gasoline Sales

H. J. Claycamp

Knowledge of the dynamic pattern of sales responses to short duration differentials between prices of competing products is important to price leaders and price followers alike. Price leaders must determine whether the sales response is adequate to justify continuing the price at the new level, while price followers must decide if and when the new price should be countered. Since the rate of information diffusion and the extent of information seeking by consumers at the time of purchase may cause the sales effect to lag, vary with item or carry over after prices have been returned to former levels or equalized by competitors, dynamic rather than static estimates of price elasticities are required for informed decision making.

This study was designed:

1. Show how regression analysis can be used to obtain statistical estimates of the dynamic sales effect of short-term price differentials on competing products.
2. Provide some first approximations of the magnitude of the sales effect of unusual[1] price differentials on the sales of gasoline at retail outlets.

In retail distribution of gasoline, operators who do not follow a policy of price leadership must frequently decide whether to ignore or react to lower prices of competition.[2] The operator who is not a price leader and who wishes to maximize his revenue can choose the optimal strategy if he has accurate estimates of the daily cross elasticity of demand and the carry-over effect. For example, as long as the cross-elasticity coefficient of daily sales is algebraically greater than -1.0 and the carry-over effect is insignificant, the

operator should ignore the lower prices of competitors. However, when the coefficient becomes less than -1.0, he should react to the competitive price. Note that the latter strategy may be appropriate even if the elasticity coefficients indicate otherwise. If enough consumers make purchase decisions based on price differentials no longer in existence, the carry-over effect would be large enough to cause a net loss in revenue for the entire period.

The model used in this study permits estimation of:

1. The cross-elasticity coefficient for the first day of a price differential.
2. The cross-elasticity coefficient for subsequent days of a price differential.
3. A coefficient for the short run carry-over effect.
4. And a coefficient for the effect of serial correlation.

The Data

Operators of five retail service stations selling a nationally advertised brand of gasoline in a metropolitan area of the Southeastern United States were asked to provide the following data for a 90-day period:

1. Gallons sold each day.
2. Price per gallon each day.
3. Price per gallon for the same grade posted at the outlet which the operator considered as his primary competitor.
4. Incidents which would result in an unusual increase or decrease in sales.

All operators chose competitors selling nationally advertised brands, and no sample outlet chose another sample outlet as its primary competitor. The normal price condition was one of equality on like grades of gasoline. All stations used large uniform signs posted on the premises to advertise the current price.

Stations 1, 2 and 3 were neighborhood stations which presumably drew most of their business from residents of the

---

[1] Price differentials other than those usually present between major nationally advertised brands and independent or regional brands.

[2] The occurrence of differentials at competing outlets is more frequent than most observers believe. See: S. Morris Livingstone and Theodore Levitt, "Competition and Retail Gasoline Prices," *Review of Economics and Statistics*, XLI (May 1959), 119–32.

Reprinted from *Journal of Marketing Research*, published by the American Marketing Association, Vol. 3 (May 1968), pp. 175–178.

area. Stations 4 and 5 were located close to major traffic arteries and presumably sold to customers from a wider area.

Weather and business conditions were highly stable over the period, and none of the stations showed a significant upward or downward trend in sales. In approximately 10 percent of the 450 station-days, the competitive price was less than the price at the sample station. Although none of the sample stations lowered its price before its competitor, on several occasions sample stations attempted to lead prices to higher levels. If the major competitor failed to follow, the price was returned to its former level. Most differentials were less than three cents per gallon and lasted for one or two days. There was only one occurrence of a four-cent differential and only one instance where a differential lasted as long as four days.

The Model

The following model was specified and tested on each of the five stations:

$$\frac{X_{i,t} - \overline{X}_{i,dt}}{\overline{X}_{i,dt}} = a_0 + b_1 \left[\frac{X_{i,t-1} - \overline{X}_{i,dt-1}}{\overline{X}_{i,dt}} \right]$$

$$+ b_2 \left[D_1 \frac{P_{i,t} - P_{c,t}}{P_{c,t}} \right] + b_3 \left[D_2 \frac{P_{i,t} - P_{c,t}}{P_{c,t}} \right]$$

$$+ b_4 D_3 + U_t, \qquad (1)$$

where

a_0 = intercept

$X_{i,t}$ = gallons sold by station i on day t

$\overline{X}_{i,dt}$ = average gallons sold by station i on the day of the week corresponding to t

$P_{i,t}$ = price per gallon at station i on day t

$P_{c,t}$ = price per gallon at primary competitor on day t

D_1 = dummy variable

= 1.0 for first day in which $P_{i,t} \neq P_{c,t}$

= 0.0 for all other days

D_2 = dummy variable

= 1.0 for second day or subsequent days in which $P_{i,t} \neq P_{c,t}$

= 0.0 for all other days

D_3 = dummy variable

= 1.0 for first day after a price differential in which $P_{i,t} = P_{c,t}$

= 0.0 for all other days

U_t = error term.

The dependent variable was specified in terms of the relative deviation from the station's normal gallonage for each day of the week to eliminate variance attributable to the day-of-week cycle and to permit comparisons of stations of different sizes.

The serial correlation term (the first variable on the right side of Equation 1) was included to account for the suspected interdependence between daily sales at a specific station. Because of the wide range of day-of-week normal gallonages, deviations on day t-1 were related to normal

gallonages on day t. Although this formulation deviates from the usual formulation in a distributed lag model, the regression coefficient for the serial correlation term can be interpreted as a summary of residual effects of past price variations and the effect of deviations from normal sales on day t-1.

To obtain separate estimates for first and subsequent day effects of a price differential, two price terms involving dummy variables were specified. The first price term, involving dummy variable D_1, was non-zero only on the first day of a price differential, while the second price term, involving dummy variable D_2, was non-zero only on subsequent days of a differential.[3] Since the price variables were specified in terms of the relative change of the primary competitor's price, and the dependent variable for sales at the sample station was also specified in relative terms, the partial regression coefficients b_2 and b_3 in Equation (1) can be interpreted as coefficients of the cross-elasticity of price.

It is important to note that the existence of only positive price differentials, i.e., sample station price greater than competitor price, during the data collection period simplified the model. If negative differentials had occurred, additional price terms involving two new dummy variables (say D_4 and D_5) would have been required. Under this condition D_1 and D_2 would be used to represent first and subsequent days of positive differentials, while D_4 and D_5 would designate first and subsequent days of negative differentials. Note that the partial regression coefficients for terms involving D_4 and D_5 would then be interpreted as ordinary price elasticity coefficients rather than cross-elasticity coefficients, and there would be an implicit assumption that the increment in gallonage comes from the primary competitor whose price is used as a proxy for the market price.

Two assumptions were made when specifying a variable for the carry-over effect. First, it was assumed that if such an effect were present it would have its maximum value immediately after prices were brought into equality and would become less important as information about the parity of prices became common knowledge. Second, since there was no downward trend in gallonage for any of the stations during the period, it was assumed that frequent existence of a positive price differential produced no long term carry-over effect. Hence the dummy variable D_3 was specified as nonzero only on the first day of price equality after a price differential.

In order to test the reliability of the findings, the model was replicated on data for each station independently and on the combined data for all stations.

Results

Analysis of results presented in Table 1 reveals the following:

---

[3] Inclusion of the observations for days in which sample station prices equalled competitive prices circumvented the problem of perfect negative correlation between $D_1 + D_2$.

1. There is little serial correlation between deviations from day-of-week normal gallonages.
2. In spite of low values for R^2, a high degree of consistency exists in estimates of the first day effect of price differentials in four of the five replications.
3. Only one station failed to show a higher subsequent day effect than the first day effect.
4. There is little or no short term carry-over effect of price differentials.

The first finding is contrary to *a priori* expectations. Although the combined analysis indicates a slight negative serial correlation, estimates of this effect for individual stations show little consistency. Only Station 1, the smallest of the neighborhood stations, shows a strong relationship between deviations from normal on day *t*-1 and day *t*. The absence of a strong serial correlation term, particularly for the neighborhood Stations 1, 2, and 3, is surprising since purchases of gasoline can be, in most cases, accelerated or deferred by one day, and all the stations make sales to customers using credit cards.

Since little serial correlation appears in the data, and price differentials existed on only 10 percent of the sample days, the low values of R^2 are to be expected. Given that the model accounts for less than ten percent of the variance in sales of each station, the similarity of estimates of the first day cross-elasticity coefficients is surprising. Obtaining four of five separate estimates of the coefficient within a range of −1.409 to −1.860 seems more important than individual tests of significance of the regression or determination coefficients.

Although the range of estimates of subsequent day elasticity coefficients is greater than that of the first day effect, in all cases except Station 1 the subsequent day coefficients have negative signs and indicate a greater effect on sales than do first day coefficients. The greater variability of subsequent day estimates is undoubtedly due in part to the fact that data were too sparse to permit separate estimation of second, third, and fourth day coefficients. Hence, the estimates actually represent an average daily effect for price differentials days after the first day.

Price changes at stations other than the primary competitor could also cause the variability of the estimates. However, given the available data, there was no way to estimate the extent of this influence.

The absence of important negative coefficients for D_3 indicates that the carry-over effect of price differentials is negligible. Apparently information about differentials which existed at an earlier date has little effect on consumers' choice of outlets at the time of purchase.

This result could reflect the following behavior:

1. Consumers who are likely to switch outlets in response to price do not perceive price differentials when they do not need to make a purchase.
2. If consumers are aware of price differentials as they occur, they verify the fact before switching outlets.

Additional information from a consumer survey would be required to verify whether consumers perceive gasoline price information when the purchase is not needed.

The results of this study clearly indicate that operators of the sample stations should counter lower competitive prices immediately if they wish to maximize revenue. For example, the expected loss for the operator of Station 5 is .743 percent of his normal daily revenue for each percentage point of the price differential. On subsequent days the expected daily revenue loss is 2.72 percent for each percentage point of the unmatched price differential.

Summary and Limitations

Results of this study indicate that short term price differentials between competing retail outlets produce greater than proportional losses in the normal gallonages of price followers. Although the effect increases with the duration of the differential, there does not appear to be a measurable carry-over effect. Contrary to *a priori* expectations there does not appear to be a significant amount of interdependence between daily deviations from normal gallonages — even for neighborhood stations.

Table 1
Regression Results

Station	Serial Correlation	First Day Price Elasticity	Subsequent Day Price Elasticity	Carry-Over Effect	R^2	N
1	−0.193 (1.810)*	−2.971 (1.068)	1.473 (0.344)	0.056 (0.432)	.062	87
2	0.870 (0.679)	−1.708 (1.196)	−4.624 (1.040)	0.034 (0.348)	.045	73
3	−0.043 (0.468)	−1.409 (0.545)	−1.927 (0.563)	0.136 (1.073)	.032	75
4	0.052 (0.463)	−1.860 (0.853)	−4.919 (1.745)	−0.061 (0.597)	.058	77
5	−0.014 (0.121)	−1.743 (1.421)	−3.720 (1.766)	0.033 (0.308)	.072	72
Combined	−0.053 (1.114)	−1.843 (2.227)	−2.916 (2.037)	0.031 (0.622)	.027	384

* *T* values

Several limitations which may influence generalizations of these results should be noted. First, the sample was taken in one geographic location and represents interactions between stations selling only major brands of gasoline.

Second, since the data did not include observations of price differentials greater than ten percent, and most differentials existed for less than four days, no conclusions can be drawn about larger differentials and longer time periods.

Third, all stations in the sample were price followers. Hence it would be improper to infer that the same effects would be present if they attempted a policy of price leadership.

Fourth, this analysis has not attempted to measure possible "halo" effects on other products sold by the outlet. To the extent that sales of other products are affected, the impact of the price differential on total station revenue may be understated.

For Discussion

1. Evaluate how the independent variables were operationalized. Interpret the parameter estimates in Table 1. What is a T-value and how is it interpreted? Since the T-values are relatively low, the independent values may well have no impact on the dependent variable. Comment.

2. This model, unlike the first four, is a time series model which means that the data represent successive time periods. In such a model the analyst should be concerned with serial correlation — the error terms are correlated, a large positive error or residual in one period is likely to be followed by another positive error in the next period. Serial correlation will not bias the parameter estimates but it can lead to understated estimates of parameter variances (and T-values). Was there serial correlation in this study? The Aaker-Day paper provides another example of a time-series model.

Part 1

The Analysis of Dependence

Section B
SIMULTANEOUS EQUATION
REGRESSION ANALYSIS

7

A Recursive Model of Communication Processes

David A. Aaker
George S. Day

A durable model of the communication process is based upon the hierarchy-of-effects hypothesis. According to this hypothesis, the effect of a perceived advertisement is to move an individual from unawareness to awareness and then to knowledge, preference, and, finally, purchase (Lavidge and Steiner, 1961). The simplicity and intuitive reasonableness of the resulting communication process model has led to its wide acceptance in marketing circles. At the same time, it has been sharply criticized (Palda, 1966), mainly on the grounds that the progression is not necessarily a one-way sequence from unawareness to purchase and not all individuals will proceed through each step in the hierarchy. Further, the ability of advertising to influence movement through the hierarchy will depend upon many variables, including the appeals, the brand, and the hierarchy level involved. This paper will examine the communication process, with emphasis on the applicability of the hierarchy process and on the role of advertising.

An earlier paper (Assael and Day, 1968) showed that aggregate brand attitude change tended to lead to changes in brand sales. This current paper extends that analysis by using a recursive model that includes the contributions of price and advertising. In addition, a different model formulation and an improved data base substantially increase the scope and reliability of the results.

Hypotheses about Communication Effects

In this study we will consider market behavior (*market share*), two intervening variables (*awareness* and *attitude*), and two external or exogenous variables (*price* and *advertising*). In developing alternate hypotheses, we will first focus upon the hierarchy variables — awareness, attitude, and market share.

Attitude and Behavior

The hierarchy-of-effects model in Figure 1 makes explicit the assumption that awareness (change) is a precursor of attitude (change), which, in turn, leads to sales (as a change in market share). In other words, attitude is assumed to predict behavior.

A major competing hypothesis (shown in Figure 2) is that attitude (change) may follow a behavior (change). Since this hypothesis is somewhat counter-intuitive, it is useful to look at the various theoretical and methodological reasons advanced for this possibility.

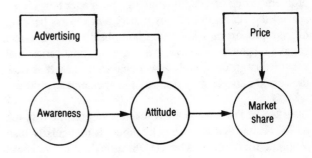

Figure 1
The Hierarchy-of-Effects Hypothesis
Hypothesis (1)

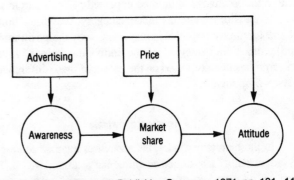

Figure 2
A Competing Hypothesis of the Communication Process
Hypothesis (2)

Cognitive Dissonance Theory.   One view is that attitude change gives meaning to prior behavior change — as in the case of the buyer who has to justify a prior choice or usage experience to himself. For example, "imagine a purchasing situation in which advertising, effective as a reminder of a particular brand name, caused the consumer to select this rather than another brand. Satisfaction with the consequences of the purchase evoked a favorable attitude where none existed before, or strengthened a weak preference" (Palda, 1966). Without attitude change, the beliefs of favorable use experience and weak or nonexistent brand preference are inconsistent, a condition that most people cannot tolerate. Wherever behavior is induced by environmental situations — such as a coupon, or a free sample, or an out-of-stock of a favorite brand — we can expect attitude change to follow behavior change.

Learning without Involvement.   A second conceptual argument for a reverse flow of influence follows from Krugman's (1965) observation that television messages are usually received under conditions of low involvement when perceptual defenses are absent or reduced. The consequence is a shift in the cognitive structure but no corresponding attitude change. The acts of shopping, purchase, or subsequent use release new attitudes that support the prior cognitive change.

Methodological Problems.   The attitude change triggered by pre-purchase shopping is likely to appear to follow the behavior change for yet another reason (Ramond, 1965). The problem is one of interview timing. No matter how closely spaced the successive surveys, there will always be a significant proportion who change both their attitude and their behavior between surveys. An aggregate time-series analysis of this group would show a change in market share in the period between surveys, and a later change in attitude.

The Effect of Product and Brand Differences.   Lipstein (1968, p. 14) argues that the hierarchy model is particularly inappropriate for products where (1) the attitude structure is well defined as a consequence of recent prior purchasing and usage experience, (2) there is relatively little economic or psychological risk in a single purchase, and, consequently, (3) there is little pressure to acquire information prior to purchase. This is an apt description of the instant coffee market to be studied in this paper, which suggests that relatively little attitude change should be expected prior to purchase.

Even within a single product category, the applicability of the hierarchy hypothesis may vary with the positioning and promotion strategies of the individual brands. Little research has been reported on the extent of these differences between brands.

The Awareness Variable

In the hierarchy model, the awareness increase achieved by advertising is assumed to influence attitude, which, in turn, is expected to affect market position. The idea that learning represented by awareness or by brand comprehension precedes and "causes" attitude change was challenged by Haskins (1964). He suggested that the importance of fact learning is overrated by both advertisers and fourth-grade teachers. More important, he surveyed advertising and psychological journals covering a ten-year period noting research projects that reported changes in knowledge and in attitudes or behavior. The results were illuminating. Out of 21 studies in communication research, mostly in controlled laboratory settings with small samples, two showed a positive relationship between changes in knowledge or factual recall and changes in attitudes or behavior, two showed a negative relationship, and the rest showed little or no relationship. Haskins found seven relevant studies conducted by advertising people, but in all cases the expected positive relationship was found to be absent. Thus, there is some question whether awareness is a relevant variable on which advertising should operate. Further, if awareness is relevant, does it operate through an attitude construct or does it operate directly upon market behavior?

The Dynamics of the Process

There is another set of relevant questions about the process that will be considered in this research. How lasting is the impact of advertising on the hierarchy variables? Does any impact tend to dissipate rapidly or does it decay rather slowly instead?

The Role of Exogenous Variables

The expected impacts of the exogenous variables are included in Figures 1 and 2. Price is assumed to affect mainly the market share — reflecting the brand-switching of price-sensitive buyers. It may have some effect upon attitude — particularly in Hypothesis (2) — in that price is an important product attribute for some segments. Price should not have much impact upon awareness.

Theoretically, advertising can operate on awareness, attitude, or directly upon market behavior. However, it is often assumed that advertising is more effective in creating awareness than in affecting attitudes, and that it is least effective in directly affecting market behavior. It will be of interest to explore this assumption and to determine what differences emerge with the different brands. It should be noted that advertising, in this case, is primarily directed at attitude and behavior, since the brands are well established.

Description of the Data

Two data sources were used in this study of the instant coffee market. A national store audit was used to provide estimates of average retail price and dollar market share during 19 successive bi-monthly periods. The estimates of aggregate attitude, awareness, and advertising exposure were obtained from 19 independent cross-section telephone surveys, timed to coincide with the beginning of an audit

Table 1
Variable Definition

Variable Type	Variable	Abbreviation	Description
Endogenous	Awareness	AW(t)	% of households aware of brand at t (unaided recall)
Endogenous	Attitude	ATT(t)	Weighted average of % saying brand is best at t and % saying brand is one of several better brands at t*
Endogenous	Market share	MS($t, t+1$)	Average dollar market share during period t to $t+1$
Exogenous	Price	PR($t, t+1$)	Price (in cents) that brand is above or below the average price for all brands in the market during the period t to $t+1$
Exogenous	Advertising	ADV(t)	% of households who correctly recalled specific copy claims at t

* The attitude score ATT(t)$_t$, for each brand m, is based on the following weighted sum of responses:

$$\frac{\text{Proportion of total sample saying brand } m \text{ is better than the rest of the brands in the market}}{2.00} + \frac{\text{Proportion saying brand } m \text{ is one of several better brands}}{3.86}$$

The weights are based on the judgments of an independent sample of housewives of the degree of favorableness or unfavorableness of the item on an 11-point scale, using Thurstone's scaling procedures 5. Theoretically, this score can range from zero, if no users of the product thought the brand had any merit, to 50.0, if everyone agreed the brand was the best.

period. The variable descriptions are summarized in Table 1. Each survey was based upon a national probability sample of approximately 1,200 households prequalified as users of the product class within the preceding 60 days. The 19 data points used in this study compare to 14 used in the earlier study.

During the three-year period of this study, the total dollar and unit sales were relatively stable; thus any increase in the sales of one brand came primarily at the expense of other brands. This study is confined to the top five nationally distributed and promoted brands; none had less than a 5 percent share at any time during the study.

The hypotheses suggested above were developed primarily from a consideration of the behavior of individuals. Clearly, people differ, and the same ones do not behave identically in all situations. Since aggregate data are used in this study, we are asking which hypotheses have enough general application to emerge in the face of the aggregation. It should be emphasized that conflicting hypotheses can indeed be simultaneously operating in the market.

Model Specification

The three hierarchy variables of awareness, attitude, and market share are considered *endogenous* — they are explained by the model. Each appears as a dependent variable in the system of equations which defines the recursive model. In contrast, advertising and price are treated as *exogenous*;[1]

they are determined by forces outside the process being modeled and are not influenced by the other model variables. Lagged endogenous variables (i.e., those from previous time periods), together with exogenous variables, form the *predetermined* variables. These latter variables are not determined by the model in the time period under study.

The general model for exploring the various hypotheses is defined by the following three equations:

$$\begin{aligned} AW(t) = a_0 &+ a_1 AW(t-1) + a_2 ATT(t-1) \\ &+ a_3 MS(t-1,t) + a_4 ADV(t) \\ &+ a_5 PR(t, t+1) + u_a(t) \end{aligned} \quad (1)$$

$$\begin{aligned} ATT(t) = b_0 &+ b_1 AW(t-1) + b_2 ATT(t-1) \\ &+ b_3 MS(t-1,t) + b_4 ADV(t) \\ &+ b_5 PR(t, t+1) + u_b(t) \end{aligned} \quad (2)$$

$$\begin{aligned} MS(t, t+1) = c_0 &+ c_1 AW(t) + c_2 ATT(t) \\ &+ c_3 MS(t-1,t) + c_4 ADV(t) \\ &+ c_5 PR(t, t+1) + u_c(t) \end{aligned} \quad (3)$$

This model overcomes many of the deficiencies of past research in this area by considering lagged variables and a system of equations. Further, this model has several characteristics distinguishing it from most other applications of simultaneous equation analysis in marketing — it is a recursive model and it avoids an a priori specification of the model structure.

A model is defined by Malinvaud (1966: p. 60) to be recursive "if there exists an ordering of the endogenous variables and an ordering of the equations such that the ith equation can be considered to describe the determination of the value of the endogenous variable during period t as a function of the predetermined variables and of the endogenous variables of index less than i. A model is said to be 'inter-

---

[1] The use of change in all-commodity distribution as a third exogenous variable was considered. Independent examination showed so little variability over time for any of the brands that it was decided to limit it entirely.

dependent' if it is not recursive."[2] Clearly, the model defined by the three equations satisfies this definition.

Recursive models have an important statistical property that interdependent models lack. The parameters can be estimated by applying ordinary least squares to each equation, and the resulting estimates are unbiased (Malinvaud, 1966, p. 514). Thus, we need not consider alternate estimation techniques — a convenient circumstance considering the difficulty that other researchers have had in applying and interpreting alternate estimation methods (e.g., Farley and Leavitt, 1968).

Perhaps more important, recursive models using lagged endogenous variables permit direction-of-influence interpretations to emerge. Malinvaud has summarized the position of Wold (1954), who contributed in the mid-fifties to the development of the theory of recursive models, as follows: "Herman Wold supported the thesis that a good model should describe causal chains and therefore be recursive, since in reality one quantity cannot be at the same time cause and effect of another" (Malinvaud, 1966, p. 60).

A second characteristic of the model defined by Equations (1), (2), and (3) is that any one of several behavioral hypotheses is permitted to emerge. In contrast, most researchers, in using simultaneous equation models (e.g., Bass, 1969; Farley and Leavitt, 1968; and Farley and Ring, n.d.), specify a structure compatible with some "model" or hypothesis and deduce parameter values which are then compared with resulting parameter estimates. The underlying model is deemed supported if a suitable number of estimates are "reasonable." In this research, we avoid the a priori specification of a structure. Rather, the parameter estimates are permitted to suggest a posteriori the structure-defining constraints. The objective is to avoid inhibiting the empirical phase wherever possible.

The model is also in a distributed-lag format, since in each equation the dependent variable, lagged one period, is included among the independent variables. Distributed-lag models have been applied in marketing by Palda (1964), Massy and Frank (1965), and others. The assumption of the most common single-equation version of this model is that the independent variables have an immediate impact, and also a carry-over (or "distribution" over time) effect, that decays geometrically. In the case of two variables, the model would appear as:

$$MS(t, t + 1) = a + b_1 ATT(t) + b_2 \lambda ATT(t - 1)$$
$$+ b_3 \lambda^2 ATT(t - 2) + \cdots$$
$$+ c_1 AW(t) + c_2 \lambda AW(t - 1)$$
$$+ c_3 \lambda^2 AW(t - 2) + \cdots . \quad (4)$$

If we multiply Equation (4), lagged one period, by λ and subtract it from Equation (4), we get:

$$MS(t, t + 1) = a + \lambda MS(t - 1, t)$$
$$+ b_1 ATT(t) + c_1 AW(t). \quad (5)$$

Thus, the coefficient, λ, of the lagged endogenous variable becomes a measure of the extent to which the influence of the independent variables is dissipated quickly. If it is large, then their influence is distributed over many time periods.

In summary, the model is conceived to contain the types of evidence relevant to causation studies (Green and Tull, 1966, pp. 96–98), associative variation, sequence of events (the lagged endogenous variables), and the absence of other possible causal factors (via the inclusion of relevant exogenous variables and the lack of an a priori imposed structure).

Results

The Quality of the Results. Scatter diagrams of a sample of the data did not suggest any nonlinearities, so no transformations were performed. The price variable was available only for Brands 3, 4, and 5. Consequently, the model with the price variable deleted was first estimated using ordinary least squares (OLS) for each of the five brands individually, and for all five brands combined. The results are shown in Table 2. The model with the price variable included was then run on Brands 3, 4, and 5 individually, and on the three brands combined. These results are presented in Table 3.

When the brands were aggregated, dummy variables were inserted to compensate for the different variable levels at which the brands operate. An assumption of the model when applied to this aggregate data is that each coefficient is the same for all brands. A gross comparison of the individual brand coefficients and their standard deviations indicates that this assumption is not extremely unreasonable.[3]

The R^2 values for the individual brands are certainly respectable. The lowest R^2 is 0.30, and in two thirds of the equations it is over 0.50. Further, in over half of the equations the lagged endogenous variable is not significant, so the remaining variables are explaining most of the variance. The R^2 for the equations with aggregated data are deceptively high. The three brands had relatively small variation around different levels, reflecting the fact that they had very different average market shares. Thus, the total variance went up enormously when the brands were combined. The standard error of regression is the more appropriate indicator of the performance with the aggregated set.

A common problem in time series studies is serial correlation, which leads to inefficient coefficient estimates and understated estimates of coefficient variances. The Durbin-Watson statistics shown in the tables indicate that this statistical problem is not troublesome in this research. Over half of the values are above the upper limit of the Durbin-Watson test, and none are close to the lower limit at which the hypothesis of serial independence is rejected. However, this test is biased when lagged dependent variables are used. This bias, of course, is small when the lagged dependent

---

[2]This definition is sufficient for a deterministic model. With the error terms included, we must also assume that the covariance matrix of the error terms is a diagonal.

[3] The model was also run with the data divided by the appropriate mean for each brand. The results were not affected significantly. Thus, we have reported the results using the original data so that the results will have more meaning.

Table 2
Regression Results, Price Excluded* (*t* Values in Parentheses)

Brand	Dependent Variable	Independent Variables					R^2†	Standard Error	Durbin-Watson	Sample Size
		AW($t-1$)	ATT($t-1$)	MS($t-1, t$)	ADV(t)	a_0				
1	AW(t)	0.39 (1.80)	3.30 (1.20)	−2.01 (1.40)	2.85 (2.42)	21.8 (3.65)	0.50	3.96	1.84	19
2	AW(t)	0.01 (0.06)	−0.18 (0.11)	2.13 (1.44)	2.6 (3.82)	11.2 (1.6)	0.62	1.42	1.52	19
3	AW(t)	0.30 (1.06)	0.75 (0.47)	−0.33 (0.26)	0.16 (0.81)	23.2 (2.41)	0.42	1.81	1.98	19
4	AW(t)	0.26 (0.96)	−4.13 (1.30)	0.95 (0.57)	1.2 (2.6)	33.61 (1.97)	0.38	4.67	2.10	19
5	AW(t)	0.61 (2.56)	−0.08 (1.52)	0.08 (0.24)	0.42 (2.67)	24.5 (1.5)	0.57	1.42	1.52	19
All	AW(t)	0.37 (3.60)	−0.09 (0.86)	0.33 (0.71)	0.46 (3.01)	—	0.977	3.20	1.90	95
		AW($t-1$)	ATT($t-1$)	MS($t-1, t$)	ADV(t)	b_0				
1	ATT(t)	−0.01 (0.68)	0.45 (1.84)	0.07 (0.57)	0.13 (0.92)	0.88 (1.70)	0.30	0.35	1.84	19
2	ATT(t)	−0.01 (0.15)	−0.18 (0.53)	0.68 (2.07)	0.10 (0.68)	0.48 (0.32)	0.30	0.39	1.77	19
3	ATT(t)	0.11 (1.89)	−0.08 (0.26)	0.09 (0.34)	0.03 (0.85)	−0.21 (0.11)	0.55	0.37	1.55	19
4	ATT(t)	0.01 (0.67)	0.16 (0.70)	−0.03 (0.27)	0.11 (3.37)	2.51 (2.02)	0.54	0.34	1.98	19
5	ATT(t)	0.23 (1.28)	0.02 (0.49)	0.13 (0.51)	0.27 (2.3)	−13.5 (1.09)	0.51	1.07	2.70	19
All	ATT(t)	0.01 (0.36)	0.03 (1.70)	0.26 (3.00)	0.10 (3.60)	—	0.986	0.60	2.20	95
		AW($t-1$)	ATT($t-1$)	MS($t-1, t$)	ADV(t)	c_0				
1	MS($t, t+1$)	0.05 (1.23)	0.70 (1.40)	0.03 (0.18)	0.01 (0.04)	2.45 (1.80)	0.40	0.65	1.03	19
2	MS($t, t+1$)	−0.05 (1.26)	0.35 (2.20)	0.76 (5.20)	−0.76 (0.07)	1.27 (1.86)	0.79	0.20	1.98	19
3	MS($t, t+1$)	0.06 (1.12)	0.03 (0.14)	0.70 (3.30)	0.02 (0.68)	−0.31 (0.16)	0.80	0.32	1.68	19
4	MS($t, t+1$)	0.05 (1.27)	0.71 (1.27)	0.23 (1.05)	−0.08 (0.80)	−4.34 (1.38)	0.34	0.72	2.36	19
5	MS($t, t+1$)	0.23 (1.77)	0.66 (3.35)	0.34 (2.07)	−0.12 (1.37)	−4.33 (0.46)	0.78	0.83	2.40	19
All	MS($t, t+1$)	0.05 (6.05)	0.40 (5.77)	0.51 (6.92)	0.06 (1.63)	—	0.998	0.52	2.34	95

* Dummy variables for each brand were inserted in the aggregate equations.   † R^2 is unadjusted.

variables are insignificant, as they often were in this research, especially in the awareness and attitude equations. Further, several of the equations were run with the dependent variable omitted. The results suggest that if the bias were removed from the test, the hypothesis of serial independence would still not be rejected at the 0.05 level.

Testing Specific Hypotheses. First, consider Table 2. The influence of AW upon ATT seems extremely low. In the aggregate, the *t* value is only 0.36. Only Brand 3 has a positive coefficient significant at the 0.10 level, and Brands 1 and 2 have negative coefficients. In contrast, AW seems to be much more significant in the MS equation. In the aggregate, the *t* value is 6.05, and all the coefficients except that of Brand 2 are positive, with *t* values exceeding 1.0. This

result casts some doubt upon the hierarchy concept as portrayed in Hypothesis 1. However, it is undoubtedly also reflecting the fact that there is a longer time lag between AW($t-1$) and ATT(t) than between AW(t) and MS($t, t+1$). It may be that a shorter time lag between AW($t-1$) and ATT(t) would show a greater relationship. Nevertheless, the minimal impact of lagged AW on ATT and the strong link between AW and MS are surprising.

As expected, neither the ATT nor the MS variable seemed to influence the AW variable to any significant degree. The relevant *t* values in the aggregate case were both below 1.0. It should be noted that Brand 2 has a relatively high positive MS coefficient in the AW equation. Thus, there is some suggestion in the Brand 2 case, especially noting the negative AW coefficient in the MS equation,

Table 3
Regression Results, Price Included,* Brands 3–5 (*t* Values in Parentheses)

Brand	Dependent Variable	Independent Variables						R^2†	Standard Error	Durbin-Watson	Sample Size
		$AW(t-1)$	$ATT(t-1)$	$MS(t-1, t)$	$ADV(t)$	$PR(t)$	a_0				
3	$AW(t)$	0.28	0.79	−0.40	0.16	0.06	24.10				
		(0.85)	(0.47)	(0.29)	(0.79)	(0.15)	(2.05)	0.42	1.90	2.00	19
4	$AW(t)$	0.22	−3.24	0.42	1.15	−0.21	38.8				
		(0.80)	(0.92)	(0.23)	(2.50)	(0.30)	(2.05)	0.41	4.7	2.13	19
5	$AW(t)$	0.61	−0.07	0.14	4.6	−0.15	21.8				
		(2.50)	(1.43)	(0.39)	(2.5)	(0.47)	(1.23)	0.58	1.5	1.5	19
All	$AW(t)$	0.17	−0.04	0.16	0.44	−0.26	—				
		(1.33)	(0.40)	(0.33)	(3.27)	(1.72)		0.982	3.06	2.08	57
		$AW(t-1)$	$ATT(t-1)$	$MS(t-1, t)$	$ADV(t)$	$PR(t)$	b_0				
3	$ATT(t)$	0.13	−0.12	0.15	0.03	−0.05	−1.04				
		(1.96)	(0.37)	(0.53)	(0.82)	(0.66)	(0.44)	0.57	0.37	1.62	19
4	$ATT(t)$	0.02	0.05	0.04	0.12	0.03	1.83				
		(0.91)	(0.20)	(0.29)	(3.60)	(1.30)	(1.41)	0.59	0.33	2.31	19
5	$ATT(t)$	0.23	0.01	−0.06	0.16	0.46	−5.4				
		(1.40)	(0.33)	(0.26)	(1.40)	(2.15)	(0.46)	0.64	0.96	2.80	19
All	$ATT(t)$	0.02	0.03	0.24	0.09	0.06	—				
		(0.58)	(1.33)	(2.25)	(2.70)	(1.82)		0.985	0.70	2.10	57
		$AW(t-1)$	$ATT(t-1)$	$MS(t-1, t)$	$ADV(t)$	$PR(t)$	c_0				
3	$MS(t, t+1)$	0.06	0.03	0.68	0.02	0.07	−0.22				
		(1.05)	(0.14)	(2.96)	(0.65)	(0.11)	(0.10)	0.80	0.33	1.66	19
4	$MS(t, t+1)$	0.03	1.05	0.12	−0.10	−0.06	5.68				
		(0.69)	(1.69)	(0.49)	(1.00)	(1.16)	(1.72)	0.40	0.72	2.43	19
5	$MS(t, t+1)$	0.28	0.49	0.25	−0.17	0.29	−2.36				
		(2.13)	(2.16)	(1.43)	(1.80)	(1.37)	(0.25)	0.81	0.81	2.47	19
All	$MS(t, t+1)$	0.05	0.62	0.41	−0.24	−0.45	—				
		(1.64)	(4.46)	(3.95)	(0.67)	(0.12)		0.997	0.67	2.39	57

* Dummy variables for each brand were inserted in the aggregate equations.   † R^2 is unadjusted.

that usage is preceding and perhaps ''causing'' changes in the awareness level. There are at least two possible explanations for this finding. First, impulse buying may be particularly important for this brand. Second, it might indicate that for this brand the link between AW and MS influences purchase behavior very quickly. If AW and MS were affected in the same time period, the AW would appear to follow the MS change, since it was measured at the end of the time period. Brand 2 differed from the others in that it had a higher emphasis upon quality. It was also available as a regular coffee. Further, it was the smallest brand studied and did grow slightly during the time periods involved.

We now consider the ATT and MS terms which are at the heart of the two major competing hypotheses summarized in Figures 1 and 2. Does an attitude change precede and cause a behavioral change, or does the reverse occur? It seems clear that ATT is a significant influence on MS in this study. In the aggregate, the *t* value of the ATT coefficient in the MS equation was 5.77, and the *t* values for Brands 2 and 5 were over 2.2. Only for Brand 3 was the *t* value low. In the ATT equation, the conclusion is not so clear. The coefficients and *t* values are lower. Only Brand 2 had a significantly positive coefficient. These results thus offer some support to the hierarchy-of-effects hypothesis. However, there is certainly evidence of some influence moving in the opposite direction. In the aggregate, the MS *t*

value in the ATT equation was 3.0, and for Brand 2 it was 2.07. Also, the effect of MS on ATT seems higher than that of AW. However, there is a methodological bias, as mentioned before, which tends to emphasize the MS to ATT flow of influence. It is caused by the fact that an MS and ATT change in the same time period will appear as an MS to ATT flow of influence. With this in mind, the ATT to MS flow of influence predicted by the hierarchy model does seem to appear more dominant in this study.

These conclusions do not seem to be affected by the addition of the price variable in Table 3. For example, the AW coefficients in the ATT equation are slighly higher, but still only those of Brand 3 are significantly positive.

The *advertising* variable was expected to influence AW, and to a lesser extent ATT, but to have little direct impact upon MS. These hypotheses seem to be supported. In Table 2, the impact of ADV upon MS seems small. It is negative, in fact, for three of the five brands. When price is added in Table 3, the negative coefficient for Brand 5 becomes significant. In contrast, ADV is a strong influence upon AW and ATT. In the AW equation there is only one case where the ADV variable is not significantly positive. In the ATT equation the results for the individual brands are less significant, but the overall results are still strong. ADV for Brands 1 and 2 seemed to have more impact on AW than on ATT. We have already noted that Brand 2 was the smallest studied, Brand 1 was similar in market size to Brand 2, and Brands 4 and 5 were the largest. Here, ADV seemed to have an equal impact upon AW and ATT. Again it should be noted that these results could partially by reflecting the nature of the time lags actually operating.

The *price* variable was expected to primarily influence MS. Since a price decline should create a positive MS change, the coefficients should be negative. The empirical results are somewhat puzzling. Price seemed to have little influence on market share — a *t* value of 0.12 in the aggregate. There was an apparent impact of price upon AW and ATT. It seemed to have a slight positive impact upon AW (represented by a negative coefficient). Perhaps price reductions accompanying promotions attract sufficient attention to influence AW. Conversely, the impact of price upon ATT tended to be negative (a positive coefficient). Perhaps these same promotions had an image-tarnishing effect upon the brand which canceled the increase in awareness. The net result on MS was, consequently, very small. There is a competing explanation. It is possible that price declines follow and thus are associated with weak demand instead of preceding and being associated with strong demand. In the tradition of simultaneous-equation analysis, this suggests considering price as an endogenous variable.

The coefficients of the lagged endogenous variables in the recursive equations are also of interest. In general, lagged effects were more important in the MS equations. Thus, the effect of the independent variables on awareness and attitude seems to dissipate rather rapidly, whereas their impact on behavior is of a longer-run nature. This conclusion, where confirmed, suggests that advertising campaigns addressed solely to awareness and attitude may not have the long-term impact they desire unless the campaign's impact is felt fairly soon in market behavior.

It should be noted that this study was conducted under the handicap of significant multicollinearity. Thus, the regression coefficients tend to have higher variances and covariances than would be desirable. Fortunately, the *t*-test is still appropriate, and conclusions based upon it are still valid. However, one must realize that misspecification could distort these findings. Two further qualifications concern the generally crude nature of the attitude and advertising effects variables, which tend to mask subtle changes in the market, and the mature but highly competitive character of the instant coffee market. Other measures and markets may yield different communication processes when subjected to this type of time series analysis. Nonetheless, the consistency of the effects across five brands enhances the validity of the conclusions.

Summary and Conclusions

It appears that neither of the basic hypotheses of communication effects is an accurate representation of the empirical results of this study. A more appropriate description would be the model suggested by Figure 3. We have omitted price, since the results in this area were inconsistent.

The first conclusion is that advertising can influence behavior (market share) by working through awareness. There are undoubtedly those to whom brand awareness is an important determinant of purchase for this product class. But advertising can also affect behavior through its influence upon attitude — probably by reaching a different type of buyer. These observations held across the five brands studied here. Thus, it appeared that all brands had advertising campaigns that affected both awareness and attitude simultaneously. One surprising result was that the influence of advertising seems to go from awareness directly to behavior and does not operate through the attitude construct. Relatively strong support for the hypothesis that attitude change precedes behavior change was found in this study. Not surprisingly, the reverse effect also emerged, although it was relatively less significant.

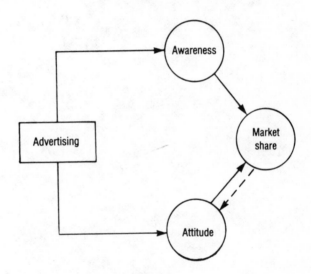

Figure 3
A Revised Model of Communication Effects

References

1. Assael, Henry, and George S. Day. "Attitudes and Awareness as Predictors of Market Share," *Journal of Advertising Research*, 8 (December 1968), 3–12.
2. Bass, Frank M. "A Simultaneous Regression Study of Advertising and Sales of Cigarettes," *Journal of Marketing Research*, 6 (August 1969), 291–300.
3. Claycamp, Henry J., and Lucien E. Liddy. "Prediction of New Product Performance: An Analytical Approach," *Journal of Marketing Research*, 6 (November 1969), 414–420.
4. Edwards, Allen L. *Techniques of Attitude Scale Construction*. New York: Appleton-Century-Crofts, 1957.
5. Farley, John U., and Harold J. Leavitt. "A Model of the Distribution of Branded Personal Products in Jamaica," *Journal of Marketing Research*, 5 (November 1968), 362–369.
6. Farley, John U., and L. Winston Ring. "An Empirical Test of the Howard-Sheth Model of Buying Behavior," unpublished Working Paper. New York: Columbia University, n.d.
7. Green, Paul E., and Donald S. Tull. *Research for Marketing Decisions*. Englewood Cliffs, N.J.: Prentice-Hall, 1966.
8. Haskins, Jack B. "Factual Recall as a Measure of Advertising Effectiveness," *Journal of Advertising Research*, 4 (1964), 2–8.
9. Krugman, Herbert E. "The Impact of Television Advertising: Learning without Involvement," *The Public Opinion Quarterly*, 29 (Fall 1965), 349–356.

10. Lavidge, Robert J., and Gary A. Steiner. "A Model for Predictive Measurement of Advertising Effectiveness," *Journal of Marketing,* 25 (October 1961), 59–62.

11. Lipstein, Benjamin. "Anxiety, Risk, and Uncertainty in Advertising Effectiveness Measurements," in L. Adler and I. Crespi (eds.), *Attitude Research on the Rocks.* Chicago: American Marketing Association, 1968.

12. Malinvaud, E. *Statistical Methods of Econometrics.* Chicago: Rand McNally & Co., 1966.

13. Massy, William F., and R. E. Frank. "Short-Term Price and Dealing Effects in Selected Market Segments," *Journal of Marketing Research,* 2 (May 1965), 171–185.

14. Maloney, John C. "Attitude Measurement and Formation," paper presented at the Test Market Design and Measurement Workshop, American Marketing Association, Chicago, April 21, 1966.

15. Palda, Kristian S. *The Measurement of Cumulative Advertising Effects.* Englewood Cliffs, N.J.: Prentice-Hall, 1964.

16. _____. "The Hypothesis of a Hierarchy of Effects: A Partial Evaluation," *Journal of Marketing Research,* 3 (February 1966), 13–25.

17. Ramond, Charles K. "Must Advertising Communicate to Sell?" *Harvard Business Review,* 43 (September-October 1965), 148–161.

18. Wold, H. "Causality and Econometrics," *Econometrica* (April 1954).

For Discussion

1. Why might behavior be hypothesized to cause or influence attitude?

2. Explain what is the defining characteristic of a recursive model and of a distributed lag model.

3. Develop a set of hypotheses and a revised model (like that of Figure 3) using only the Brand 4 data. Also do it for only the Brand 3 data. Why do you think your conclusions differed from that of Figure 3 (if they did differ)?

8

Causal Path Analysis in Market Research

M. G. Christopher
C. K. Elliott

It would not be an exaggeration to say that of all the concerns of the investigative sciences causality ranks the highest. The desired end product of any research is usually a statement concerning the causes and effects of various actions or activities, whether these events occur in a test-tube or in a test market. Market research is obviously no exception to this and the empirical nature of most market research lends itself to causal analysis and prediction.

Market research, calling as it does on the techniques and ideas of many disciplines, has not been slow to subject the results of its empirical observations to rigorous and sophisticated procedures. Nevertheless analysis has tended to stop short at multivariate methods and does not take the next short step to causal analysis. Multivariate techniques can isolate factors contributing to a causal process but do not arrange these in a testable causal pattern.

We may distinguish two requirements in market research concerning causality: first we must be able to say that this factor contributes to this event; second we must be able to specify a hierarchy of causal agents, in other words we will wish to say that A precedes B which precedes C which then causes event D. It has always been possible to formulate hypotheses based on intuitive judgement and/or empirical evidence but usually these hypotheses have only been subjected to the flimsiest of tests. The fundamental requirement, as the authors see it, is for a hypothesis generating and validating device, in other words a mechanism that will enable the researcher to postulate certain aspects of behavior possibly connected with the event under study and then refine and reduce the data concerning these aspects, suggest a hypothesis based upon a statistical examination of the data and then test this hypothesis. Alternatively it may

The authors gratefully acknowledge the programming assistance given by Geraint Roberts of the University of Bradford Management Centre who has also contributed much in the way of advice during the development of this technique. These findings are the development of work originally sponsored by Product Research Ltd.

be desired to test alternate competing hypotheses and so the mechanism must be capable of giving an indication of which is the most likely.

Such a mechanism is the basis of the Causal Analysis Package. Mainly as a result of the nature of the data used in the initial experiments using the techniques the first stage incorporates a cluster analysis although this is not necessarily the only, or the best, way of reducing a large data field down to a smaller and more easily handled number of variables. In effect it is possible to input the raw data from a questionnaire at one end of the process and output a tested hypothesis concerning causal patterns at the other.

The applications of such a package to market research are obviously manifold. A typical application could be a readership study — why do readers read a particular newspaper or periodical? A questionnaire could be designed to cover as many dimensions of readership as are thought relevant, using, as far as possible, objective techniques for deriving constructs. The more these initial questions are refined and the more factor-pure self-rating scales are, then the more accuracy they will have as a predictive battery. It is obvious that the choice of dimensions to be studied will affect the outcome of the experiment and no matter how sophisticated the technique described may be, the accuracy of the output is solely a function of the relevance and completeness of the input.

Conceptual Background

The concept of causality has a dubious status in the philosophy of science, and many urge its complete rejection. We tend still to think in terms of events being caused by other events, however, and so it is necessary not to outlaw the concept but to purify it, rigorously defining it in operational terms so that the philosophy of science may parallel the scientist's everyday thinking.

Attempts to rehabilitate causality have a long history,

and one such attempt appears to have borne useful fruit for the applied scientist. The idea of causal path analysis was developed by Wright (1934, 1960) to assist in the prediction of genetic changes and to calculate the genetic similarity of relatives of given degrees of relationship. Wright further showed how it was possible to estimate the magnitude of paths[1] linking variables which would account for observed relationships in such diverse areas as the influence upon intelligence of heredity and environment (1931), and the linked supply and demand for corn and hogs (1934).

Simon (1957) indicated that it has become customary to avoid statements of causality and instead to speak of 'functional relationships' or 'interdependence.' He showed, however, that interdependence implies a symmetrical relationship between variables whereas causation implies asymmetry; and so if asymmetry of relationship makes sense in our thinking about the world, then a concept of causality is necessary.

We obviously observe asymmetric relationships between variables (e.g., age of a customer influences probability of buying pop records but not vice versa) and Simon demonstrated how causality may be defined in terms of asymmetric relationships amongst variables or sets of variables within a self contained model. Thus, any attempt to use a causal model must specify a finite set of variables, although error terms may be introduced to represent the effects upon the dependent variable of variables outside the model.

Blalock (1964) developed the practical uses of Simon's ideas, showing that causal models may be evaluated using methods very similar to those of Wright. Although experimentation is the strongest test of a causal model, this is not always practically possible and we frequently have to use non-experimental data, and Blalock was particularly concerned with causal inferences in such situations. He distinguished direct and indirect causation: X is a direct cause of Y if (and only if) a change in X produces a change in Y ($X \rightarrow Y$) whereas X may be an indirect cause of Z by producing a change in Y which produces a change in Z ($X \rightarrow Y \rightarrow Z$), and thus a causal route may be identified. Two uses of the causal path method were distinguished by Blalock:

(i) it can test hypothetical models previously generated
(ii) it can help to generate new causal models.

Hypothetical causal models are tested by comparing their predictions with observed data. If there is a good fit between the two, one is justified in saying that the model is a good one, but not necessarily the only correct one unless all possible models have been evaluated. New models may be generated by showing which independent variables directly and indirectly cause variation in the dependent variable.

Duncan (1966) attempted to make the method of path analysis more accessible to social scientists and showed its uses by re-analysing previously published data. He stressed that the method requires linear, additive, asymmetric relations which may be used to generate a recursive system of equa-

tions (i.e. there is no reciprocal reaction of variables).

The relationship of path analysis to regression analysis is clear. It is essentially a development of multiple regression analysis to show which independent variables and which combinations of these variables best explain the dependent variables. It is an extension of multiple regression analysis in that it can aid the interpretation of a multiple regression. Furthermore path analysis can show both the direct and indirect effects of independent variables on the dependent variable. It is this latter attribute of path analysis which enables the investigator to build complex models of causal relationships of a type unattainable by conventional multiple regression analysis.

The diagrammatic representation of causal models helps to reveal their structure (see Figure 1). Each variable is represented by a point and each significant relationship between variables by a unidirectional arrow. The strength of the relationship between each pair of variables is expressed by a path coefficient, which is the β used in multiple regression. The basic theorem of path analysis as demonstrated by Duncan (op. cit.) shows that a correlation between two variables can be written in terms of the routes linking them via other variables in the model. As the model may be complex, a useful technique to establish all the possible routes is to trace a route from one variable to the other variable as indicated by the direction of the arrows, making sure that any one variable is not used more than once in each route. The path coefficients linking each pair of variables along the route are multiplied. When every possible route between the two variables is traced in this way, and the products of path coefficients obtained, the resulting expression indicates the single direct path and all possible indirect paths between the two variables. The sum of these path coefficient products should equal the correlation between the two variables, and if it does not, the causal model must be modified. Blalock suggests two heuristics to assist the modification:

"(1) make changes where there are the largest discrepancies between actual and predicted values
"(2) where possible make changes first in causal relationships among variables presumed to be operating near the beginning of the causal sequence."

Blalock (op. cit. p. 80)

Figure 1

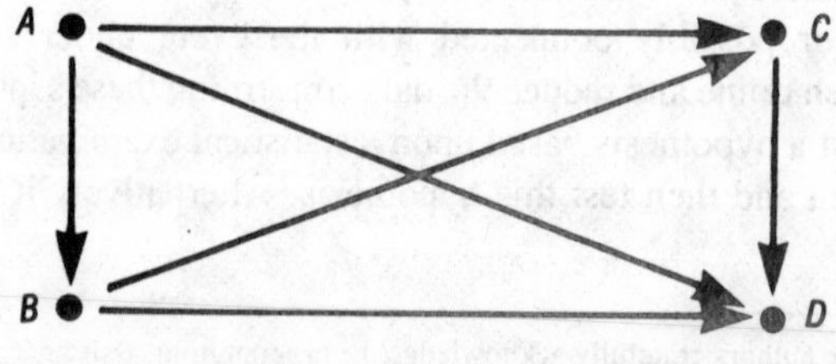

For example in Figure 1, if D is the dependent variable and ABC independent variables, then routes from A to D in this model are

AD   direct

$\left.\begin{array}{l}\text{AB BD} \\ \text{AB BC CD} \\ \text{AC CD}\end{array}\right\}$ indirect

then

$$r_{AD} = \beta_{AD} + \beta_{AB} \cdot \beta_{BD} + \beta_{AB} \cdot \beta_{BC} \cdot \beta_{CD} + \beta_{AC} \cdot \beta_{CD}.$$

If this equation is not satisfied within pre-specified limits, say plus or minus 5%, then one of the paths should be removed.

For example, if the path AC is removed then the model is shown in Figure 2

Figure 2

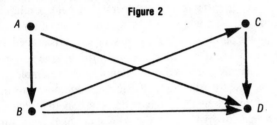

and routes from A to D are

AD   direct

$\left.\begin{array}{l}\text{AB BD} \\ \text{AB BC CD}\end{array}\right\}$ indirect

then

$$r_{AD} = \beta_{AD} + \beta_{AB} \cdot \beta_{BD} + \beta_{AB} \cdot \beta_{BC} \cdot \beta_{CD}.$$

The development of digraph theory (Harary *et al* 1965) has implications for the construction of causal models, as was shown by Huff (1959) who developed a topological model of consumer space preferences. The use of matrix algebra facilities computer manipulation of complex models and the Causal Analysis Package, based as it is on the sequential comparison of matrices, uses these techniques to identify complex causal routes.

Identification of Relevant Independent Variables and the Imput to the Causal Analysis Package

The input to the model is in the form of correlation coefficients between variables; these variables being those which it is thought are the major factors or features contributing in a causal manner to the occurrence or outcome under investigation. Thus if it is thought that the occurrence D is a function of events A, B and C then these events must be numerically evaluated, usually by some method of observation. Often the problem is not so much one of quantifying these variables but the actual identification of those variables that are relevant to the causal process. It is at this stage that the success or failure of meaningful causal identification is in the balance. For example it may be observed that two events

are closely linked, in a correlative sense, with the dependent outcome; the digraph below illustrates such a possibility:

At this initial stage of thinking only in terms of correlation we may not be correct in ascribing directionality to the link between A and B but an even greater hazard is that we may be introducing spurious relationships by failing to identify a third independent variable (C) which effects both A and B:

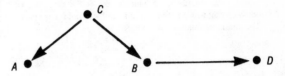

In this example a change in C will induce a change in A and a change in B such that changes in A will appear to be linked with changes in B, yet as far as causal influences on D are concerned A is irrelevant: the causal chain here is simple

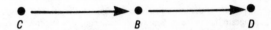

It is therefore apparent that unless all the relevant variables have been correctly identified the causal model will be at best incomplete and at worst totally misleading. The initial selection of variables must obviously be made on a subjective basis, although of course this does not mean that such choice need not have a logical basis for inclusion in the battery. In some cases it may be possible to utilise existing procedures to identify the relevant variables, for example, the Repertory Grid technique as developed by Kelly could be used in a situation where it was thought that some aspect of personal behaviour was a function of personal constructs arranged in some hierarchial, causal manner. Rather than risking the danger of excluding an important variable it may be advisable to cast the net wide and then eliminate for irrelevancy and/or redundancy later.

Path analytic techniques have been developed only for those situations where the relationship between independent and dependent variables is thought to be linear. Similarly, it is dependent upon the additive nature of the predictors. In common with many other analytic and predictive methods causal path analysis is constrained by certain underlying assumptions:

(1) The normality of underlying variables.
(2) Errors in the data must be uncorrelated.
(3) Linearity of regressions.
(4) It must be assumed that variables outside the system (i.e. those not measured) do not influence the causal pattern, i.e. the dependent variable must be completely explained in terms of the independent variables (although error terms may be used to account for unexplained influence of outside variables.)
(5) There may only be one dependent variable.
(6) Data should be derived from large samples in order that the sampling error is small. (This requirement is in order that the path coefficients (β) may be tested for significance against the standard error of the coefficient.)

Program Details

Computer programs have been written to identify significant causal paths and to generate causal routes. Two levels of sophistication of input data are handled:

> Type (1): The investigator must be able to determine a likely hierarchy of causal influences. This hierarchy can then be used to specify the direction of causality linking each pair of input variables, or to state that a pair of variables are not causally linked. Such a procedure is illustrated in the example appended. The program uses matrix methods to identify the causal routes and up to twenty-nine independent variables may be used. This information is input in the form of an influence matrix (a square matrix with one row and one column for each variable, in which a cell = 1 if there is a causal link between that row and that column, and = 0 if there is no causal link). The influence matrix for Figure 1 is

	A	B	C	D
A	0	1	1	1
B	0	0	1	1
C	0	0	0	1
D	0	0	0	0

> Type (2): If the investigator cannot specify direction of causality the program has to identify all possible causal paths and then all possible combinations of paths to form all possible causal routes. Although a series of heuristics are used, the number of independent variables has to be limited to six because of the large storage capacity required by the program when generating combinations of paths. In view of the complexity of this program discussion of the procedures must await communication in a further paper.

The raw data for the program may be a mixture of binary (e.g. yes/no answers to questions) and continuous variables (e.g. a numerical scale of strength of attitude). The program computes the appropriate correlation coefficient between all variables and tests their statistical significance at a given level. Only statistically significant correlations are used to generate causal paths.

With type 1 data the correlation matrix is combined with the influence matrix to yield a new matrix with entries only for cells which represent statistically significant correlations and meaningful causal influences. This significant influence matrix is then used to generate the routes. With type 2 data the combinations of causal paths are generated. Path coefficients (i.e. β coefficients) are computed by taking each adjacent pair of variables in a causal route and holding constant prior variables along the route. For example:

the route ABCDE

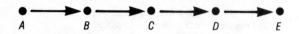

uses

$$\beta_{BA}, \ \beta_{CB \cdot A}, \ \beta_{DC \cdot BA}, \ \beta_{ED \cdot CBA}.$$

The sums of products of path coefficients (i.e. β coefficients) are then computed for each causal route, and output together with the appropriate correlation coefficient between the starting independent variable and the dependent variable so that the investigator can check the balance between these

values, and decide whether to accept or further amend the causal model. In addition, the model is output in matrix form (cf. input influence matrix) together with a matrix of all significant β coefficients.

Causal Path Analysis in Action

Working on data generated by Johan Arndt in his work on word-of-mouth communication (1968) it is possible to illustrate quite dramatically how the technique of causal path analysis can be used to generate hypotheses which are supported, in this instance, by empirical research.

The role of risk in product purchase has been given great attention in recent years. Bauer (1960) has suggested that there is a degree of risk, real or apparent, in many purchasing situations, the amount of risk being a function of the 'risk-style' of the purchaser and the product itself. It is argued that in order to avoid social or economic injury the low-risk taking potential purchaser will often take considerable precautions, usually in the form of acquiring additional information, before making the purchase decision. Sheth (1968) has shown that low-risk innovations (i.e. products with little associated risk) are more likely to achieve adoption more quickly and at a higher level. In addition Perry and Hamm (1969) using canonical methods have shown that the higher the socio-economic risk involved in a particular purchase decision, the greater the importance of personal influence, as compared with other sources of influence.

In his study of the adoption of a new brand of coffee Arndt (1968) interviewed 416 housewives in an apartment complex and determined their scores on the following dimensions:

Social variables:
1. *Opinion leadership:* How often the interviewers were referred to by the other housewives for advice on new food products.
2. *Social integration:* How often they were referred to by the other housewives as being friends.

Psychological variables:
1. *Inner-other directedness:* Derived from the Kassarjian Social Preference Scale.
2. *Generalised self-confidence:* A measure of feelings of inadequacy.
3. *Perceived risk:* A multiplicative function of the importance and uncertainty components of the consumers' perception of risk.

Purchasing variables:
1. *General innovativeness for food products:* Number of new food products tried in a given period.
2. *Deal-proneness:* Susceptibility to below-the-line promotions.
3. *Usage rate of coffee.*
4. *Brand loyalty.*

(For the scoring procedures employed see Arndt (op. cit.).)

Demographic data relating to the respondents (age, number of children, length of marriage) were collected by Arndt but not reported. Although the data were not collected by the authors it seems reasonable in view of Arndt's use of correlation analysis that they conform to the assumptions stated earlier.

The nine variables above were arranged by the present authors into a likely hierarchy of causation. It seems reasonable to assume that psychological variables precede social variables which in turn precede purchasing variables. Within each of these three groups the ordering of influence is debatable but on intuitive reasoning the following ordering was made:

Inner-other directedness	(2);
Generalized self-confidence	(3);
Perceived risk	(4);
Social integration	(5);
Opinion leadership	(6);
Innovativeness	(7);
Deal-proneness (8); Brand loyalty (9);	
Usage rate	(10);
Product Adoption (1, Dependent variable).	

(Numbers refer to computer print-out, see below.)

It should be noted that the two variables deal-proneness and brand loyalty could not be ordered and thus no causal influence is postulated in either direction. On the basis of this hierarchy the following influence matrix was constructed.

Table 1
Original Influence Matrix

	1	2	3	4	5	6	7	8	9	10
1	0	0	0	0	0	0	0	0	0	0
2	1	0	1	1	1	1	1	1	1	1
3	1	0	0	1	1	1	1	1	1	1
4	1	0	0	0	1	1	1	1	1	1
5	1	0	0	0	0	1	1	1	1	1
6	1	0	0	0	0	0	1	1	1	1
7	1	0	0	0	0	0	0	1	1	1
8	1	0	0	0	0	0	0	0	0	1
9	1	0	0	0	0	0	0	0	0	1
10	1	0	0	0	0	0	0	0	0	0

Arndt's correlations are reproduced in Table 2.

The cells significant at the 0.5 level in the correlation matrix were combined with the appropriate cells in the influence matrix to yield a 'significant influence matrix.' '1' indicates a significant causal influence, '0' the absence of significance or causality.

Table 3
Significant Influence Matrix

	1	2	3	4	5	6	7	8	9	10
1	0	0	0	0	0	0	0	0	0	0
2	1	0	0	0	0	0	0	0	0	0
3	0	0	0	0	0	0	0	0	0	0
4	1	0	0	0	1	1	0	0	1	1
5	0	0	0	0	0	1	1	0	0	0
6	1	0	0	0	0	0	1	1	0	0
7	0	0	0	0	0	0	0	0	0	0
8	1	0	0	0	0	0	0	0	0	0
9	1	0	0	0	0	0	0	0	0	0
10	1	0	0	0	0	0	0	0	0	0

Figure 3

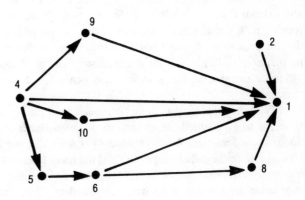

Table 2
Correlation Matrix

	1	2	3	4	5	6	7	8	9	10
1	1.00	0.10	−0.05	−0.14	0.06	0.12	0.02	0.22	0.27	0.15
2	0.10	1.00	0.08	0.05	0.03	−0.01	0.01	0.03	−0.04	−0.09
3	−0.05	−0.08	1.00	−0.03	0.06	−0.05	0.01	−0.06	−0.01	0.07
4	−0.14	0.05	−0.03	1.00	−0.10	−0.10	0.00	0.09	−0.16	0.17
5	0.06	0.03	0.06	−0.10	1.00	0.56	0.17	0.06	−0.02	0.06
6	0.12	−0.01	−0.05	−0.10	0.56	1.00	0.17	0.17	0.02	0.07
7	0.02	0.01	0.01	0.00	0.17	0.17	1.00	0.00	0.02	0.09
8	0.22	0.03	−0.06	0.09	0.06	0.17	0.00	1.00	0.12	0.02
9	0.27	−0.04	−0.09	−0.16	−0.02	0.02	0.02	0.12	1.00	−0.01
10	0.15	−0.09	0.07	0.17	0.06	0.07	0.09	0.02	−0.01	1.00

Table 4
Path Coefficient Matrix

	1	2	3	4	5	6	7	8	9	10
1	0.00	0.00	0.00	0.00	0.00	0.00	0.00	0.00	0.00	0.00
2	0.12	0.00	0.00	0.00	0.00	0.00	0.00	0.00	0.00	0.00
3	0.00	0.00	0.00	0.00	0.00	0.00	0.00	0.00	0.00	0.00
4	−0.15	0.00	0.00	0.00	−0.10	−0.04	0.00	0.00	−0.16	0.17
5	0.00	0.00	0.00	0.00	0.00	0.56	0.11	0.00	0.00	0.00
6	0.06	0.00	0.00	0.00	0.00	0.00	0.11	0.22	0.00	0.00
7	0.00	0.00	0.00	0.00	0.00	0.00	0.00	0.00	0.00	0.00
8	0.19	0.00	0.00	0.00	0.00	0.00	0.00	0.00	0.00	0.00
9	0.23	0.00	0.00	0.00	0.00	0.00	0.00	0.00	0.00	0.00
10	0.19	0.00	0.00	0.00	0.00	0.00	0.00	0.00	0.00	0.00

Table 5
Products of Routes

Product	Routes			
0.1227	1	2		
−0.1514	1	4		
−0.0025	1	6	4	
−0.0033	1	6	5	4
−0.0018	1	8	6	4
−0.0024	1	8	6	5	4
−0.0376	1	9	4	
0.0324	1	10	4	

Table 6
Sum of Products

1	0.0000
2	0.1227
3	0.0000
4	−0.1664
5	0.0000
6	0.0000
7	0.0000
8	0.0000
9	0.0000
10	0.0000

The computer output is shown in Table 4, page 45.

A diagrammatic representation of the model would appear as in Figure 3, page 45.

The sum of the products of path coefficients for all routes between variable 4 and the dependent variable (1) is given in Table 6 as being −0.1664.

The coefficient of correlation between these two variables (from Table 2) is −0.14. Reference to the basic theorem of path coefficients postulated earlier would indicate that the proximity of these two coefficients suggests that this particular model gives a good explanation of the causal influence on product adoption in these particular circumstances.

The remarkable aspect of this particular example is that is seems to give added credence to the ideas of Bauer and Sheth quoted earlier. Risk (variable 4) is seen to have a crucial role in the influence process and the role of personal influence (variable 5 and 6) is seen to be of some importance in relation to risk along the lines suggested by Perry and Hamm (1969). It may have been expected that inner-other directedness would have had a more pronounced influence on other variables in the model rather than merely a direct influence on product adoption. Whilst such an influence was allowed for in the influence matrix this was eliminated as a result of the non-significant correlations reported by Arndt.

If the assumption may be made that what has happened in the past, i.e. at the time of investigation, will be repeated in the future then this technique may be used predictively as well as analytically.

The output of causal path analysis in this particular form lends itself to hypothesis testing and hypothesis refining as we have seen but it may also lead the experimenter to the discovery of relationships previously unrecognized and so to the postulation of new hypotheses. The method discussed here is still very much in a stage of development and should be used with caution but the possible implications for marketing management could be great.

References

1. Arndt, J. (1968). "Profiling Consumer Innovators" in J. Arndt (ed.) *Insights into Consumer Behavior*. Allyn & Bacon.
2. Bauer, R. A. (1960). "Consumer Behavior as Risk Taking" in R. S. Hancock (ed.) *Dynamic Marketing for a Changing World*. American Marketing Association.
3. Blalock, H. M. (1964). *Causal Inferences in Non-experimental Research*. Chapel Hill: University of North Carolina Press.
4. Duncan, O. D. (1966). "Path Analysis: Sociological Examples," *American Journal of Sociology*. 72, 1–16.
5. Harary, F., Norman, R. Z., Cartwright, D. (1965). *Structural Models: An Introduction to the Theory of Directed Graphs*. John Wiley and Sons.
6. Huff, D. L. (1959). *A Topological Model of Consumer Space Preferences*. Occasional paper No. 11, Bureau of Business Research. Seattle: University of Washington.
7. Perry, M. & Hamm, B. C. (1969). "Canonical Analysis of Relations between Socioeconomic Risk and Personal Influence in Purchase Decisions." *Journal of Marketing Research*, 6, 3, 351–354.
8. Sheth, J. N. (1968). "Perceived Risk and Diffusion of Innovations" in J. Arndt (ed.) *Insights into Consumer Behaviour*. Allyn & Bacon.
9. Simon, H. A. (1957). *Models of Man*. London: John Wiley and Sons.
10. Wright, S. (1931). "Statistical Methods in Biology." *American Statistical Association* XXVI (suppl.), 155–163.
11. Wright, S. (1934). "The Method of Path Coefficients." *Annals of Math. Stats*. 5, 161–215.
12. Wright, S. (1960). "Path Coefficients and Path Regressions: Alternative or Complementary Concepts." *Biometrics*, 16, 189–202.

For Discussion

1. What is the difference between an association between two variables and a causal relationship? What is a spurious relationship?
2. Identify the inputs and outputs in the path analysis approach described by Christopher and Elliott. How does one generate the influence matrix? What is the most critical assumption of path analysis? Comment upon the validity of the indirect paths in Figure 3.

9

Causation, Path Analysis and The Old Sausage Machine

Paul Duncan-Jones

It is rather curious that market researchers did not latch onto path analysis long ago. It has been fashionable among sociologists since Duncan's seminal article (Duncan, 1966), and was used by Emery and his co-workers in a field closely related to marketing (Emery et al., 1968). Now Christopher and Elliott have provided this journal with a clear exposition (*JMRS*, April, 1970), and we shall no doubt see a rash of applications at the next two annual conferences.

This is all to the good, provided the "new" tool is used with insight and understanding. Unfortunately Christopher and Elliott rather create the impression of one more procedure, like factor analysis or cluster analysis, for routine or (eventually) somnambulist application. Thus they write that "the fundamental requirement . . . is for a hypothesis *generating* and validating device . . ." (my italics), and later mention a computer algorithm for scrutinizing *all possible* path models that could be generated from a given correlation matrix. This suggests a fundamental misconception about the nature and uses of path analysis. It seems worth trying to set the record straight.

A path analysis consists of three essential ingredients or aspects. All three must be isomorphic with each other.

1. A *theory* spelling out the causal connections among a set of variables, and justifying assertions that one variable is (partially) or is not determined by another.

2. A path *diagram* or arrow scheme showing the connections amongst the variables.

3. A set of *equations* containing the path coefficients together with rules and supplementary equations for estimating the coefficients, if the estimation procedures are not obvious.

Christopher and Elliott have discussed the diagrams and equations, but rather glossed over the need for a theory. However, the arrows in one's path diagram assert directions of causal determination and these directions must come from "outside" the statistical calculation, which (at least in "just-identified" recursive systems) will fit equally well irrespective of the direction of the arrows. In Figure 1 below we may argue about the existence of the path marked *A* ("Do people

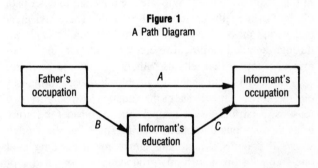

Figure 1
A Path Diagram

really have a direct influence on their sons' jobs? Is it just that they influence their education?"), but no-one is going to question seriously whether the arrows are running in the right direction. Why is this? Rosenberg (1968) and Stinchcombe (1968) have suggested the following guides to the direction of causal ordering.

a. Temporal order (as in Figure 1). We just do not believe Father's job twenty or thirty years ago was influenced by Informant's present job. But are we so sure about "self-confidence" vis-à-vis "social integration" (cf. Christopher and Elliott, loc. cit.)?

b. The relative fixity or lability of the variables. Thus we are more likely to believe that alienation is determined by sex or race than the other way around.

c. Ideally, classical experimentation, manipulating X and noting the effect on Y. We all know the difficulties in the way of this in market research. But sometimes laboratory experiments may suggest we "pencil in" an arrow in one direction rather than another.

d. Experimental manipulation of Y to show the *absence* of effect on X when we already know they co-vary. Thus if we happen to know that extraverts are more addicted to smoking than introverts, hypnotically inhibit their smoking and find their level of extraversion unaffected we may conclude that extraversion causes smoking rather than vice-versa.

e. If external knowledge provides a *complete* account of the causes of X, without mentioning Y, then if X and Y are correlated, we can assume X determines Y rather than vice-versa. There simply is not room for Y among the determinants of X. I doubt if we shall ever encounter this situation in marketing analysis.

f. We may know that Y is caused by (rather than causes) some third variable Z. If X and Z are uncorrelated, the presumption is that Y is not a cause of X, and any correlation between X and Y can better be explained by X causing Y.

These heuristics are useful in building theories and mapping them into path models, but (apart from experimentation under ideal conditions) they do not provide conclusive evidence. A path model is only useful to the extent that it represents a carefully-developed theory. Path analysis may sometimes help us decide between two or three alternative models of the situation — so long as there are only minor differences between them — but it is not the philosopher's stone —the grand substitute for thought in data analysis — that some people always yearn for. Path analysis usually is quite simply the formalisation of a theory, and without the theory one would not know how to draw the path diagram. Consider Figure 2. This represents the familiar case of "spurious correlation." X and Y only appear to be correlated because they are both dependent on Z (the double headed, curved arrow is conventionally used to indicate a "non-causal" correlation). This could quite well be Figure 1, with path C in that diagram deleted. Why are we reluctant to delete path C? Not principally on statistical grounds. There is a great and varied mass of evidence — from common observation, through detailed empirical research to wide-ranging sociological theory — that tells us path C "ought" to be there.

So why is path analysis valuable, it if only formalises our theoretical knowledge of the situation? Broadly for two reasons. First, because it compels one to consider the structural assumptions that one is making. In doing so, it often shows that one's assumptions are more far-reaching (and one's conclusions less firmly grounded) than one had supposed. Second, because it helps us to forecast. If we have a firmly-based path model, well grounded in theory, checked for statistical consistency and with good estimates of the path coefficients, and if we believe our model really incorporates all the important features of the situation, we can (at last!) draw conclusions about what will happen if we interfere with the situation at given points and in given ways. Thus we may be able to say *quantitatively* that the effect of altering one part of the system (say point-of-sale promotion) will be to leave retailer confidence almost unaffected, to have a slight negative effect on the images of competing brands and to increase sales of one's own brand by a given amount.

This is not the occasion for an extended exposition of path analysis. Excellent introductions are available in Blalock (1969a) and the first three or four chapters of Borgatta (1969). Our main purpose has been to emphasize (in contrast to Christopher and Elliott's presentation) the importance of prior knowledge, theory and sheer hard thinking in setting up a path diagram. There are one or two minor points in Christopher and Elliott's article that also call for comment. First, they note that variables should be normally distributed. This is quite unnecessary. The mathematics of path analysis (like that of multiple regression on which it is based) works just as well without any stringent distributional assumptions. But perhaps they have in mind the validity of "t" tests and standard error calculations. Again they are wrong both because the tests are robust against departures from assumption (see, e.g., the references given by Labovitz (1967)), and also because this type of test is normally inappropriate with market research data, typically gathered from multi-

Figure 2
Another Path Diagram

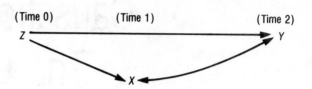

stage samples. Jack-knifed confidence intervals will usually be more appropriate (Brillinger, 1966). They make several further misleading statements or implications because they have only considered the simpler kinds of path diagram. Thus, path models can be and have been developed which allow for non-linearity, for reciprocal interaction and for estimating relationships between unobserved hypothetical variables from correlations among indicators. The first two points have been most fully explored by econometricians (see particularly Fisher, 1966) and the latter by Costner (1969), Blalock (1969b) and Duncan (e.g. in Borgatta, 1969).

References

1. Blalock, H. M. (1969a). *Theory Construction*. Prentice-Hall. Methods of Social Science Series.
2. _____ (1969b). "Multiple Indicators and the Causal Approach to Measurement Error." *American Journal of Sociology*, 75, 264–272.
3. Borgatta, E. F. (ed.) (1969). *Sociological Methodology 1969*. Jossy-Bass.
4. Brillinger, D. R. (1966). "The Application of the Jack-knife to the Analysis of Consumer Surveys." *Commentary* (now *Journal of the Market Research Society*), 8, 74–80.
5. Christopher, M. G. and Elliott, C. K. "Causal Path Analysis in Market Research" *Journal of the Market Research Society*, 12, 112–124.
6. Costner, H. L. (1969). "Theory, Deduction and Rules of Correspondence." *American Journal of Sociology*, 75, 245–263.
7. Duncan, O. D. (1966). "Path Analysis: Sociological Examples." *American Journal of Sociology*, 72, 1–16.
8. Emery, F. E., Hilgendorf, E. L. and Irving, B. L. (1968). *The Psychological Dynamics of Smoking*. Tobacco Research Council, Research Paper 10.
9. Fisher, F. M. (1966). *The Identification Problem in Econometrics*. McGraw-Hill.
10. Labovitz, S. (1967). "Some Observations on Measurement and Statistics." *Social Forces*, 46, 151–160.
11. Rosenberg, M. (1968). *The Logic of Survey Analysis*. Basic Books.
12. Stinchcombe, A. L. (1968). *Constructing Social Theories*. Harcourt, Brace and World.

For Discussion

Path analysis according to Duncan-Jones should be used to represent a well-grounded theory. Can it be used to test a theory that is only tentative? Can it be used in exploratory research when the goal is to develop theories? How can you prove causation?

10

Unobservable Variables in Structural Equations Models: with an Application in Industrial Selling

David A. Aaker
Richard P. Bagozzi*

An econometric model consists of a set of independent variables and one or more dependent variables. The relationships between the variables are normally specified by an equation for each dependent variable. These relationships can represent empirical associations or causal links. When causal links are involved, the econometric model is termed a structural equation model [22, p. 2]. In such models each variable represents a theoretical construct. The assumption is that the theoretical construct is measured without error by a single variable or indicator. Such an assumption seems naive on its face. In most contexts any single indicator will be biased, and multiple indicators are a logical way to reduce the biasing effect of any one indicator [13]. Further, econometricians have shown that even if an indicator is an unbiased representation of a theoretical construct, measurement error can still lead to biased conclusions [25].

The assumption of single indicators without measurement error may be justified under some conditions. In particular, there are situations where there is only one indicator available, where the indicator has a high degree of validity and reliability, and when problems of construct and relationship specification dominate. There are many situations, however, in which such an assumption is not justified, but is made because there is no perceived alternative.

One purpose of this article is to present the use of an alternative: the use of unobservable variables to represent theoretical constructs in structural equation models. This approach allows the use of multiple indicators of the theoretical constructs. Further, it explicitly introduces measurement error and formally specifies the relationship between the theoretical construct and the observable indicators. A second purpose of this paper is to show how competing structural equation models can be evaluated and to explain how a hypothesis test can be used to help compare them. A third purpose is to illustrate this methodology in the context of a study on an industrial sales force.

The use of unobservable variables in structural equation models and the associated statistical methodology can be credited to a variety of disciplines including sociology, statistics, econometrics, and psychometrics. It can be viewed as a synthesis of econometrics and factor analysis. In this article the approach will be described first. In the second section it will be viewed from a factor analysis perspective. The third section will set forth several examples of how it can be used in the context of a personal selling study. Parameter estimation and identification will be addressed in the fourth section. The model testing and theory development issues will be discussed in the fifth section. Finally, alternative approaches to the measurement error problem will be discussed.

Structural Equations and Unobservable Variables

In Figure 1A, a simple model is shown where a single dependent variable, y, is affected by two independent variables, x_1 and x_2. This model can be written mathematically through the well-known linear regression model as:

$$y = \beta_1' x_1 + \beta_2' x_2 + \varepsilon' \qquad (1)$$

where β_i' is a standardized regression coefficient (termed a beta weight) and is interpreted as the change in standard deviations of y that would result from a change in one standard deviation of x_i. Throughout this article we adopt the path

*The authors would like to acknowledge the helpful comments of Ronald S. Burt, James M. Carman, and Robert A. Meyer.

analysis assumption that all variables are standardized.[1] The error term, ε', represents the amount of variance in y not explained by the independent variables.

Notice that the model is limited to a system of relationships between observable variables since y, x_1, and x_2 are actual measurements performed on some population. In effect, the model assumes that all variables are measured without error and that the parameters represent relationships between empirical observations. Our example could, of course, include additional dependent (and independent) variables. The result would be a system of equations representing a set of cause-effect relationships. Several researchers in marketing have worked with such models [cf., 1, 4, 6, 18].

In Figure 1B, a model is portrayed in which two independent unobservable variables, x_1^* and x_2^*, impact upon the dependent unobservable variable, y^*. In this figure and succeeding ones, the unobservable variables (except error terms) are indicated by circles, observable variables (i.e., indicators, measurements, operationalizations) are shown as squares, and causal relationships are depicted as straight-line segments with arrowheads. The curved line between x_1^* and x_2^* indicates that they may be correlated. The causal relationships in the model can be represented by two sets of equations.

The first set of equations represents the hypothesized relationships in one's theory:

$$(2) \qquad y^* = \beta_1 x_1^* + \beta_2 x_2^* + \varepsilon.$$

Notice that this equation expresses relationships only among unobservable variables (or theoretical constructs) and thus constrasts to the model of Equation (1) which is limited exclusively to relationships among observable variables. Notice further that the coefficients and error term in Equation (2) — β_1, β_2, and ε — will, in general, differ from those in Equation (1) — i.e., β_1', β_2' and ε'.

The second set of equations captures the relationships between theoretical constructs and their indicators (the observable variables):

$$y_1 = \lambda_1 y^* + v_1 \qquad\qquad x_2 = \alpha_2 x_2^* + u_2$$
$$y_2 = \lambda_2 y^* + v_2 \qquad\qquad x_3 = \alpha_3 x_2^* + u_3$$
$$x_1 = \alpha_1 x_1^* + u_1 \qquad\qquad x_4 = \alpha_4 x_2^* + u_2.$$

The linking parameters (i.e., λ_i and α_i) are measures of the degree of correspondence between the theoretical constructs and their indicators or measurements. When an λ_i or α_i is less than one in magnitude (given the standardization convention adopted above), the indicator will be an imperfect measure of the theoretical construct, and the corresponding error term (v_i or u_i) will formally reflect other sources of variation in the respective indicator. The error terms for the indicators are known as "errors in variables."

In effect there are now two "theories." The first is the theory providing causal links between the theoretical constructs. The second is what Blalock terms the auxiliary theory which defines the rules of correspondence between the theoretical constructs and their indicators [10].

Figure 1
An Econometric Perspective

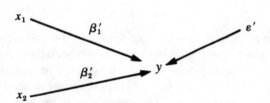

A. A Simple Structural Equation Model

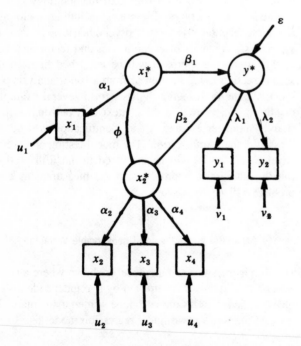

B. A Structural Equation Model with Unobservable Variables

The Factor Analysis Perspective

Unlike econometrics in which the use of multiple indicators of unobservable variables is rare (see [23]), factor analysis began with the concept of an unobservable variable as a central part of its model.[2] Factor analysis has evolved in

---

[1] For an introduction to path analysis, see [9, 17, 37]. For a discussion of the trade-offs for using standardized versus unstandardized coefficients, see [36, 45, 38]. One result of standardization is that there is no intercept term in the linear model.

[2] Griliches [25] notes that econometricians have largely ignored the errors in variables problem. He hypothesizes that the reasons are, among others, that economic data tend to be aggregated (so that random errors will cancel) and collected by others (so responsibility is not felt), that identification and simultaneity have been the major intellectual problems, that the theoretical constructs were somewhat fuzzy, and that there was no perceived cure.

two directions. Early work in factor analysis had as its goal the extraction of a small number of "theoretical" constructs from a larger set of observed variables. Typically, the researcher had no theoretical hypothesis in mind when using factor analysis in this sense but was searching for a structure underlying his or her data. This use of factor analysis is termed "exploratory factor analysis" in the literature and is the type most frequently used by marketers.

A newer model of factor analysis — termed "confirmatory factor analysis" — has been developed in recent years as a means of discovering an underlying structure in one's data, given some prior theoretical or empirical information. To date, at least three marketing studies have employed this methodology [3, 4, 41]. Confirmatory factor analysis will be described here because it will provide the reader, especially one familiar with exploratory factor analysis, with some insight into unobservable variables in structural equation models, because of its methodological relevance and because it illustrates the role of prior theory specification.

It is useful to begin by reviewing the exploratory factor analysis model shown in Figure 2A. The terms f_1, f_2, and f_3 represent uncorrelated (orthogonal) factors which are unobservable. It would also be possible to consider an exploratory factor analysis model in which the factors were permitted to be correlated (oblique). Correlated factors would be linked by a curved line in the representation. In Figure 2A each of the x's is an observable variable which measures to some extent the three factors. Since their variance is not entirely due to the three factors, an error term is included to account for the remaining portions of their variance. The error terms are assumed to be independent. Algebraically the model is represented by equations such as:

$$x_1 = \alpha_1 f_1 + \alpha_7 f_2 + \alpha_{13} f_3 + u_1$$

$$x_2 = \alpha_2 f_1 + \alpha_8 f_2 + \alpha_{14} f_3 + u_2$$

$$x_3 = \alpha_3 f_1 + \alpha_9 f_2 + \alpha_{15} f_3 + u_3$$

$$x_4 = \alpha_4 f_1 + \alpha_{10} f_2 + \alpha_{16} f_3 + u_4$$

$$x_5 = \alpha_5 f_1 + \alpha_{11} f_2 + \alpha_{17} f_3 + u_5$$

$$x_6 = \alpha_6 f_1 + \alpha_{12} f_2 + \alpha_{18} f_3 + u_6$$

$$\phi_{12} = \phi_{13} = \phi_{23} = 0$$

where ϕ_{ij} = the correlation factor i and factor j.

A factor analysis program can estimate the α's, the factor loadings. The loading of x_1 on factor 1, for example, reflects the degree to which x_1 is a measure of the unobservable variable f_1. If all variables are standardized and the factors are uncorrelated, the loadings are correlations between the observable variables and the factors. After the estimation has occurred, and often after factor rotation, judgments are made as to which variables are measuring which factors. In fact, judgments about the identity of the factors and even the number of factors are made only after parameter estimation. One shortcoming with exploratory factor analysis is that the meaning or interpretation of factors is often difficult to ascertain.

In contrast to this familiar description of exploratory factor analysis, confirmatory factor analysis represents a completely different approach. In confirmatory factor analysis the factors are conceptualized and interpreted and the variables which measure each factor are identified prior to the estimation of parameters. Theory is thus employed prior to the estimation phase to impose structure. In practice, this usually means that some of the factor loadings and some (but not necessarily all) of the correlations between factors are set equal to zero.[3] These restrictions are not ad hoc but rather reflect one's theory, past research, or methodology and in any case are *hypotheses* to be tested on data.

In Figure 2B an example of confirmatory factor analysis is shown. The factor f_1 is shown as being measured by the observable variable x_1. The links between f_1 and the other observable variables are set equal to zero. Similarly, the factor f_2 is measured only by the observable variables x_2, x_3, and x_4 and the factor f_3 is measured only by x_5 and x_6. Further, the factor f_3 is permitted to be correlated (denoted by the curved lines) with both f_1 and f_2. The α_i coefficients linking the theoretical constructs and the observable variables still have the familiar interpretation of factor loadings. The error terms are assumed uncorrelated. Algebraically the model of Figure 2B is represented by:

$$x_1 = \alpha_1 f_1 \qquad\qquad + u_1$$

$$x_2 = \qquad \alpha_8 f_2 \qquad + u_2$$

$$x_3 = \qquad \alpha_9 f_2 \qquad + u_3$$

$$x_4 = \qquad \alpha_{10} f_2 \qquad + u_4$$

$$x_5 = \qquad\qquad \alpha_{17} f_3 + u_5$$

$$x_6 = \qquad\qquad \alpha_{18} f_3 + u_6$$

$$\phi_{12} = 0$$

Even in exploratory factor analysis it is common to consider correlated factors. In fact, it is possible to conduct factor analyses of factors, termed second order factor analysis [24, Ch. 11]. However, it is not natural to think of factors as being causally related. The focus is rather upon operationalizing constructs rather than exploring causal relationships. However, it is actually a rather small step methodologically to extend the confirmatory factor analysis to a structural equation with unobservables. The factors are simply considered to be causally related instead of being correlated and an errors in equations term is added. Note the similarity between Figures 2B and 1B where f_1, f_2, and f_3 correspond to x_1^*, x_2^*, and y^*, respectively.

We have attempted here to make a strong distinction between exploratory and confirmatory factor analysis in order to motivate Figure 2B which is closely related methodologically and conceptually to unobservable variables in

---

[3] It can be shown that failure to include such constraints will result in biased and inefficient parameter estimates and, in fact, in some contexts an elegant expression can be derived for the bias and loss of efficiency introduced [21, pp. 256–57].

Figure 2
A Factor Analytic Perspective

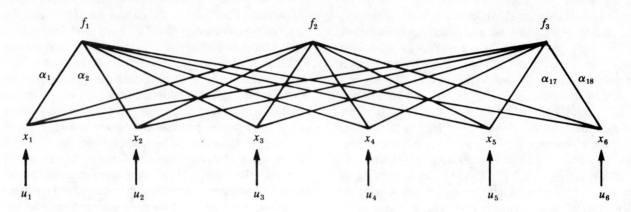

A. An Exploratory Factor Analysis Model

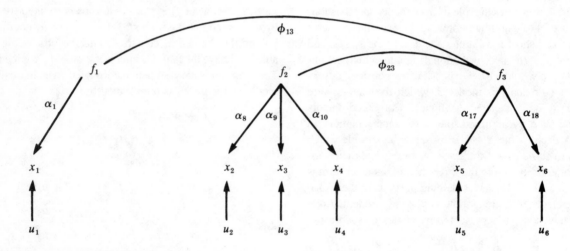

B. A Confirmatory Factor Analysis Model

structural equations. However, the reader should be aware that there is actually a continuum running from exploratory to confirmatory factor analysis that is analogous to the process of science moving from the exploration of phenomena to the confirmation of general hypotheses. Pure exploratory factor analysis is represented by the researcher who collects a set of variables and subjects them to factor analysis with no knowledge of what to expect. Pure confirmatory factor analysis might be represented by the researcher who could, from prior theory, specify the exact structure and all the parameters and was only interested in seeing, as an hypothesis, if the model fit a particular data set. Actually the pure forms are very rare. The exploratory factor analyst usually has some idea of appropriate theoretical constructs when selecting variables, and the confirmatory factor analyst can usually specify only some of the parameter restrictions [43, pp. 361–64].

Applying the Model in Industrial Selling

In this section three models will be introduced to illustrate the use of unobservable variables in structural equation models.

The theoretical and empirical setting is a study of the industrial sales force of a company which sells steel and plastic strapping tools and materials [2]. Each of the 106 salesmen participating in the study has a selling position requiring considerable skill, initiative, and product knowledge. Table 1 defines ten variables from the study that will be employed in the models presented in this section and in the balance of the article. The first variable, dollar sales, was determined from internal records. The other variables were obtained from a self-administered questionnaire. A correlation matrix appears as an appendix.

Consider first Figure 3 which illustrates a multiple-indicator/multiple-cause (MIMIC) model [28, 33]. The unobservable variable y^* has three causes (x_1, x_2, and x_3) and three indicators (y_1, y_2, and y_3). The indicators are dollar sales and two measures of self-satisfaction. The unobservable variable is conceptualized as self-fulfillment since it includes sales performance which is hypothesized to be a surrogate for self-performance appraisals as well as two measures of job satisfaction. The three causes are job tension (x_1), specific self-esteem (x_3), and role ambiguity (x_1).

Table 1
Definitions of Variables Used in Analyses

Symbol	Name	Description
y_1	Sales	*Dollar Sales*—Dollar volume of sales achieved by each salesperson for year following administration of questionnaire. Steps were taken to adjust for salespeople who quit or were transferred, changes in territory size, shifts in accounts between territories, windfall accounts, and other confounds.
y_2	SAT 1	*Job Satisfaction #1*—Four six-point Likert items measuring degree of satisfaction with promotion, pay, and the overall work situation.
y_3	SAT 2	*Job Satisfaction #2*—Four six-point Likert items measuring degree of satisfaction with opportunity to demonstrate ability and initiative; job security; belief that work is challenging and gives one a sense of accomplishment; and felt degree of control over aspects of job.
y_4	SAT	*Job Satisfaction #1 & #2*—Composite of *Job Satisfaction #1* and *Job Satisfaction #2*.
x_1	TEN 1	*Job Tension #1*—Eight five-point Guilford self-rating items indicating how frequently the salesperson feels bothered with limits of authority, opportunities for advancement, supervisor demands and decisions, how the amount of work interferes with its quality, and how work interferes with family life.
x_2	TEN 2	*Job Tension #2*—Seven five-point Guilford items indicating how frequently the salesperson feels bothered with the scope and responsibilities of the job, work load, the qualifications required for the job, difficulty of obtaining information necessary to perform the job, relations with co-workers, and decisions conflicting with one's values.
x_3	EST 1	*Specific Self-esteem #1*—Two nine-point and one five-point self-rating scales measuring each salesperson's attributions (relative to other salespeople in the company) of the quantity of sales they achieve, their potential for achieving the top 10% in sales in their company, and the quality of their performance with regard to planning and management of time and expenses.
x_4	EST 2	*Specific Self-esteem #2*—Three nine-point self-rating scales measuring each salesperson's ability to reach quota, feeling as to the quality of customer relations, and self-regard as to knowledge of own products and company, competitors' products, and customers' needs.
x_5	RA 1	*Role Ambiguity #1*—Six five-point Likert items indicating degree of uncertainty with limits of authority, call norms, supervisor expectations for management of time and activities, customer expectations on frequency of calls, and family expectations on time to spend on job.
x_6	RA 2	*Role Ambiguity #2*—Six five-point Likert items indicating degree of uncertainty with freedom to negotiate on price, power to modify delivery schedules, evaluation of supervisor, overall expectations and satisfaction of customers, and family expectations with respect to performance.

The figure shows the estimated coefficients and their standard errors. The estimation method will be discussed later as will the interpretation of the χ^2 statistic also shown in the figure.

Consider the indicator coefficients. The indicator's y_2 and y_3 have about equal coefficients while the indicator y_1 has a smaller coefficient. Thus the indicator y_1 has a smaller role in indicating y^* than the other two. These indicator coefficients are interpreted just like factor loadings. The difference is that factor loadings are based only upon the intercorrelations among the indicators whereas these indicator coefficients are also based upon the links to the causal variables.

The causal coefficients can be used to explore specific causal hypotheses. The significant x_1 coefficient supports the hypothesis that there is an inverse relationship between felt job tension and self-fulfillment. Further, the hypothesis that there is a positive relationship between specific self-esteem and self-fulfillment is supported by the significant x_2 coefficient. Finally, the x_3 coefficient does not support the hypothesis that there is an inverse relationship between role ambiguity and self-fulfillment. For a more detailed discussion of these hypotheses and others introduced in this paper see [2, 5, 14].

A second model, shown in Figure 4, is the two-indicator/two construct model. In this model the unobservable variable role ambiguity, x^*, measured by x_5 and x_6, is hypothesized to have an inverse influence on self-fulfillment measured by y_1 (sales) and y_4 (job satisfaction). The significant coefficient between x^* and y^* supports the hypothesis. Note that x_6 is the superior indicator of x^* in the context of this model. Similarly, y_4 is the better indicator of y^*. Again the χ^2 statistic will be discussed below.

The third model, shown in Figure 5, is more complex, containing four constructs. The self-fulfillment construct has now been broken into two constructs, sales and job satisfaction. Further, a model hypothesis that is only very weakly supported, is that sales influences job satisfaction. An hypothesis that is supported is that job tension (x_1^*) has a negative influence on job satisfaction and on sales. Another supported hypothesis is that the other independent variable, self-esteem (x_2^*), influences both job satisfaction and sales. Again, the indicator coefficients reflect the relative ability of the indicator to measure the unobservable construct.

Identification and the Estimation of Parameters

The first step in constructing structural equation models is to propose relevant theoretical constructs, their indicators, and the structure or pattern of relationships. This set of procedures is known as *specification*. Specification depends fundamentally upon the theory one hopes to develop and test, the observable variables available, the results of past research, the creativity and acumen of the researcher, and a number of other factors. Given that one has specified a theory, two additional steps come to the fore: *identification* and *estimation*. Both are introduced below.

To illustrate identification, consider the simple system consisting of one unobservable variable, y^*, and two indicators, y_1 and y_2, as shown in Figure 6A. The unobservable variable might now represent overall job satisfaction which is employed here for discussion purposes. In this simple model, only one piece of information – the sample correlation $r_{y_2 y_3}$, between y_1 and y_2 – is provided, yet two parameters (i.e., α_2 and α_4) are to be estimated. Since unique solutions of the paramters can not be found without making further assumptions, the system is termed underidentified.[4]

Two methods can be used to achieve identification for the model of Figure 6A. First, constraints can be added to the system. For example, if one has reason to believe that $\alpha_2 = \alpha_3 = \alpha$, then the model will be exactly identified with

$$\alpha = \sqrt{r_{y_2 y_3}} = .80.$$

A second approach is to add information to the model. For instance, a third indicator of y^* can be employed as shown in Figure 6B. Although the addition of y_1 introduces another parameter to be estimated (i.e., α_1), there are now three pieces of information available in the model (i.e., $r_{y_1 y_2}$, $r_{y_1 y_3}$, $r_{y_2 y_3}$), and the system will be exactly identified and parameter estimates will be uniquely determined.

If we keep adding information and/or constraints to an identified system it will become over-identified. The result is that there will be several estimates of the same parameter. For example, suppose we include the third indicator and the constraint that

$$\alpha_1 = \alpha_2 = \alpha.$$

The result is two different estimates of the α_3 parameter:

$$\alpha_3 = \frac{r_{x_1 x_3}}{\sqrt{r_{x_1 x_2}}}, \quad \text{and} \quad \alpha_3 = \frac{r_{x_2 x_3}}{\sqrt{r_{x_1 x_2}}}.$$

With an overidentified system and therefore more than one estimate for at least one of the parameters, there are several alternatives available to the researcher. The second estimate can be used to "test" the model. The problem is that it is not clear what represents an acceptable fit [28, p. 83]. Another approach is to somehow average the two estimates. Most estimation techniques in factor analysis and econometrics are effectively techniques to average competing estimates in overidentified models. One such technique, maximum likelihood estimation, rates high on statistical criteria and also leads to a useful goodness-of-fit test (to be discussed later). Jöreskog has developed a practical maximum likelihood estimation program, termed LISREL, which can handle the most general structural equation problem including both errors in equations and errors in variables [30, 31, 32, 35]. The availability of this program and its predecessors is in part responsible for the consideration of this class of model.

Thus, a first step of analysis is to determine if a proposed structural model is identified. A necessary condition is that the number of correlations (which is equal to $\frac{1}{2}(w)(w-1)$,

where w is the number of observable variables) exceed the number of parameters. Unfortunately it could happen that not all of the correlations provide an independent piece of information and thus this condition is not a sufficient condition for identifiability.[5] For some special cases such as the MIMIC model [33], structural equation systems without measurement error [19], and a small number of other models [20, 26, 27, 47], general rules do exist for determining identifiability. For example, in the MIMIC model with q causes and p effects, the model will be identified if the degrees of freedom are nonnegative:

$$\text{d.f.} = q(p-1) + p(p-3)/2 \geqq 0.$$

The model of Figure 3 therefore has six degrees of freedom of six overidentifying pieces of information. Unless one of these special cases is involved, the only sure way to prove identifiability is to algebraically show that each parameter can be estimated. Since such an approach can get involved for a complex model, identification can be a practical problem. However, it is possible to obtain some diagnostics from the LISREL program that will help to discover underidentifiability.

Model Testing and Theory Development

Ideally, one's theory will dictate a unique structural equation model, and a program such as LISREL can be used to estimate parameters. In practice, however, the researcher will more often begin with a tentative model as an hypothesis which then needs to be tested, refined, and retested before a satisfactory model can emerge. Further, it is also more likely that a researcher will have several structural equation models to investigate as rival hypotheses. This is so partly as a result of the immaturity of theory in marketing and the social sciences and partly as a consequence of the complexity of marketing problems and the uncertainty inherent in all phases of the research process. The researcher thus would like to know which, if any, of his or her models are or are not supported by the data.

An overall goodness-of-fit test of any structural equation model is provided by the maximum likelihood estimation procedure. To describe this test, it is useful to explain the estimation procedure from another perspective. We start with R, the sample correlation matrix of observable variables.[6] Corresponding to R is a true, population correlation matrix Σ. Each element in the true correlation matrix can be determined (if the system is identified) from the model

---

[4] For a presentation of the algebra of path analysis leading to such estimation equations, see [37].

[5] The system is underidentified if one or more of the parameters is underidentified. It could happen that some parameters in a system could be identified and others underidentified. For example, in Figure 1B the parameters α_1 and μ_1 are not identified, but the remaining parameters are identified. If α_1 was set equal to 1 and μ_1 was set equal to zero (implying zero measurement error in x_1^*), the system would be over-identified with seven degrees of freedom.

[6] Or the sample variance-covariance matrix if the variables are not standardized.

parameters. Maximum likelihood estimation effectively attempts to find parameter estimates which will generate an estimated correlation matrix, $\hat{\Sigma}$, that will come as close as possible to the actual sample correlation matrix, R. If the model is just identified, then there will be a perfect match. If, however, the model has one or more overidentifying restrictions then the match probably will not be perfect in the presence of sample errors. A chi-square statistic is generated in the maximum likelihood estimation procedure that provides the probability that the differences between R and $\hat{\Sigma}$ would be that large under the null hypothesis that the specified model was correct.[7] The alternative hypothesis is that there are no restrictions on the matrix Σ.[8]

The test is thus whether the hypothesized model fits the data. Like most hypothesis tests, it is sensitive to sample size. Further, it does not provide any indication why the model does not fit the data, only that it does not fit. Similarly, if the model fits the data, it does not by itself suggest which other models might also fit the data. The existence of such a test is most important since in a general structural equation model there is not commonly used statistic like R^2 in a regression context to evaluate the overall model.[9]

The χ^2 statistics presented in Figures 3, 4, and 5 may now be examined. The χ^2 value for the MIMIC model of Figure 3 was 23.5 indicating a poor fit or a very large sample. Since the sample size, 106, is not excessive and the p value is so low, a judgment that the model did not fit this data is appropriate. The interpretation of the various model coefficients presented earlier should be tempered with the knowledge of the poor fit and the implication that the model structure is faulty. One way the structure could be faulty is if constructs and/or indicator have been omitted.

The χ^2 for the model in Figure 4, in contrast, suggests an extremely good fit and tends to confirm and support the judgments made about the model coefficients. The χ^2 value for the Figure 5 model, 13.3, is more borderline. The p-value of about 0.10 means that a χ^2 value of over 13.3 would appear about one time in ten if the proposed structure is true. To illustrate an important use of the χ^2 goodness-of-fit measure in hypothesis testing and theory construction, the analysis of the Figure 5 model is continued below.

Exploring Nested Models. One model is said to be nested or contained within a second if the latter can be obtained by adding causal paths to the former. By continuing to add paths a sequence of nested models can be obtained. Nested models provide a mechanism to explore alternative theories. A researcher can begin with a model that is most consistent with theory. If this model is not compatible with the data (i.e., is rejected) then causal paths can be added to the inadequate

model in order to construct a better performing model. If, on the other hand, the original model performs adequately, then causal paths might be deleted to see if a more parsimonious model might also fit the data. The particular deletion or addition should be theoretically justifiable, of course. The adequacy of the new model(s) so constructed can be determined from the comparison of the individual chi-squared statistics.

To illustrate, assume that in the Figure 5 model the strongest theoretical evidence exists only for the β_1 and β_5 links. Thus the researcher begins with a Figure 5 model in which:

$$\beta_1 = \beta_2 = \beta_3 = 0.$$

The resulting model, as noted in Table 2, has a χ^2 value at 45.84 indicating an extremely poor fit to the data and suggesting that the model is incorrectly specified. Perhaps needed constructs were omitted, the indicators were invalid, the errors were not independent (to be considered below), or relevant causal paths were omitted. This last possibility will now be explored.

Table 2

Summary of Hypothesis Tests for Selected Nested Models of Figure 5

Model	χ^2	d.f.	p-value	Change in χ^2
1. $\beta_1 = \beta_2 = \beta_3 = 0$	45.84	11	.00	—
2. $\beta_2 = \beta_3 = 0$	19.45	10	.03	26.39
3. $\beta_3 = 0$	14.57	9	.10	4.88
4. Full Model of Figure 5	13.33	8	.10	1.24
5. $\beta_5 = 0$	13.47	9	.14	.14
6. $\beta_3 = \beta_5 = 0$	16.25	10	.10	2.92

The procedure is to add a set of paths thereby specifying a new model. The usefulness of the additional paths may be judged by the difference in the chi-square statistics. The difference for large samples is, in fact, also distributed as a chi-square distribution with degrees of freedom equal to the number of added paths.[10] A large chi-square value (and small p-value) provides evidence that the paths should be included.

To continue the example, suppose that of the omitted paths β_1 had the greatest theoretical support. Adding β_1 provides Model 2 in Table 2 which generates a reduction in chi-square from Model 1 of 26.39. This chi-square value has one degree of freedom associated with it because on path was added. Thus, strong evidence that the β_1 path should be included is provided.

Model 2 still has an unsatifactory fit so it may be useful to add another causal path assuming it would be theoretically justified. In fact, there is theoretical support for a negative link between job tension and sales represented by β_2 [2, 5]. Adding the link yields Model 3 which is shown in Table 2 to generate further chi-square reduction of 4.88, a reduction which is significant at the .02 level. Thus, empirical support is provided for the inclusion of the β_2 link.

---

[7] Lawley and Maxwell indicate that the chi-square test can probably be trusted when the sample size exceeds the number of observable variables by about 50 although they do recommend that a correction factor be applied to improve the chi-square approximation [38, p. 36].

[8] The matrix does have to be positive semi-definite.

[9] In the MIMIC model several useful statistics are available one of which has an interpretation similar to R^2 in regression [33].

---

[10] This test is based upon the likelihood ratio test. See [42, p. 298].

Figure 3
A MIMIC Model

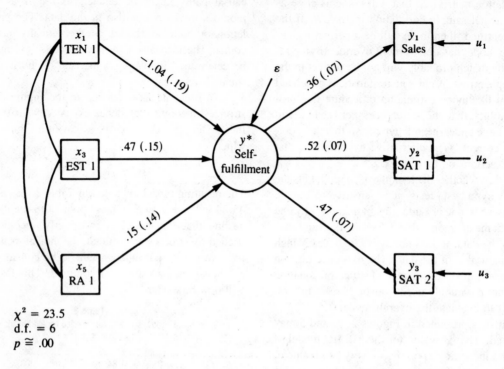

$\chi^2 = 23.5$
d.f. = 6
$p \cong .00$

Note: Standard errors are in parentheses.

Figure 4
A Two Indicator/Two Construct Model

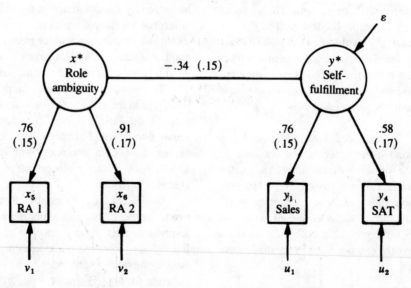

$\chi^2 = 0.001$
d.f. = 1
$p \cong .98$

Note: Standard errors are in parentheses.

Figure 5
A Four Construct Model

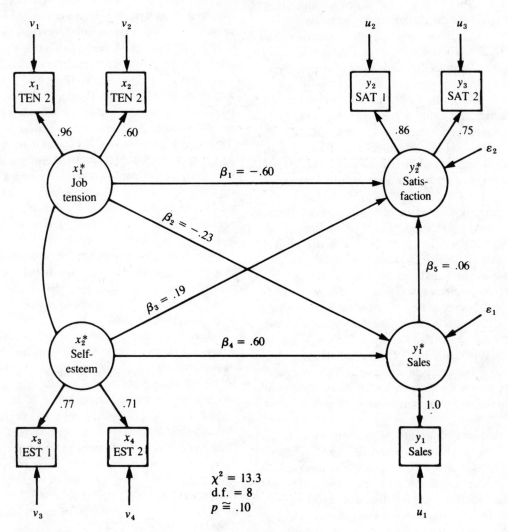

$\chi^2 = 13.3$
d.f. $= 8$
$p \cong .10$

Note: All coefficients are significant at the 0.05 level except that of $|\beta_5|$.

Figure 6
One Construct Models

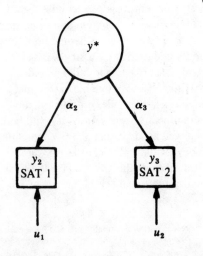

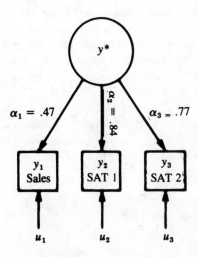

A. Two Indicators   **B. Three Indicators**

Finally, the inclusion of β_3, generating the complete Figure 5 model, provides an insignificant improvement in chi-square, 1.24. Thus, it is concluded that without strong theoretical support for the β_3 link, it should be omitted.

The use of hypothesis tests to explore nested models can, of course, also proceed in the other direction (see [44] for an example). If a model fits well it might be possible to delete paths in order to generate a more parsimonious model that will also fit the data. Thus, the researcher will attempt to theoretically justify eliminating some model paths to see if the model performance will thereby be affected. Paths which have small or nonsignificant coefficients associated with them (the standard t-test applies) are candidates for omission, assuming that their presence is not mandated by theory.

To illustrate, consider again the Figure 5 model. Given the relatively low β_5 path magnitude, it seems appropriate to consider a model with it deleted. Such a model, termed Model 5 in Table 2, barely increases the chi-square statistic. The next candidate for deletion is the β_3 link. The resulting Model 6 in Table 2 increases the chi-square by 2.92. Since a chi-square of 2.92 with one degree-of-freedom is just significant at the 0.10 level, the empirical conclusion on the marginal inclusion of the β_3 link, given that the β_5 link is deleted, is not very definitive.[11] Of course, the researcher can remove more than one path at a time. If both the β_3 and β_5 links were removed together, the chi-square difference would be 3.06 and the appropriate degrees of freedom would be two.

A few additional comments are in order. First, if the researcher selects in advance a particular nested model to test, the theory is relatively clear. Suppose, however, a series of models is tested and then, after the results are examined, one hypothesis test is selected to support a particular model. The researcher should know that the selected hypothesis test may appear impressive in part because it was selected from a group of tests, and it should be interpreted accordingly. A second and related comment is that this procedure (like stepwise regression) is not a mechanism to mechanically generate a theory, although it can suggest hypotheses. There should be competing theories which are being evaluated at each step. Third, since the p-level is sensitive to sample size it is often difficult to interpret when large sample sizes are present. Further, the maximum likelihood estimation approach is best suited for large samples so that the large sample case should be the norm. A solution is to work with the chi-square statistic. Although it will not have any meaning in an absolute sense, it will provide a good indication of the relative fit of the various submodels and can thus be used as an aid in theory construction.

Measurement Errors

In the foregoing an assumption has been that the measurement errors have been independent. There are situations in which it is appropriate and useful to relax that assumption.

To illustrate, consider the two construct models in Figure 7, with job tension as the independent variable and self-fulfillment as the dependent variable. The χ^2 value indicates a marginal fit ($p_i \cong .07$). There are, of course, a variety of possible reasons why the model did not fit better. Self-fulfillment needs to be divided into two constructs as was done in the Figure 5 model. Another is that the error terms of y_2 and y_3 are correlated. Correlated errors within constructs arise from the presence of some unmeasured third variable causing an association between y_2 and y_3. Perhaps y_2 and y_3 are indicators of not only self-fulfillment but some other unobservable not in the model. In any case, the Figure 7B model with correlated errors can be formally tested and compared with the model without correlated errors. The reduction in the χ^2 value is 3.30 which (with one degree of freedom) is significant at the 0.10 level and provides empirical support (but, of course, does not prove) that a link should be made between u_2 and u_3.

Errors can also be correlated across constructs (e.g., v_1 and u_1). Such an occurrence is particularly common in longitudinal studies [34]. Suppose two unobservable constructs are attitude and lagged attitude. The attitude indicators may have correlated errors due to the use of a common scale, common response sets or memory effects. Costner and Schoenberg show how in some models the existence of correlated errors across constructs can be detected [16]. Still another possibility is a path between an unobservable construct (i.e., x^* in Figure 7) and an error term associated with another construct (i.e., u_1). If an observable variable were an indicator of two constructs in the model, such a link would be appropriate [34].[12]

Alternative Approaches to Unobserved Variables

A number of alternatives are available other than the structural equation approach to unobserved variables. As noted at the outset, a common and often inappropriate approach is simply to assume that the unobserved variable is measured without error by a single indicator.

Another approach is to build an index of an unobservable construct based upon indicators that are considered relevant and use this index in the structural equation. The index might be a simple sum or it could be more complex involving weights and a nonadditive structure. The internal consistency of the index can be measured by a reliability coefficient such as the Cronbach α [32]. Hopefully, the index will serve to cancel the effects of nonrandom errors

---

[11] For Model 6 the revised path coefficients are:

$$\beta_1 = -.751$$
$$\beta_2 = -.260$$
$$\beta_3 = .570.$$

---

[12] The researcher will normally strive to have each measurement be an indicator for only a single theoretical construct, however, in order to avoid ambiguities in interpretation. Theoretical constructs, of course, can have multiple indicators without posing problems in interpretation.

Figure 7
Modeling Correlated Errors

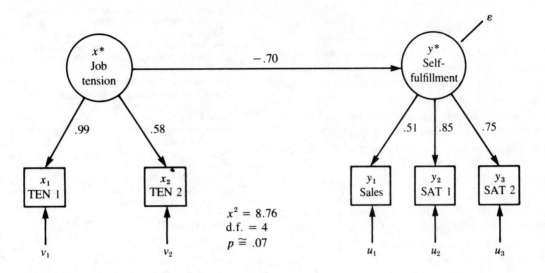

A. Uncorrelated Errors

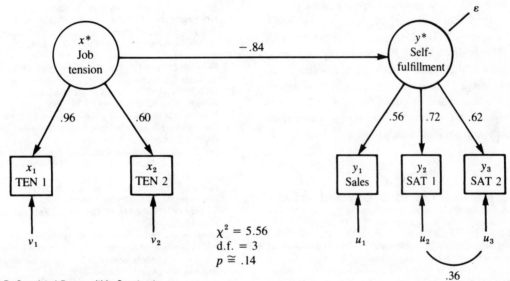

B. Correlated Errors within Constructs

associated with the various indicators. However, the use of an index requires the a priori establishment of the weighting scheme and functional form, a demanding task in many contexts. An index will also tend to both create and obscure specification errors. Further, in part because the error terms are not explicitly introduced, the resulting interpretation of the system is less precise and complete than it might be.

Still another approach involves conducting a factor analysis and then using the resulting factor scores in the structural model [33]. Such an approach contains all the characteristics of exploratory factor analysis. The constructs and their indicators are not specified from prior theory and experience but rather are generated by the data which contain sampling and nonsampling errors. Often this can be a relatively subjective and unreliable procedure. If the analyst has any prior information whether from theory, past research, or the particular research design at hand, the use of

unobservable variables in the structural equation context should be more appropriate.

It is possible to decompose the parameter estimation procedure and obtain prior estimates of the "factor loadings" in a multiple indicator model. For example, in Figure 1B the terms λ_1 and λ_2 and v_1 and v_2 can be estimated in a confirmatory factor analysis sense using only the correlations among the two indicator variables for y^*. Then the other model parameters can be estimated with λ_1 and λ_2 and v_1 and v_2 prespecified. Burt [12] points out that such an approach can often result in different estimates of the "factor loadings." When the complete model is estimated the other exogenous and endogenous variables help to define the y^* construct and therefore influence λ_1, λ_2, v_1, and v_2. If the rest of the model is ignored, then y^* must be defined solely in terms of its indicators. If the analyst has more confidence and knowledge about the indicators than about the total model structure, this decomposition approach might be reasonable.

Conclusions

It will be useful in conclusion to highlight some of the assumptions and limitations of the approach described in this paper. First, the relationships are postulated to be linear and additive although suitable transformations can relax this assumption in some contexts. Second, the variables are assumed to be intervally scaled (see [21, p. 248]) and normally distributed. The use of nominally scaled dependent variables can cause substantial problems. Third, the maximum likelihood estimate and the goodness-of-fit test based upon it may not perform well if a small sample is used (i.e., for $n \lesssim 50$). Fourth, on the other hand, the χ^2 statistic on which the goodness-of-fit test is based has no clear interpretation by itself and its associated significance level will not be useful when the sample size is so large that all results are "significant." Finally, although the approach does provide ways to guide theory development, it is predicated upon the researcher starting with some theory to specify and test.

The use of unobservable variables in structural equations seems to have exceptional potential to help marketing researchers. The reality is that, for marketing problems, single indicators of theoretical constructs tend often to be biased and unreliable. A reasonable solution is to use multiple indicators and to explicitly model the errors in variables rather than have them confounded with errors in equations resulting from a misspecified theory.

References

1. Aaker, David A., and Day, George S. 1974. "A Dynamic Model of Relationships, Advertising, Consumer Awareness, Attitudes and Behavior." *Journal of Applied Psychology* 59; 281–286.
2. Bagozzi, Richard P. 1976. "Toward a General Theory for the Explanation of the Performance of Salespeople." Unpublished doctoral dissertation. Northwestern University. Evanston, Illinois.
3. ———. 1977a. "Convergent and Discriminant Validity by Analysis of Covariance Structures: The Case of the Affective Behavioral, and Cognitive Components of Attitude." In *Advances in Consumer Research.* Edited by W. D. Perreault, Jr. Vol. 4. Association of Consumer Research.
4. ———. 1977b. "Structural Equation Models in Experimental Research." *Journal of Marketing Research* 14 (May), 209–226.
5. ———. "Salesforce Performance and Satisfaction as a Function of Individual Difference, Interpersonal, and Situational Factors," *Journal of Marketing Research,* 15 (forthcoming, 1978).
6. Bass, Frank M. 1969. "A Simultaneous Equation Regression Study of Advertising and Sales of Cigarettes." *Journal of Marketing Research* 6 (August), 291–300.
7. Bielby, William T. and Robert M. Hauser, "Structural Equation Models." *Annual Review of Sociology,* forthcoming.
8. Blalock, Hubert M., Jr. 1967a. "Path Coefficients Versus Regression Coefficients." *American Journal of Sociology* 72, 675–676.
9. ———. 1967b. "Causal Inferences, Closed Populations, and Measures of Associations." *American Political Science Review* 61, 130–136.
10. ———. 1968. "The Measurement Problem: A Gap Between the Languages of Theory and Research." In *Methodology in Social Research.* Edited by Hubert M. Blalock, Jr. and Ann B. Blalock, 5–27. New York: McGraw-Hill Book Company.
11. Burt, Ronald S. 1973. "Confirmatory Factor-Analytic Structures and the Theory Construction Process." *Sociological Methods and Research* 2 (November), 131–190.
12. ———. 1976. "Interpreting Confounding of Unobserved Variables in Structural Equation Models." *Sociological Methods and Research* 5 (August), 3–52.
13. Campbell, D. T. and Fisk, J. D. 1959. "Convergent and Discriminant Validation by the Multitrait-Multimethod Matrix," *Psychological Bulletin,* 56, 81–105.
14. Churchill, G. A., Jr., Ford, N. M. and Walter, O. C., Jr. 1976. "Organizational Climate and Job Satisfaction in the Salesforce." *Journal of Marketing Research,* 13 (November), 323–32.
15. Costner, H. L. 1969. "Theory, Deduction and Rules of Correspondence." *American Journal of Sociology* 75 (September), 245–263.
16. Costner, H. L. and Schoenberg, R. 1973. "Diagnosing Indicator Ills in Multiple Indicator Models." In *Structural Equation Models in the Social Sciences.* Edited by A. S. Goldberger and O. D. Duncan. New York: Academic Press.
17. Duncan, Otis Dudley, 1975. *Introduction to Structural Equation Models.* New York: Academic Press.
18. Farley, John U., Howard, John A., and Lehman, Donald R. 1976. "A 'Working' System Model of Car Buyer Behavior." *Management Science* (November), 235–247.
19. Fisher, F. M. 1966. *The Identification Problem in Econometrics.* New York: McGraw-Hill.
20. Geraci, V. J. 1974. "Simultaneous Equation Models with Measurement Error." Unpublished Ph.D. dissertation, Department of Economics, University of Wisconsin.
21. Goldberger, Arthur S. 1964. *Econometric Theory,* New York: John Wiley & Sons, Inc.
22. ———. 1973. "Structural Equation Models: An Overview." In *Structural Equation Models in the Social Sciences.* Edited by A. S. Goldberger and O. D. Duncan, New York: Seminar Press. 1–18.
23. ———. 1974. "Unobservable Variables in Econometrics." In *Frontiers in Econometrics.* Edited by P. Zarembka, New York: Academic Press. 193–213.
24. Gorsuch, Richard L. 1974. *Factor Analysis.* Philadelphia, Pa.: W. B. Saunders Company.
25. Griliches, A. 1974. "Errors in Variables and Other Unobservables." *Econometrica* 42 (November), 971–998.
26. Hsiao, C. 1976. "Identification for a Linear Dynamic Simultaneous Error-Shock Model." Working Paper. Berkeley: Department of Economics, University of California.
27. ———. "Identification and Estimation of Simultaneous Equation Models with Measurement Error." *International Economic Review* forthcoming.
28. Hauser, R. M. and Goldberger, Arthur S. 1971. "The Treatment of Unobservable Variables in Path Analysis." In *Sociological Methodology 1971.* Edited by H. L. Costner, San Francisco: Jossey–Bass, 81–117.
29. Jacobson, Alvin L., and Lalu, N. M. 1974. "An Empirical and Algebraic Analysis of Alternative Techniques for Measuring Unobserved Variables." In *Measurement in the Social Sciences.* Edited by H. M. Blalock, Jr., Chicago: Aldine, 215–242.
30. Jöreskog, Karl G. 1969. "A General Approach to Confirmatory Maximum Likelihood Factor Analysis." *Psychometrika* 34, 183–202.
31. ———. 1970. "A General Method of Analysis of Covariance Structures." *Biometrika* 57, 239–251.
32. ———. 1973. "A General Method for Estimating a Linear Structural Equation System." In *Structural Equation Models in the Social Sciences.* Edited by A. S. Goldberger and O. D. Duncan, New York: Seminar Press, 85–112.
33. Jöreskog, Karl G. and Goldberger, Arthur S. 1975. "Estimation of a Model with Multiple Indicators and Multiple Causes of a Single Latent Variable." *Journal of the American Statistical Association* 70, (September), 631–639.
34. Jöreskog, Karl G., and Sörbom, D. "Statistical Models and Methods for Analysis of Longitudinal Data." In *Latent Variables in Socioeconometric Models.* Edited by D. J. Aigner and A. S. Goldberger. Amsterdam: North-Holland, forthcoming.
35. Jöreskog, Karl G., and van Thillo, M. 1972. "LISREL: A General Computer Program for Estimating a Linear Structural Equation System Involving Multiple Indicators of Unmeasured Variables." RB-72-56. Princeton, N. J.: Educational Testing Service.
36. Kim, J. and Mueller, C. W. 1976. "Standardization and Unstandardized Coefficients and Causal Analysis." *Sociological Methods and Research* 4 (May), 423–438.
37. Land, K. C. 1969. "Principles of Path Analysis." In *Sociological Methodology 1969.* Edited by E. F. Borgatta, San Francisco: Jossey–Bass, 3–37.

38. Lawley, D. N. and Maxwell, A. E. 1971. *Factor Analysis as a Statistical Method*. London: Butterworth.

39. Lord, F. C. and Novick, M. R. 1968. *Statistical Theories of Mental Test Scores*. Reading, Mass.: Addison-Wesley.

40. Massy, William F. 1969. "What is Factor Analysis?" In *Proceedings of the 1964 Conference of the American Marketing Association*, Chicago: American Marketing Association, 291–307.

41. Mitchell, A. A. and Olson, J. C. 1975. "The Use of Restricted and Unrestricted Maximum Likelihood Factor Analysis to Examine Alternative Measures of Brand Loyalty." Working Paper No. 29. Pennsylvania State University.

42. Mood, Alexander M. and Graybill, Franklin A. 1963. *Introduction to the Theory of Statistics*, New York: McGraw-Hill Book Company.

43. Mulaik, Stanley, A. 1972. *The Foundations of Factor Analysis*. New York: McGraw-Hill Book Company.

44. Nan, Lin and Burt, Ronald S. 1975. "Differential Effects of Information Channels in the Process of Innovation Diffusion." *Social Forces* 54 (September), 265–274.

45. Tukey, J. W. 1954. "Causation, Regression and Path Analysis." In *Statistics and Mathematics in Biology*. Edited by O. Kempthorne, T. A. Bancroft, J. W. Gowen and J. L. Lush, Ames, Iowa: Iowa State College Press, 35–66.

46. Werts, C. E., Jöreskog, K. G. and Linn, R. L. 1973. "Identification and Estimation in Path Analysis with Unmeasured Variables." *American Journal of Sociology* 78, 1469–1484.

47. Wright, Sewall. 1970. "Path Coefficients and Path Regressions: Alternatives or Complementary Concepts?" *Biometrics* 16, 189–202.

For Discussion

1. What is an unobservable variable? Illustrate your answer.
2. What is the MIMIC model? Develop your own example of a MIMIC model. What is the difference between an underidentified and overidentified model?
3. Explain how a χ^2 value is used to test a model.
4. Interpret a *p*-level of .06 associated with a χ^2 test.
5. What are nested models?
6. The insertion of unobservable variables complicates. Why add them?

Appendix

Pearson Product-Moment Correlations for Observations of Variables Used in Analyses

Variables	y_1	y_2	y_3	y_4	x_1	x_2	x_3	x_4	x_5	x_6
Dollar Sales, y_1	1.000									
Job Satisfaction #1, y_2	.395	1.000								
Job Satisfaction #2, y_3	.364	.647	1.000							
Job Satisfaction #1 and #2, y_4	.420	.929	.884	1.000						
Job Tension #1, x_1	−.438	−.589	−.491	−.600	1.000					
Job Tension #2, x_2	−.383	−.290	−.324	−.337	.572	1.000				
Specific Self-esteem #1, x_3	.536	.297	.288	.322	−.273	−.392	1.000			
Specific Self-esteem #2, x_4	.494	.254	.284	.294	−.248	−.267	.548	1.000		
Role Ambiguity #1, x_5	−.187	−.134	−.137	−.149	.307	.260	−.294	−.289	1.000	
Role Ambiguity #2, x_6	−.222	−.139	−.191	−.179	.293	.391	−.364	−.425	.696	1.000

$m = 106$

11

A Model of the Distribution of
Branded Personal Products in Jamaica

John U. Farley

Harold J. Leavitt

Introduction

A behavioral model of a developing economy's distribution system might be useful to governments and private businesses. Governments sometimes channel little public capital into the distribution sector; therefore, balanced development depends on response of this private distribution structure to external change. Similarly, private industry interested in tapping substantial and growing markets of developing countries must understand how the merchandising structure functions and how it responds to various elements inside and outside the structure.

Such a model has been developed for Jamaica. This Caribbean island nation, an independent member of the British Commonwealth since 1961, is representative of a group of relatively poor countries experiencing rapid economic development. Encouraged by government support and trade protection, a growing manufacturing sector complements the economic mix including agriculture, bauxite production, and tourism. In 1964, the population of 1.8 million had a per capita income of $441 and ranked among nations in the fourth quintile of the world's income distribution, near such nations as Malta, Mexico, and Chile [18]. The 1950–64 estimated growth rate in GNP per capita was a substantial 5.43 percent — comparable to the stellar growth rate for Puerto Rico during the same period [7].

Description of the Model

The model involves key decisions for each member of the three-level structure:

1. Manufacturers and importers who sell either through wholesalers or directly to retail outlets. A single firm may manufacture or package part of its line and import another part.
2. Wholesalers, located in various parts of the island, who often retail and wholesale. They are supplied by manufacturers and importers.
3. Retailers, including several general merchandisers and fewer other kinds of outlets. For reasons discussed in the appendix, this analysis focuses on general merchandisers.

The model's structure is based on pilot interviews and analysis of data collected at various stages of a cross-sectional field study but not used in the testing phase. The key decisions for retailers are whether to stock a product and whether to stock more than one brand of the product; for manufacturers and importers, to call directly on retailers or to deal through wholesalers; and for wholesalers, to compete with wholesalers of related products that might otherwise be supplied by a single wholesaler. These decisions depend on each other and on sales through feedback on other decisions.

The model has five dependent variables that are influenced by several other elements in the system:

1. Distribution is f_1 (sales, manufacturer-importer merchandising, wholesaler merchandising).
2. Sales is f_2 (distribution, multiple brand stocking, income, population).
3. Manufacturer-importer merchandising activity is f_3 (sales, distance from Kingston).
4. Wholesaler merchandising activity is f_4 (sales, distance from nearest wholesaling center).
5. Multiple brand stocking is f_5 (sales, manufacturer-importer merchandising, wholesale merchandising).

The definitions of these elements and of the dependent variables follow.

Distribution. Measured distribution of a product is the proportion of all interviewed retailers who stock the product. Retailers' short-run decisions to stock are based on perceived sales potential for the product; current sales are used as a proxy for short-run expected sales. The product can be supplied and promoted either directly or by importers or manu-

Reprinted from *Journal of Marketing Research*, published by the American Marketing Association. V, November 1968, pp. 362–368. Mr. and Mrs. C. W. Wilson of Caribbean Research, Ltd., aided all aspects of the study, and computations were facilitated by the Northern European University Computation Center, Technical University, Lyngby. The Ford Foundation Research Grant in Operations Management to GSIA partially supported the study.

facturers who are aggressive merchandisers, or less directly through repeated contact with more than one wholesaler. Intensity of direct contact is defined as the percentage of all retailers stocking the product who are supplied directly by manufacturers and importers. The index is product specific. An index of wholesale merchandising activity is the number of wholesalers identified by retailers as suppliers for a set of products (discussed later) by all those retailers stocking these products. This measure is area specific. Both indexes of merchandising intensity are, themselves, dependent variables in other relationships.

Sales. Monthly sales rates depend on basic demand determinants of population and income and on certain aspects of merchandising activities. The data indicated that retailers generally adopt fixed markup rules and that suppliers' prices are quite homogeneous; hence there is negligible average retail price variation in Jamaica. Real prices vary, of course, but are affected much more by consumers' income than by nominal price differentials. Population is defined for each product by a supplier-defined target group; men over 15 years old for shaving cream, women 15 to 65 years old for skin cream and sanitary napkins, and the total population for toothpaste. Merchandising practices that affect sales are the availability of product and of alternative brands, that is, ease of access to supply.

Manufacturer-Importer Merchandising Activity. Importers and manufacturers perform similar merchandising activities. They maintain sales forces that put special effort where sales potential exists. As with retailers' stocking decisions, current sales are used as a proxy for short-run expectations. All such firms are located in the capital, Kingston, and their cost of reaching other parts of Jamaica is approximated by distance from the center of Kingston to the approximate population center of gravity of these areas.

Wholesaler Merchandising Activity. As with manufacturers and importers, wholesalers' activities seem to depend on sales potential described earlier and on the distance from customers. Distance is measured from the approximate population center of gravity of a sample area to the nearest wholesaling center. A wholesaling center is a location where more than one retailer identified a wholesaler whose address could be determined independently.

Brand Stocking Practices. As with distribution, retailers will stock more than one brand of any product that has substantial local sales. They also respond to sales contacts with distributors and wholesalers. The depth index of brand stocking is the average number of brands of the product stocked by stores carrying the product.

Distribution and multiple brand stocking are complementary and correspond to the extensive and intensive margins of the distribution system [4]. These margins are analogous to economic concepts, i.e., the extensive margin marks the limit where new land can economically be brought

into use, and the intensive margin marks where output can be economically increased on land already in use. Here, the extensive margin (distribution) determines whether the product is stocked at all, and the intensive margin (the brand stocking index) indicates how much the line is stocked by retailers who stock the product. External influences affect the margins similarly, but they are nontheless separable empirically.

The sales feedback relationship, strong in the empirical results, discussed later, enters all aspects of the model. Using current sales as a proxy for short-term expected sales in the relationships can be justified in two ways. First current sales volume is, in fact, an excellent predictor of short-run future sales volume [17]; models of rational [12] and static [10] expectations are often formulated in this way. Interview results determine the second rationale. For example, the reason for stocking a new product or brand usually cited by retailers [5] and almost universally cited by wholesalers was that they had been asked for the item. Since stocking decisions can be implemented quickly, they rapidly feed back through the sales equation and into the other relationships. This is the behavioral kind of decision making discussed by Cyert and March in connection with behavioral theory of the firm [1]. Interviews revealed that behavior patterns, particularly those connected with decisions to introduce new items, include pervasive elements of problem-oriented and localized search for alternatives and feedback response to request rather than planned response to the environment. Although the sales feedback formulation in the model is a reasonable approximation of the situation, more detailed fieldwork on expectation formation is required.

Identification

The interactions of sales and the marketing decision rules imply an interdependent system of relationships. The variables can be divided into two sets — those determined within the system (endogenous) and those determined outside (exogenous or predetermined). Four endogenous variables cover the merchandising activities of the distribution system's three levels. The fifth endogenous variable, sales, is the key link to the exogenous variables related to basic demand.

Endogenous	Exogenous
Y_1 is percent of stores stocking the product	X_1 is target population for the product
Y_2 is sales in units per month	X_2 is income per capita in the parish where the area is
Y_3 is index of direct contact with importer and manufacturer for the product	X_3 is distance from population center of gravity to Kingston
Y_4 is index of wholesale activity in the area	X_4 is distance from population center of gravity to nearest wholesale town
Y_5 is index of depth of brand stocking for the product	

Since scatter diagrams revealed no obvious nonlinearities, the model was formulated as a set of linear relationships. Define y' as a column vector of observations of endogeneous variables, x' as a column vector of observations of exogenous variables augmented by unity in the last position, u' as a vector of errors, and B and Γ as the matrices of coefficients of the endogenous and exogenous variables, respectively [8].[1] The well-known matrix equation expression for the model is:

$$By' + \Gamma x' = u'.$$

The actual matrices are:

$$B = \begin{bmatrix} -1 & \beta_{12} & \beta_{13} & \beta_{14} & 0 \\ \beta_{21} & -1 & 0 & 0 & \beta_{25} \\ 0 & \beta_{32} & -1 & 0 & 0 \\ 0 & \beta_{42} & 0 & -1 & 0 \\ 0 & \beta_{52} & \beta_{53} & \beta_{54} & -1 \end{bmatrix}$$

$$\Gamma = \begin{bmatrix} 0 & 0 & 0 & 0 & \gamma_{15} \\ \gamma_{21} & \gamma_{22} & 0 & 0 & \gamma_{25} \\ 0 & 0 & \gamma_{33} & 0 & \gamma_{35} \\ 0 & 0 & 0 & \gamma_{44} & \gamma_{45} \\ 0 & 0 & 0 & 0 & \gamma_{55} \end{bmatrix}$$

The last column in the Γ matrix contains the constant term, unrestricted in value, in each equation. The second column in B shows how greatly all the decision rules are oriented toward sales, (Y_2), a variable that shows up in every equation. Similarly, the link of sales to the basic determinants $(X_1$ and $X_2)$ of demand through the second equation is shown in the second row of Γ. The first and fifth rows in the B matrix, both involving decisions by retailers, are unusual because the corresponding rows in Γ are all zero, except for the constant. The first and fifth equations thus involve no exogenous variables. Despite this, necessary and sufficient conditions for identification are met, and estimation of the structural parameters is feasible [18]. Equation 2 is exactly identified and the others are overidentified.

Normalization of the diagonal elements of B to -1 means that the hypothesized signs of the coefficients correspond to their natural influence on the dependent variables. All coefficients are, by hypothesis, positive except γ_{33} and γ_{44}, the coefficients of the two distance variables approximating travel costs for wholesalers and retailers.

The Data

This article reports the results of fitting the model to data on shaving cream, skin cream, sanitary napkins, and toothpaste. These products were chosen for several reasons. First, preliminary inquiries and coincident pretests showed that markets for these products are in various stages of development throughout the island. Second, because the product classes are narrowly defined and have relatively few brands, suppliers and manufacturers are easy to identify. Third, there are no special public policy or excise problems associated with the products' internal distribution, though there are some tax incentives that encourage domestic production. Domestic production has apparently had little impact on the brand structure. Fourth, the products are in the same expenditure class in previous Jamaican budget analyses [16], personal and medical care. This makes analysis of the four products replicative to some extent. Fifth, marketing strategy for each product has been similar — heavy emphasis on distribution and negligible advertising at this point of market development.

The model is fit to cross-sectional data from 30 of the 32 constituencies into which Jamaica is divided for census and administrative purposes. The sampling plan and sources of subsidiary data are described in the appendix. This formulation assumes implicitly that various parts of Jamaica are in different stages of a homogeneous process of each product's market development [11], although the pattern may be different for different products. This is a palatable assumption, given the geographic, climatic, and cultural homogeneity of the relatively small island.

Ordinary Least-Squares Estimates

The coefficients' signs are generally consistent with those hypothesized since 46 of 56 coefficients, excluding constants, have the expected signs and 23 of these are statistically significant at $\alpha = .05$ or better (Table 1). The coefficients of determination for 18 of the 20 equations are significant at the .05 level and most at much higher levels, although the fits vary substantially over products.

The most apparent particular effect is the impact of sales on the structure at all levels. The sales variable occurs as an independent variable 16 times; 15 coefficients are positive and 12 are significant at $\alpha = .05$ or higher. It thus appears that all members of the structure — retailer, wholesaler, manufacturer, and importer — are indeed responding with decision rules geared to sales or near-run expected sales.

All eight coefficients for manufacturer-importer merchandising activities are positive and four are significant at least at $\alpha = .05$. This influence is therefore felt both through distribution (the extensive margin in Equation 1) and through brand stocking (the intensive margin in Equation 5). These results suggest that any group, public or private, interested in stimulating activity in the private retailing sector should look to the community of manufacturers and importers. This group is small, geographically concentrated, and highly influential on the remainder of the structure. Interviews also indicated that all firms in this group have ties — corporate, personal for the managers, or both — to agents of change, both at home and abroad. For stimulating these firms, subsidies for wider

---

[1] Editor's Note. The matrix equation represents five equations. The coefficients for the ith equation are given by the ith rows in the matrixes. For example, the third equation is: $0Y_1 + \beta_{32}Y_2 - 1Y_3 + 0Y_4 + 0Y_5 + 0X_1 + 0X_2 + \gamma_{33}X_3 + 0X_4 + \gamma_{35}X_5 = u_3$ which can be rewritten as: $Y_3 = +\beta_{32}Y_2 + \gamma_{33}X_3 + \gamma_{35}X_5 - u_3$ where now the endogenous variable in the third equation, y_3, appears alone on the left side. The term x_5 is defined to be 1.

Table 1
Ordinary Least-Squares Estimates of Parameters in Five Equation Model

Dependent Variable	Independent Variable	Shaving Cream	Sanitary Napkins	Skin Cream	Toothpaste
Distribution (Y_1)	Sales (Y_2)	20.67*	.0314†	.0737†	.0128
	Importer-manufacturer activity (Y_3)	3.29†	30.89‡	16.60	35.58*
	Wholesale activity (Y_4)	7.61‡	−26.765	−10.69	−28.96
	Constant	−3.18	33.124	30.08	69.34
	R^2 (unadjusted)	.797*	.491*	.270†	.401*
Sales (Y_2)	Distribution (Y_1)	.0275*	3.040‡	2.148*	5.023‡
	Multiple brand stocking (Y_5)	.0284	133.37‡	−34.642	553.7‡
	Income (X_1)	.0317	1.167‡	.5467†	.779
	Population (X_2)	.0599	.9839†	−.0021	.130
	Constant	.1209	.1736	.1139	.1470
	R^2 (unadjusted)	.897*	.675*	.352*	.548*
Importer-manufacturer activity (Y_3)	Sales	1.069*	.6829*	1.074*	4.164*
	Distance from Kingston	−.0502	−.2044*	−1.682*	.0218*
	Constant	.1209	.1736	.1139	.1470
	R^2 (unadjusted)	.365*	.6825*	.5391*	.6364*
Wholesale activity (Y_4)	Sales (Y_2)	.2775*	.3010*	.3767†	.2649*
	Distance from nearest wholesale center (X_4)	−.0409	−.2347	−.2139	.0636
	Constant	.6851	.4437	.6810	.4067
	R^2 (unadjusted) .409*	.407*	.156	.3686*	
Multiple brand stocking index (Y_5)	Sales (Y_2)	2.231*	.6578*	−.0861	.0735
	Importer-manufacturer activity (Y_3)	.6354*	.5780‡	.1127	.5671*
	Wholesale activity (Y_4)	−.3546	−1.501†	.1235	.0559
	Constant	.4379	1.963	.992	.9385
	R^2 (unadjusted) .749*	.314†	.0624	.7436*	

* Significant at 1 percent level.
† Significant at 5 percent level.
‡ Significant at 10 percent level.

coverage are particularly appropriate since distribution appears sensitive to any such contact. In turn, manufacturers and importers appear to be sensitive to distances they must travel to reach customers. (The distance coefficient in Equation 3 is always negative and highly significant in three cases.) A subsidy would reduce costs associated with traveling these distances.

However, interviews with wholesalers showed that they are rather passive order takers and that they do very little active soliciting for business. This is supported by the eight coefficients of the wholesale contact index distributed about zero. The wholesalers thus appear inert, for both securing distribution and actively encouraging retailers to stock new brands. The distance variable appears to have only a weak negative effect, probably because the wholesalers are spread over the island instead of concentrated in Kingston as the manufacturers are. It is possible that, despite clustering of wholesalers in market towns, individual wholesalers hold considerable monopolistic power over retailers because of institutional factors such as credit arrangements. This can be especially true outside main metropolitan areas where multiple wholesaler arrangements are fairly rare and where credit arrangements may be crucial to small-scale retailers. Field work is planned to examine these issues more deeply.

The exogenous demand variables in the sales equation

are population and income. All income coefficients are positive, and one is significant at $\alpha = .05$. Three population coefficients are positive and one is significant at $\alpha = .05$. Collinearity problems between these variables, discussed later, are probably related to the apparent weak effects of the two variables.

Simultaneous Estimation Procedures

The discussion has, thus far, skirted an important set of methodological issues related to the model's involving a set of interdependent equations rather than a single relationship. Ordinary least-squares estimates of parameters are biased for small samples and are inconsistent when used to estimate the structural parameters of such a system. Even an infinite sample size will not remove the bias [8]. Lack of bias and consistency are not necessarily attractive properties for an estimator but, other things being equal, consistency is more desirable than inconsistency. Various adjustments that take into account interdependencies among the equations produce consistent estimates. Three such procedures were used to fit the equations of the model simultaneously. Two techniques estimate the equations one at a time — two-stage least squares and limited information maximum likelihood. Each is a linear procedure in which certain matrices are adjusted before the normal equations are solved. The third technique, full information maximum likelihood, involves solution by iteration of a system of nonlinear equations to estimate all coefficients simultaneously. The three methods appear to break down because of a problem plaguing many single-equation analyses — multicollinearity.

These three multiple-equation methods will generally yield estimates which for small samples are biased but consistent — approach the true value asymptotically in probability as the sample size increases. Asymptotic properties, especially consistency, offer little relief for dealing with small bodies of data, but they are desirable, other things being equal. Knowledge of the small sample properties of these methods comes chiefly from Monte Carlo studies of known systems of equations subjected to known errors — usually specification errors [8]. Ordinary least squares generally performs somewhat worse than the other methods for squared error, mainly because of greater bias. Recently,

Table 2

Structural Parameters for Equation 1,
Estimated by Alternative Methods for Shaving Cream

| | Independent Variable | | | |
Coefficients Estimated by	Sales	Importer-Manufacturer Activity	Wholesale Activity	Constant
Ordinary least squares	20.67 (4.11)*	3.29 (1.89)*	7.61 (5.91)*	−3.18
Two-stage least squares	58.76 (42.2)*	−4.45 (9.68)*	−31.11 (68.2)*	14.33
Limited information maximum likelihood	65.48 (52.34)*	−4.47 (11.1)*	−41.38 (83.38)*	18.91
Full information maximum likelihood	67.86†	−7.37 (7.81)*	−33.94†	15.4

* Standard errors.
† Estimated variances negative.

however, studies of nonnormal errors and collinearity indicate ordinary least squares is more capable than the other methods in overcoming these difficulties [13]. This robustness appears important in estimating structural parameters of

this model. For example, the behavior of the four methods for the shaving cream distribution equation (Table 2) is typical of the results of procedures for all the products and for all equations.

Table 2 shows that, for all three multiple-equation methods, standard errors increase and some signs change. None of the coefficients is significant. Nearly collinear variables in single equations often produce similar estimation problems. The negative estimated variances of the full information coefficients provide more evidence of near singularity of at least one of the many matrices that must be inverted in this procedure. Of course, there is no such thing as a negative variance. The variances were approximated by an iterative procedure that involves matrices of derivatives, which may be singular up to, perhaps, computer rounding error.

The matrix of simple correlation coefficients (Table 3) — again for shaving cream — provides additional insight. The simple correlations between pairs of variables that appear in each equation are high, but many others are also large enough to warn of potential difficulty even in single-equation estimation. Wide disparity of the eigenvalues of the covariance matrix for the exogenous variables — one of many submatrices to be inverted in the multiple-equation methods — provides further evidence of potential matrix arithmetic problems [3]. (The largest eigenvalue is 10^6 times the smallest.) Collinearity between income and population (both exogenous) may also partially explain why these variables had such weak effects in the sales equation.

A final matter related to collinearity involves the full information procedure that did not converge in 25 minutes of 7,090 computations for two products and converged in 15 and 19 minutes, respectively, for the other two. This enormous amount of computation time for a small system of equations [15] is another symptom of the near-singularity of some submatrices.

Similar estimation dilemmas are reported elsewhere, and multiple-equation methods are generally considered more sensitive to multicollinearity than are ordinary least squares [9]. Here the choice of estimation procedures lies

Table 3

Simple Correlation Coefficients of Nine Variables for Shaving Cream

Variable	Sales	Importer-Manufacturer Activity	Wholesale Activity	Multiple Brand Stocking	Income	Population	Distance to Kingston	Distance to Nearest Market Town
Endogenous variables								
Distribution	.867	.655	.684	.745	.596	.183	−.600	−.371
Sales		.587	.666	.703	.657	.304	−.570	−.356
Importer-manufacturer activity			.493	.675	.631	.493	−.392	−.463
Wholesale activity				.483	.668	.398	−.602	−.329
Multiple brand stocking					.488	.313	−.604	−.327
Exogenous variables								
Income						.603	−.531	−.385
Population							−.407	−.498
Distance to Kingston								.454

between biased results and consistent results that are not interpretable because of an external problem. The decision favored the more flexible ordinary least-squares procedure, noting of course the salient characteristics of the alternative procedures.

Summary

A five equation model of the Jamaican distribution structure was developed. The structural parameters were estimated with ordinary least squares for four branded personal product markets in various stages of development — shaving cream, skin cream, sanitary napkins, and toothpaste. Some difficulties apparently caused by multicollinearity in connection with methods of simultaneous estimation of the structural parameters led to the choice of ordinary least squares as the primary estimation technique.

The signs of the estimated parameters generally corresponded to those hypothesized, and the fits were generally satisfactory. For the products studied, it appears that all parties in the structure — manufacturers and importers, wholesalers and retailers — respond sensitively to decision rules based on sales or short-run expected sales. It also appears that wholesalers are relatively inactive merchandisers and that the entire structure is sensitive to manufacturer-importer sales effort. The structure's characteristics indicate that aggressive introduction or demand stimulation programs should include incentives for manufacturers and importers to increase the number of retailers to which their sales forces sell directly.

These four products are, of course, not necessarily representative of branded goods or of branded personal products. Nevertheless, although the numerical estimates of the parameters range widely, the general structure appears similar over products.

Appendix

Sampling. The sampling was carried out in three stages.

1. *Interviews with Importers and Manufacturers.* All identifiable large importers and manufacturers were interviewed in 1965 on the basis of business registration directories, conversations with other suppliers, and the advice of an independent research agency. There were 13 such firms dealing in these products.
2. *Interviews with Retailers.* Jamaica is divided for census purposes into small areas called enumeration districts, each with from 200 to 900 inhabitants. Sets of three contiguous enumeration districts were drawn from the detailed Jamaican census of 1960 [2]. Of the 2,661 enumeration districts, 234 were drawn; these were supplemented by 37 districts from a random sample drawn in connection with another study, plus two districts contiguous to each. The latter were included for special reasons outside the scope of the present report [14]. In all, 345 districts were included. Within each district, all retailers of food, drug, and grocery products were interviewed in 1964. The refusal rate in this group was zero.
3. *Interviews with Wholesalers.* As part of the interviews, retailers were asked to identify suppliers of the products that they stocked. (The business registers are much less complete and reliable in their listing of wholesalers than of importers and manufacturers.)

From the list of 137 different suppliers identified in the retailer interviews, a sample of 21 was drawn randomly for interviews in the wholesale sector. One wholesaler refused to participate. Always, the wholesalers identified importers or manufacturers as their suppliers, giving evidence of a three-level distribution system.

The sampling plan, which represented retailers randomly by area, led to underweighting of large retail outlets. This could have been remedied by using a sampling frame of outlets weighted by sales; unfortunately, no list of outlets was available for Jamaica. It also could have been remedied by a two-stage sampling plan, the first stage an area sample to verify strata, and the second a stratified sample with probabilities proportionate to outlet size [6]; it was infeasible to follow this procedure after the initial sample was drawn and the problem discovered. A disparity of some 20 percent exists between total industry volumes estimated by the importers and manufacturers and projections of retailer's sales to total sales in each product class. (The importers and manufacturers may also err, of course.) The underrepresented large outlets are chiefly modern drug stores and supermarkets, and the actual sample mainly covers more traditional, general merchandise retailers.

The enumeration districts are aggregated into 32 constituencies that became the study's basic sampling units and that also meshed conveniently with census demographic data. Reliable income data are available only for the 14 parishes, each of which contains two or three constituencies with no overlap; constituency income was approximated by the parish income. Thirty of the 32 constituencies are included in the sample. Evident interviewer errors in one constituency in the skin cream data could not be corrected with followup, so the sample for that product contains 29 not 30 points.

References

1. Richard M. Cyert and James G. March, *A Behavioral Theory of the Firm*, Englewood Cliffs, N.J.: Prentice-Hall, Inc., 1963, 114–28.
2. Department of Statistics, *Census of Jamaica*, Kingston, Jamaica, 1960.
3. Harry Eisenpress, *Forecasting by Econometric Systems*, White Plains, N.Y.: IBM Data Processing Division, Share General Program Library, 1963.
4. John U. Farley, "Intensive and Extensive Margins as Summary Measures of Consumer Brand Choice Patterns," in L. G. Smith, ed., *Reflections on Progress in Marketing*, American Marketing Association, 1964, 258–66.
5. _____ and Harold J. Leavitt, "Private Sector Logistics and Population Control: A Case in Jamaica," Working paper, GSIA, Carnegie-Mellon University, 1968.
6. Robert Ferber, *Market Research*, New York: McGraw-Hill Book Co., 1949, 69–76.
7. International Bank for Reconstruction and Development, *World Bank Atlas of Per Capita Product and Population*, Washington: IBRD, 1966.
8. J. Johnston, *Econometric Methods*, New York: McGraw-Hill Book Co., 1963, 246–57.
9. Lawrence Klein and M. Nakamura, "Singularity in the Equation Systems and the Problem of Multicollinearity," *International Economic Review*, 3 (September 1962), 274–99.
10. Robert E. Lucas, "Adjustment Costs and The Theory of Supply," *Journal of Political Economy*, 75 (August, 1967), 321–34.

11. William F. Massy, "Television Ownership in 1950: Results of a Factor Analytic Study," in Ronald E. Frank, Alfred A. Kuehn, and William F. Massy, ed., *Quantitative Techniques in Marketing Analysis*, Homewood Ill.: Richard D. Irwin, Inc., 1962, 440–61.

12. John F. Muth, "Rational Expectations and the Theory of Price Movements," *Econometrica*, 29 (July 1961), 315–35.

13. Thomas Sargent, "Simultaneous Equation Systems with Non-Normal Disturbances: A Pilot Study," Unpublished working paper, GSIA, Carnegie-Mellon University, 1967.

14. J. Mayone Stycos and Kurt W. Back, *The Control of Human Fertility in Jamaica*, Ithaca, N.Y.: Cornell University Press, 1964.

15. Richard Summers, "A Capital Intensive Approach to the Small Sample Properties of Various Simultaneous Equation Estimators," *Econometrica*, 33 (January 1965), 1–41.

16. LeRoy Taylor, *Consumers Expenditure in Jamaica*, University of the West Indies, 1964.

17. Lester G. Telser, "The Demand for Branded Goods as Estimated from Consumer Panel Data," *Review of Economics and Statistics*, 44 (August 1962), 300–24.

18. J. H. Weaver and L. P. Jones, "International Distribution of Income 1950–1964," Unpublished manuscript, American University, Washington, 1967.

For Discussion

Evaluate the operationalization of the variables. Draw a figure (like that in the Aaker-Day selection) tracing out the hypothesized paths of influence between the constructs.

Part 1

The Analysis of Dependence

Section C
AID ANALYSIS

12

Segmenting Markets
By Group Purchasing Behavior:
An Application of The AID Technique

Henry Assael

In a recent article, Bass, Tigert, and Lonsdale contend that regression techniques are poor indicators of the value of socioeconomic variables in segmenting markets by behavior [2]. Past studies demonstrating low R^2 values between demographics and purchase rate suggest a large within-group or unexplained variance. Yet regression relies on the individual as the unit of observation. As the authors suggest, it is the variance between groups, not individuals, that is critical in market segmentation: grouped data should be the unit of analysis.

Given the need to examine variations in grouped data, Bass, Tigert, and Lonsdale propose multiple cross-classification analysis. A number of contingency tables are constructed to study the simultaneous effects of two variables at a time on mean usage rates. Yet more than two variables may be required to define the groups with the widest variation in usage. As the authors recognize, in such cases "the number of cells becomes large enough to overwhelm even very large samples."

Clearly, a multivariate method going beyond cross-classification analysis is required to define the large number of alternative methods of segmentation at the point of greatest discrimination in group means.

The Automatic Interaction
Detector Program

The Automatic Interaction Detector (AID) program, developed by Sonquist and Morgan [1, 3, and 4], partially overcomes the restrictions associated with cross-classification analysis; AID is a multivariate

technique for determining what variables and categories within them combine to produce the greatest discrimination in group means by the dependent variable (purchase frequency, brand last purchased, advertising recall, etc.). The program divides the sample through a series of binary splits into mutually exclusive subgroups. The group means account for more of the total sum of squares of the dependent variables than the means of any other combination of predictor variables.

AID can examine up to 35 independent variables simultaneously. The independent variables require coded intervals, with a maximum of 63 categories per variable. There are no coded interval requirements for the dependent variable, which is assumed to be continuous. Dichotomous data (purchasers of Brand X vs. nonpurchasers) are frequently used as the dependent variable since they can be transformed into a continuous variable by treating one of the categories as a proportion (e.g., percentage of purchasers).

In operation, the program splits the sample into two subgroups to provide the largest reduction in the unexplained sum of squares of the dependent variable. This is accomplished as follows: group means are determined for each classification of all independent variables, and all dichotomous groupings of each variable are examined. Using region as an example, the group mean for those living in the East, Northcentral, South, and West is first computed. The group means for all dichotomous groupings are then examined—East vs. rest of U.S., East and Northcentral vs. South and West, etc. Each predictor variable is split into two non-overlapping subgroups providing the

Reprinted from *Journal of Marketing Research,* published by the American Marketing Association, Vol. 7 (May 1970), pp. 153–158.

largest reduction in unexplained variance. The split is chosen to maximize the between sum of squares for the ith group (the group to be split), so that

$$BSS_i = (n_1 \bar{y}_1^2 + n_2 \bar{y}_2^2) - N_i \bar{Y}_i^2$$

where:

n = size of split subgroup
N = size of parent group being split (ith group)
$\bar{y}$ = mean value of the predictor for the split subgroup
$\bar{Y}$ = mean value of the predictor for the parent group being split.

The division will take place at the point of greatest discrimination in group means. Thus respondents might be divided by region into Northcentral vs. rest of U.S., by income into $12,500 and under vs. over $12,500, etc.

At this point, binary splits have been formed for each predictor variable, maximizing the between sum of squares. The between sum of squares for each variable is divided by the total sum of squares for the group to be split (BSS_i/TSS_i). This ratio is computed for each of the independent variables. AID then selects that variable with the highest BSS_i/TSS_i. The first iteration is completed when the sample is divided into two groups accordingly. All dichotomous splits defined by the other predictor variables are discarded.

Figure 1 illustrates the output of the program. The proportion of respondents defining Brand X as their usual brand is the dependent variable. Eight socioeconomic characteristics and level of product usage are the independent variables. When the total sample is examined, the maximum reduction in the unexplained sum of squares is obtained by splitting the sample by sex. The proportion of usual brand purchasers in the total sample was 16.7%. Yet 24.3% of the females considered Brand X their usual brand, compared to only 6.7% of the males. Since sex could yield only one dichotomous grouping, the division of the variable was predetermined. Yet before selecting sex, all other variables were dichotomized at their most significant point and the BSS/TSS ratio computed.

Once the population is divided into two subgroups, the program treats each subgroup as a separate popu-

Figure 1
Socioeconomic Segmentation by Usual Purchasers of Brand X

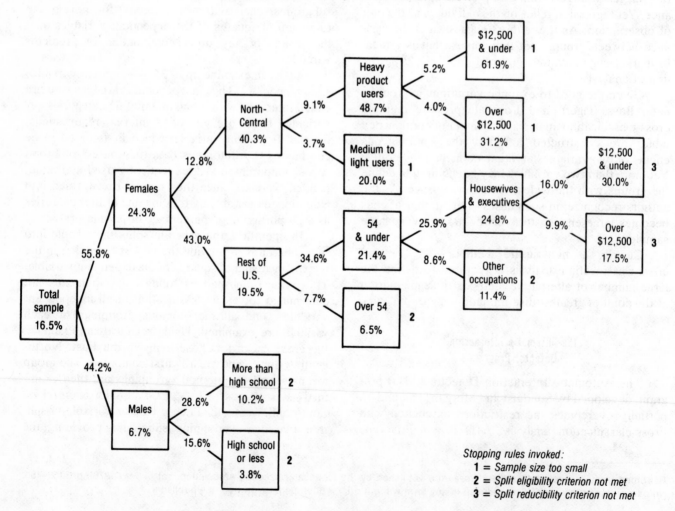

Stopping rules invoked:
 1 = Sample size too small
 2 = Split eligibility criterion not met
 3 = Split reducibility criterion not met

lation and the same process is repeated. Within the female subgroup, the program dichotomizes the remaining independent variables at the optimal point, computes a BSS_i/TSS_i for each variable, and selects the variable with the highest ratio of between to total sum of squares for the next split. In Figure 1, a split by region into Northcentral vs. rest of U.S. provided a maximum reduction of unexplained variance within the female subgroup. Females living in Northcentral states comprised 12.8% of the sample. Yet within this subgroup, 40.3% were usual purchasers of the brand, compared to 24.3% for all females. Similarly, the first split off the male subgroup is by education. Given a 6.7% male market share, the proportion drops to 3.8% if males did not enter college.

After the second series of splits, four subgroups have been formed. The program again treats each subgroup as a separate population, and another iteration determines which predictor variable, when split, will best reduce the unexplained sum of squares for that subgroup. The subgroup chosen for the next iteration is that unsplit sample group which has the largest total sum of squares (TSS_i). The number of iterations in the program is controlled by three stopping rules which limit the number of subgroups formed:

1. A minimum sample criterion (set at $N = 25$ in the example cited).
2. A split eligibility criterion requiring that a group must contain a minimum percentage of the total original sum of squares if it is to be considered eligible for splitting ($TSS_i \geq .05 \, TSS_t$ in the above example). This requirement prevents groups with little variation from being split.
3. Presuming the group is eligible for a split, a split reducibility criterion requiring that the size of the between group sum of squares for the ith group has to be a minimum percentage of the total original sum of squares ($BSS_i \geq .02 \, TSS_t$). This criterion is applied when none of the predictor variables in the group sufficiently reduces the unexplained variance.

The eventual output is a "tree diagram" developing subgroups of the samples by combinations of variables. By the fourth iteration in the female branch of Figure 1, the subgroup contained only 5.2% of the sample, defined as females in Northcentral states who are heavy users of the product category with family income $12,500 and under. The proportion of usual purchasers within this group was 61.9%, compared to the sample average of 16.5%. Thus, given these four characteristics, the probability of purchasing Brand X increases by almost four times. Similarly, given the fact the respondent is a male laborer or foreman, the probability of purchasing is less than one-fourth the sample average.

Figure 1 may be regarded as an optimal socio-economic segmentation of the market by purchasing behavior. It is up to the analyst to determine at what point the segments should be defined. Delineating the market with 5.2% of the sample may not be operational. On the other hand, 5.2% of the sample may represent such a large proportion of total volume that it deserves separate attention.

Limitations of the Program. By considering a large number of variables simultaneously, defining the most significant combinations of variables, and demonstrating the joint effects of the predictor variables, the AID program overcomes many of the limitations inherent in standard cross-classification analysis. It represents a more effective method of segmentation than regression analysis, since it determines the joint effects by analyzing variance between grouped (rather than individual) data.

Yet several restrictions remain. First, the program relies on dichotomous splits. A three or four-way split may reduce the unexplained variance more than a two-way split. This problem is partially resolved in that the program can split the same variable at the next iteration. The first split may be high vs. middle-low income; the next split off the latter subgroup could then be middle vs. low income, having the same effect as an initial three-way split. Yet the first step is still development of dichotomous splits for all variables, possibly eliminating a three-way grouping that might have otherwise been more discriminating. The program may have selected income as the first two-way split over education. Yet had the variables been defined in a trichotomous manner, the sample might have been split by education on the first iteration.

This illustrates another problem. The program selects the variable with the highest BSS/TSS by which to split the sample. All subsequent splits are contingent on the subgroups formed by the first split. Yet it is possible a second variable was almost as discriminating as the first. Had the program split by the second variable, the subsequent tree diagram might have been totally different. In Figure 1, sex was the first split with a BSS_i/TSS_i ratio of .056. Occupation had a ratio of .053, an insignificant difference. In this case, a split by occupation would have made little difference, since the division would have been by housewives vs. all others. Yet other "near misses" could markedly change the character of progressive iterations.

This problem can be partially resolved by judicious use of the program. The program could be run again, eliminating the variable which defines the first two subgroups, to give an alternate variable a chance to split. Subsequent subgroups can then be examined to determine if they differ markedly from the original run. If the structures produced by such a sensitivity analysis differ, then criteria of face validity will have to be applied to determine the most logical basis for segmenting the market.

A third problem is that the supposedly independent variables may be closely interdependent. As noted, the potential split by occupation in the first group was merely a reflection of the significance of sex. Such interdependencies may create spurious splits, defeating the purpose of the program. One method of insuring the independence of the variables is to run a prior factor analysis and input pre-classified factor scores for each respondent rather than the original values. Yet the difficulties of interpreting average factor scores for a subgroup inhibits such a solution. Segmentation by factor scores may not provide clear-cut implications for media scheduling or promotional appeals.

Socioeconomic Segmentation

Figures 1 and 2 illustrate the results of the program in a socioeconomic segmentation of a consumer packaged goods market. Four hundred users of the product category were interviewed. The dependent variable was the proportion of respondents defining Brand X as their usual brand. Eight socioeconomic variables were utilized as predictor variables:

Sex	Region
Occupation	Education
Income	Race
Age	Number in household

In addition, level of product usage was included as an independent variable.

One important advantage of AID is that variables such as occupation, race, and region can be treated as nominal rather than scaled variables. Since the program examines all dichotomous groupings of a vari-

able's attributes, there need be no assumption of monotonicity—that is, an assumed ascending or descending sequence in the order of the variable's attributes—as might be the case for age, income, frequency of purchase, etc.

The tree diagram in Figure 1 presents a series of profiles by usual purchasers of Brand X. The 5.2% of the sample represented by females living in the North-central region who are heavy users of the product with income under $12,500 has a 61.9% probability that Brand X is their usual brand, compared to a sample average of 16.5%. Figure 2 demonstrates that this group accounts for 20% of all usual purchasers of Brand X. The least likely user is effectively defined by only two characteristics: sex and education. The 15.6% of the sample who were males who did not complete high school had a 3.8% probability of claiming Brand X as their usual brand. This group accounts for only 3.5% of Brand X usual purchasers. An individual in the extreme high probability group had 16 times as much chance of being a usual purchaser of Brand X as an individual in the extreme low probability group. Similarly, intermediate segments can be identified with purchaser probabilities ranging from 6.5% to 31.2%.

As a representation of existing market potential, Figures 1 and 2 may be a valuable guide to media selection. Bass, Tigert, and Lonsdale suggest that an important criterion in media selection is the proportion of the vehicle's audience in high or low market potential segments. If vehicles can be selected based on the interaction of sex, region, income, and educa-

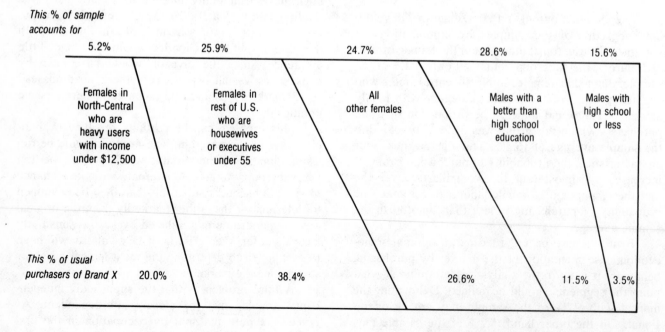

Figure 2
Market Concentration of Usual Purchasers of Brand X

tion, then the cost per unit of market potential delivered may be minimized. This is particularly valid when one-twentieth of the sample accounts for one-fifth of the market.

The AID program is most valuable in demonstrating the interaction between variables. Region was a discriminator only within the female group. Income and level of usage were important only within the female-Northcentral subsegment. Moreover, education had an opposite effect on usage level for males compared to females in the Northcentral states.

The female orientation of the brand was well known prior to the analysis. Yet the sharp interaction between sex, region, rate of use, and income was not suspected, nor could it have been uncovered without a multivariate program for data reduction.

Attitudinal Segmentation by AID

In some cases, perceptual rather than socioeconomic segmentation of the market may be desirable

as a first step. In one application, the objective was to define differences in attitudes for a commonly used beverage by usage rate. Thirteen attitudinal criteria were developed. A national sample of 2,000 housewives was then asked to rate the degree to which the beverage satisfied each criterion on a ten point scale, with ten being the ideal. The thirteen criteria were:

1. Good tasting
2. Good for serving guests
3. Good at mealtimes
4. Refreshing
5. Easy to prepare
6. Provides lift and pickup
7. Good for the family
8. Low in calories
9. Economical
10. Good as year-round drink
11. Restores energy
12. Thirst-quenching
13. Pure ingredients.

Figure 3 presents the delineation of segments by these criteria. The dependent variable is the number

Figure 3
Attitudinal Segmentation by Usage Level

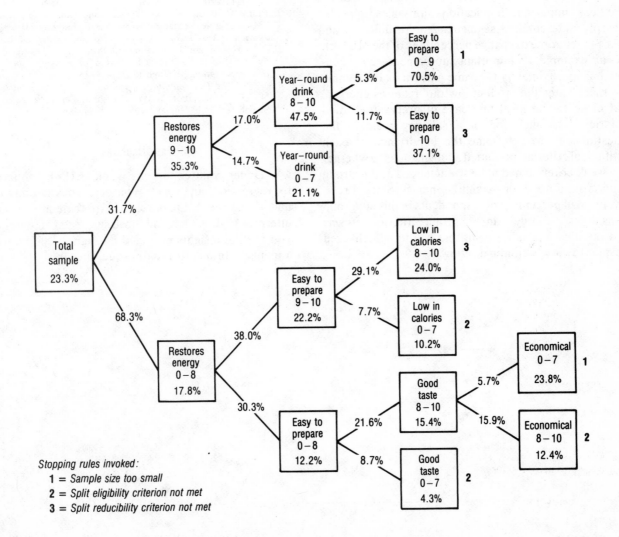

Stopping rules invoked:
1 = Sample size too small
2 = Split eligibility criterion not met
3 = Split reducibility criterion not met

of units consumed by the family in the last week. "Restores energy" was the criterion that most sharply differentiated usage rates. Those rating the drink close to the ideal on this criterion drank twice as much of the beverage. Once again, the interactions demonstrated were the most important output. The 5.3% of the sample that rated the beverage close to the ideal on both "year-round drink" and drink that "restores energy," yet less than ideal on "ease of preparation," consumed 70.5 units compared to the sample average of 23.3. Not surprisingly, the 8.7% of the sample rating the beverage low on energy, "ease of preparation," and taste consumed only 4.3 units. As before, the usage rate between the most and least concentrated segments was 16 to one.

Examination of the detailed output also revealed:

1. "Year-round drink" is an important discriminator only within the subgroup that rates the beverage high on energy.
2. "Ease of preparation" increases usage only among those who rate the beverage intermediate to low on energy.
3. "Good tasting" is an important discriminator primarily among those rating the beverage low on "ease of preparation."

In segmenting usage rates by attitudes, Figure 3 provides important implications for sales appeals. Sharply differentiated segments require different appeals to reinforce or change perceptions of the product. As an example, an important subsegment — 29% consuming approximately the same amount as the sample average — rates the product low on "restores energy," yet close to the ideal on "ease of preparation" and calories. The inclusion of a saliency scale in the questionnaire to determine the importance of each attitudinal criterion permitted a judgment as to whether the weak criterion had to be strengthened or the strong criteria reinforced for maximum impact. Since a relatively small percentage of respondents in this subgroup considered "energy" an important criterion, it was obvious this was not a point that had to be delivered despite the low attitudinal rating.

Summary and Conclusion

Both regression and cross-classification analysis are inadequate means of segmenting markets. Correlation coefficients may not reflect significant differences between grouped data. Cross-classification analysis may demonstrate such differences, yet is extremely limited in going beyond the two variable case and demonstrating interactions among a large number of potential market discriminators.

Although having certain serious defects, the AID program is a significant improvement over standard cross-classification analysis. It is capable of analyzing and reducing large combinations of data to produce the greatest discrimination between subgroups. The program was effective in segmenting product and brand usage by demographic and attitudinal variables, producing strategic implications for media selection and the delivery of copy appeals to concentrated market segments.

References

1. Henry Assael, John H. Kofron and Walter Burgi, "Advertising Performance as a Function of Print Ad Characteristics," *Journal of Advertising Research,* 7 (June 1967), 20–6.
2. Frank M. Bass, Douglas J. Tigert and Ronald T. Lonsdale, "Marketing Segmentation: Group Versus Individual Behavior," *Journal of Marketing Research,* 5 (August 1968), 264–70.
3. J. N. Morgan and J. A. Sonquist, "Problems in the Analysis of Survey Data and a Proposal," *Journal of the American Statistical Association,* 58 (June 1963), 415–35.
4. ——, *The Determination of Interaction Effects,* Monograph No. 35, Ann Arbor: Survey Research Center, Institute for Social Research, University of Michigan 1964.

For Discussion

Under what conditions would AID be preferred to regression analysis? What are the assumptions underlying the AID approach? Are there any ways to interpret Figure 3 beyond those suggested? How could you use the insights provided by Figure 3 if you were a manager of a soft drink product line?

13

The Pitfalls of AID Analysis

Peter Doyle

Ian Fenwick

The Automatic Interaction Detector (AID), pro-posed formally by Morgan and Sonquist [9] in 1964, has become widely used in the analysis of survey data. The purpose of this study is to evaluate the use of this technique. Our investigations suggest that, as preva-lently employed and interpreted, AID is both mis-leading and unreliable to an unexpected degree. Further, even when used correctly at a preliminary stage of data analysis it is subject to considerable bias and its use without validation tests can never be justi-fied. In this article a more critical use of AID and similar programs is encouraged.

The Data Analyzed

The analysis is based upon a 1972 study of the Sunday reading habits of a representative sample of over 2000 adults in the United Kingdom. In personal interviews, respondents provided information about media usage, attitudes, and a large number of socio-economic characteristics. This article relates to one aspect of media usage—time spent reading newspa-pers. Heavy readers are important to publishers and advertisers because such readers have a higher proba-bility of seeing an advertisement. They are also likely to have a stronger commitment to the vehicle, thus reading time may indicate the degree to which editorial content influences the effectiveness of an advertise-ment [5]. A goal of the research reported here was to determine the characteristics of these readers.

Alternative Analysis Methods

Formally our problem relates to studying a rela-tionship of the form:

$$y = f(x_1, \ldots x_n) + e \qquad (1)$$

where y is readership time; $x_1, \ldots x_n$ are the predictors or correlates of y, and e is an error term. A good model is a formulation of (1) which includes the most signifi-cant correlates and combines the variables in an accu-rate structural form. Prior knowledge or theory will usually suggest an approach to selecting the variables, but in general, the functional form, nonlinear effects and interactions among the independent variables will be more difficult [9]. An incorrectly specified model will lead to a greater unexplained variance, and bias the estimates of the effects of the predictors.

Nonlinearities can usually be identified through straightforward graphical procedures or transforma-tions. Interactions have presented a more complex problem. An interaction exists where the effects of one predictor depend upon the value of another. For instance, education may affect time spent reading among men but not among women. Graphically this is represented by the two slopes in Figure 1. If this inter-action is ignored, the effect of education will be under-estimated. Morgan and Sonquist [9, 11, 12] have shown that such interactions are common in social research.

The advantage of *cross-classification* tables is that such interactions can be isolated [10]. This feature plus their general simplicity have made them the most widely used method of presenting the results of a survey analysis. The main problem with cross-classi-fication tables is that it is difficult to extend the analysis beyond two predictors: the analysis becomes too cum-bersome and the sample is soon segmented into sub-groups too small for study [7]. If significant predictors have to be left out, then the model will fail to explain a significant proportion of the variance. If the predictors are correlated, omission of one or more will also lead to biased estimates of the effects of those included.

* Peter Doyle is Professor of Marketing and Ian Fenwick is Lecturer in Marketing, University of Bradford Management Centre, England. They wish to thank the Surveys Division of the Interna-tional Publishing Corporation for providing the data on which this study is based.

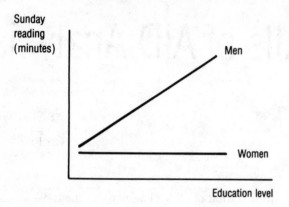

Figure 1
Interaction between Education and Sex
in Predicting Sunday Reading

Regression analysis permits these multiple predictors to be handled and their significance levels and partial contributions to be estimated. However, this gain is made at the expense of more restrictions as to the form of the model. Frequently, this means assuming that the effects of the independent variables are linear and additive. While nonlinearities and interactions can be estimated, it is necessary that these be specified a priori. A second problem, persuasively argued by Bass, Tigert, and Lonsdale [4], is that regression analysis is commonly unsuitable as a technique for predicting behavior. In general one is interested in identifying groups with significant differences in behavior. Regression analysis, however, uses the individual rather than the group as the unit of observation, and within-group rather than between-group variation as the criterion for fitting the model. Consequently, regression coefficients may not reflect important differences between grouped data.

Assael [3] and others offer AID as a method of overcoming these problems. It permits multiple predictors to be handled in the explanation of group behavior, and at the same time avoids restrictive assumptions about the structure of the model.

The AID Technique

The comparisons of AID with cross-classification and especially regression analysis [3, 8, 12] have been more misleading than helpful. The objective of AID is not to solve the problem represented by (1), but simply to delineate its structure. Unlike regression analysis, AID provides no reliable information about the relative importance or the statistical significance of the predictors. Its prime function is to search for the nature of the relations between variables—whether they are additive or interactive. As such, it is clearly a *preliminary* to a regression formulation or some similar technique [11].

The basic strategy employed by AID is to divide the total sample into the most homogeneous groupings in terms of the dependent variable. All independent variables are treated as categorical, the user specifying the number of categories and their range for each variable. The algorithm considers each variable in turn as the possible basis for dichotomizing the sample. Thus for each variable that partition is found which maximizes between-group sum of squares:

$$BSS_i = N_1\bar{Y}_1^2 + N_2\bar{Y}_2^2 - N_i\bar{Y}_i^2$$

where Y is the dependent variable and subscripts 1 and 2 refer to split subgroups and i to the parent group. The program then splits the sample on that variable affording the largest such between sum of squares.

The two groups so formed become themselves candidates for splitting. The output can conveniently be represented by a tree, each branch bifurcating until terminated by one of three stopping rules: (1) a group becomes so small as to cease to be of interest; (2) a group becomes so homogeneous that further division is unnecessary; (3) there is no possible division that significantly reduces BSS.

Limitations of AID.   The intuitive and visual appeal, no doubt, accounts for the popularity of AID, but many applications have failed to recognize some of the severe limitations of AID:

Sample size. Since the group rather than the individual is the unit of analysis, large sample sizes are required. Sonquist, Baker, and Morgan [12] advise at least 1000 cases if meaningful results are to be obtained. Even this is an underestimate since search techniques should always be validated. If a split-sample analysis is used, then 2000 cases are required for useful results.

Intercorrelated predictors. Unlike multivariate techniques, AID takes no account of intercorrelated predictors. As is illustrated below, where correlated predictors are present, one of them is likely to be chosen exclusively. Not only will one of the variables have to be chosen "first," but having been chosen, its correlates will be less likely to be selected. Thus order of appearance of variables is no indication of relative importance, and exclusion does not necessarily imply insignificance. This last caveat makes the simple and prevalent interpretation of the AID tree extremely foolhardy.

Skewed variables. If the *dependent* variable is heavily skewed, the program may tend repeatedly to split off small groups. Sonquist [11] reports that skewedness in *predictors* reduces their power to increase BSS making their appearance in the AID tree unlikely. In fact, the effect on BSS is dependent on the direction of skew—if the predictor is skewed toward high values of the dependent variable, BSS can be greatly increased by splits on the skewed variable. However, the program refuses splits generating groups with fewer than, in our case, 25 members. Thus heavily skewed variables tend to be eliminated particularly in the later stages of analysis. In both cases a log or square root transformation can sometimes help.

Noise. Both correlated predictors and noise in the data make it unlikely that the same tree will be obtained from different samples from the same population. Sonquist [11] finds the composition of end groups to be stable even though the order of appearance of variables changes. However, Doyle [6], working with correlated predictors, finds problems of unstable trees. Tree stability can be tested by noting for each split that variable offering the next best BSS; the program can then be re-run forcing this variable to appear. If the resulting trees are unstable, the analyst can either purge his data of intercorrelations by factor analysis, or the overall structure suggested by the set of trees can be incorporated into the final regression equation.

Significance tests. Although early versions of AID give a significance test for splits, they ignore the basic search strategy followed by the algorithm. Sonquist, Baker, and Morgan admit "because of the large number of possible splits examined there is no point asking about statistical significance" [12, p. 10].

Interactions. Despite the explicit goal of identifying structure, AID is found to be insensitive to various forms of interaction. Since AID only examines the immediate effect of a predictor on BSS and not future possible splits, any interactions which are not "one-stage" will not be identified. Thus if $E(Y/X_1 \& X_2)$ $\neq E(Y/\bar{X}_1 \& \bar{X}_2)$ where X_1 denotes presence and $\bar{X}_1$ absence of a characteristic, but $E(Y/X_1) = E(Y/\bar{X}_1)$ and $E(Y/X_2) = E(Y/\bar{X}_2)$, then although X_1 and X_2 interact and affect Y, neither will appear in the AID analysis because they have no individual effect. In the latest versions of AID (AID-III), a look-ahead option is available which does examine some of these interactions, but this facility greatly increases computer time.

Stopping rules. Because of the problems caused by correlated predictors, the decision concerning the specification of stopping rules becomes important. If the rules lead to an early truncation of the tree, then important variables may not be used. On the other hand, with low stopping rules, there is an increased probability of noise leading to spurious splits.

AID as a Preliminary to Regression Analysis. These problems mean that the use of AID alone in data analysis cannot be justified. Despite the occasional recognition of this fact [7, 11] virtually all previous applications have concentrated on the AID tree alone without proceeding to the regression stage [3, 13], or even used AID *after* stepwise regression analysis [8]. Validation, too,

has been the exception rather than the rule. As a preliminary to regression or multiple classification analysis [2], AID serves to identify interactions which can be incorporated into an equation linear in coefficients by the use of dummy variables.

Interactions may be indicated in three ways:

1. The structure of the tree: variables entering one branch and not another give a crude indication of interaction.
2. The profile of means: as illustrated below, for each predictor at each split attempt, the mean value of the dependent variable can be plotted for each predictor category. If the predictor has only additive effects then profiles will be similar; marked divergence from congruence then indicates interactions.
3. The BSS/TSS ratio: the ratio of between to total sum of squares for each predictor at each split attempt shows the proportion of the total variation explained by such a split. Sharp changes in this ratio indicate interactions.

A visual inspection of the tree is therefore inadequate. The regression analysis which incorporates identifiable interactions has three significant uses: (1) variables need not be categorized — their effects may be estimated throughout their range of values and not simply by a dichotomy; (2) multicollinearity, unless severe, can be handled by the estimators; (3) the variables may be assigned importance, either in terms of significance or from the relative size of their effects. None of these results are, of course, possible from AID alone.

Analysis

The dependent variable was the respondent's estimate of minutes spent reading the major popular Sunday papers (i.e., *News of the World, Sunday Mirror, Sunday Express, Sunday People*). The attitudinal data measuring interest in 25 topics covered by the media were factor analyzed to remove extreme multicollinearity.[1] Six factors were found with eigenvalues greater than 1, explaining 65% of the total variance (an underestimate in that the data are strictly ordinal). Table 1 shows the factor interpretations after varimax rotation.

An initial AID run was performed to examine the characteristics of the data and to eliminate variables lacking a useful causal interpretation [11, pp. 191–201]. Low parameter values were used on the algorithm to extract the maximum information. The six factors and six other variables shown in Table 2 were retained for further analysis.

As noted above AID is particularly subject to upward bias due to sampling error and to the nature

---

[1] Ed. Note: A factor is a combination of variables that are correlated. Factor Analysis is described in Part II of this book.

Figure 2
Correlates of Readership: the AID Tree

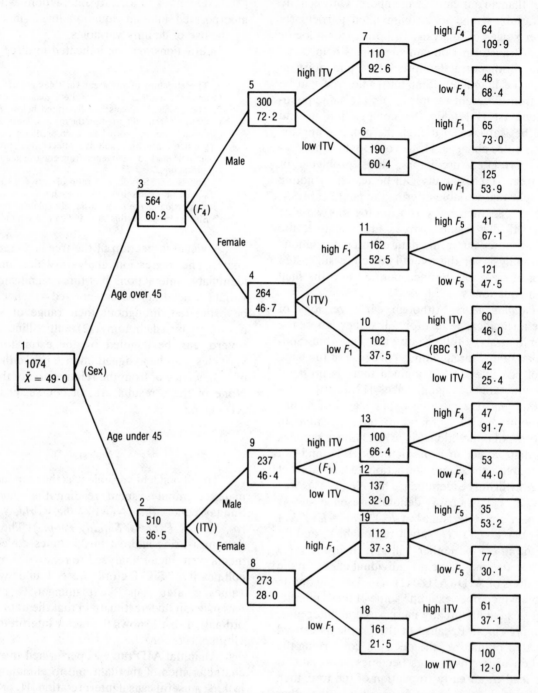

of the search procedure. Consequently, it is essential to build in a validation procedure. Here the sample was randomly halved to give just over 1000 respondents each for analysis and validation. Figure 2 shows the final tree derived from the analysis sample. The stopping rules were: where group size fell below 100; where group variance was below .01% of total variance; or where no split led to BSS of above .001% of total variance.

The heaviest readers are older males, are heavy watchers of ITV, and have strong "male interests." By contrast, younger women who were low ITV viewers and interested in articles about "people" read on average little more than one tenth of the time spent by the heaviest readers. The characteristics of various reading categories can easily be identified.

Moving from description to the prime goal of formulating structural relationships, several interac-

Table 1
Factor Analysis of Interest Ratings

Factor number	High variable loading	Factor interpretation
F1	Articles on film personalities	People
	Advice and help	
	Stories and gossip	
	Letters	
	Horoscope	
	TV guide	
F2	Local news	News
	UK news	
	Political news	
	International events	
	News comment	
	Exposes	
F3	Ads and shopping news	Home and
	Fashion advice	leisure
	Women's items	
	Furniture and home	
	Holiday advice	
F4	Cars and motoring	Male interests
	Pictures of girls	
	Cartoons	
	News pictures	
F5	Crosswords	Puzzles
	Competitions	
F6	Football	Sport
	Horse-racing	

Table 2
Variables Used in AID Analysis

Variable	Description
Age	14–65+ in 7 categories
Sex	Male, female
Social class	5 categories
	A: Upper middle class (3% of UK adults)
	B: Middle class (9%)
	C1: Lower middle class (22%)
	C2: Skilled working class (31%)
	D: Working class (26%)
	E: Lowest level (9%)
BBC 1 viewing	Average Sunday viewing (minutes) 0–210+ in 6 categories
BBC 2 viewing	Average Sunday viewing (minutes) 0–94+ in 6 categories
ITV viewing	Average Sunday viewing (minutes) 0–400+ in 6 categories
6 factors	See Table 1, each in 3 categories

tions were identified from the output of the program. Sex, although entering both branches with similar profiles, interacts with those variables following it. Thus for males television viewing is important, whereas it only affects females with low scores on factor 1. Figure 3 shows the profile of mean readership levels against ITV viewing categories for group 4 (females aged 45+) and group 5 (males aged 45+). The divergence in profiles clearly indicates the sex/TV interaction. A more

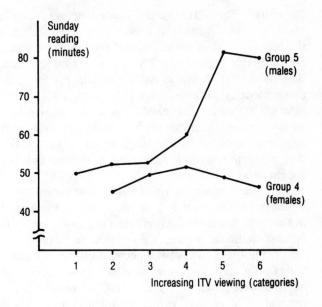

Figure 3
Mean Profile for ITV Viewing for Groups 4 & 5

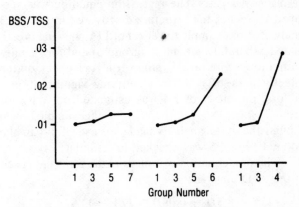

Figure 4
Explanatory Power of Factor 1

Note: For a description of group composition see Figure 2.

complex interaction is shown in Figure 4 which plots the explanatory power of factor 1 for three routes through the AID tree. The route to group 7 (males aged 45+, with high ITV viewing) shows factor 1 as a relatively unimportant variable. However that to group 6 (males aged 45+, with low ITV viewing) shows a sharp rise in the power of factor 1. Thus factor 1 only acquires significance for males if they are low ITV viewers. The plot for group 4 (females aged 45+), on the other hand, indicates the importance of factor 1 for this group—irrespective of ITV viewing level.

In contrast, age, which provides the initial split, appears to be linear and additive. Mean profiles are approximately congruent throughout the tree and the partial effects of other variables are about equal in upper and lower branches.

Comments. The AID output immediately reveals a number of the difficulties discussed earlier. To illustrate the problem caused by correlated predictors, where a rival variable produced a BSS close to that selected, this variable is shown in parentheses in Figure 2. In many cases, rival candidates (BSS within 1% of the selected variable) did exist. For example, F1 was almost chosen in group 9, but finally did not even appear in this branch. The stopping rules exacerbated this problem; several significant variables did not appear at all in the tree.

Another important point concerning interactions which has not previously been recognized is illustrated in the tree. Some interactions turn out to be spurious on distributional grounds. Factor 4, for example — "male interests" — is skewed because only males score highly on it. This results in the effect of the interaction being underestimated. By contrast, F4 only appears for high ITV viewers within the male branch; this is a genuine rather than a distributional interaction.

Regression Analysis. The regression equation was specified to reflect the structure discovered in the AID analysis. For example the effect of ITV viewing is estimated separately for males (group 5) and for females with a low score on F1 (group 10). As a check on the effectiveness of AID in identifying significant predictors, the effect of F4 was estimated not only for group 7 but also for the rest of the sample, even though the AID analysis made no use of F4 in the latter. Factor F5 was checked in a similar way.

The first equation was fitted to the same data used in the AID analysis:

$$y = -18.5 + 8.5D_5 + 0.08D_5 * ITV + 13.9D_7 * F_4$$
$$(1.0) \quad (3.3) \quad\quad (4.6)$$

$$+ 11.7D_6 * F_1 + 5.6(1 - D_5) * F_1 + 0.01D_{10} * ITV$$
$$(3.7) \quad\quad (1.6) \quad\quad (0.4)$$

$$+ 7.8D_{11} * F_5 + 2.2(1 - D_7) * F_4$$
$$(3.1) \quad\quad (1.1)$$

$$+ 3.2(1 - D_{11}) * F_5 + 6.7 \text{ Age}$$
$$(1.4) \quad\quad (8.5)$$

$$\bar{R}^2 = 0.52$$

where $D_i = 1.0$ if respondent is in group i, 0 otherwise. The t-statistics are shown in parentheses. Four out of the six true interactions are significant and contribute to explained variation, and the two "test" interactions are insignificant at the 5 percent level.[2] Overall the

---

[2] A linear form of the model, ignoring interactions, had an $\bar{R}^2 = 0.21$.

equation is not unsatisfactory, accounting for about 50% of the variation in reading time.

Validation

The significance of the regression equation is, however, not an adequate test of the bias and limitations of AID described earlier, all of which lead to an overestimate of the power of the model. A true test of the predictive power of the model must be based upon validation. One method is to compare the tree from the analysis sample (Figure 2) with that generated from the validation sample. The model fails this test. The new tree looks very different from the original. A different age split occurs and the variable no longer enters in a simple additive form; sex is only used in one branch and there are substantial differences in the structure of the terminal groups. Precise replication is, however, unlikely. Intercorrelated predictors, sampling error, and arbitrary stopping rules all make replication unlikely. A more appropriate test is one of the *predictive* value of the model. This can be performed by using the analysis equation to generate readership levels for the validation sample. This reduced the coefficient of determination by 50% ($\bar{R}^2 = 0.25$) — a reduction much greater than can be attributed to chance (see [1, p. 76]). The search procedure, therefore, greatly overestimates the predictive power of the AID-regression model.

Further insight into the robustness of the interaction terms generated by AID can be obtained by *fitting* the original equation structure to the validation sample:

$$y = -24.3 + 16.6D_5 + 0.14D_5 * ITV + 3.13D_7 * F_4$$
$$(1.5) \quad (4.6) \quad\quad (0.7)$$

$$+ 16.2D_6 * F_1 + 10.3(1 - D_5) * F_1 + 0.02D_{10} * ITV$$
$$(4.3) \quad\quad (2.4) \quad\quad (0.7)$$

$$+ 6.19D_{11} * F_5 + 1.6(1 - D_7) * F_4 + 4.2(1 - D_{11})F_5$$
$$(2.1) \quad\quad (1.7) \quad\quad (2.0)$$

$$+ 6.9 \text{ Age}$$
$$(7.3)$$

$$\bar{R}^2 = 0.40$$

The coefficients are very different from the analysis sample, although not all these differences are statistically significant. In addition, the two "test" interactions now turn out to be significant. These results confirm that AID leads to upward bias in prediction and that the search procedure tends to generate artificial interaction terms.

Conclusions

As a widely available technique AID is extraordinarily prone to misuse. The authors are unaware of any previous article in the marketing literature which illustrates the construction of the regression formulation from the AID model and effectively validates the results. Yet without these stages, AID is virtually useless!

Even when used correctly as a simple descriptive device or as a preliminary to regression, AID is still easily misinterpreted. This is caused by two related factors: the inability of the technique to handle correlated predictors and the lack of restrictive assumptions in the model which make its interpretation prone to idiosyncrasies caused by sampling and measurement errors. Little trust therefore can be placed on results which are not validated.

References

1. Anderson, T. W. *An Introduction to Multivariate Statistical Analysis*. New York: Wiley, 1958.
2. Andrews, F. M., James N. Morgan, and John A. Sonquist. *Multiple Classification Analysis*. Ann Arbor: Survey Research Center, University of Michigan, 1967.
3. Assael, Henry. "Segmenting Markets by Group Purchasing Behavior: An Application of the AID Technique," *Journal of Marketing Research*, 7 (May 1970), 153–8.
4. Bass, Frank M., Douglas J. Tigert, and Ronald T. Lonsdale. "Market Segmentation: Group Versus Individual Behavior," *Journal of Marketing Research*, 5 (August 1968), 264–70.
5. Brown, Michael, "Print Media Research Objectives and Applications," in Robert M. Worcester, ed., *Consumer Market Research Handbook*. London: McGraw-Hill, 1972, 548–76.
6. Doyle, Peter. "The Use of AID and Similar Search Procedures," *Operational Research Quarterly*, 24 (September 1973), 465–7.
7. Frank, Ronald E., William F. Massy, and Y. Wind. *Market Segmentation*. Englewood Cliffs, N.J.: Prentice Hall, 1972.
8. Heald, Gordon I. "The Application of AID and Multiple Regression Techniques to the Assessment of Store Performance and Site Selection," *Operational Research Quarterly*, 23 (June 1972), 445–54.
9. Morgan, James N. and John A. Sonquist. "Problems in the Analysis of Survey Data and a Proposal," *Journal of the American Statistical Association*, 58 (September 1963), 415–34.
10. Moser, C. A. and G. Kalton. *Survey Methods in Social Investigation*. London: Heinemann, 1971.
11. Sonquist, John A. *Multivariate Model Building*. Ann Arbor: Survey Research Center, University of Michigan, 1970.
12. _____, Elizabeth L. Baker, and James N. Morgan. *Searching for Structure*. Ann Arbor: Survey Research Center, University of Michigan, 1971.
13. Staelin, Richard A. "Another Look at AID," *Journal of Advertising Research*, 11 (October 1971), 23–8.

For Discussion

What are the limitations of AID? Which do you feel is the most serious one? The second most serious? Explain the validation procedure. What do the authors mean by an "upward bias in prediction"? Why might AID have such a bias?

The Analysis of Dependence

14

New Way to Measure Consumers' Judgments

Paul E. Green
Yoram Wind

Taking a jet plane for a business appointment in Paris? Which of the two flights described below would you choose?

A B-707 flown by British Airways that will depart within two hours of the time you would like to leave and that is often late in arriving in Paris. The plane will make two intermediate stops, and it is anticipated that it will be 50% full. Flight attendants are "warm and friendly" and you would have a choice of two movies for entertainment.

A B-747 flown by TWA that will depart within four hours of the time you would like to leave and that is almost never late in arriving in Paris. The flight is nonstop, and it is anticipated that the plane will be 90% full. Flight attendants are "cold and curt" and only magazines are provided for entertainment.

Are you looking for replacement tires for your two-year-old car? Suppose you want radial tires and have the following three options to choose from:

Goodyear's, with a tread life of 30,000 miles at a price of $40 per tire; the store is a 10-minute drive from your home.

Firestone's, with a tread life of 50,000 miles at a price of $85 per tire; the store is a 10-minute drive from your home.

Or Sears's, with a tread life of 40,000 miles at a price of $55 per tire; the store is located about 10 minutes from your home.

How would you rank these alternatives in order of preference?

Both of these problems have a common structure that companies and their marketing managers frequently encounter in trying to figure out what a consumer really wants in a product or service. First, the characteristics of the alternatives that the consumer must choose from fall along more than a single dimen-

sion—they are multiattribute. Second, the consumer must make an overall judgment about the relative value of those characteristics, or attributes; in short, he must order them according to some criterion. But doing this requires complex trade-offs, since it is likely that no alternative is clearly better than another on every dimension of interest.

In recent years, researchers have developed a new measurement technique from the fields of mathematical psychology and psychometrics that can aid the marketing manager in sorting out the relative importance of a product's multidimensional attributes.[1] This technique, called conjoint measurement, starts with the consumer's overall or global judgments about a set of complex alternatives.[4] It then performs the rather remarkable job of decomposing his or her original evaluations into separate and compatible utility scales by which the original global judgments (or others involving new combinations of attributes) can be reconstituted.[2]

Being able to separate overall judgments into psychological components in this manner can provide a manager with valuable information about the relative importance of various attributes of a product. It can also provide information about the value of various

---

[1] R. Duncan Luce and John W. Tukey, "Simultaneous Conjoint Measurement: A New Type of Fundamental Measurement," *Journal of Mathematical Psychology,* February 1964, p. 1.

[2] The first marketing-oriented paper on conjoint measurement was by Paul E. Green and Vithala R. Rao, "Conjoint Measurement for Quantifying Judgmental Data," *Journal of Marketing Research,* August 1971, p. 355.

[4] Ed. Note: Conjoint analysis is sometimes called trade-off analysis reflecting the fact that the procedure is concerned with trade-off judgments.

levels of a single attribute. (For example, if price is the attribute under consideration, conjoint measurement can give the manager a good idea of how sensitive consumers would be to a price change from a level of, say, 85¢ to one of 75¢ or even 95¢.) Indeed, some models can even estimate the psychological trade-offs consumers make when they evaluate several attributes together.

Exhibit I
Experimental Design for Evaluation of a Carpet Cleaner

Package designs

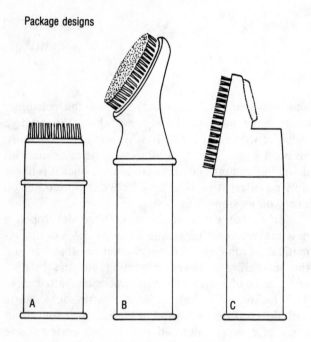

Orthogonal array

	Package design	Brand name	Price	Good Housekeeping seal?	Money-back guarantee?	Respondent's evaluation (rank number)
1	A	K2R	$1.19	No	No	13
2	A	Glory	1.39	No	Yes	11
3	A	Bissell	1.59	Yes	No	17
4	B	K2R	1.39	Yes	Yes	2
5	B	Glory	1.59	No	No	14
6	B	Bissell	1.19	No	No	3
7	C	K2R	1.59	No	Yes	12
8	C	Glory	1.19	Yes	No	7
9	C	Bissell	1.39	No	No	9
10	A	K2R	1.59	Yes	No	18
11	A	Glory	1.19	No	Yes	8
12	A	Bissell	1.39	No	No	15
13	B	K2R	1.19	No	No	4
14	B	Glory	1.39	Yes	No	6
15	B	Bissell	1.59	No	Yes	5
16	C	K2R	1.39	No	No	10
17	C	Glory	1.59	No	No	16
18	C	Bissell	1.19	Yes	Yes	1*

* Highest ranked

The advantages of this type of knowledge to the planning of marketing strategy are significant. The knowledge can be useful in modifying current products or services and in designing new ones for selected buying publics.

In this article, we first show how conjoint measurement works from a numerical standpoint. We then discuss its application to a variety of marketing problems, and we demonstrate its use in strategic marketing simulations.

How Conjoint Measurement Works

In order to see how to apply conjoint measurement, suppose a company were interested in marketing a new spot remover for carpets and upholstery. The technical staff has developed a new product that is designed to handle tough, stubborn spots. Management interest centers on five attributes or factors that it expects will influence consumer preference: an applicator-type package design, brand name, price, a *Good Housekeeping* seal of endorsement, and a money-back guarantee.

Three package designs are under consideration and appear in the upper portion of Exhibit I. There are three brand names under consideration: *K2R, Glory,* and *Bissell.* Of the three brand names used in the study, two are competitors' brand names already on the market, whereas one is the company's present brand name choice for its new product. Three alternative prices being considered are $1.19, $1.39, and $1.59. Since there are three alternatives for each of these factors, they are called three-level factors. The *Good Housekeeping* seal and money-back guarantee are two-level factors, since each is either present or not. Consequently, a total of $3 \times 3 \times 3 \times 2 \times 2 = 108$ alternatives would have to be tested if the researcher were to array all possible combinations of the five attributes.

Clearly, the cost of administering a consumer evaluation study of this magnitude—not to mention the respondents' confusion and fatigue—would be prohibitive. As an alternative, however, the researcher can take advantage of a special experimental design, called an *orthogonal array,* in which the test combinations are selected so that the independent contributions of all five factors are balanced.[3] In this way each factor's weight is kept separate and is not confused with those of the other factors.

---

[3] A nontechnical discussion of this special class of designs appears in Paul E. Green, "On the Design of Experiments Involving Multiattribute Alternatives," *Journal of Consumer Research,* September 1974, p. 61.

The lower portion of Exhibit I shows an orthogonal array that involves only 18 of the 108 possible combinations that the company wishes to test in this case. For the test the researcher makes up 18 cards. On each card appears an artist's sketch of the package design, A, B, or C, and verbal details regarding each of the other four factors: brand name, price, *Good Housekeeping* seal (or not), and money-back guarantee (or not). After describing the new product's functions and special features, he shows the respondents each of the 18 cards (see Exhibit I for the master design), and asks them to rank the cards in order of their likelihood of purchase.

The last column of Exhibit I shows one respondent's actual ranking of the 18 cards; rank number 1 denotes her highest evaluated concept. Note particularly that only *ranked* data need be obtained and, furthermore, that only 18 (out of 108) combinations are evaluated.

Computing the Utilities. Computation of the utility scales of each attribute, which determine how influential each is in the consumers' evaluations, is carried out by various computer programs.[4] The ranked data of a single respondent (or the composite ranks of a group of respondents) are entered in the program. The computer then searches for a set of scale values for each factor in the experimental design. The scale values for each level of each factor are chosen so that when they are added together the *total* utility of each combination will correspond to the original ranks as closely as possible.

Notice that two problems are involved here. First, as mentioned previously, the experimental design of Exhibit I shows only 18 of 108 combinations. Second, only rank-order data are supplied to the algorithms. This means that the data themselves do not determine how much more influential one attribute is than another in the consumers' choices. However, despite these limitations, the algorithms are able to find a *numerical* representation of the utilities, thus providing an indication of each factor's relative importance.

In general, more accurate solutions are obtained as the number of combinations being evaluated increases. Still, in the present case, with only 18 ranking-type judgments, the technique works well. Exhibit II shows the computer results.

As can be observed in Exhibit II, the technique obtains a utility function for each level of each factor.

4. As an illustration, see Joseph B. Kruskal, "Analysis of Factorial Experiments by Estimating Monotone Transformations of the Data," *Journal of the Royal Statistical Society,* Series B, March 1965, p. 251.

Exhibit II
Results of Computer Analysis of Experimental Data of Exhibit I

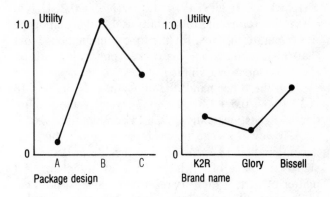

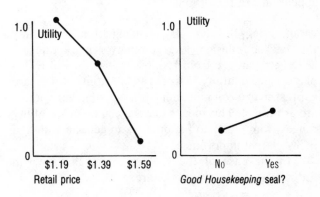

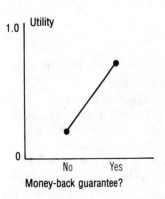

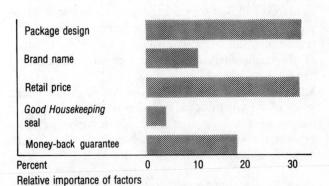

Relative importance of factors

For example, to find the utility for the first combination in Exhibit I, we can read off the utilities of each factor level in the five charts of Exhibit II: $U(A) = 0.1$; $U(K2R) = 0.3$; $U(\$1.19) = 1.0$; $U(No) = 0.2$; $U(No) = 0.2$. Therefore the total utility is 1.8, the sum of the five separate utilities, for the first combination. Note that this combination was ranked only thirteenth by the respondent in Exhibit I.

On the other hand, the utility of combination 18 is 3.1 $(0.6 + 0.5 + 1.0 + 0.3 + 0.7)$, which is the respondent's highest evaluation of all 18 combinations listed.

However, as can be easily seen from Exhibit II, if combination 18 is modified to include package Design B (in place of C), its utility is even higher. As a matter of fact, it then represents the highest possible utility, even though this specific combination did not appear among the original 18.

Importance of Attributes.   By focusing attention on only the package design, the company's marketing researchers can see from Exhibit II that Design B displays highest utility. Moreover, all utility scales are expressed in a common unit (although their zero points are arbitrary). This means that we can compare utility ranges from factor to factor so as to get some idea of their relative importance.

In the case of the spot remover, as shown in Exhibit II, the utility ranges are:

Package design $(1.0 - 0.1 = 0.9)$
Brand name $(0.5 - 0.2 = 0.3)$
Price $(1.0 - 0.1 = 0.9)$
Good Housekeeping seal $(0.3 - 0.2 = 0.1)$
Money-back guarantee $(0.7 - 0.2 = 0.5)$

How important is each attribute in relation to the others? The lower portion of Exhibit II shows the relative size of the utility ranges expressed in histogram form. As noted, package design and price are the most important factors, and together they account for about two thirds of the total range in utility.

It should be mentioned that the relative importance of a factor depends on the levels that are included in the design. For example, had price ranged from $1.19 to a high of $1.89, its relative importance could easily exceed that for package design. Still, as a crude indication of what factors to concentrate on, factor importance calculations provide a useful by-product of the main analysis regardless of such limitations.

Managerial Implications.   From a marketing management point of view the critical question is how these results can be used in the design of a product/marketing strategy for the spot remover. Examination of Exhibit II suggests a number of points for discussion:

- Excluding brand name, the most desirable offering would be the one based on package Design B with a money-back guarantee, a *Good-Housekeeping* seal, and a retail price of $1.19.
- The utility of a product with a price of $1.39 would be 0.3 less than one with a price of $1.19. A money-back guarantee which involves an increment of 0.5 in utility would more than offset the effect of the higher price.
- The use of a *Good Housekeeping* seal of approval is associated with a minor increase in utility. Hence including it in the company's product will add little to the attractiveness of the spot remover's overall offering.
- The utility of the three brand names provides the company with a quantitative measure of the value of its own brand name as well as the brand names of its competitors.

Other questions can be answered as well by comparing various composites made up from the utilities shown in Exhibit II.

The Air Carrier Study.   What about the two Paris flights you had to choose between? In that study, the sponsor was primarily interested in how air travelers evaluated the B-707 versus the B-747 in transatlantic travel, and whether relative value differed by length of flight and type of traveler—business versus vacation travelers. In this study all the respondents had flown across the Atlantic at least once during the preceding 12 months.

Exhibit III shows one of the findings of the study for air travelers (business and vacation) flying to Paris. Without delving into details it is quite apparent that the utility difference between the B-707 and the B-747 is very small. Rather, the main factors are departure time, punctuality of arrival, number of stops, and the attitudes of flight attendants.

The importance of type of aircraft did increase slightly with length of flight and for business-oriented travelers versus vacationers. Still, its importance to overall utility was never greater than 10%. It became abundantly clear that extensive replacement of older aircraft like the B-707 would not result in major shifts in consumer demand. On the contrary, money might better be spent on improving the scheduling aspects of flights and the attitudes and demeanor of flight personnel.

The air carrier study involved the preparation of some 27 different flight profiles (only two of which appear at the beginning of the article). Respondents simply rated each flight description in terms of its desirability on a seven-point scale. Only the order properties of the ratings were used in the computer run that resulted in the utility scales appearing in Exhibit III.

The Replacement Tire Study.   The conjoint measurement exercise in the replacement tire study was part of a larger study designed to pretest several television commercials for the sponsor's brand of steel-belted radial tires. The sponsor was particularly interested in

Exhibit III
Utility Functions for Air Travelers to Paris

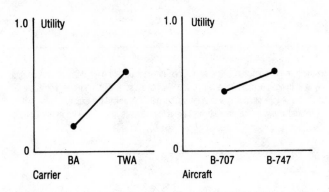

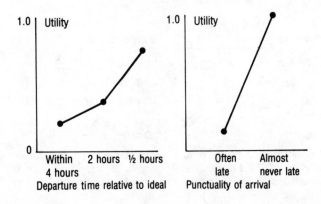

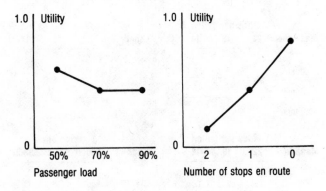

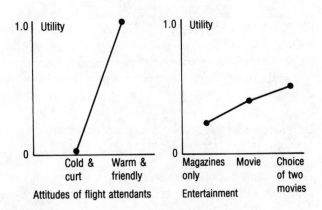

the utility functions of respondents who expressed interest in each of the test commercials.

The respondents considered tread mileage and price as quite important to their choice of tires. On the other hand, brand name did not play an important role (at least for the five brands included in the study). Not surprisingly, the most popular test commercial stressed tread mileage and good value for the money, characteristics of high appeal to this group. What was surprising was that this group represented 70% of the total sample.

This particular study involved the preparation of 25 profiles. Again, the researchers sorted cards into seven ordered categories. The 25 profiles, also constructed according to an orthogonal array, represented only one twenty fifth of the 625 possible combinations.

Potential Uses of Conjoint Measurement

The three preceding studies only scratch the surface of marketing problems in which conjoint measurement procedures can be used. For example, consumer evaluations can be obtained on:

- New product formulations involving changes in the physical or chemical characteristics of the product
- Package design, brand name, and promotional copy combinations
- Pricing and brand alternatives
- Verbalized descriptions of new products or services
- Alternative service designs

Moreover, while the three preceding examples emphasized preference or likelihood-of-purchase orderings, any explicit judgmental criterion can be used. For example, alternatives might be ordered by any of these criteria:

- Best value for the money
- Convenience of use
- Suitability for a specified type of consumer or for a specified end use
- Ruggedness, distinctiveness, conservativeness, and other "psychological images"

Designing Bar Soaps. In one recent study researchers related the psychological imagery of physical characteristics of actual bars of soap to end-use appropriateness; this study was conducted for the laboratory and marketing personnel of a diversified soap manufacturer.

While the designing of a bar of soap—by varying wieght, size, shape, color, fragrance type and intensity, surface feel, and so on—may seem like a mundane exercise, the fact remains that a cleverly positioned bar soap (for example, Irish Spring) can rapidly become a multimillion-dollar enterprise. Still, the extent of knowledge about the importance of such imagery is woefully meager. The researchers formulated actual bars of soap in which color, type of fragrance, and intensity of fragrance were constructed according to

Exhibit IV
A Two-at-a-Time Factor Evaluation Procedure

What is more important to you?

There are times when we have to give up one thing to get something else. And, since different people have different desires and priorities, the automotive industry wants to know what things are most important to you. We have a scale that will make it possible for you to tell us your preference in certain circumstances—for example, gas mileage vs. speed. Please read the example below which explains how the scale works—and then tell us the order of your preference by writing in the numbers from 1 to 9 for each of the six questions that follow the example.

Example:
Warranty vs price of the car

Procedure:

Simply write the number 1 in the combination that represents your first choice. In one of the remaining blank squares, write the number 2 for your second choice. Then write the number 3 for your third choice, and so on, from 1 to 9.

Price of car	Years of warranty 3	2	1
$3000	1		
$3200			
$3400			

Price of car	Years of warranty 3	2	1
$3000	1		
$3200	2		
$3400			

Price of car	Years of warranty 3	2	1
$3000	1	3	
$3200	2		
$3400			

Price of car	Years of warranty 3	2	1
$3000	1	3	6
$3200	2	5	8
$3400	4	7	9

Step 1 (Explanation)

You would rather pay the least ($3000) and get the most (3 years). Your first choice (1) is in the box as shown.

Step 2

Your second choice is that you would rather pay $3200 and have a 3-year warranty than pay $3000 and get a 2-year warranty.

Step 3

Your third choice is that you would rather pay $3000 and have a 2-year warranty than pay $3400 and get a 3-year warranty.

Sample:

This shows a sample order of preference for all possible combinations. Of course, your preferences could be different.

For each of the six questions to the right, please write in the numbers from 1 to 9 to show your order of preference for your next new car.

Price of car	Miles per gallon 22	18	14
$3000			
$3200			
$3400			

Max speed	Miles per gallon 22	18	14
80 mph			
70 mph			
60 mph			

Length	Miles per gallon 22	18	14
12 feet			
14 feet			
16 feet			

Roominess	Miles per gallon 22	18	14
6 passenger			
5 passenger			
4 passenger			

Made in	Miles per gallon 22	18	14
Germany			
U.S.			
Japan			

Made in	Price of car $3000	$3200	$3400
Germany			
U.S.			
Japan			

a design in which all possible combinations of the experimental factors appeared. All the other characteristics of the soap were held constant.

Respondents examined the soaps and assigned each bar to the end use that they felt best matched its characteristics—moisturizing facial soap, deep-cleaning soap for oily skin, woman's deodorant soap, or man's deodorant soap. The data were then analyzed by conjoint measurement techniques, leading to a set of psychophysical functions for each of the characteristics.

The study showed that type of fragrance was the most important physical variable contributing to end-use appropriateness. Rather surprisingly, the type of fragrance (medicinal) and color (blue) that appeared best suited for a man's deodorant soap were also found to be best for the deep-cleaning soap, even though deep-cleaning soap had been previously classed for marketing purposes as a facial soap. On the other hand, fragrance intensity played a relatively minor role as a consumer cue for distinguishing among different end uses.

In brief, this study illustrated the feasibility of translating changes in various physical variables into changes in psychological variables. Eventually, more detailed knowledge of these psychological transformations could enable a laboratory technician to synthesize color, fragrance, shape, and so forth to obtain soaps that conjure up almost any desired imagery. Moreover, in other product classes—beers, coffees, soft drinks—it appears possible to develop a psychophysics of taste in which such elusive verbal descriptions as "full-bodied" and "robust" are given operational meaning in terms of variations in physical or chemical characteristics.

Verbalized Descriptions of New Concepts. In many product classes, such as automobiles, houses, office machines, and computers, the possible design factors are myriad and expensive to vary physically for evaluation by the buying public. In cases such as these, the researcher usually resorts to verbalized descriptions of the principal factors of interest.

To illustrate, one study conducted among car owners by Rogers National Research, Inc. employed the format shown in Exhibit IV. In this case the researchers were interested in the effects of gas mileage, price, country of manufacture, maximum speed, roominess, and length on consumer preferences for new automobiles. Consumers evaluated factor levels on a two-at-a-time basis, as illustrated in Exhibit IV. Market Facts, Inc. employs a similar data collection procedure.[5]

In the Rogers study it was found that consumer evaluations of attributes were highly associated with the type of car currently owned and the type of car desired in the future. Not surprisingly, gas mileage and country of manufacture were highly important factors in respondent evaluations of car profiles. Somewhat surprising, however, was the fact that even large-car owners (and those contemplating the purchase of a large car) were more concerned with gas economy than owners of that type of car had been historically. Thus, while they fully expected to get fewer miles per gallon than they would in compact cars, they felt quite strongly that the car should be economical compared to others in its size class.

Organizations as Consumers. Nor is conjoint measurement's potential limited to consumer applications. Evaluations of supply alternatives by an organizational buyer are similar to benefits sought by the consumer. Thus, one can argue, these evaluations are among the most important inputs to industrial marketing strategy.

As an illustration, the management of a clinical laboratory was concerned with the problem of how to increase its share of laboratory test business. It had a study conducted to assess how physicians subjectively value various characteristics of a clinical laboratory in deciding where to send their tests.

Each physician in the study received 16 profiles of hypothetical laboratory services, each showing a different set of characteristics, such as reliability of test results, pick-up and delivery procedures, convenience of location, price range of services, billing procedures, and turnaround time. Utility functions were developed for each of these factors. On the basis of these results the management of the laboratory decided to change its promotion by emphasizing a number of convenience factors in addition to its previous focus on test reliability.

Marketing Strategy Simulations

We have described a variety of applications of conjoint measurement, and still others could be mentioned.[6] What has not yet been discussed, and is more important, is the role that utility measurement can play in the design of strategic marketing simulators. This type of application is one of the principal uses of conjoint measurement.

As a case in point, a large-scale study of consumer evaluations of airline services was conducted in which consumer utilities were developed for some 25 dif-

[5] Richard M. Johnson, "Trade-Off Analysis of Consumer Values," *Journal of Marketing Research,* May 1974, p. 121.

[6] Paul E. Green and Yoram Wind, *Multiattribute Decisions in Marketing: A Measurement Approach* (Hinsdale, Ill.: Dryden Press, 1973).

ferent service factors such as on-ground services, in-flight services, decor of cabins and seats, scheduling, routing, and price. Moreover, each utility function was developed on a route (city-pair) and purpose-of-trip basis.

As might be expected, the utility function for each of the various types of airline service differed according to the length and purpose of the flight. However, in addition to obtaining consumers' evaluations of service profiles, the researchers also obtained information concerning their *perceptions* of each airline (that is, for the ones they were familiar with) on each of the service factors for which the consumers were given a choice.

These two major pieces of information provided the principal basis for developing a simulation of airline services over all major traffic routes. The purpose of the simulation was to estimate the effect on market share that a change in the service configuration of the sponsor's services would have, route by route, if competitors did not follow suit. Later, the sponsor used the simulator to examine the effect of assumed retaliatory actions by its competitors. It also was able to use it to see what might happen to market share if the utility functions themselves were to change.

Each new service configuration was evaluated against the base-period configuration. In addition, the simulator showed which competing airlines would lose business and which ones would gain business under various changes in perceived service levels. Thus, in addition to single, ad hoc studies, conjoint measurement can be used in the ongoing monitoring (via simulation) of consumer imagery and evaluations over time.

Prospects and Limitations

Like any new set of techniques, conjoint measurement's potential is difficult to evaluate at the present stage of development and application. Relatively few companies have experimented with the approach so far. Capability for doing the research is still concentrated in a relatively few consulting firms and companies.

Conjoint measurement faces the same kinds of limitations that confront any type of survey, or laboratory-like, technique. First, while some successes have been reported in using conjoint measurement to predict actual sales and market share, the number of applications is still too small to establish a convincing track record at the present time.

Second, some products or services may involve utility functions and decision rules that are not adequately captured by the models of conjoint measurement. While the current emphasis on additive models (absence of interactions) can be shifted to more complex, interactive models, the number of combinations required to estimate the interactions rapidly mounts. Still, little is known about how good an approximation the simpler models are to the more elaborate ones.

Third, the essence of some products and services may just not be well captured by a decomposition approach that assumes that the researcher can describe an alternative in terms of its component parts. Television personalities, hit records, movies, or even styling aspects of cars may not lend themselves to this type of reductionist approach.

While the limitations of conjoint measurement are not inconsequential, early experience suggests some interesting prospects for measuring consumer tradeoffs among various product or service characteristics. Perhaps what is most interesting about the technique is its flexibility in coping with a wide variety of management's understanding of consumers' problems that ultimately hinge on evaluations of complex alternatives that a choice among products presents them with.

For Discussion

Provide your rank ordering of the three tire choices given at the outset. How did you generate the ordering? What thought process? Which was the most important attribute? What is the model? Would it fit your choice process? Interpret the utilities given in Exhibit II. What are the advantages and disadvantages of the two-at-a-time evaluation approach?

15

Trade-Off Analysis of Consumer Values

Richard M. Johnson

Introduction

This article develops and describes a method for evaluating the value systems of consumers. The three components of this method are: (1) a technique of data collection requiring a respondent to consider "trade-offs" among desirable alternatives; (2) a computational method which derives "utilities" accounting as nearly as possible for each respondent's choice behavior; and (3) a simple market simulation model which attempts to determine those characteristics of a product which will maximize its share of preference within any particular competitive context. This method has been used in several problem areas in the recent past. These include pricing of condominium units [2] and forecasting air traffic between cities [1].

Much marketing research activity is directed toward trying to find out what consumers want. Consumers are often asked what product attributes are most important to them, or what their "ideal" levels of various product attributes are. Neither of these traditional approaches is entirely satisfactory. For instance, judgments concerning the importance of various attributes are usually ambiguous unless great care is taken in defining attributes. Odor, for instance, may be an "important" attribute when considering products which differ noticeably in odor, but may be quite unimportant with a different sample of products *from the same category* if they all happen to smell the same. Safety may be regarded as an overpoweringly important attribute of airlines, when considered in the abstract. Yet, if airlines are not considered to differ in degree of safety, it cannot affect a passenger's choice of airline. Importance judgments are therefore not necessarily meaningful unless discussed in a highly specific context.

The identification of "ideal levels" of attributes is also frequently inadequate. There are many product attributes for which ideal levels do differ from consumer to consumer, such as saltiness of pretzels, lightness of beer, or sudsiness of detergent. For attributes such as convenience, economy, or level of performance, however, we can safely assume that every consumer would prefer a product having as high a level of each attribute as possible. What is needed in such cases is information about consumer "trade-offs"; since no manufacturer can afford to sell an infinitely convenient and high performing product for a price of zero, it becomes relevant to determine how consumers value various levels of each attribute and the extent to which they would forego a high level of one attribute to achieve a high level of another. The method to be described here is based on the premise that each consumer's choice behavior is governed by such trade-off values and that, although he or she may be unable to articulate them, they may be revealed by choices among product concepts having characteristics which are varied in systematic ways.

Techniques of conjoint measurement have generated much interest in the field of mathematical psychology in the last few years, where the notion was first enunciated by Luce and Tukey [7]. Green and Rao [3] describe the application of such methods to marketing research problems. The basic idea is that by providing consumers with stimuli from among which to choose we can make inferences about their value systems based upon behavior rather than upon self-reports. The word "conjoint" has to do with the fact that we can measure relative values of things considered jointly which might be unmeasurable taken one at a time.

Conjoint measurement is fundamentally different from those types of measurement with which most market researchers are familiar. It requires a basic assumption, or "measurement model," regarding the ways in which attributes of objects are related. Although it requires only rank-order data, it produces measurements which are "stronger" than rank orders. Conjoint measurement is similar in this respect to several nonmetric scaling procedures.

---

* Richard M. Johnson is Vice-President of Market Facts, Inc.

Reprinted from *Journal of Marketing Research,* published by the American Marketing Association, Vol. 11 (May 1974), pp. 121–127. No part of this article may be reproduced in any form without prior written permission from the publisher.

Measurement of Consumer Values

Suppose that we wish to assess the "importance" or "utility" to a prospective car buyer of each level of several car attributes. As a way of collecting data we might give a respondent a pair of attributes and ask for his rank order of preference for cars differing on these two attributes. He would thus be asked to "trade-off" these attributes against one another.

Consider cars differing only in price and top speed, and suppose a respondent were to state his rank order of preference for cars with nine combinations of price and top speed. Such data could be arranged as follows:

Price	Top Speed (MPH)		
	130	100	70
$2,500	1	2	5
$4,000	3	4	6
$6,000	7	8	9

If we were to examine these data one attribute at a time, we would conclude that this respondent prefers lower prices to higher prices, and faster cars to slower cars, other things being equal. Although we can obtain such potentially valuable information by examining these attributes separately, we can learn much more by examining them jointly. For instance, we see that while this respondent's preferred car will cost $2,500 and go 130 MPH, his second choice shows that he would rather drop to a top speed of 100 MPH than pay the higher price of $4,000. Thus by considering these two attributes jointly, we can learn something about their relative importance in influencing his preferences. If we wished to investigate this respondent's value system more generally, we could have him express his preferences for cars differing in warranty and seating capacity, warranty and price, and so on. If he were very highly motivated, we could ask him to provide trade-off data for all possible pairs of attributes in which we were interested.

One possible data-gathering procedure consists of giving each respondent a booklet in which each page contains a trade-off matrix with rows representing various levels of one attribute and columns representing levels of a second attribute. The respondent is asked to rank those combinations of attributes presented in each matrix according to his preferences.

This data collection approach is considerably different from another technique described by Green and Rao [3]. With that procedure, which might be called a "concept evaluation" technique, respondents provide rank orders of preference for product concepts which differ simultaneously with respect to all attributes being studied. Each approach has advantages. The concept evaluation approach has the

Table 1
One Respondent's Trade-off Data
(Rank Orders of Preference)

	Top Speed			Seating Capacity			Months of Warranty		
	130	100	70	2	4	6	60	12	3
Price									
$2,500	1	2	5	2	1	3	1	3	4
$4,000	3	4	6	5	4	6	2	5	6
$6,000	7	8	9	8	7	9	7	8	9
Top speed									
130 MPH				2	1	3	1	2	5
100 MPH				5	4	6	3	4	6
70 MPH				8	7	9	7	8	9
Seating capacity									
2							2	5	8
4							1	4	7
6							3	6	9

advantages of greater "realism," since respondents are choosing among concepts which are more elaborately specified, and at least theoretically, of being able to quantify interactions among attributes.

However, for many product categories it is desirable to study upwards of a dozen product attributes. It is hard to handle this many attributes if all concepts are to be given a specified level of each attribute. The pairwise approach has the advantage that the number of attributes to be studied is limited only by constraints of interview length and respondent endurance. A second advantage of the pairwise approach is that respondents provide information about trade-offs among pairs of attributes in such a direct form that one can infer relative "importances" of attributes by simple tabulations of the data.

We shall now provide a numerical example of how conjoint measurement can be used to infer consumer values from pairwise trade-off data. Let us suppose that automobiles could be described adequately in terms of four attributes, each with three levels. Rank order of preference data for an actual respondent are shown in Table 1, in which are shown six trade-off matrices, one for each pair of attributes.

Consider a simple model of preference formation which assumes that each respondent has a positive "utility" value for each level of each attribute, and that the relative degree of his "liking" for a specific car is obtained by multiplying together his utilities for the attribute levels describing that car. If we knew a respondent's utilities for the relevant attributes we could predict his rank order of preference for specific cars. A set of utilities for this respondent is provided in Table 2.

This person's relative liking for a $4,000, 130 MPH car would be $.33 \times .51 = .1683$. This is only a relative value and will have meaning only when com-

Table 2
Estimated Utility Values for One Respondent

	Level	Utility
Price	$2,500	.57
	$4,000	.33
	$6,000	.10
Top speed	130 MPH	.51
	100 MPH	.34
	70 MPH	.15
Seating capacity	2 persons	.31
	4 persons	.42
	6 persons	.27
Warranty	60 months	.49
	12 months	.31
	3 months	.20

pared with other similarly-derived values for cars having other levels of price and top speed. For this person a $2,500, 100 MPH car would have a relative value of .57 × .34 = .1938. Therefore, this respondent should prefer the $2,500, 100 MPH car. In choosing among cars differing in all four attributes, our respondent's relative values would be obtained by computing the products of four utility values at a time rather than two at a time.

This respondent's utilities are estimated so as to account simultaneously for all six of his pairwise trade-off matrices in Table 1. By way of illustration, Table 3 indicates the computations of pairwise products for the price versus speed comparison. This respondent's utilities for the three price levels are shown at the left margin, and his utilities for the three speeds are shown at the top. The value in each cell is obtained by multiplying together his utilities for that row and column. The rank orders of the numerical values in the cells of this table are indicated by the numbers in parentheses. We find that these pairwise products have nearly the same rank order as the data themselves, the single exception being the cells ranked 6 and 7. Thus, the estimated utilities are quite consistent with the data and may be taken as a summary. These utility values are only meaningful in a relative sense. If we were to raise them to any positive exponent (such as squaring them or taking their square roots) their meaning would be unchanged. Also, since their absolute magnitudes are arbitrary, they are scaled so that the sum for each attribute is unity.

Although the model underlying this computation is a multiplicative one, it is not different in any important sense from additive models in more common use. By taking logarithms of these values we could get new values for which sums rather than products would have the desired rank orders. Even considering the arbitrariness of scaling conventions, these particular utility values are not unique; other values obtained by slight modifications of these will still provide pairwise products having almost the same rank order as the data. However, if the respondent had reacted to several pairs involving each attribute and we were to solve simultaneously for utilities "best fitting" all his preference data, there is likely to be a unique solution apart from scaling.

Computation

The numerical techniques available to convert the observed rank orders into estimates of utilities are similar to techniques of nonmetric scaling in [4, 5, 6]. The computing method used most frequently here is an iterative procedure which attempts to minimize a measure of "badness of fit" of the utilities to the data. Since the data consists of only rank orders, the measure of fit must indicate the extent to which the pairwise products of utilities have rank orders similar to the data.

Two measures have been helpful; the first of these is Kentall's tau. Suppose we have n objects which have been approximately rank ordered from largest to smallest. The tau statistic is the difference between proportions of pairs in "right order" and "wrong order." A tau of 1.0 indicates a perfect rank order, a tau of −1.0 indicates a perfect negative relationship, and a value of zero indicates an unrelated ordering.

Suppose that a respondent has filled out a trade-off matrix of size 3 × 3, and we have estimated utilities for him which are multiplied together to produce a "theoretical" value for each cell of the matrix as in Table 4. With 9 cells there are 36 pairs of cells. Tau would be the number of these pairs of cells for which the difference between theoretical values is in the right direction (the same direction as his data for that

Table 3
Pairwise Products of Utilities

		130 MPH .51 (1)	100 MPH .34 (2)	70 MPH .15 (5)
$2,500	.57	.2907 (3)	.1938 (4)	.0855 (7)
$4,000	.33	.1683 (6)	.1122 (8)	.0495 (9)
$6,000	.10	.0510	.0340	.0150

Table 4
Actual versus Predicted Preferences
for Five Optical Product Concepts

Concept	Actual first choice votes	Predicted first choice votes
A	43	28
B	101	114
C	157	117
D	204	252
E	152	146
Total	657	657

pair of cells) minus the number in the wrong direction, all divided by 36. If a respondent had filled out six such matrices and we wished to measure the overall extent to which his utilities fit his data, we would cumulate the numerator and denominator of tau over all 6 matrices. When the utilities in Table 2 are applied to explain the data in Table 1, we get a tau of .935, indicating a reasonably close but not perfect fit.

The tau statistic is based on a count of numbers of errors without regard to their size. A second measure, phi, takes into account the sizes of errors. For each pair of trade-off cells we consider the ratio of the computed values. If this ratio is denoted by the symbol r, then the quantity $[r + (1/r) - 2]$ may be regarded as a measure of the "distance" of the ratio from one. This quantity is zero if the ratio is one and increases as the ratio becomes either larger or smaller than one. The statistic phi is defined by the expression:

$$\phi = \frac{\Sigma[r + (1/r) - 2]\delta}{\Sigma[r + (1/r) - 2]}$$

$$\delta = \begin{cases} 1 \text{ if the computed difference is in} \\ \quad \text{the "wrong" direction.} \\ 0 \text{ otherwise.} \end{cases}$$

This index would have a value of zero if there were no errors of fit, and a value of one if the order of every pair of cells were incorrectly predicted. The most successful computing algorithm currently available uses a "gradient" technique to minimize phi. Normally, those respondents with low values of phi also have high values of tau, suggesting that either of these indices may work reasonably well in practice as a measure of lack of fit.

Assumptions

The model of preference formation underlying this method assumes that the attributes studied are independent. This assumption has two ramifications. The first is that the attributes must be nonredundant, or more accurately, they must all be equally redundant. The utility for a collection of attributes is considered to be the product of the utilities of each of its attributes. If an attribute were represented twice, for instance, its utility would figure into the overall as its square, rather than its first power. Lacking any good way to measure the extent of redundancy among the attributes in a list, it seems prudent to conduct preliminary research to formulate attribute lists which are as nonredundant as possible.

The second ramification of the independence assumption is one regarding interaction among variables. The model assumes, for instance, that the extent to which a respondent prefers a red car to a black one will be independent of size, price, and model type. It

seems possible that red may be someone's preferred color for a convertible while black may be his preferred color for a limousine. This assumption of no interaction is most certainly false when applied to such extreme cases; however, it appears to be tenable under ordinary circumstances. If such interactions do exist in a specific set of data, they will be indicated by unfavorable values of tau and phi.

Determining Optimal Product Characteristics

A simple model of preference formation has been described which expresses an individual's theoretical relative preferences as products of sets of utilities. A method for estimating these utilities from rank order data has also been suggested. We next consider the problem of converting these relative values to something more nearly approaching shares of the market.

Suppose a market currently consists of products A, B, C, . . . , etc. We wish to predict the relative sales of a new product, X, if X were to become available. The most natural approach would seem to consist of estimating each respondent's overall liking for each product and then to count the number of respondents for whom X has the highest value. This approach assumes that an individual restricts his purchases to his preferred product. This may be nearly true in product categories with high brand loyalties, such as cigarettes, or with infrequent "large ticket" purchases, such as houses. In other product categories it may be more appropriate to employ a probabilistic model which distributes an individual's probability of purchase in some way over his several most preferred products.

Suppose that an appropriate sample of respondents has provided the necessary data and that utilities have been computed for each respondent. We may also have gathered demographic, product consumption, media exposure, and other information about each individual. Suppose we have several experimental versions of a product in mind (which do not necessarily yet exist). We assume that these versions are all feasible from a manufacturing and pricing standpoint, that we *could* produce any of them, and we wish to choose the "best" version.

We compute each individual's overall liking for the first version of the experimental product, determining whether or not it would have a value higher than any currently available product. If it would have a higher value than any current product, we conclude that this individual would in fact buy it if it were available. If our respondent sample is well chosen, if we weight individuals appropriately to reflect individual differences in consumption, and if we have included the relevant product attributes, then the resulting proportions of respondents with predicted preferences for each product should correspond approximately to actual market shares for currently available products (apart from differences caused by variables unaccounted for, such as advertising and sales force effectiveness). We could then estimate: (1) how many respondents would choose the experimental product X, in the context of A, B, C, . . . , etc.; (2) what the likely volume of consumption would be; (3) what products such individuals are now using and from which they would be switched if X were introduced; (4) who they are, demographically, and how they may be contacted by advertising. By repeating the process for experimental versions $X_1, X_2, \ldots$, etc., we can determine which of these optimizes whichever criterion we wish.

Since computations are done on a respondent-by-respondent basis, it is possible to study interactions among products. For instance, that pair of experimental products could be selected involving relatively little overlap with one another which will theoretically maximize total profitability for the corporation. Likewise, a companion product or line extension can be chosen which appears capable of producing the greatest net increase in total corporate profit.

Evidence Regarding Appropriateness of the Model

Although the procedures described here have been in use for a fairly short time, a number of methodological studies have been conducted, three of which will now be described briefly.

Content Dependence.   Even with as few as seven or eight attributes it becomes impractical to have a respondent fill out trade-off matrices for all attribute pairs. It is therefore relevant to inquire whether the utilities obtained for an attribute depend upon the other attributes with which it is compared. In one experiment, involving 24 product attributes, respondents were divided randomly into 2 groups. Respondents in each group filled out trade-off matrices for a subset of 18 attributes. Only 12 attributes were common to both questionnaires, and no pair of attributes appeared in both questionnaires.

It was possible to examine the mean utilities for each level of each attribute to see whether different utilities were produced by the experimental groups as a function of context. The 12 common attributes had a total of 46 levels. A t-test was conducted for each of these to determine whether the means were significantly dissimilar. We would have expected between 4 and 5 differences to appear significant at the 90% level of confidence due to chance alone, but only 3 values this large were observed, somewhat less than chance. Therefore this experiment failed to demonstrate any difficulty with context dependence,

and lends support to the practice of exposing respondents to subsets of attribute pairs.[1]

External Validation — Prediction of Preference.   The most critical question regarding validity of the model is whether a respondent's utilities, when multiplied together properly, do in fact provide an accurate prediction of his preferences. This question was examined in two experiments. In the first of these, respondents filled out 6 trade-off matrices comprising all possible pairings of 4 attributes. Each attribute had 3 levels so that 12 utilities were computed for each respondent. It would have been possible to specify $3^4 = 81$ possible hypothetical product descriptions using these attributes. A subset of 12 of these was chosen, each having the characteristic that it had the "best" level of one attribute, the "worst" level of another, and "middle" levels of the remaining two attributes. The same respondents also provided rank orders of preference for these 12 hypothetical products. We were interested in determining how closely the actual rank orders of preference for these 12 concepts would be predicted by the model.

It should be noted that the model was being asked to work under exceptionally difficult circumstances. The 12 hypothetical products were chosen so as to be as nearly equivalent in overall desirability as possible. If a product had been included with the "best" level of each attribute and/or one with the "worst" level of each attribute, the prediction of preference would most surely have been easier.

In order to assess the goodness of prediction, a rank order correlation coefficient was computed between the actual and predicted rank orders of preference for each respondent. The median of these values was .80. This was felt to constitute a reasonable level of prediction, given the unreliability inherent in the measure being predicted.

Since the fit was not perfect, however, it seemed prudent to inquire whether the errors tended to be random or systematic. If, for instance, the model tended systematically to over- or underpredict level of preference for any of the 12 concepts, we would have evidence of its failure to account for some aspect of the respondents' preferences. The respondents' rank orders of preference were therefore averaged, as were the rank orders of their predicted preference. The rank order correlation between these two sets of averages was .91. This appeared to be an acceptably

---

[1] The t-statistic is not strictly appropriate for this purpose, since it involves a normality assumption which utilities probably do not satisfy (although their logarithms might). However, the t-statistic is generally considered to be relatively robust under this condition, a property not so characteristic of multivariate analysis of variance, which might otherwise have been a more appropriate technique.

high value, and inspection of the differences between the two sets of averages provided no evidence of systematic over- or undervaluing any attribute.

In another study respondents filled out 15 trade-off matrices dealing with 10 attributes of products in a "hard goods" category. The same respondents were also presented with five concept statements describing hypothetical products from this category and asked to rank these concepts in order of their preferences. Each respondent's trade-off data were used to estimate his utilities for the 10 attributes, and these were used in turn to predict the rank order of his preferences for the 5 concepts.

The distribution of actual and predicted first choices is given in Table 4. The distribution of first choice votes estimated from the trade-off data is similar to the actual distribution ($r = .92$), with the exceptions that Concept D is overpredicted by about 25%, while Concept C is underpredicted by a similar amount. The fit is less impressive on a person-by-person basis, however. With 5 products we should expect to predict a respondent's first choice correctly 1 time in 5, or 20% of the time. The actual number of "hits" is 294, representing a success rate of approximately 45%. Thus the similarity of the distributions of actual and estimated first choices is partially caused by compensating errors. This corresponds to experience in other product categories, where the success rate at predicting first choice has ranged from a low of about 40% (twice the chance level with 5 products) to a high of 85% (about 6 times the chance level with 7 products).

An analysis was also conducted to determine whether prediction was more successful among most and least preferred products than among products in the middle of the preference distribution. For each respondent the five concepts were arranged in order of stated preference, from first choice to last choice. For each pair of positions a check was then made to see whether the model made the correct prediction of pairwise order. Cumulating over respondents, we can determine the accuracy with which the model predicts pairwise preference for any two actual preference ranks. These percentages are provided in Table 5.

With these data the model was successful in predicting preference of the most preferred over the

second most preferred concept only 64% of the time, while it correctly predicted the preference of the most preferred over the least preferred concept 82% of the time. The lowest percent accuracy figures are for discrimination between rank orders 2 versus 3 and 3 versus 4, as might be expected. The success rate increases in general as the spread between rank order positions increases, and is somewhat higher for most and least preferred concepts than for those more in the middle. Perhaps surprisingly, the model is somewhat more successful at predicting least preferred product than most preferred, though this may be a specific characteristic of these data.

Evaluation and Conclusions

The greatest strength of the procedure seems to be its ability to generate rather refined predictions from quite primitive data. This is a characteristic of all the nonmetric scaling methods. A second strength is its apparently wide applicability. Not only can the model provide predictions about levels of buying interest for new concepts, but it can also provide information about the "trade-offs" among product attributes. For instance, the model can estimate how much price might be increased when a new feature is included without loss of market share, or whether one feature might be substituted for another without loss of share. The procedure is by no means limited to verbalized product dimensions. It is possible to study color, odor, texture, size, shape, and other physical product attributes with the aid of visual or other sensory aids. Indeed, the simulation procedure can easily be generalized to incorporate each respondent's *perceptions* of current products or new product concepts on such subjective attributes as "beauty" or "satisfaction."

A third important benefit of the procedure is that the concepts tested need not actually exist in concept form. Even if there were only 10 relevant attributes with only 2 levels each, a total $2^{10} = 1024$ possible concept statements would be definable. Using traditional concept testing procedures, several hundred tests might be required to explore all the attractive possibilities. Using a model such as that described here, all 1024 of them could be evaluated in some sense without ever exposing even one concept to any respondent. The cost of this strength is the rather heroic assumption of no interaction among attributes. The model assumes that the whole is equal to the sum (literally, the product) of its parts and, to whatever extent this assumption is false, it will produce misleading results.

It is clear that the usefulness of the procedures described here will ultimately be judged on an empirical basis. At this time there are not yet any clear predictions made by the model which have had time to be

Table 5
Percent Accuracy for Pairwise Preference Predictions

Rank order of less preferred concept	Rank order of more preferred concept			
	1	2	3	4
2	64			
3	67	60		
4	75	69	59	
5	82	82	75	70

proven either true or false in the marketplace. Such information should soon become available, however, since the model has been applied in a number of subject areas.

References

1. Davidson, J. D. "Forecasting Traffic on STOL," *Operational Research Quarterly*, 24 (1973), 561–9.
2. Fiedler, John A. "Condominium Design and Pricing: A Case Study in Consumer Trade-Off Analysis" in M. Venkatesan, ed., *Proceedings*. Third Annual Conference, Association for Consumer Research, 1972, 279–93.
3. Green, Paul E. and Vithala Rao. "Conjoint Measurement for Quantifying Judgmental Data," *Journal of Marketing Research*, 8 (August 1971), 355–63.
4. Johnson, Richard M. "Pairwise Nonmetric Multidimensional Scaling," *Psychometrika*, 38 (March 1973), 11–8.
5. Kruskal, Joseph B. "Multidimensional Scaling by Optimizing Goodness of Fit to a Nonmetric Hypothesis," *Psychometrika*, 29 (March 1964), 1–27.
6. _____. "Analysis of Factorial Experiments by Estimating Monotone Transformations of the Data," *Journal of the Royal Statistical Society*, Series B, 27 (March 1965), 251–63.
7. Luce, R. Duncan and John W. Tukey. "Simultaneous Conjoint Measurement: A New Type of Fundamental Measurement," *Journal of Mathematical Psychology*, 1 (February 1964), 1–27.

For Discussion

What are the key assumptions of conjoint measurement? What is the difference between a multiplicative and additive model? Explain and illustrate the implications of the assumption that the attributes are independent. Interpret Tables 4 and 5. What attributes would be needed to model your choice of automobile? What attribute levels would you use?

16

New Product Evaluation: Electric Vehicles for Commercial Applications

George Hargreaves
John D. Claxton
Frederick H. Siller

A general requirement of an electric utility is to maintain an accurate forecast of the future demand for electrical power. This necessitates keeping abreast of potential power-demanding innovations. Electrically powered commercial vehicles, if widely adopted, would clearly influence future power demands.[1] Therefore, research was conducted to evaluate the future usage of electrically powered vehicles by commercial fleets.

This study had two principal objectives: (1) to identify the number of commercial applications that were compatible with electric vehicles in terms of technical requirements such as speed, range, and loads; and (2) to assess the perceived importance of these technical requirements as compared to other vehicle characteristics such as initial costs and pollution levels. Conjoint measurement was a key tool in the research process.

Method

Data Collection. The data collection was done in two parts. The preliminary collection assessed the technical compatibility of electric vehicles with current truck usage patterns. This was done by questioning a random sample of fleet personnel responsible for truck operations. The sample was drawn from the vehicle registration list for a metropolitan area of approximately 1,200,000 people and was stratified to insure representation of a cross section of fleet sizes. Interviewers obtained information on operating characteristics such as daily miles traveled, number of business calls, speeds, and cargo loadings.

An important feature of this phase of the data collection was that the operating chacteristics for each fleet were segmented by fleet application. That is, when a fleet used one set of trucks for one application and another set for a second application, two sets of operating characteristics were obtained. Therefore, although a fleet's average requirements might not be compatible with electric vehicles, a subset of the fleet could be.

The second data collection involved fleet personnel directly responsible for vehicle purchase decisions and assessed the perceived positive and negative characteristics of electric vehicles. Of particular concern was the relative impact of technical capabilities as compared to other criteria on the purchase decision. For example, would a fleet operator give up truck capabilities to gain reduced operating costs? Or pay a higher initial price to gain reduced pollution? This information was gathered by inviting fleet operators to electric vehicle seminars and questioning them by means of focus group interviews. The seminar approach allowed the respondents to gain some understanding of the nature of electric vehicles, to operate an electrically powered van,[2] and to answer a questionnaire dealing with the relative merits of electric versus conventional vehicles. Conjoint measurement

---

[1] See "Postal Service Plugging Into E. V. Mail Delivery," *Electric Vehicles News,* November 1973, pp. 20–22; and *The Potential Market for On-The-Road Electric Vehicles* (New York: Electric Vehicle Council, 1973).

[2] The test vehicle was a Battronic Minivan, produced by Boyertown Auto Body Works of Boyertown, Pennsylvania.

was used to assess the relative importance of various vehicle characteristics.[3]

Conjoint Measurement. When making a purchase decision, a buyer must compare products that differ on a number of attributes. In effect, he decides which combination of attributes will give the most satisfaction. Conjoint measurement can be used to assess the relative importance of various levels of the attributes being considered.

This procedure involves asking respondents to rank a set of alternatives from most to least desirable. For example, suppose truck purchases were based solely on two criteria, amount of seat padding and number of chrome knobs on the dashboard. Using conjoint measurement, truck buyers would be presented with a set of hypothetical trucks that differed in terms of these two characteristics and would be asked to rank the alternatives from most to least preferred.

---

[3] For discussion of conjoint measurement, see: Paul E. Green, "Marketing Applications of MDS: Assessment and Outlook," *Journal of Marketing*, Vol. 39 (January 1975), pp. 24–31; Richard M. Johnson, "Trade-Off Analysis of Consumer Values," *Journal of Marketing Research*, Vol. 11 (May 1974), pp. 121–127; and Paul E. Green and Yoram Wind, *Multiattribute Decisions in Marketing: A Measurement Approach* (Hinsdale, Ill.: Dryden Press, 1973).

Unlike a direct rating of padding and ornamentation, the ranking of alternatives forces the decision maker to make trade-offs (as he must do in an actual truck purchase decision). For example, he must decide whether he would rather have four-inch padding and three chrome knobs, or six-inch padding and one chrome knob. Since we have assumed that both criteria are important, the choice would not be trivial.

Findings

Technical Compatibility. Information from the preliminary sample of 440 fleets was used to evaluate the compatibility of electric vehicles with current truck usage patterns. Across this sample there were a total of 693 sets of trucks, each set being used for a specific application. Usage patterns in terms of requirements such as miles, stops, and loads were measured for each of the 693 truck applications and then compared with electric vehicle capabilities.

The standard used to represent electric vehicle capability was: a maximum range of 40 miles, a maximum of 40 business stops en route, a maximum payload of 1500 pounds, and seldom requiring freeway speeds. As indicated in Figure 1, 11% of the truck applications operated within the capabilities of the standard electric vehicle. An increase in range capability to 60 miles increased the compatible applications

Figure 1
Technical Compatibility of Commercial Truck Applications

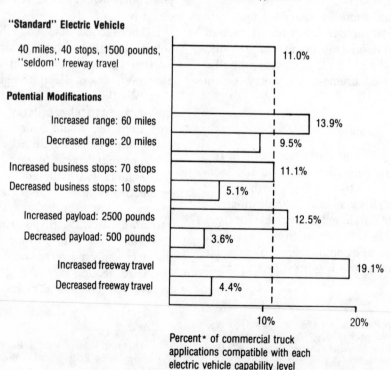

"Standard" Electric Vehicle

40 miles, 40 stops, 1500 pounds, "seldom" freeway travel — 11.0%

Potential Modifications

Increased range: 60 miles — 13.9%
Decreased range: 20 miles — 9.5%

Increased business stops: 70 stops — 11.1%
Decreased business stops: 10 stops — 5.1%

Increased payload: 2500 pounds — 12.5%
Decreased payload: 500 pounds — 3.6%

Increased freeway travel — 19.1%
Decreased freeway travel — 4.4%

Percent* of commercial truck applications compatible with each electric vehicle capability level

* The percentages are weighted averages calculated to take into consideration the proportion of Metro fleets in each of four fleet size categories.

by approximately 3%. Increasing the number of business stops to 70, or payload to 2500 pounds, had very little impact. However, increasing the electric vehicles' ability to travel at freeway speeds almost doubled the number of compatible truck applications, from 11% to 19%.

Attribute Trade-offs between Electric and Conventional Vehicles. It is clear that even when an electric vehicle could meet usage requirements, a truck buyer might not switch from a conventional truck. Several additional attributes come into consideration. Electric vehicles represent a new propulsion system that some buyers may consider desirable, but that others may be unwilling to try. Electric vehicles, at least initially, will be priced at a premium. On the other hand, electrics will have lower operating costs and will offer very low levels of air and noise pollution.

The second phase of this study used conjoint measurement to assess the relative importance of these attributes. The data represented rankings of sixteen alternative truck designs. Analysis of these data was done with Kruskal's MONANOVA program,[4] resulting in a utility (or importance) rating for each attribute. The results, shown in Table 1, indicate that "unlimited speed and range" of conventional vehicles was seen as the most important consideration, followed by "reduced operating costs," "standard initial price," and "zero pollution." Buyers were relatively indifferent in terms of "new propulsion system" versus "conventional propulsion."

Table 1 also shows the aggregate utilities of the particular characteristics for both electric and conventional vehicles. This analysis indicates that con-

ventional trucks are more desirable than current electric vehicles, with net utilities of +0.836 and −0.836 respectively. It should also be noted that electric vehicles would be more desirable than conventional vehicles if they were sold at standard prices, *or* if they were not constrained by limited speed and range.

Conclusions

This study addressed the question of new product evaluation in a relatively mature market: electrically powered delivery vans in commercial fleet applications. Although 11% of the commercial applications were compatible in terms of the technical capabilities of electric vehicles, when additional attributes were considered the product was not acceptable in its present form. That is, the negative attributes—reduced technical capabilities and premium price—more than offset the positive attributes—reduced pollution and lower operating costs. Thus, general commercial acceptance of electric vehicles will depend either on increased vehicle capabilities or on competitive prices.

In general, the use of conjoint measurement to assess attribute trade-offs is seen as a promising methodology for addressing questions of new product evaluation. This approach makes it possible to consider both the technical capabilities of the new product and the perceptual attributes of importance to potential buyers. The particular strength of this measurement approach is that it forces the recognition of trade-offs among product attributes and thus can be used to establish the perceived value of various possible product designs.

For Discussion

Interpret Figure 1. Interpret and consider the implications of Table 1. What are the key assumptions underlying Table 1?

---

[4]Joseph B. Kruskal, "Analysis of Factorial Experiments by Estimating Monotone Transformations of the Data," *Journal of the Royal Statistical Society,* Series B, Vol. 27 (March 1965), pp. 251–263.

Table 1
Relative and Net Utilities of Conventional versus Electric Vehicles

Conventional		Electric	
Characteristic	Utility	Characteristic	Utility
Unlimited speed and range[a]	+1.426	Limited speed and range	−1.426
Standard operating costs[b]	−0.928	Reduced operating costs	+0.928
Standard initial price[c]	+0.901	Premium initial price	−0.901
Standard pollution[d]	−0.544	Zero pollution	+0.544
Conventional propulsion[e]	−0.019	New propulsion system	+0.019
Net utility	+0.836	Net utility	−0.836

[a]Speed and range capabilities compared were "unlimited" and "40 mph & 40 miles."
[b]Operating costs compared were "Standard: 10¢/mi." and "Reduced: 5¢/mi."
[c]Initial prices compared were "Standard: $5000" and "Premium: $8000."
[d]Pollution levels compared were "Standard: gasoline engine" and "Zero."
[e]Propulsion systems compared were "Conventional: gasoline engine" and "New system: electric."

17

The Design of Test Marketing Experiments

Benjamin Lipstein

There are two levels at which test market experiments must be designed: one is the arrangement and selection of markets, the other is the measurement system to be used within the market. This paper is concerned with the structure and selection of markets for experimentation.

Although test marketing of a new product may be undertaken for a number of reasons, there are two purposes most of us would consider of paramount importance and which have clear design implications: one is to derive an estimate of the brand share which the product may achieve on a national level; the second is to evaluate alternative strategies for subsequent use on a national scale. The brand share projection problem is essentially a problem of estimation in contrast with the second which is a test of a specific set of alternatives or hypotheses. While the projection problem may also be regarded as a test of a hypothesis, the problem of estimation remains dominant in its implications for design.

The Evaluation of Alternative Strategies

It is in the area of alternative strategies that experimental design has much to contribute to the test market experiment. The issue is the relative performance of two different marketing activities. For example, which will be more effective, a coupon or a sample, in the introduction of a new product? Should the price be set at $.75 or $.98? Will one kind of copy approach produce a more rapid trial rate than an alternative copy approach? In these situations one is not so much concerned with the absolute share achievement, though this kind of information is often estimated, as with the relative performance of the two strategies in terms of brand share, consumer awareness, and consumer trials.

Within the context of this problem, it is meaningful to talk about the consequences and the cost of an erroneous decision. For example, if we choose couponing in preference to sampling, and if the decision is incorrect, the consequences may be a specific dollar cost of marketing or a lower achievement in brand share. It is these risks that must be related to what statisticians refer to as the Type I and Type II errors. A Type I error is the case in which no difference exists between two merchandising approaches, but we erroneously believe there to be a difference. A Type II error is committed when we fail to recognize a difference that exists. There are different cost consequences for each of these two kinds of errors, and the probabilities must accordingly be fixed against these costs. The fixing of these probabilities is a joint responsibility of the researcher and marketing management. They are often arrived at by negotiation. The ultimate value of a test may depend upon management's awareness of the likelihood of these two probabilities. This does not call for confounding management with technical jargon—management is often quite familiar with these issues—the problem is only one of communication.

Treatment Variations within the Market

Once these probability levels have been fixed we are prepared to tackle the specific questions of the design of a test market experiment. One of the first issues to be considered is, can the alternative strategies such as couponing and sampling be tested in the same market? One cannot mix two different copy strategies within the same media market and hope to measure any differences. If the issue *can* be tested within the market, such as the case of couponing and sampling, then we have much greater latitude in the choice of cities for experimental purposes. From a design point of view, such an experiment is concerned with comparisons within the experimental block or city.

Typically in such a situation the city might be divided into two, three, or four parts. Coupons would be used in one part, samples in another part, and perhaps no promotions in still another part of the city. Separate measurements would be taken in each part of the city and comparisons could then be made between each of the parts to provide an estimate of the effect of one versus the other. Such results could then be combined over a number of test cities. The important thing is that the comparisons are always made within the city and hence the city effects or city differences do not confound or conceal the experimental effects.

Many arrangements of treatments can be used in a complete block design. The randomized complete block design might call for a division of the city into two or more segments for the application of separate treatments. For instance, in Syracuse, the railroad divides the city and the metropolitan area into two halves (north and south) which are fairly comparable on a demographic basis. In the case of Columbus, such a division can be made on the north/south axis and again, very conveniently, the railroad divides the metropolitan area into two approximately equivalent parts.

The effect of testing couponing versus sampling in the same city is best observed by examining the experimental design model. The model identifies the following variables:

U = Overall mean of the entire city
B = City or block effect
S = Sampling effect
C = Couponing effect.

Let us assume that we are estimating brand share using retail store audits in both halves of the city. The observed share for the coupon half of the city is represented by X_c and for sample half by X_s.

The observed shares have the following model representation:

$$X_c = U + B + C + e \tag{1}$$

$$X_s = U + B + S + e \tag{2}$$

where e is the random error. To compute the effect of the couponing versus sampling, we subtract one equation from the other to obtain:

$$X_c - X_s = C - S. \tag{3}$$

We can thus measure the effect of couponing versus sampling within the city or block, subject only to sampling variation. A variation of the split city design is to use a checkerboard design where segments of the city are randomly selected and assigned to sample or coupon exposure. In this kind of application a consumer panel would be needed to measure the effects since retail store audits could not be clearly attributed to the effects of couponing or sampling.

If it is desired to vary two factors simultaneously, a factorial arrangement might be used, say, two levels of sampling and two price levels if they can be controlled within the same market. Such an arrangement would provide estimates of the differential effects of sampling levels, prices, and the possible interaction of the two.

Assuming that we have divided a test city into four parts for purposes of this factorial design, we would have the following equations:

$$X_1 = U + SP_1 + e \tag{4}$$

$$X_2 = U + SP_2 + e \tag{5}$$

$$X_3 = U + CP_1 + e \tag{6}$$

$$X_4 = U + CP_2 + e \tag{7}$$

where X_1, X_2, X_3, and X_4 represent the brand shares for each segment of the city, U, S, and C are as defined above, and P_1 and P_2 represent the lower and higher prices in the test. One estimate of price effect is equation (4) minus equation (5):

$$X_1 - X_2 = SP_1 - SP_2. \tag{8}$$

Similarly, we have for equations (6) and (7):

$$X_3 - X_4 = CP_1 - CP_2. \tag{9}$$

Since both are equally acceptable estimates of price we can combine equations (8) and (9) to obtain the effect of the price difference, namely:

$$\text{Effect} \atop \text{of price} = \tfrac{1}{2}[(SP_1 - SP_2) + (CP_1 - CP_2)]. \tag{10}$$

Similarly, by subtracting equation (6) from (4) and (7) from (5) and averaging the results we have:

$$\text{Effect of sample} \atop \text{versus coupon} = \tfrac{1}{2}[(SP_1 - CP_1) + (SP_2 - CP_2)]. \tag{11}$$

Lastly, adding equations (4) and (7) and subtracting equations (5) from (6) provides an estimate of the interaction of couponing/sampling with changes in price:

$$\text{Interaction effect} = \tfrac{1}{2}[(SP_1 + CP_2) - (SP_2 + CP_1)]. \tag{12}$$

The statistical analysis of this experiment is very direct. The details are readily available in most books on design of experiments. The reader should be cautioned, however, that at least two markets are required with these experiments to provide a bona fide error term for testing of the effects.

If the market can only absorb two treatment variations, but three are under consideration, an incomplete block design using groups of three cities can be used. In such a case, let us assume that one test market contains a test of sampling versus couponing, another contains sampling versus control, and the third contains couponing versus control. If sampling proves to be superior to couponing in the first market and couponing is superior to control in the second market, and couponing is superior to control in the third market, then we have a unique ranking:

Sampling > Couponing > Control.

In effect, although all treatments are not included in the same block, comparisons can be made between the three experimental variations.

A great many test variations can be considered within the context of viewing the test city as an experimental block. The key to such designing is that the variation between cities, which is generally very large, is excluded from the comparisons. However, this type of experiment provides only relative performance of the treatment. It is of course understood that all other factors such as dollars of advertising and sales effort are held constant. Throughout this section I have assumed that at least two markets with the same treatment arrangements will be used so that variances and tests of significance can be computed. The size of the Type I and Type II errors one is willing to accept, and the order of difference sought, will determine the number of test markets.

Treatment Variations between Markets

Where the issue to be tested affects the entire market, such as copy or levels of advertising expenditures, the entire test market becomes the experimental unit. The design must then contend with and attempt to control between city variation. In general, for a given level of reliability, the number of test cities for this type of problem is substantially greater than for test market variables which can be tested in the same market.

Since the comparisons are to be made between markets, every effort must be made to reduce the variability which is a function of the selected markets. In this case, many of the dictums which we frequently hear are relevant. Ideally, markets to be used in the test should be as similar as possible. Where possible, the following restraints should be placed upon the selection of markets. They should be similar in population size, family income, demographic characteristics, and ethnic background; similar in trade factors and media facilities; and, hopefully, all in the same geographic region. Our willingness to forego any of these controls will be related to our evaluation of the degree to which differences in these characteristics may affect the test results. It now becomes self-evident why certain cities are used repeatedly for test market operations.

Having selected the cities for the test, the next step is the selection of the experimental design. Latin squares are frequently useful because they provide a means for controlling variations between cities, which could not be controlled by selection. For example, the rows of the Latin square might control for geographic variation, while the columns could be used for controlling competitive activity or media facility

Table 1
Latin Square

Competitive Activity	Geographic Region		
	East	North Central	West
Level 1	A	B	C
Level 2	B	C	A
Level 3	C	A	B

where A = High level of advertising expenditure
B = Medium level of advertising expenditure
C = Low level of advertising expenditure

variations. The treatments within the Latin square in this case might be three levels of advertising expenditures or three different kinds of copy. The Latin square design implies independence of controls and treatments or that an interaction effect is not present. By way of example, we may obtain from retail store audits an estimate of brand share for each segment of the Latin square as in Table 1.

These brand shares are functions of geographic region, competitive activity, and the experimental level of advertising. By summing the rows we would be averaging out the effect of regions and levels of advertising; by summing the columns, the average effect of competitive activity and levels of advertising would be eliminated; and lastly, by summing the advertising expenditure level for each of the treatments we would average out the effect of geographic region, and competitive activity for a direct comparison of levels of advertising. The Latin square design operates to reduce the variation in the experiment in the same way that stratification does for sample surveys. In this case, the experimental error which is derived from the experiment for testing the treatment effects is due to the variation between cities. We would expect that the variation between cities would be substantially greater than the within variation to be found in the complete block experiments described above.

If the test issues are levels of advertising versus levels of promotion, a factorial arrangement might be considered. The advantage of the factorial design is that it would provide an estimate of the interaction of these two treatment variations with no additional increase in sample size.

The structure of factorial designs when the entire city is used as the experimental unit is similar to the factorial design described above. However, only one treatment is used for each city, in contrast with complete block designs in which all treatments are used within a single city. The main problem when the entire city is used as the experimental unit is again the variation which cities contribute to the experimental error.

The experimental variations for these situations are many and varied. Because the between city variation is likely to be large, it is always desirable that advance estimates of variation be made to indicate the reasonableness of the sample of cities for the decision issues. Again, consideration must be given to the expected magnitude of the Type I and Type II errors as well as the degree of difference expected.

Other Considerations in Design

There are a great variety of experimental designs and estimation procedures, such as covariance analysis and regression methods, which the statistician can draw upon for designing test market experiments. The variations in design and estimation are only limited by our imagination and the cost restraints of the project. In addition, there are a number of other important considerations in test market design which are beyond the scope of this paper, such as length of test, benchmark measurements, related measurements, policing of your own activities, and competition.

External Disturbances to Test Markets

Since the problems of test marketing are not only in design, but also in execution, there is some merit in enumerating some of the things that may obscure the effects to be measured in a test market.

1. The sales force may discover that they have a poor brand showing in one of the cities, and may decide to improve the picture.
2. The test product may go out of stock, and not be replenished in time.
3. A newspaper strike may affect the media program.
4. Your competitor may be in an overstocked position.
5. Price cutting to clear stocks may be the pattern of the day.
6. Your competitor may be out of stock for the test period. This, of course, would exaggerate the success of the audit.

7. Special promotions or deals may be run by your competitor. This may have the effect of obscuring the normal success of the new product or test feature.
8. Competitor changes in price, whether up or down, would have an impact.
9. Unusual climatic conditions or other natural phenomena would obviously interrupt the progress of the test.

The main point of this listing of some of the causes of disruption of a test city audit is that we cannot, and should not, attempt to analyze the data without consideration of all of these unpredictable events. Awareness of these occurrences in a test city program provides the opportunity for evaluating these uncontrollable and extraneous events in a test market experiment.

The simple facts of life are that we never have enough test cities from a statistical point of view. Hence, it is all the more important to recognize factors which could distort the test results.

Test marketing can be a dangerous and misleading tool, but if designed and used intelligently it can provide management with essential guidance which will assure success in the long run.[1]

For Discussion

What is an experimental treatment? How does it differ from a block effect? What is an interaction effect? What is a Latin square design and why is it used?

---

[1] Editor's note: In a section deleted due to space constraints, Dr. Lipstein stressed the importance of using multiple test markets which are representative of significant segments if reliable national market share projections are to be obtained. He also suggested that multiple measurements be built into the test markets to ensure against erroneous interpretation.

18

Factorial Design in a Pricing Experiment

William D. Barclay

Introduction

This article describes an application of factorial design to a pricing experiment conducted at the retail store level. Although factorial design has long been applied in biological and industrial experimentation [2, 3, 4, 6], comparatively few marketing research applications have been reported [1, 5].

The need for the pricing experiment discussed here arose as follows:[1] For one of its product lines, the Quaker Oats Company manufactures three items: A, B, and C. These items comprise a "line" since they fulfill a similar, broad consumer need. They compete with one another and with other brands in the same general category.

Financial analysis of these items revealed a wide discrepancy in profit productivity. Item C was evaluated as adequately profitable, but neither A nor B was so judged. Translated to retail price levels, increases of four cents per package for A and four cents per package for B were desired.

Given this marketing background, the research problem was formulated this way. Assuming that total line profits (of A, B, and C combined) are the suitable criterion:

1. What would be the effect on total line profits of increasing the price of A by four cents per unit at retail?
2. What would be the corresponding effect of increasing the price of B by four cents per unit?
3. Is there interaction between these two factors, i.e., would the effect of increasing one price depend on the level of the other price?

This article describes the experimental design used to answer these questions (a factorial design in randomized blocks) and the analysis. The focus will be on a description of methodology and its rationale. For full computational detail, the reader will be referred to appropriate sources.

[1] The situation has been modified for simplicity and security.

The Experimental Design and Its Execution

Because two factors were of interest here (the consequences of increasing the prices of A and B), the study might have been designed as two separate experiments, each dealing with one factor. This classical, single-factor-at-a-time approach was rejected in favor of a complete factorial design [1, 3, 4, 5, 6] that involved the use of four treatment combinations as shown below.

Treatment Combination	Symbol	Description of Package Prices	
		Price of A	Price of B
1	a_1b_0	Present	Present
2	a_0b_1	Present	Present $+4¢$
3	a_1b_0	Present $+4¢$	Present
4	a_1b_1	Present $+4¢$	Present $+4¢$

Factorial design was adopted principally because we anticipated the possibility of interaction between the two price increases. Detecting interaction would have been impossible with the single factor approach, since factors are not simultaneously varied in that method. If (as later developed) there were no interaction, then factorial design would be more efficient.

Experimental Layout and Its Development. A completely randomized experimental layout would have been inefficient. The Latin Square layout and similar designs, involving changing treatments over time, were eliminated because of administrative difficulty and possible consumer confusion about shifting prices. The randomized block design [1, 2, 3, 4, 5, 6] was chosen because it was more efficient than complete randomization and avoided the problems associated with Latin Square type designs.

For sample size, no directly relevant information about the magnitude of experimental error was available. However, related knowledge indicated that 30 test stores per treatment combination, or 120 in all,

Reprinted from *Journal of Marketing Research*, published by the American Marketing Association, Vol. 6 (November 1969), pp. 427–429. The author acknowledges the advice and participation of James L. Spangenberg, Carolyn Cleath, and H. Maurice Jones, all of Quaker Oats, in the development and conduct of the experiment.

were needed for comparisons among pairs of treatment combinations. The 120 test stores were chosen from among medium to large grocery stores in an area with high distribution on test items.

With 120 stores and randomized blocks of four treatments, there were 30 blocks to be constructed. A three-week sales audit of the stores provided a stratification basis. For each store, Quaker sales and market share were calculated. Stores were listed in order of Quaker sales divided into consecutive groups or eight. Within each group, stores were then ranked by Quaker share. Finally, successive subgroups of four stores were defined as blocks. Within each block, randomization was used to decide which store would receive each treatment combination.

Physical Conduct of the Experiment. Three weeks after pretest audit, experimental price changes were made. Simultaneously, some distribution gaps in test stores were filled so that the experiment was conducted under 100 percent distribution conditions. Prices assigned to products introduced at this time equalled average high or low prices specified by the treatment assigned.

Three monthly sales audits were conducted. Standard procedures were used to maintain Quaker items in stock at correct prices.

Analysis of Data

The key response observation in this experiment was line profits. However, the analysis was conducted in terms of the logarithms of profits rather than the original observations on the following rationale:[2]

1. Since test stores varied widely in size, it was anticipated that treatment effects would more likely be additive on a log scale than on the original scale.
2. For each level of B pricing the sum of the two A price observations in each block was plotted against their difference. For each B price level the plot was approximately linear, suggesting that these observations should be transformed to a log scale for analysis.[3]

Also, the main analysis was in log profits for the combined second and third test months. First month's data was omitted so that consumers could adapt to experimental changes.

Estimates of Factor Effects. The analysis was standard for a 2×2 factorial in randomized blocks [4, 6]. Denoting the treatment combination means (in coded log profit units) by the same symbols used earlier to identify the treatment combinations, the experimental

means were: $a_0b_0 = 3.0128$ units, $a_0b_1 = 3.0255$, $a_1b_0 = 2.9863$, and $a_1b_1 = 2.9441$ units. Factor effects were estimated as follows:

1. Increasing the price of A by four cents was estimated to change profits by:

$$\tfrac{1}{2}(a_1b_0 - a_0b_0) + \tfrac{1}{2}(a_1b_1 - a_0b_1) = -0.0540 \text{ units.}$$

2. Increasing the price of B by four cents was estimated to yield:

$$\tfrac{1}{2}(a_0b_1 - a_0b_0) + \tfrac{1}{2}(a_1b_1 - a_1b_0) = -0.0148 \text{ units.}$$

3. The interaction between the two factors was evaluated to be:

$$\tfrac{1}{2}(a_1b_1 - a_0b_1) - \tfrac{1}{2}(a_1b_0 - a_0b_0) = -0.0274 \text{ units.}$$

Confidence Intervals for Factor Effects. The preceding estimates of factor effects are, of course, subject to sampling fluctuations. From the variance analysis below the experimental error variance was estimated to be $s^2 = 0.030334 = (0.174)^2$ with 87 degrees of freedom.

Source	Degrees of Freedom	Sum of Squares	Mean Square
Blocks	29	3.922590	
Treatments	3	0.116546	
Error	87	2.639099	.030334

Ninety percent confidence intervals were constructed using the formula:

$$\text{Estimated effect} \pm ts/(r)^{\frac{1}{2}}$$

where

$t = 1.66$ is Student's t value for 87 degrees of freedom and 90 percent confidence
$s = 0.174$ units
$r = 30$ blocks.

Since the width of the half-interval was $(1.66)(0.174)/5.477 = 0.0528$ units, the 90 percent confidence intervals were as shown below.

Effect	90% Confidence Interval (Log Units)
Price of A	-0.0012 to -0.1068
Price of B	-0.0676 to $+0.0380$
Interaction	-0.0802 to $+0.0254$

From the standpoint of questions in this experiment, these confidence intervals may be interpreted as follows:

1. Increasing the price of Item A by four cents at retail would (with 90 percent confidence) reduce total line profits. In log units, the loss in profits would range from 0.0012 to 0.1068 units per store. In percentage terms (obtained by taking the antilogarithms of these losses), the profit reduction would be between less than 0.1 percent and about 22 percent. (The magnitude of the probable loss is poorly determined because of high experimental error, but its existence is well established.)

---

[2] See Cox [3, Chapter 2] and Snedecor and Cochran [6, Chapter 11] for further discussion.
[3] See Bliss [2, Chapter 11] for discussion of graphical evaluation of additivity.

2. There was no evidence that increasing the price of *B* would significantly change total profits. Similarly, interaction between the two factors was not statistically established.

Commentary

It is believed that the factorial approach is worth consideration whenever a marketing experiment evaluates two or more factors, each at two or more levels. It would appear especially useful for pricing experiments involving several items in a line, in which the possibility of interaction of effects is usually present.

The experiment was somewhat disappointing because the results were subject to comparatively high experimental error, but this is generally true in marketing experimentation. In any case, the results of the experiment were sufficiently precise to be used for the pricing decisions that were made.[4] It was decided to hold the price of A at the lower level and to

---

[4] To conserve space, only part of the analysis has been reported. Covariance analysis was also used to improve results.

increase the price of B, but by less than the amount tested.

References

1. Seymour Banks, *Experimentation in Marketing*, New York: McGraw-Hill Book Co., 1965.
2. Charles I. Bliss, *Statistics In Biology*, Volume One, New York: McGraw-Hill Book Co., 1967.
3. David R. Cox, *Planning of Experiments*, New York: John Wiley & Sons, Inc., 1958.
4. Owen L. Davies, ed., *The Design and Analysis of Industrial Experiments*, London: Oliver and Boyd, 1956.
5. Paul E. Green and Ronald E. Frank, *A Manager's Guide to Marketing Research: Survey of Recent Developments*, New York: John Wiley & Sons, Inc., 1967.
6. George W. Snedecor and William G. Cochran, *Statistical Methods*, Ames: The Iowa State University Press, 1967.

For Discussion

Interpret the estimates of factor effects. What is a factorial design? How might the design be extended to simultaneously test the effect of three levels of advertising?

19

The Effects of Shelf Space
Upon Sales of Branded Products

Keith K. Cox

One of the scarcest resources in a self-service store is shelf space. In allocating shelf space, many food manufacturers and supermarket retailers employ decision rules which assume a positive relationship between the amount of shelf space given to a product and its sales [5, 13]. The ideal decision rule for shelf space allocations for retailers would consider contribution to profit and opportunity cost concepts. A brand should be given more shelf space if (1) its additional revenue is greater than its additional cost (contribution to profit concept), and (2) there are no other alternative uses of that additional shelf space that will add more profit (opportunity cost concept). The same concepts imply that manufacturers should strive for additional shelf space for their brands if (1) the additional revenue gained is greater than the additional cost to acquire the shelf space, and (2) there are no alternative ways of increasing revenue for their brands that will add more contribution to profit.

A retailer may be considered as a seller of shelf space to various buyers. Cairns shows how this idea can be combined with the appropriate cost concepts [4, p. 34]:

> To induce a retailer to sell him space, a supplier must offer a price for a unit of space which exceeds the "opportunity cost" of this space. This opportunity cost of a unit of retail space is the gross profit the retailer can obtain by allocating this space to the most profitable item not now in his assortment, or to the most profitable combination of items already stocked.

Therefore, it is the marginal revenue and not the average revenue that should be considered in the decision rules for retailers and manufacturers.[1] There is very little published information on measuring the additional revenue an individual brand gains when given additional shelf space.

In the absence of much empirical data, a "battle of the shelf space" occurs frequently between manufacturers and retailers. The manufacturer is interested in maximizing the revenue and profit of his brand, but the retailer is interested in maximizing the revenue and profit of the total product category. Previous research by the author has shown that the retailer's increasing the amount of shelf space for a product category beyond a certain minimal level may be an inefficient method of space allocation [6].

The objective of this article is to measure the relationship between sales of an individual product brand and its shelf space. Therefore, this research is primarily oriented toward a manufacturer with a national brand or a retailer with a private brand who is interested in maximizing sales of his own brand. Three hypotheses were tested in a field experiment.

1. There is no relationship between the amount of shelf space given to a staple product brand and total unit sales of that product brand.

This hypothesis is based on the assumption that consumers buy staple goods primarily by habit. Consequently, the amount of shelf space allocated to a staple brand is a very weak stimulus as long as the brand has some minimum amount of shelf space.[2]

2. There is a relationship between the amount of shelf space given to an impulse product brand that has high consumer

---

[1] Kotler [14] discusses the appropriate decision rules for allocation of marketing effort, pp. 274–6.

[2] Buzzell, *et al.* [3] shows how a minimum level of shelf space should be allocated to any brand. See Exhibit 7, pp. 51–52.

Reprinted from *Journal of Marketing Research*, published by the American Marketing Association, Vol. 7 (February 1970), pp. 55–58. The author expresses his appreciation to Mr. Bernard Weingarten and Mr. Virgil Reynolds, President and Vice President of Weingarten Supermarkets, for their permission to use six supermarkets in the field experiments. Mr. John Burton assisted in the daily audit of the experiments. No part of this article may be reproduced in any form without prior written permission from the publisher.

acceptance and total unit sales of that product brand.[3]
3. There is no relationship between the amount of shelf space given to an impulse product brand that has low consumer acceptance and total unit sales of that product brand.

Merely by classifying a brand as an impulse brand, one which may influence the consumer in a spur-of-the-moment decision, it is a logical assumption that sales of that brand should be influenced by changing amounts of shelf space. However, a product brand with high consumer acceptance may have a lower threshold level in terms of the influence of shelf space than would a product brand with low consumer acceptance.

Because past research has shown that the effect of shelf space upon product sales may be relatively minor, a 25% level of significance was selected in testing the three hypotheses.[4] Although this higher level of significance increases the probability of a Type I error, it decreases the probability of a Type II error. A Type II error would occur if the hypothesis that there was no relationship between the amount of shelf space and product brand sales was accepted when, in reality, there was a relationship between the amount of shelf space and product brand sales.

Research Methodology

The present experiment measured the relationship between the sales of a product brand (i.e., Coffeemate) and shelf space, whereas a previous experiment measured the relationship between the sales of a product category (i.e., all powdered coffee cream) and shelf space [6]. The two product categories chosen for the test were powdered coffee cream and salt, with powdered coffee cream considered an impulse product and salt considered a staple product. Two leading brands were tested in each product category. Morton and Food Club salt brands were selected to test the first hypothesis; Coffeemate powdered coffee cream was selected to test the second hypothesis; and Creamora powdered coffee cream was selected to test the third hypothesis.

Selection of Research Design. Many past field experiments in supermarkets have utilized some type of Latin square design [2, 9, 11, 12]. This is a logical design, since differences among stores and among time periods can be statistically controlled through a randomized process and replication of the test treatments. In the present experiment, the Latin square design was not selected because of its limitation that the number of treatments, stores, and time periods have to be equal.

Table 1
Shelf Treatments for Powdered Coffee Cream and Salt Experiments

Treatment	Powdered Coffee Cream		Salt	
	Coffeemate	Creamora	Morton	Food Club
	Proportion of shelf space			
1	⅓	⅔	⅓	⅔
2	½	½	½	½
3	⅔	⅓	⅔	⅓

Based upon past experimental results, the decision was made not to control for time differences.[5] A randomized blocks design was selected, with the stores treated as the blocks, so that one important type of extraneous variation (differences among stores) could be separated from the experimental error.

Six large supermarkets within the Weingarten food chain in Houston, Texas, were selected as test stores. Each store was assigned all test treatments on a random basis, with each treatment lasting for one week. A shelf inventory of the test products was made each day during the life of the experiment.

Selection of Shelf Treatments. The total shelf space for the two product categories was kept constant throughout the experiment. Different allocations of shelf space were made between the two brands of salt and powdered coffee cream (Table 1). Although most food manufacturers would not normally consider such a wide variation of shelf space alternatives for their brands, the test treatments ranged from a low of one-third to a high of two-thirds of the total shelf space available for the top two brands; these extremes were intended to make the experimental results as powerful as possible.

To obtain the necessary shelf treatments, all test stores had to have some multiple of six in total shelf space for the two brands tested within each product category. For example, if the total shelf space allocation was 24 shelf facings for the two brands, the test treatments for each brand would be 8, 12, and 16 shelf spaces. If a test store actually had 22 spaces before the experiment started, the amount of space for the two brands would be adjusted to 24 spaces for the life of the experiment.

The experiment lasted three weeks in October and November of 1968.

Experimental Model. A fixed effect model for a randomized blocks design was selected for the experiments, where a single observation is given by

$$Y_{ij} = M + T_j + B_i + E_{ij}$$

---

[3] One operational way to classify whether a product brand has high consumer acceptance is by using a share of market criteria.
[4] See Cox and Enis [7, pp. 9–11], Richmond [17, Chapter 10], and Banks [1, pp. 223–5].

[5] See Cox [6], especially Table 2, p. 65.

where

Y_{ij} = the jth observation in the ith block
M = overall mean
T_j = effect of jth treatment
B_i = effect of ith block
E_{ij} = effect of experimental error in the ith block subjected to jth treatment
$i = 1, 2, \ldots, n$
$j = 1, 2, \ldots, t$.

In the randomized blocks design, the following statistical relationships are used:

Total sum of squares = Treatment sum of squares
+ Block sum of squares
+ Residual error sum
of squares

$$\sum_i^n \sum_j^t (Y_{ij} - M)^2 = n \sum_j^t (\bar{Y}_{.j} - M)^2$$
$$+ t \sum_i^n (\bar{Y}_{i.} - M)^2 + \sum_i^n \sum_j^t (Y_{ij} - \bar{Y}_{.j} - \bar{Y}_{i.} + M)^2$$

where

$\bar{Y}_{.j}$ = treatment mean
$\bar{Y}_{i.}$ = block mean
t = number of treatments
n = number of replications.

Each sum of squares is divided by the appropriate degrees of freedom to obtain the mean square. The F-ratio formula is

$$F = \frac{\text{Treatment mean square}}{\text{Residual error mean square}}$$

Using a 25% level of significance with 2 and 10 degrees of freedom, the null hypothesis should be rejected when the F-ratio is greater than 1.60.

Test Results

The test results of the supermarket experiments are shown in Tables 2 and 3. Table 2 summarizes the total unit sales of each product brand for each shelf space treatment in the experiment. Table 3 gives the

Table 2
Total Unit Sales of Product Brands
in Six Supermarkets over Three Weeks

Brands	Shelf Space		
	$\frac{1}{3}$	$\frac{1}{2}$	$\frac{2}{3}$
Coffeemate	366	409	442
Creamora	155	158	146
Morton salt	672	639	675
Food Club salt	249	286	283

degrees of freedom, mean squares, and F-ratio for all four product brands tested. The following are the results.

Hypothesis 1 was accepted. There was no relationship between the amount of shelf space given to Morton and Food Club salt and total unit sales of the two product brands.

Hypothesis 2 was accepted. There was a relationship between the amount of shelf space given to Coffeemate and its total unit sales. The F-ratio was 3.49 greater than required for the 25% level of significance.

Hypothesis 3 was accepted. There was no relationship between the amount of shelf space given to Creamora and total unit sales of Creamora.

The F-ratio for differences in product sales among stores was significant at the 1% level for all four brands. These results point out how difficult it is to execute a quasi-experimental design, where a group of equivalent control stores and test stores are used in the experiment.

Analysis and Implications of Results

Using the contribution to profit and opportunity cost concepts, what decisions might be implied to retailers and manufacturers from the research results? For staple products and impulse brands with low consumer acceptance, the additional marginal revenue gained from additional space was insignificant. Given this information retailers should limit their shelf allo-

Table 3
Mean Squares and F-Ratios for Four Brands Tested

Source	Degrees of Freedom	Coffeemate		Creamora		Morton		Food Club	
		Mean Square	F-Ratio	Mean Square	F-Ratio	Mean Square	F-Ratio	Mean Square	F-Ratio
Blocks (stores)	5	1,644.8	23.70*	400.0	7.94*	5,817.2	16.29*	912.8	9.78*
Treatments (shelf spaces)	2	242.0	3.49†	6.5	.13	66.5	.19	70.5	.76
Residual error	10	69.4		50.4		357.1		93.3	
Total	17								

*Significant at .01 level.
†Significant at .10 level.

cations for these brands to some minimal level; such a level for any brand should be influenced by such constraints as out-of-stock conditions and the ability to stock a full case at one time.

Suppose that Morton salt sold twice as much as Food Club salt, and that the minimal level for any brand of salt was six shelf spaces. One decision rule would be to give the Morton brand twice as much shelf space as the Food Club brand, since it sold twice as much. If there were eighteen spaces allocated to salt, Morton salt would be allocated twelve spaces and Food Club salt would get six spaces. The Dillon study suggests the use of this decision rule for allocating shelf space to products based upon past sales history [8].

Using the contribution to profit and opportunity cost concepts, an alternative decision rule would be for the retailer to give both Morton and Food Club brands the minimum six shelf spaces, and stock the Morton brand twice as often. The extra six spaces would then be available for new products or other alternatives (opportunity cost) which would contribute more profit to the retailer.

For many manufacturers, the additional revenue generated by extra shelf spaces for a brand may not compensate for the cost of obtaining the shelf space. In terms of opportunity cost, the brand salesman may need to spend more time keeping his brand in stock and seeing that the retailer carries his full product line rather than spending his time obtaining more shelf space beyond a minimal level.

Conclusions

There are a number of limitations to the present experiment. First, sale of many other brands may respond differently to changes in shelf space than the brands tested in this experiment. Also, this experiment was conducted in six stores of one supermarket chain in only one city. Still, the results imply that many of the existing decision rules in use by manufacturers and retailers in allocating shelf space may need to be reevaluated.

References

1. Seymour Banks, *Experimentation in Marketing*, New York: McGraw-Hill, 1965.
2. D. G. Burgoyne and C. B. Johnston, "Are Shelf Space and Shelf Location Really Important?" *The Business Quarterly*, (Summer 1968), 56–60.
3. Robert D. Buzzell, Walter J. Salmon, and Richard F. Vancil, *Product Profitability Measurement and Merchandising Decisions*, Boston: Harvard University, 1965.
4. James P. Cairns, "Suppliers, Retailers, and Shelf Space," *Journal of Marketing*, (July 1962), 34–6.
5. *COSMOS*, National Association of Food Chains, 1968.
6. Keith Cox, "The Responsiveness of Food Sales to Supermarket Shelf Space Changes," *Journal of Marketing Research*, (May 1964), 63–7.
7. _____ and Ben M. Enis, *Experimentation for Marketing Decisions*, Scranton, Pa.: International Textbook, 1969.
8. *The Dillon Study*, Progressive Grocer, New York: The Butterick Co., 1960.
9. Bennett Dominick, Jr., *An Illustration of the Use of the Latin Square in Measuring the Effectiveness of Retail Merchandising Practices*, Methods of Research in Marketing, Paper No. 2, Cornell University, June 1952.
10. James F. Engel, David T. Kollat, and Roger D. Blackwell, *Consumer Behavior*, New York: Holt, Rinehart and Winston, 1968, Chapters 21 and 22.
11. Peter Henderson, James Hind, and Sidney Brown, "Sales Effects of Two Campaign Themes," *Journal of Advertising Research*, (March 1961), 15–22.
12. William S. Hoofnagle, "Experimental Designs in Measuring the Effectiveness of Promotion," *Journal of Marketing Research*, (May 1965), 154–62.
13. "How to Allocate Shelf Space and Maintain Inventory Controls," *Food Topics*, May 1961.
14. Philip Kotler, *Marketing Management*, Englewood Cliffs, New Jersey: Prentice Hall, 1967.
15. Wayne Lee, "Space Management in Retail Stores and Implications to Agriculture," in Wenzil K. Colva, ed., *Marketing — Key to Profits in the 1960's*, American Marketing Association, 1960, 523–33.
18. *McKinsey — General Foods Study*, General Foods Corporation, October 1963.
17. Samuel B. Richmond, *Statistical Analysis*, (2nd ed.), New York: Ronald Press, 1964.
18. U.S. Department of Agriculture, *Better Utilization of Selling Space in Food Stores*, Marketing Research Report No. 30, November 1952.

For Discussion

What is a randomized block design? What is the block effect in this experiment? Interpret the footnotes in Table 3.

20

New Uses of Covariance Analysis

Lionel C. Barrow, Jr.

Research is frequently conducted to determine which of several possible treatments (such as several themes, packages, products, commercials, advertising expenditure levels, and ad campaigns) produces the best score on some key criterion. These criteria may be brand awareness, beliefs about the product, interest in buying it, sales, etc.

Researchers know that the treatments to be manipulated are not the only phenomena that can affect these criteria. For example, a person's past experience with a brand or service will probably have as pronounced an effect upon awareness and beliefs, and upon intent to use or buy the product, as seeing one or more commercials. Therefore, a researcher typically tries to design the studies to control for the effects of these other factors or covariates. Having done so to the best of his ability, the researcher then proceeds to apply his different treatments and infers that the differences he observes in, for example, interest in buying the test product, are due to the differences in the treatments administered rather than to any inherent differences in the kinds of people who received a particular treatment.

The usual way of trying to make "other things equal" is to assign respondents randomly to each treatment. However, it is just as unreasonable to expect random assignment to yield a perfect match as it is to expect exactly 50 heads and 50 tails in every 100 tosses of an unbiased coin. Just as the actual values obtained from such an experiment will vary by chance from the theoretical 50–50 value, so the actual values of the key covariates will vary by chance in an advertising experiment. With small samples, this random fluctuation can be quite large. Thus, for example, there are five chances in 100 that they will vary from six to 11 percentage points if the samples contain 150 respondents, and from eight to 14 percentage points if the samples contain only 100 respondents.

Attempts are therefore made to improve on the basic assignment procedures by making sure that an equal number of respondents with key characteristics receive each treatment.

But often sampling does not do the job. Randomly dropping or replicating a few respondents to equalize the distribution for one key variable quite often creates disproportionality in other variables.

What, then, can be done when sampling fails, when our treatment groups—whatever they are—are not comparable, are not matched on one or more key variables?

At Foote, Cone & Belding, we have been using analysis of covariance to match treatment groups as part of the normal computerized tabulation and analysis procedures in studies requiring matched groups.

Green and Tull (1966) present an excellent discussion of the rationale for using covariance analysis and of the mathematics involved. This present article summarizes some of FC&B's experiences with the procedure (which we recommend highly) and, in addition, presents some of the situations not covered by Green and Tull in which the procedure should not be used. Cochran (1957) and Smith (1957) both credit the noted British statistician, R. A. Fisher, with being the first to introduce analysis of covariance in 1934. Cochran quotes Fisher as saying that the procedure "combines the advantages and reconciles the requirements of two very widely applicable procedures known as regression and analysis of variance."

The technique equates samples for the effects of as many key variables (such as previous usage of a brand) as we are able to identify and measure. It therefore enables us to say with confidence that a given treatment is or is not better than another treatment because we have, to the best of our ability, made "all other things equal" by controlling for the influence of those extraneous variables.

The extent to which statistical controls are exercised depends upon two factors:

1. The *size* of the relationship between the matching variable (or covariate) and the dependent variable (as determined by a regression coefficient).
2. The extent to which a given group average differs on the covariate from the average for the entire sample.

Thus, let:

$\bar{Y}_a$ and $\bar{Y}_b$ = the *unadjusted* scores by each of two groups (Group A and Group B) on the dependent variable

$\bar{Y}_a'$ and $\bar{Y}_b'$ = the *adjusted* scores for the same groups on the same variable

$\bar{X}_a$ and $\bar{X}_b$ = the scores obtained by each group on the covariate

$\bar{X}$ = the scores obtained by the entire sample on the covariate

b_{xy} = the regression coefficient indicating the size of the relationship.

Then, a simplified formula for the adjustment would be:

$$\bar{Y}_a' = \bar{Y}_a - b_{xy}(\bar{X}_a - \bar{X})$$
$$\bar{Y}_b' = \bar{Y}_b - b_{xy}(\bar{X}_b - \bar{X}).$$

Covariance may also be used to reduce sampling or experimental error thereby enabling an experimenter to discover significant differences that might otherwise have been missed.

The reduction in the estimate of sampling or experimental error is affected only by the extent to which the covariate is correlated with the dependent variable.

As Winer (1962) points out, "if this correlation is equal to p, and the experimental error per unit, disregarding the covariate, is σ_y^2, then the experimental error after the adjustment is:

$$\sigma_y^2(1 - p^2)\left[1 + \frac{1}{f_e - 2}\right]$$

where f_e represents the degrees of freedom for the estimation of σ_y^2."

Use of Covariance to Correct Mismatched Samples

Table 1 presents the results of analysis of covariance adjustments on the first eight FC&B copy research studies in which the procedure was used.

These scores represent the expression of interest in buying the test product, using the seven-point scale below.

Scale Position	Index Score	Code for Machine Analysis
Definitely will buy	100	6
Almost definitely will buy	83	5
Probably will buy	67	4
Not sure will buy or not	50	3
Probably will not buy	33	2
Almost definitely will not buy	17	1
Definitely will not buy	00	0

As Table 1 indicates, on the average the adjustments were minor (less than one index point). This is probably because the copy research sampling procedures (random selection of sampling points; interviewing at every nth household; rotating the order in which respondents are assigned to a test or control group; and obtaining an equal number of interviews in each sampling cluster for each test and control group) were designed to achieve as close a match as is possible "in the field."

Thus, in most instances, the adjustments did not lead to a change in our conclusions. However, this was

Table 1

Effect of Covariance Adjustment on Purchase Intent Scores

Study Number	Purchase Intent Index Scores		
	Unadjusted	Adjusted	Difference
I			
Test Group	43	39	−4
Control Group	18	22	+4
II			
Test Group A	30	30	—
Test Group B	36	35	−1
III			
Test Group A	70	70	—
Test Group B	65	65	—
IV			
Test Group A	80	81	+1
Test Group B	80	80	—
Test Group C	79	79	—
Test Group D	81	81	—
V			
Test Group A	76	76	—
Control Group	69	69	—
VI			
Test Group A	64	63	−1
Test Group B	57	57	—
Control Group	51	52	+1
VII			
Test Group A	73	72	−1
Test Group B	70	69	−1
Control Group	65	67	+2
VIII			
Test Group A	52	51	−1
Control Group	41	42	+1
Average change*			.9*

* Computed without regard to the plus or minus sign.

not always the case. For example, the data for Study VII were taken from a copy research test of two commercials. In this study two groups of 150 housewives were interviewed to obtain their interest in buying the product and their beliefs about the product after seeing a commercial. The same data were obtained from a third (control) group of housewives who did not see a test commercial. The interviews were conducted in the home in four cities (New York, Chicago, St. Louis, and Los Angeles). Each test group respondent saw one and only one of the test commercials on an 8 mm. rear-screen projector along with a short entertainment film.

The key covariate was the response to the five-point brand usage scale below which bore a high relationship (beta weight = .926 for the coded scores) to purchase intent.

Scale Position	Index Score	Code for Machine Analysis
Always	100	4
Often	75	3
Sometimes	50	2
Seldom	25	1
Never	00	0

The unadjusted purchase intent data indicated that both commercials significantly increased interest in buying the test product. If no adjustments had been made we would have concluded that both commercials were good enough to run, on the strength of the following data:

Commercial	Unadjusted Purchase Intent Differences between Test and Control Groups
"A"	+8*
"B"	+5*

* Significant at .05 level

However, the control group contained fewer users of the test product than did either of the test groups and, as a result, had a lower brand usage score. When covariance adjustments were made for this and other differences, the control group score went up and the score for test group "B" went down. The adjusted difference was an insignificant two index points. The adjusted difference of +5 index points between Commercial "A" and the Control, while smaller than the unadjusted difference, was still large enough to be significant. Thus, the adjustments resulted in a change in our conclusions. "A" was deemed good enough to run but "B" was not.

The correctness of these adjustments was partially confirmed by an FC&B validation study. These respondents were reinterviewed six weeks later to ascertain what products and brands they had purchased since the original interview. Commercial "A" produced a significant increase in reported purchasing of the test brand while Commercial "B" did not. More Commercial "A" respondents than control group respondents reported buying the test brand. (The difference was 12 percentage points.) The Commercial "B" difference over the control group, on the other hand, was an insignificant two percentage points.

Failure to match samples can also lead to picking the wrong winner. McNemar (1955) gives such an example. He reports a study in which the unadjusted means were:

Test Treatment	Unadjusted Score
1	7.30
2	5.60
3	4.40

From the above data it would appear that Treatment I was the clear winner. However, the group that received Treatment 1 also had a higher score on a covariate which bore a close relationship to the criterion (beta weight = .687). When the criterion scores were adjusted for the difference on the covariate, the adjusted means became:

Treatment	Adjusted Score
1	5.95
2	4.86
3	6.48

In other words, Treatment 3 was the better treatment, *not* Treatment 1. Treatment 1's score was spuriously inflated by the covariate, and its apparent superiority disappeared as soon as an adjustment was made for the difference on the covariate.

Covariate analysis can thus prevent a researcher from making erroneous judgments about findings from supposedly matched samples. It can also give him more confidence in the judgments that he does make.

Improving the Chances of Finding Significant Differences

The term "precision" is used in research to refer to the preciseness or accuracy with which one measures some variable (such as interest in buying the product, beliefs about the product, etc.). Since in advertising research we are dealing with data gathered from samples (rather than with data gathered from everyone in the population) some of the variation observed is due to sampling error. That is, the proportions saying that they are "willing to buy Product X" may not be exactly the same in any two samples of housewives. Thus, there is a certain amount of sampling "error" in any of our estimates of the effects of any of the advertising treatments being assessed.

As Green and Tull (1966) point out, covariance procedures can be used to reduce experimental error, and thereby increase the preciseness of one's measurements. In fact, in the eight FC&B research studies previously mentioned, covariance procedures have resulted in an error reduction of from five per cent to 63 per cent for the key measure (purchase intent), with the average reduction being 33 per cent.

The covariates responsible for this have for the most part been those related to a respondent's previous experience with and/or awareness of the test brand. Demographic characteristics have not played an important role to date in reducing error in FC&B research studies.

Obviously there are other ways of attempting to obtain the same end. One could (for example) reduce sampling error by:

1. Stratifying the sample beforehand on the key covariates into meaningful subgroups and randomly assigning members of each subgroup to the test and control conditions.
2. Increasing sampling size.

The first procedure complicates matters for an already overburdened interviewer and may not be feasible, especially if one wishes to match on several variables at the same time.

The second procedure is feasible but quite costly. Snedecor (1956) offers a method of estimating the difference in cost afforded by a change in experimental procedure. He computes an efficiency index by reversing the procedures used in Table 2 and dividing the unadjusted error mean square by the adjusted. In an example he uses, the unadjusted mean square = 0.0270 while the adjusted mean squares = 0.0214. The ratio between the two equaled 126 per cent.

Snedecor concludes that without covariance, 26 per cent more sampling units (pigs in his example) "would have been required to achieve the same precision."

Following the same logic, the efficiency index for covariance ranged from 106 per cent to 273 per cent, and averaged 164 per cent.

To accomplish a similar reduction in error by increasing sampling size would have required an average increase of 64 per cent or 90 additional interviews per group. Depending on the incidence of eligible respondents, FC&B pays, on the average, from $9 to $12 an interview for the field work on a copy research job. Since usually one control and at least one test group is included in every job, the extra cost for the typical job could range from $1728 to $2304. Covariance analysis seldom costs more than $200. The cost advantage of the procedure is, therefore, considerable.

Limitations

Covariance analysis may be used:

1. When one wants to make sure the different samples are matched on key covariates.
2. When one wishes to reduce error variance and thereby increase one's chances of finding significant differences.

However, the blind use of the procedure will not guarantee that either of the above goals will be reached.

It should be obvious that covariance analysis is usable only if the covariates can be measured. When the covariates cannot be measured, the only way to increase the precision of your study is to increase sample size.

It should be equally obvious that covariance analysis may lead to improper results if, as Green and Tull point out, the basic assumptions of the procedures are not met. Covariance procedures assume that the relationship between the covariate and the criterion is the same for all samples in the study.

Although Atiqullah (1964) indicates that violating this assumption "does not seem to have serious effect" when large samples are used, it is our recommendation that problems of this sort be handled wherever possible by including the covariate as a secondary factor.

Covariance analysis also assumes that the relationships between the covariates and the dependent variable are linear. Thus, an inspection of the crosstabs prior to doing the covariance analysis might indicate that some transformation of the data will increase the extent of the relationship and thereby increase the usefulness of the covariance analysis.

However, there are two less obvious circumstances in which covariance analysis should definitely

Table 2
Effect of Covariance Adjustments on Experimental Error

Study Number	Error Mean Square		Per Cent Reduced*	Covariance Efficiency†
	Unadjusted	Adjusted		
I	3.3100	2.0143	61%	164%
II	3.2116	2.3079	22	139
III	2.3024	1.9141	17	120
IV	1.4886	1.4072	5	106
V	3.7347	1.8189	51	205
VI	3.3723	1.7592	48	192
VII	3.7527	1.3729	63	273
VIII	2.7760	2.5251	9	110
Average			33%	164%

*Adjusted/Unadjusted.
†Unadjusted/Adjusted.

not be used which were not discussed by Green and Tull. H. Fairchild Smith (1957) points out these two problem areas:

1. When the potential covariates are themselves affected by the experimental manipulation.
2. When the variation in the covariate is imposed along with the experimental manipulation.

With reference to the first problem area, in FC&B's copy research studies, brand usage or brand awareness data gathered before exposure to a test commercial are prime candidates for use as covariates. Experience has shown that they are related to the basic copy research criteria (purchase intent and beliefs about the product), and they cannot be affected by the experimental manipulation (showing or not showing a given commercial) since they are gathered before the manipulation takes place.

However, it would not be appropriate to use these as covariates in a study of the effect of an advertising campaign (measured at several points in time). The campaign may not only be affecting purchase intent, it may also be affecting brand usage and awareness.

Smith (1957) says that under these conditions, covariance analysis is not only meaningless but might be misleading.

He says:

When treatments induce simultaneous variation in all characters to estimate their effects on one while "holding another constant" is artificially fictitious. To my mind such estimates are anything but illuminating. The commonly occurring phase "corrected means," with its implication that more correct comparisons are thereby made, is misleading; "fictitious means" might be less deceptive. In absence of experimental control to demonstrate what in fact would happen if a given character were "held constant," one can seldom demonstrate that actually false conclusions are reached, but treatment means "adjusted" by error regressions seem to yield no information which cannot be gleaned from simpler statistics unconfused by distortions whose interpretation is dubious.

Smith also discusses the other instance in which covariance analysis is neither proper nor useful. This occurs if the covariate is imposed with the treatment. For example, in a study of advertising weights one might establish:

1. A "normal" weight spot schedule (i.e., where the schedule is one that would normally be purchased for this client).
2. A spot schedule that varies from the normal such as a "double" weight schedule.

The usual method for establishing a "double" weight schedule would be to try to buy twice as many "impressions" as purchased for the "normal" sched-

ule. However, it probably will not be possible to do this on the same programs with the same adjacencies. An attempt would then be made to buy comparable programs and/or time periods but ultimately one may wind up buying the additional impressions wherever one can—even if it means buying in fringe time or on fringe stations that ordinarily would not be considered for the client's schedule.

Thus, the advertising weight study may involve not only a test of different potential impressions, but it may also involve a test of different types of schedules.

At first glance it would seem that analysis of covariance could be used—if desired—to "control" for the last unintended variation. Not so, says Smith:

If one wants to use an observed regression to allow for an ancillary environmental effect which cannot conveniently be randomized with treatments and may vary systematically from one treatment to another, the only safe procedure is to arrange for it to be deliberately varied. . . . The ideal arrangement, if an ancillary factor may seriously affect results, is to factorize it with treatments even if its levels may not be precisely controlled.

In spite of the problems discussed above, there are a sufficiently large number of cases where covariance analysis is both proper and useful. It is, therefore, recommended highly to researchers faced with the twin problems of matching samples and reducing experimental error.

References

1. Atiqullah, M. The Robustness of the Covariance Analysis of a One-Way Classification. *Biometrika,* Vol. 51, Nos. 3 and 4, 1964, pp. 365–372.
2. Cochran, Willam F. Analysis of Covariance: Its Nature and Use. *Biometrics,* Vol. 13, September 1957, pp. 261–281.
3. Green, Paul E. and Donald S. Tull. Covariance Analysis in Marketing Experimentation. *Journal of Advertising Research,* Vol. 6, No. 2, June 1966, pp. 45–53.
4. McNemar, Quinn. *Psychological Statistics.* 2nd Edition, New York: John Wiley, 1955.
5. Smith, H. Fairfield. Interpretation of Adjusted Treatment Means and Regressions in Analysis of Covariance. *Biometrics,* Vol. 13, September 1957, pp. 281–308.
6. Snedecor, George W. *Statistical Methods.* 5th Edition, Ames, Iowa: The Iowa State College Press, 1956.
7. Winer, B. J. *Statistical Principles in Experimental Design.* New York: McGraw-Hill, 1962.

For Discussion

A factor can be controlled by adding a block effect or by the analysis of covariance. Explain the difference. When would one approach be preferred over the other? Interpret Table 2.

The Analysis of Dependence

Section F
DISCRIMINANT ANALYSIS

21

Discriminant Analysis of Audience Characteristics

William F. Massy

How similar are the audiences of two or more advertising vehicles? While most would agree, for example, that *Life* and *Look* readers are more nearly alike than those of *Life* and *New Yorker*, methods for quantifying these differences are rather unwieldy. The usual procedure is to collect data for each audience group on several interesting variables, compute the means of the variables, and then compare them among the audience groups. Thus, it might be found that "*Life* readers show more preference for Brand X than do those of *New Yorker*," or "*Life* readers tend to be drawn from the Y socioeconomic class, whereas *New Yorker* readers tend to be in the Z class."

While statements like these are very useful for sorting out gross differences in audience characteristics, they do not readily combine into a compact index of overall audience similarity. It is difficult to look at two columns of means and decide how different, on balance, they really are. The problem becomes much more complicated when comparing three or more audiences.

The method of *N*-way multiple discriminant analysis discussed in this paper can provide a set of aggregate similarity indices for a given number of audiences. Basically, the procedure attempts to "predict" which audience group an individual belongs to, based on the sets of group means discussed above, together with the set of sample variances and co-variances of the variables. That is, the individual is assigned to the audience group whose characteristics are most like his own. Since it is known beforehand which group the person actually belongs to, we can prepare a table of correct and incorrect classifications. This "score sheet" of correct and incorrect classifications, or *confusion matrix*, then provides the basis for the desired similarity indices. That is, the fewer the misclassifications of individuals to audience groups, the more distinct or dissimilar the audience groups.

This paper describes an application of the confusion matrix method in measuring the similarity of audiences for five Boston FM radio stations. But first let us examine the statistical underpinnings of *N*-way multiple discriminant analysis, starting with two-way analysis.

Two-Way Discriminant Analysis

Two-way discriminant analysis, which deals with an arbitrary number of variables but only two populations, is becoming more common in marketing (see, for example, Banks, 1958; Evans, 1959; and Frank and Massy, 1963). The first step in this form of analysis is to estimate the coefficients in a linear discriminant function. Here is an example of this type of function, in terms of two hypothetical variables, *X* and *Y*.

$$f_i = c_X X_i + c_Y Y_i.$$

The subscript *i* runs over the individuals included in the analysis.

Reprinted from the *Journal of Advertising Research*. Copyrighted 1965 by the Advertising Research Foundation. This study was supported, in part, by funds made available by the Ford Foundation to the Graduate School of Business, Stanford University. Conclusions, opinions, and other statements are those of the author and do not necessarily represent those of the Ford Foundation. Computations were subsidized by and performed at the Western Data Processing Center, University of California at Los Angeles.

The author also expresses his appreciation to Herbert Taylor, who collected the data upon which this study is based in the Spring of 1962, as part of the requirements for the degree of Master of Science in Industrial Management at the Massachusetts Institute of Technology, and to Professor Thomas Lodahl of the Graduate School of Business and Public Administration, Cornell University, for making the information available. The data also are discussed in a previous paper by the author (Massy, 1963). No part of this article may be reproduced in any form without prior written permission from the publisher.

Figure 1
Discrimination of Two Hypothetical Populations on Two Variables

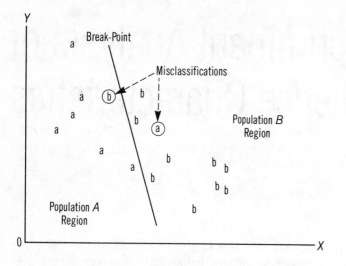

Figure 2
Probability That an Observation Will Fall in Population A or B

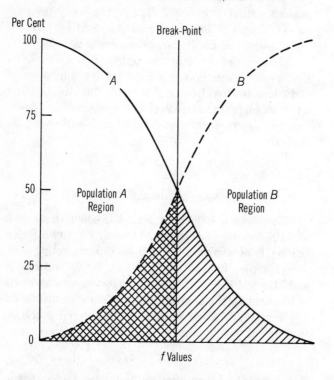

A critical value of f is determined such that if an individual's f value is above the break-point he is classified in one group and if it is below he is assigned to the other. Hence the name "discriminant analysis": the function f is defined so that it discriminates between members of the two groups in the most efficient fashion.

Let us assume we have measurements on two variables for a sample of 18 drawn equally from two populations, A and B. Figure 1 presents the hypothetical scatter diagram for this sample. Now imagine

that we draw a nineteenth observation, but do not know whether it belongs to A or B. The problem is to assign the new observation to either A or B in a way that minimizes the probability of misclassification.

In this case we would base our estimate of the coefficients (the c's) of the discriminant function on the information provided by the original 18 observations. Having values for the c's allows us to assign a value of f to any possible combination of X and Y, whether from our original sample or a new sample. Next, we use mathematical methods to estimate the probability that, given a particular value of f, the observation would fall in A. This probability distribution for A might look like the one given by the solid curve in Figure 2, which also presents a similar distribution for B, shown by a dotted curve.

Further, Figure 2 contains a vertical line which represents the discriminant or break-point value of f. The break-point is set half way between the means of f for A and B, so at this point an observation has about an equal probability of falling in A or B. The shaded areas on either side of the break-point give the total probability of misclassifying a particular observation.

The logic of two-way discriminant analysis is presented in greater detail in Frank, Kuehn, and Massy (1962), along with computing formulas. More detailed treatments can be found in the references cited in connection with N-way analysis.

N-Way Analysis. Consider three populations of individuals (A, B, and C), describable in terms of two variables (X and Y). The populations might refer to audiences of three advertising media and the variables to audience attributes, such as family size and income. Figure 3 shows a hypothetical scatter diagram for the attribute values of individuals in each of the three populations.

The discriminant problem here is to define three mutually exclusive regions (a, b, and c) which exhaust the X-Y space. The region boundaries should be set up such that when the X and Y values put an individual into a given region, it is more probable that he actually is a member of that population than of any other population. The problem is soluble provided that the variables are approximately normally distributed in each population, their respective variance-covariance matrices are about equal, and that the a priori probability for membership in each (i.e., the relative incidence of the groups in the overall population) is known. (These conditions also are required for the two-way case.)

In Figure 3, the lines separating the three regions represent loci of equal probability for their respective pairs of regions. To report that a given observation lies to one side of the threshold line is to say that the probability that the observation belongs in this region is greater than for any other region. Obviously, this

Figure 3
Acceptance Regions for Three Hypothetical Populations on Two Variables

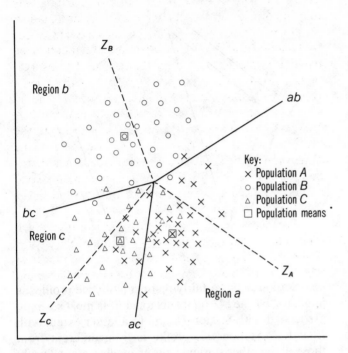

Key:
× Population A
○ Population B
△ Population C
□ Population means

Table 1
Predicted and Actual Population
Membership of Hypothetical Example

Actual	Predicted A	B	C	Total
A	20	1	6	27
B	1	25	1	27
C	7	1	19	27

for the example. The figures along the diagonal tell us that the number of correct predictions for B is greater than for either A or C. The off-diagonals indicate that a member of A is most likely to be misclassified as a C, and a member of C to be wrongly associated with A. Hence it makes sense to conclude that populations A and C are more nearly alike than are A and B, or B and C. Figure 3 corroborates this view, since the distance between the two swarms of points for the A-C pair is less than that between the points for either the B-C or B-A pair.

While the same conclusion could have been obtained by examining the six t ratios for the differences between the means of pairs of groups, this would greatly strain the analyst's ability to compare many numbers at once, even in this rather simple example. Another technique for measuring similarity, the Mahalanobis D^2 statistic (see Rao, 1952), is not as easy to understand and is not as closely related to the predictive efficacy of the discriminant analysis as the method of confusion matrices.

"maximum probability criterion" does not preclude mistakes in classification. Six population A individuals are erroneously put in group C and one in group B. On the other hand, if the classification process were repeated many times with similar samples of individuals, this procedure would result in the lowest possible proportion of errors.

How are the regions determined? As in the two-way case, the sample data are used to estimate the parameters of linear discriminant functions for the populations. These are denoted by the three broken half lines (Z_A, Z_B, and Z_C) in Figure 3. (Note: for the sake of simplicity, the discriminant function was not drawn in Figure 1; if it had been, it would be shown perpendicular to the break-point line.) Once the parameters of these functions have been estimated, the boundaries are set so that each discriminant line (Z) bisects the angle between its respective boundary lines: thus Z_A bisects the angle between ab and ac. (This is equivalent to taking half the distance between the discriminant means in the two-way case.) The analyst proceeds by first estimating the three sets of discriminant coefficients and then setting up boundaries for the acceptance regions on the basis of his initial results. While the means of the variables fall within the acceptance regions for their respective populations (this is a necessary condition), they do not have to lie on the discriminant lines.

Figure 3 also provides insight into using confusion matrices to evaluate the similarity of populations. Table 1 shows the correct and incorrect classifications

An Application

Similarity of FM Station Audiences. Confusion matrices were used to evaluate the similarities among the audiences of five FM radio stations located in the Boston Metropolitan Area. The data for the study were collected by Herbert Taylor (1962) from a sample of families who owned at least one FM radio receiver. A mail questionnaire was used to obtain information on current station selections and some 47 socio-economic and consumption variables. Respondents were given a series of scales simulating the markings on a typical FM dial, and asked to note the position of the dial(s) on each FM receiver in the home, as of the time the questionnaire was filled out.

The sample consisted of returned questionnaires from about 380 families; 280 had sent in for Station A's program guide and the rest were selected at random. The results given here are based on the 239 families for whom the station tuned to at response time could be unambiguously determined. Since the sample probably contains substantial biases, which may lead to false impressions about audience characteristics, station call letters have been withheld.

Table 2
Confusion Matrix for 12 Variates,
Assuming Equal Probabilities

Actual	Predicted Audience Membership					
Audience	A	B	C	D	E	Total
A	43	13	8	21	14	99
B	16	15	15	13	13	72
C	3	5	14	5	4	31
D	2	3	5	9	4	23
E	2	1	0	4	7	14

Total Hits = 88; Per Cent Hits = 36.8%; $\chi^2(48) = 72.4$

The first step in the analysis was to reduce the number of potential explanatory variables from 47 to some more manageable number. Factor analysis was used to obtain 12 new variates that could serve as summaries of the original set. (The definitions of the factor score variables are presented below in Table 4.) The factor loadings matrix upon which they are based is the same as that reported by Massy (1963).

The 12 summary variates were subjected to a five-way multiple discriminant analysis to predict which types of respondents listen to what radio station.

Table 2 gives the confusion matrix for the 12-variate five-way discriminant run for the sample of 239 families, under the assumption that a priori probabilities are equal for membership in any of the five audiences. Entries on the main diagonal of the matrix denote correct classifications or hits, while the off-diagonal elements represent misses. The percentage of hits is 36.8 per cent. A χ^2 test based on the Mahalanobis D^2 statistic found the differences between the means among the five groups to be significant at the .025 critical level. Thus we may conclude that at least one pair of station audiences are different on at least one of our 12 variables.

We are better able to draw conclusions from the confusion matrix if we normalize the raw misclassification counts by dividing each by its row total. The new entries, presented in Table 3, represent the probabilities that an individual who is actually in a given station's audience will be so classified. Table 3 indicates that some combinations of stations are much more alike than others, as far as we can tell.

Table 3
Normalized Confusion Matrix for 12 Variates,
Assuming Equal Probabilities

Actual	Predicted Audience Membership					
Audience	A	B	C	D	E	Total
A	.43	.13	.08	.21	.14	1.00
B	.22	.21	.21	.18	.18	1.00
C	.10	.16	.45	.16	.13	1.00
D	.08	.13	.22	.39	.17	1.00
E	.14	.07	.00	.29	.50	1.00

Figure 4
Association Diagram for 12 Variables (Arrow Indicates Direction of Misses)

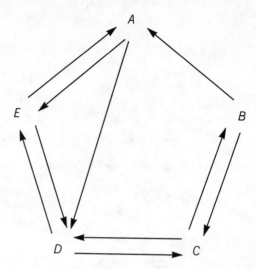

Station A has a fairly distinct audience profile, as indicated by the .43 on its diagonal; it is most strongly associated with Station D, and to a lesser extent with E and B. Station B's profile is little different from those of the other stations; it is somewhat more closely associated with A and C.

Station C has a strongly differentiated profile; its diagonal of .45 is almost three times as large as any of the misclassifications. C is weakly associated with B and D.

Station D has a fairly distinct profile, and is most nearly like Station C, followed by E. The Station E profile appears to be quite distinct, but the small sample size for E makes conclusions difficult.

It would be interesting to know whether the relationships given above are reciprocal. That is, if members of one group tend to be misclassified in a second group, are members of the second group in turn likely to be misassigned to the first group? In Figure 4 the arrows indicate the direction of misclassification for the two largest off-diagonal entries in each row of Table 3. The figure shows that, except for Station A, all relationships are reciprocal. Station A listeners tend to be disproportionately associated with Station D rather than B, even though B's listeners are more likely than D's to be associated (i.e., misclassified) with A.

Table 4 presents the coefficients of the 12 variables for the five discriminant functions. Each coefficient represents the effect of the variable on the probability of classification in the group corresponding to the particular discriminant function. As such, the coefficients are more sensitive measures of audience characteristics than a similar table of the means of the variables. Moreover, the discriminant coefficients take into account correlations among variables. For example, since older people obviously have fewer children living at

Table 4
Multiple Discriminant Coefficients for Five Stations and 12 Variates

Variables	Stations				
	A	B	C	D	E
1. Durables ownership (high scores more likely to own dishwashers, freezers, washers, dryers, second cars)	−.18	−.53	+ .27	− .74	−1.01
2. Age—older (+)	−.89	−.79	+1.18	+ .38	−1.72
3. Social class I—higher occupational status	+.41	+.90	+ .21	+1.22	+1.11
4. Music preference I—classical and opera (+) vs. popular (−)	+.03	+.06	− .26	+ .11	− .01
5. Social class II—"lower middle class" (high scorers use credit, have low income and assets, tend to have older cars)	+.20	+.29	− .34	+ .57	+ .94
6. Automobile ownership (high scorers own newer cars, tend toward foreign, lower priced, and larger models)	+.96	−.01	−1.27	−1.04	+1.10
7. Music preference II—folk (+) vs. popular (−)	−.04	+.19	+ .60	+ .18	− .27
8. Source of entertainment (high scorers seldom "go out")	+.58	+.21	− .48	+ .24	+1.04
9. Wife's status—working wife (+)	+.36	−.09	− .06	− .69	− .49
10. Music preference III—opera (+) vs. jazz (−)	+.28	+.35	− .55	− .13	+ .77
11. "Individualism" (high scorers tend to like folk music, dislike trading stamps, and not own TV set or shop in discount houses)	−.27	+.20	+ .71	+1.98	+ .20
12. Program guide—sent in for Station A's guide (−)	+.31	+.43	+ .18	+ .25	+ .22
Constant	−.26	−.19	− .38	− .38	− .33

home, the means for these two variables would tend to be highly correlated from group to group. The discriminant coefficient, on the other hand, gives us the effect of number of children at home, holding age constant, and vice versa.

Certain audience characteristics can be observed by looking at the extreme values of the discriminant coefficients for each variable in Table 4. A variable contributes most to the probability of classification in that station audience for which it is most positive. Conversely, negative coefficients indicate the extent to which high scorers on a variable are *not* likely to be associated with the particular audience. Variables whose coefficients are near zero for any group do not much affect the probability for that group.

Key Audience Characteristics.   An analysis of the extreme positive and negative coefficients in Table 4 produced the following audience profiles:

Station A   Ownership of a bigger or newer car, or more than one car, contributes most strongly to classification in A's audience. Families that seldom "go out" to movies, sports, or cultural events also are disproportionately likely to be "A's." The younger the family the higher its probability of being in the A audience.

Station B   The probability of classification in B increases as the family rises in occupational status. It is highest if the family did not send in for A's program guide. Younger families, and families that indicate a preference for opera over jazz, are more likely to be assigned to B.

Station C   Respondents assigned to C tend to be much older than average, and own fewer and/or older and smaller automobiles, and prefer jazz and popular music to opera. "Going out" contributes more to C's classification probability than to any other station. The same is true for sending in for A's program guide—Station C even is ahead of Station A.

Station D   "Individualism" contributes most strongly to the probability of classification in this audience. Next in importance is occupational status. Affluence in automobile ownership strongly inhibits the chances of being so classified.

Station E   High classification probabilities for E are strongly related to occupational status and automobile affluence, and inversely related to "going out" and durables ownership. Younger people are much more likely to be classified in this audience. The group is most likely to exhibit "lower middle class" values (Social class II). The extreme positive coefficient for opera versus jazz might best be regarded as a dislike for jazz.

Differences between pairs of coefficients indicate the extent to which the variable aids in discriminating the two audiences. The five stations permit ten different pair-wise comparisons of coefficients. Since this is an unwieldy number, we shall concentrate on the pairs that are not connected by any arrows in Figure 4. Our data indicate that the most widely separated stations in the discriminant space are A-C, B-C, B-D, and C-E.

A compared with C. A listeners are younger and much more likely to own newer, larger autos and/or more autos than C listeners. On the other hand, families that "go out" often are much more likely to be classified in C.

B compared with C. The probability of classification in B rather than C increases as automobile affluence increases, and decreases with age.

B compared with D. "Individualism" increases the probability of membership in D relative to B. On the other hand, the B's tend to be younger and more affluent on automobile ownership.

C compared with E. Age, automobile affluence, and durables ownership increase the probability of being classified in C relative to E. The same is true for a stated preference for jazz over opera. The E's tend to "go out" more than the D's, and are more likely to exhibit "lower middle class" behavior.

While a more extensive analysis of audience differences would be necessary in an actual study, the foregoing shows how the confusion matrix can be used to narrow down the comparison of pairs of discriminant coefficients. The same approach could be used to determine what pairs of means are most likely to exhibit significant differences. It represents an important reduction of the dimensions of the problem of defining essential differences between audiences, especially when a large number of audiences are to be compared.

References

1. Anderson, T. W. *Introduction to Multivariate Statistical Analysis.* New York: Wiley, 1958.
2. Banks, S. "Why People Buy Particular Brands." In Ferber, Robert, and Hugh Wales (eds.). *Motivation and Market Behavior.* Homewood, Illinois: Richard D. Irwin, 1958.
3. Cooley, W. W., and P. R. Lohnes. *Multivariate Procedures for the Behavioral Sciences.* New York: Wiley, 1962.
4. Evans, F. B. "Psychological and Objective Factors in the Prediction of Brand Choice: Ford versus Chevrolet." *Journal of Business,* Vol. 32, No. 4, October, 1959, pp. 340–369. Reprinted in Frank, R. E., A. A. Kuehn, and W. F. Massy (eds.). *Quantitative Techniques in Marketing Analysis.* Homewood, Ill.: Richard D. Irwin, 1962.
5. Fisher, R. A. "The Use of Multiple Measurements in Taxonomic Problems." *Annuals of Eugenics,* Vol. 7, 1936, p. 179.
6. Frank, R. E., A. A. Kuehn, and W. F. Massy. *Quantitative Techniques in Marketing Analysis.* Homewood, Ill.: Richard D. Irwin, 1962.
7. Frank, R. E., and W. F. Massy. "Innovation and Brand Choice: The Folgers' Invasion." *Proceedings* of the Winter Meeting of the American Marketing Association, Boston, December, 1963.
8. Kendall, M. G. *A Course in Multivariate Analysis.* London: Griffin, 1957.
9. Lipstein, B. "The Dynamics of Brand Loyalty and Brand Switching." In *Proceedings: Fifth Annual Conference.* New York: Advertising Research Foundation, 1959, pp. 101–108. Reprinted in Britt, S. H., and H. W. Boyd, Jr. (eds.). *Marketing Management and Administrative Action.* New York: McGraw-Hill, 1963.
10. Massy, W. F. "Applying Factor Analysis to a Specific Marketing Problem." *Proceedings* of the Winter Meeting of the American Marketing Association, Boston, December, 1963.
11. Rao, C. R. *Advanced Statistical Methods in Biometric Research.* New York: Wiley, 1952.

For Discussion

Interpret Figure 2. How is the break-point determined? Interpret Table 3. Interpret the coefficients in Table 4. For variable 1, for example, what does $-.18$ mean? What are the inputs and outputs to discriminant analysis? What are the key assumptions that underly Table 4?

22

Prediction of Consumer Innovators: Application of Multiple Discriminant Analysis

Thomas S. Robertson
James N. Kennedy

Introduction

The successful diffusion of new products depends on an understanding of the consumer innovator. This article reports on using multiple discriminant analysis to predict innovators and to assess the importance of several innovator characteristics.

Two multiple discriminant equations are generated. The first, a short-cut method permitting manual calculation, is based on the assumption that the variables studied are independent. The second requires a computer but considers whatever interdependence is present.

The findings here are based on an empirical inquiry into the adoption of a new small home appliance product. The characteristics studied came from literature on new product diffusion from various academic disciplines.

Innovator Characteristics

The characteristics of consumer innovators are ill-defined. Although some 800 studies on the diffusion of new ideas and practices have been reported in sociology, direct application of these findings to the marketing of consumer products is questionable.

As defined in sociology, innovators are the first 2.5 percent of the community's potential adopters to purchase. In marketing, a 10 percent figure has gained some recognition. An innovation is loosely defined as any product that consumers perceive to be new. Adoption or innovative behavior is the process of accepting and purchasing the innovation. Diffusion means the spread of the item from the manufacturer to ultimate users.

A model of innovator characteristics follows. This model is based on agricultural findings summarized by Everett M. Rogers [18], on a major research effort tracing a new drug's diffusion in the medical community [6], and on four innovative behavior studies in the marketing discipline [1, 4, 10, 16]. The characteristics selected are not exhaustive but are of most general importance in previous research.

Venturesomeness. Rogers uses venturesomeness as a summary concept to characterize agricultural innovators. "The major value of the innovator is venturesomeness. He must desire the hazardous, the rash, the daring, and the risking" [18, p. 169]. Venturesomeness is operationally defined in this study as willingness to take risks in the purchase of new products. Risk-taking by consumers has been investigated in several recent marketing studies [3, 8].

Social Mobility. The Tastemaker studies by Opinion Research Corporation conclude that innovators are

Reprinted from *Journal of Marketing Research*, published by the American Marketing Association, Vol. 5 (February 1968), pp. 64–69. The research for this article was supported by the Illinois Bell and Michigan Bell Telephone Companies and the Bureau of Business and Economic Research, UCLA. Prof. Douglas J. Dalrymple and Daniel Greeno of UCLA, C. T. Smith and E. N. Asmann, business research administrators of A. T. & T. and Illinois Bell Telephone Company, respectively, gave helpful criticism. No part of this article may be reproduced in any form without prior written permission from the publisher.

the mobiles in society [1]. Social mobility means movement on the societal status hierarchy. Here, upward social mobility is measured and defined by prior and anticipated movement on the social class ladder.

Privilegedness. Income level frequently has correlated with innovative behavior [4, 19]. Privilegedness is financial standing *relative* to other community members. Richard P. Coleman applied the privilegedness concept to the compact car and color television markets and found, for example, that color television innovators were overprivileged members of each social class [7].

Social Integration. Social integration is defined as the person's degree of participation with other community members. This variable has been important in the agricultural studies and the medical diffusion study [18, 6], but it has not been directly tested in the consumer goods area.

Interest Range. Katz and Lazarsfeld found degree of interest in a consumption area to be "strongly related" to opinion leadership [14]. A common assumption has been that innovators are more interested in the consumption area in which they innovate [22]. The Tastemaker studies further suggest that innovators may be committed to a wider range of interests or values than non-innovators [1]. The hypothesis of interest range will be studied here.

Status Concern. Status concern is the person's need to be noticed and admired. The variable is not explicitly derived from diffusion research but from Veblen's treatise on conspicuous consumption [20]. The conspicuousness of innovations and the resulting attention may prompt innovative behavior. Air-conditioners, for example, were a highly conspicuous item and this affected their pattern of diffusion in the Philadelphia nieghborhood studied by Whyte [21]. Bourne, on reference group influence, cites the product's conspicuousness as perhaps the main attribute in whether purchase will be susceptible to reference group effect [5].

Cosmopolitanism. How oriented the person is beyond his community is referred to as cosmopolitanism. Findings from the agricultural and medical studies emphasize that innovators have cosmopolitan outlooks. The physician innovator, for example, subscribed to more medical journals, attended more out-of-town professional meetings, and visited more out-of-town medical institutions and teaching hospitals [13].

Hypotheses. Innovators will have distinguishing characteristics from non-innovators. The formulation and direction of each hypothesis is based on previous research findings. Innovators will be:

1. More venturesome in their consumption behavior than non-innovators.
2. More socially mobile.
3. Relatively more financially privileged.
4. More socially integrated.
5. Interested in a wider range of consumption areas.
6. More status concerned.
7. More cosmopolitan in outlook.

Research Design

Research was done in one reasonably well defined social system, the middle class suburban community of Deerfield, Illinois. Innovators were operationally defined as the first ten percent of the community's members to adopt the small home appliance innovation under investigation. Penetration of this product in the community was 11 percent at the time of the study, one year after the product's introduction. Non-innovators were those who did not purchase the product.

The sample had 60 innovators and 40 non-innovators. This breakdown was preferred to allow more opportunity to trace the flow of information that innovators used. Innovators were chosen systematically from the community's geographic areas where the product's penetration was greatest. The sampling procedure selected every other household owning the innovation for inclusion in the sample. By a random number procedure, non-innovators were selected from each block on which an innovator was chosen. Thus it was hoped that certain demographic variables would be controlled for the innovator and non-innovator subsamples.

A telephone street-address directory was used in sample selection and interviews were arranged by telephone. Under these controlled procedures, response rate was about 80 percent. The only known biases are the exclusion of unlisted telephone number households, no telephone households, and some working-wife households.

In-home personal interviews, lasting about 90 minutes each, were done by professional interviewers. The female head of household was the spokesman for each family consumption unit because she represented the family's opinions best and she was more open to depth interviewing.

Table 1 gives the questionnaire items measuring venturesomeness and social mobility characteristics. For example, the venturesomeness characteristic is assessed by four measurement components. The answers to these components can all be arranged on seven-point scales from highly venturesome to highly

Table 1
Examples of Questionnaire Items

Characteristic	Measurement Components	Questionnaire Items
Venturesomeness	Attitude toward innovative behavior	How do you feel about buying new things that come out for the home?
	Actual adoptions of home appliances	Which of the following items do you have for your home?
	Willingness to buy hypothetical innovations	How willing would you be to buy the following items immediately after they come on the market?
	Self-perception on represented innovator characteristics	In regard to new products on the market, I am: (last-first ... leader-follower, etc.)
Social mobility	Continuity or change in friendship patterns	What about *your* friends and the friends that *you and your husband* have together. Where do you know them from? How long have you known them?
	Neighborhood mobility patterns	What do you dislike about your neighborhood? If you move, what kind of neighborhood would you like to move to? Why?
	Occupational mobility	What is your husband's occupation? What position did your husband hold before this one?
	Locational mobility	How long have you lived at this address? How often have you moved within the last five years?
	Organizational mobility	How often do you give up one organization and join another?

non-venturesome. The mean of the several components gives an overall venturesomeness score for the person. The same procedure was followed for the remaining variables.

Four coders handled the coding of the open-ended material. Over 90 percent consistency was obtained using guidelines set by the head researcher.

Linear Discriminant Function

The objective of the multiple discriminant analysis is to produce a linear function that will distinguish innovators from non-innovators. Weights are assigned to the variables such that the ratio of the difference between the means of the two groups to the standard deviation within groups is maximized. The discrete nature of the dependent variable suggests discriminant analysis rather than regression analysis, which has as an assumption that the dependent variable is a random variate.

The linear discriminant function can be expressed as [9]:

$$Z = w_1 x_1 + w_2 x_2 \cdots + w_n x_n. \qquad (1)$$

Here, $x_1 \cdots x_n$ represent the independent variables while $w_1 \cdots w_n$ represent the discriminant coefficients, or *weights*, to be applied to the independent variables. Z will be called the person's point score. Based on the point score, it should be possible to predict innovators and non-innovators.

Discriminant analysis also allows the researcher to determine the relative importance of the independent variables. The importance value, proposed by Mosteller and Wallace [17], measures the contribution of each variable to the difference in the average point scores between the two groups $(\bar{Z}_I - \bar{Z}_N)$.

Given that one mean value is exactly at the average of the innovator group and another at the average of the non-innovator group, then the difference in score is a measure of the importance $[Y_i]$ of the variables, indicating the contribution it makes to the total difference in innovator versus non-innovator point scores.

$$Y_i = w_i \bar{x}_{i_I} - w_i \bar{x}_{i_N} = w_i(\bar{x}_{i_I} - \bar{x}_{i_N}). \qquad (2)$$

Here w_i is the discriminant weight for the variable under consideration while $\bar{x}_{i_I}$ is the mean score of the innovator sample for this variable and $\bar{x}_{i_N}$ is the mean score of the non-innovator sample. The discriminant weight may be determined manually if the covariance of the variables involved is assumed to be zero. Otherwise, the computations should be made using a regression analysis or discriminant analysis program.

Thus, if independence of the variables is assumed, the weights may be computed directly from the relationship:

$$w_i = \frac{\bar{x}_{i_I} - \bar{x}_{i_N}}{\sigma_{i_I}^2 + \sigma_{i_N}^2} \quad (3)$$

where $\bar{x}_{i_I}$ is the average for the ith characteristic in the innovator sample and $\bar{x}_{i_N}$ is the average in the non-innovator sample. The respective variances of the ith characteristic are represented by $\sigma_{i_I}^2$ and $\sigma_{i_N}^2$ [17].

Significance of the point-score distributions is tested using the difference between the average point scores for innovators and non-innovators.

$$D = \bar{Z}_I - \bar{Z}_N. \quad (4)$$

Using this value and the appropriate degrees of freedom, the various significance tests can be approximated [12, p. 379].

Application

Manual Technique. The first step in the analysis was to compute discriminant weights using (3), assuming zero covariance among the variables. The objective was to quickly identify the important variables and to provide guidelines for the final computer analysis.

Mean scores and manually computed weights for innovators and non-innovators are summarized in Table 2. Means are based on a maximum possible score of 7, except for the status concern variable, where the maximum possible score is 3. Differences in mean scores from variable to variable may be com-

parable; yet, as will be seen, the importance values resulting can vary significantly as a function of the variances.

The discriminant function is designed to give high point scores (Z values) to the innovator group and to give low point scores to the non-innovator group. These Z values represent the combination of weighted characteristics for each person. It is possible to set a cutoff point so that the cost effects of misclassifying innovators and non-innovators are minimized. This cutoff point can then be used to predict innovators and non-innovators from other samples. The model's functioning, therefore, gives maximum significant difference between the means of the two groups by assigning optimum weights to the independent variables.

Based on the manually derived discriminant function and optimum cutoff points, 82 percent of the innovator group and 63 percent of the non-innovator group could be correctly classified. This discriminant function also gave importance values for the several variables, which indicated that venturesomeness and social mobility together accounted for about 62 percent of the point score difference between innovators and non-innovators.

The manually derived discriminant function, therefore, proved useful for gaining insight concerning the data. Its value is that of an approximating device. It is also helpful in evaluating the effects of various methods of coding and parameterizing the variables.

Computer Technique. The input data for the computer analysis were respondent scores on the seven characteristics (independent variables) and a dummy dependent variable. The dependent variable was assigned values of $(100)(n_2)/(n_1 + n_2)$ for innovators and $(100)(-n_1)/(n_1 + n_2)$ for non-innovators. A regression analysis program was then used to generate discriminant function weights (actually regression coefficients), the coefficient of multiple correlation, and a test of significance (F test). The covariance among the variables was, of course, considered. Discriminant function weights and importance values are in Table 3. Each importance value is also transformed into its relative importance compared with the other variables.

Venturesomeness makes the greatest contribution in discriminating between the two groups. Its importance value, 2.73, may be interpreted as the contribution this variable makes toward overall innovative behavior, or, more strictly, the contribution toward the overall difference between the average point scores of innovators and non-innovators. Its relative value is 35 percent.

The social mobility characteristic with an importance score of 2.25 accounts for 29 percent of the

Table 2
Mean Values of Characteristics, Discriminant Weights, and Importance Values*

Characteristic	Innovator Mean ($N = 60$)	Non-innovator Mean ($N = 40$)	Manual Computations	
			Weight	Importance
Venturesomeness†	4.88	4.12	3.59	2.73
Social mobility†	3.93	3.20	2.02	1.47
Privilegedness‡	3.68	3.25	1.77	0.76
Social integration‡	4.13	3.78	1.97	0.69
Status concern	2.00	1.73	1.72	0.46
Interest range	5.27	5.00	1.25	0.34
Cosmopolitanism	2.77	3.03	−1.41	0.37
Unweighted total	26.66	24.11	Difference	6.82

* Mean values based on a seven-point scale except status concern where a three-point scale was used.
† Difference between means significant at $p < .01$ (t test).
‡ Difference between means significant at $p < .05$ (t test).

Table 3
Discriminant Weights and Importance Values
by Computer

Characteristic	Weight	Importance	Relative Importance
Venturesomeness	3.59	2.73	35%
Social mobility	3.08	2.25	29
Privilegedness	2.04	0.88	11
Social integration	2.44	0.85	11
Status concern	0.95	0.26	3
Interest range	0.59	0.16	2
Cosmopolitanism	−2.86	0.74	9
Total	7.87		100%

point score difference between innovators and non-innovators, while privilegedness and social integration each have relative contribution values of 11 percent. Status concern and interest range account for only 3 percent and 2 percent, respectively, of the difference between innovator and non-innovator point scores, and are of minor importance here.

Cosmopolitanism, finally, has a negative weight with an importance value of .74. This value can be interpreted as a positive localism score and accounts for 9 percent of the difference between group point scores. A high cosmopolitanism score reduces the likelihood of innovative behavior.

The Z score distributions are in Table 4. The cutoff point that minimizes cost effects of misclassification is dependent on: (a) the proportion of innovators and non-innovators in the population and (b) the cost of misclassifying a member of either group. The two misclassification costs may be considered as: (1) the loss of profit from not selling an appliance

Table 4
Point Score Distributions

Point Score Range	Innovators Percent P_I	Innovators Cumulative	Non-innovators Percent P_N	Non-innovators Cumulative	Density Ratio P_I/P_N
57.3–60.0	1.7				∞
55.1–57.5	5.0	6.7			∞
52.6–55.0	8.4	15.1			∞
50.1–52.5	11.7	26.8	7.5		1.56
47.6–50.0	18.3	45.1	5.0	12.5	3.66
45.1–47.5	23.3	68.4	20.0	32.5	1.17
42.6–45.0	18.3	86.7	17.5	50.0	1.05
40.1–42.5	10.0	96.7	7.5	57.5	1.33
	*				
37.6–40.0	0.0	96.7	20.0	77.5	0.00
35.1–37.5	3.3	100.0	7.5	85.0	0.44
32.6–35.0			7.5	92.5	0.00
30.1–32.5			5.0	97.5	0.00
27.6–30.0			0.0	97.5	0.00
25.1–27.5			2.5	100.0	0.00

* Cutoff score that minimizes misclassification cost if the population contains 10 percent innovators and the ratio of costs, C_c/C_{LP}, is .10.

to an innovator and (2) the cost involved in canvassing a nonbuyer. Members of a population are classified as innovators if the following relationship is satisfied [2]:

$$\frac{p_{I(Z)}}{p_{N(Z)}} \geq \left(\frac{C_c}{C_{LP}}\right)\left(\frac{q_N}{q_I}\right). \qquad (6)$$

The values $p_{I(Z)}$ and $p_{N(Z)}$ are the percentages of innovators and non-innovators in the sample with point score Z. The frequency or *density ratios*, $p_{I(Z)}/p_{N(Z)}$, are in the last column, Table 4, for each of the groupings. The proportion of innovators and non-innovators are represented by q_I and q_N, respectively; the canvassing and loss-of-profit costs are C_c and C_{LP}.

For example, if the ratio of canvassing cost to loss-of-profit is .10, and ten percent of the population are innovators, the value for the right-hand side of (6) is .90. The ratios, computed in Table 4, exceed this value in the class intervals for point scores above 40. The estimated cutoff that minimizes the cost of misclassification is, therefore, 40. That is, if the point score of a particular respondent is above 40, he would be called an innovator and canvassed; if his score is 40 or below, he would be called a non-innovator and not canvassed. This strategy minimizes the cost effects of misclassification for the sample estimates.

The cutoff point that minimizes the number of respondents misclassified in the sample can also be determined by (6). Here, the cost effects are considered to be equal, the the ratio C_c/C_{LP} is, therefore, 1. Since the sample has 60 innovators and 40 non-innovators, the ratio of q_N/q_I is assumed to be .67. The optimum cutoff point, minimizing misclassification in the sample is also 40 since the ratios for point scores above 40 in Table 4 exceed .67.

It can also be seen that the density ratios do not decrease steadily, as might be expected, because of the relatively small sample number of innovators and non-innovators.

The significance of the discriminant function was evaluated by an F test [15]. The F value obtained, 2.767, suggests that the discriminant function could discriminate between innovators and non-innovators ($P < .05$). The multiple correlation coefficient was .417.

The tast of validation is not yet finished, however. As shown by Frank, Massy, and Morrison [11] and by Mosteller and Wallace [17], bias can occur in multiple discriminant analysis if the discriminant function is applied to the same sample data used to estimate the function. "The primary cause of this bias is due to errors of sampling when estimating the means of the population, upon which the discriminant coefficients are based" [11, p. 252].

A further possible source of bias is search bias which enters when a researcher seeks the best predictive variables. This bias is of no significance in this

Table 5
Results of Validation Tests

| | Total | Even Data | | Odd Data | |
		Even-Even	Even-Odd	Odd-Odd	Odd-Even
Percentage correctly classified					
Innovators (N = 60)	96.7%	83.3%	76.7%	100.0%	93.4%
Non-innovators (N = 40)	42.5	65.0	60.0	45.0	30.0
Total (N = 100)	75.0	76.0	70.0	78.0	68.0
F value	2.767	1.004		0.928	
Multiple correlation coefficient	.417	.379		.366	

study because all hypothesized variables were used in the discriminant function.

The method for validation consists of splitting the sample data and using one-half the data to derive the discriminant function and then applying this function to the remaining data [11]. This procedure can help isolate the effect of sampling errors by the decrease in discriminant power from the analysis subsample to the applied subsample.

Here, two validation runs were made. Data were divided into two series—odd and even. A linear discriminant function was computed for each series and applied against the analysis series and the applied series. Thus four combinations emerge: odd-odd, odd-even, even-even, and even-odd.

Results (Table 5) show a drop in the percentage of correct classifications when the discriminant function is applied to new data. This is caused by sampling variation in the original computation of the weights. The F tests were not significant because of reduced sample sizes. Overall results based on the discriminant function should be regarded as tentative rather than conclusive. There is evidence that predictive ability was improved. Each percentage improvement can potentially translate into an increase in sales volume.

Discussion

Review of the innovative behavior literature from several disciplines suggested probable characteristics of consumer innovators. These characteristics were measured for consumer innovators and non-innovators, and discriminant analysis was applied to test the value of the composite of characteristics for predictive purposes and the discriminating value of each characteristic.

Results of manual and computer techniques did not differ greatly, despite the assumption of zero-covariance in the manual method. The manual method is a good approximating device and at an early stage in a research project can be used to test the value of the hypotheses in discriminating ability.

For the present set of findings, it appears that two variables, venturesomeness (willingness to take new product risks) and social mobility (movement up the social class hierarchy) account for most of the innovative behavior difference between innovators and non-innovators of new home appliances. The astute marketer of such product innovations would seem to have his best chance for initial sales success with an appeal to venturesome, socially mobile people.

Characteristics also important are social integration (degree of participation with others), privilegedness (financial standing relative to other community members), and cosmopolitanism (orientation beyond the local community), the only negative related variable. The status concern and interest range variables are of minor importance here. The marketing program for an appliance innovation should perhaps further emphasize the socially integrated, privileged, and non-cosmopolitan characteristics of innovators.

The present set of findings about adoption of new home appliances suggests, therefore, promotional and market segmentation strategies. Achieving initial market penetration would seem to depend on appeals to the characteristics of importance. A revised marketing strategy would be needed after the innovator penetration level was secured in order to appeal directly to the characteristics of non-innovators. In fact, varying promotional appeals might be appropriate throughout the buildup of market share.

References

1. *America's Tastemakers,* Research Reports Nos. 1 and 2, Princeton, N.J.: Opinion Research Corporation, 1959.
2. T. W. Anderson, *An Introduction to Multivariate Statistical Analysis,* New York: John Wiley & Sons, Inc., 1958, 130–1.
3. Raymond A. Bauer, "Consumer Behavior as Risk Taking," in Robert S. Hancock, ed., *Proceedings of the American Marketing Association,* Chicago, June 1960, 389–98.

4. William E. Bell, "Consumer Innovators: A Unique Market for Newness," in Stephen A. Greyser, ed., *Proceedings of the Winter Conference of the American Marketing Association,* Chicago, 1963, 85–95.

5. Frances S. Bourne, "Group Influence in Marketing and Public Relations," in Rensis Likert and Samuel P. Hayes, Jr., eds., *Some Applications of Behavioral Science Research,* Paris: UNESCO, 1957, 217–24.

6. James S. Coleman, Elihu Katz, and Herbert Menzel, *Medical Innovation: A Diffusion Study,* Indianapolis: The Bobbs-Merrill Company, 1966.

7. Richard P. Coleman, "The Significance of Social Stratification in Selling," in Martin L. Bell, ed., *Proceedings of the 43rd National Conference of the American Marketing Association,* Chicago, December 1960, 171–84.

8. Scott M. Cunningham, "Perceived Risk as a Factor in the Diffusion of New Product Information," in Raymond M. Haas, ed., *1966 Fall Proceedings of the American Marketing Association,* Chicago, 1966, 698–721.

9. Ronald A. Fisher, *Statistical Methods for Research Workers,* London: Oliver and Boyd, 1958, 285–9.

10. Ronald E. Frank and William F. Massy, "Innovation and Brand Choice: The Folger's Invasion," in Stephen A. Greyser, ed., *Proceedings of the Winter Conference of the American Marketing Association,* Chicago, 1963, 96–107.

11. _____ and Donald G. Morrison, "Bias in Multiple Discriminant Analysis," *Journal of Marketing Research,* 2 (August 1965), 250–8.

12. Cyril H. Goulden, *Methods of Statistical Analysis,* New York: John Wiley & Sons., Inc., 1952, 378–93.

13. Elihu Katz, "The Social Itinerary of Technical Change: Two Studies on the Diffusion of Innovation," *Human Organization,* 20 (Summer 1961), 70–82.

14. _____ and Paul Lazarsfeld, *Personal Influence,* Glencoe, Ill.: The Free Press, 1955.

15. Maurice G. Kendall, *A Course in Multivariate Analysis,* London: Charles Griffin and Co., Limited, 1957.

16. Charles W. King, "Fashion Adoption: A Rebuttal to the 'Trickle Down' Theory," in Stephen A. Greyser, ed., *Proceedings of the Winter Conference of the American Marketing Association,* Chicago, 1963, 108–25.

17. Frederick Mosteller and David L. Wallace, "Inference in an Authorship Problem," *Journal of the American Statistical Association,* 58 (June 1963), 275–309.

18. Everett M. Rogers, *Diffusion of Innovations,* New York: The Free Press, 1962.

19. _____, "Characteristics of Agricultural Innovators and Other Adopter Categories," *Studies of Innovation and of Communication to the Public,* in Wilbur Schramm, ed., Stanford: Stanford University Press, 1962, 63–97.

20. Thorstein Veblen, *The Theory of the Leisure Class,* New York: The Macmillan Company, 1912.

21. William H. Whyte, Jr., "The Web of Word of Mouth," *Fortune,* 50 (November 1954), 140–3, 204–12.

22. Gerald Zaltman, *Marketing: Contributions from the Behavioral Sciences,* New York: Harcourt, Brace & World, 1965, Ch. 3.

For Discussion

Evaluate the question used to measure venturesomeness and social mobility. How are the "manual weights" determined? How do they differ from the computer techniques? Relate Table 4 to Figure 2 in the Massy selection. Why is the ratio of costs involved in selecting the cut-off point? Explain the validation test. What is the purpose of validation?

Part 1

The Analysis of Dependence

Section G
PROBIT & LOGIT ANALYSIS

23

The Application of Probit & Logit In Marketing: A Review

Peter Doyle

Probit and logit relate to the estimation of relationships involving dependent variables that are nonmetric (i.e., measured on nominal or ordinal scales).

Such relationships are ubiquitous in marketing research. Two reasons account for the use of nonmetric or qualitative dependent variables. First, consumer decisions are commonly binary (i.e., nominal scales). For example, the consumer chooses whether or not to buy a certain brand or the commuter chooses between two modes of transport. Even with more than two alternatives, the problem can still be formulated as a binary decision. These decisions can be characterized as having a threshold degree of conviction below which the consumer makes no observable response; only above the threshold can a reaction be observed. Second, measurement problems lead to the use of qualitative variables in marketing research. Psychologists have shown that consumers cannot represent accurately on continuous scales their attitudes with respect to multiple stimuli. Consequently, most surveys elicit responses in the form of ordinal or categorical scales, which purport to represent the true underlying variables.

Such problems are of interest in marketing because most studies use statistical techniques that fail to incorporate the constraints arising from qualitative or limited dependent variables. In particular, the general linear regression model is widely used since it provides a powerful tool for estimating the effects of the multiple variables usually thought to influence the dependent variable. However, this model requires three crucial *assumptions* about the model's error term, none of which can hold with qualitative dependent variables, namely, that it has an expected value of zero, a constant variance, and (if statistical inferences are to be made) a normal distribution [13].

Consequently, on qualitative dependent variables regression analysis often leads to an unnecessarily high unexplained variance, misleading estimates of the effects of the predictors, and an inability to make statements about the probability of given responses. In contrast, probit and logit not only provide better statistical models but more accurately represent the conceptual basis of many consumer decisions.

The Development of Probit and Logit

Probit and logit deal with the identical problem of predicting the level of a dependent variable that is measured on a nominal or ordinal scale. The difference lies solely in the assumption made about the frequency distribution of this response. In probit it is taken to be normally distributed; in logit, a logistic distribution is assumed.

The choice of model is largely a matter of personal preference rather than practical significance. Empirically it makes little difference, first because all the formulas and results central to probit can be simply rewritten in terms of the logistic transformation [4, 10]. Second, the results of both transformations are very close so that very large data sets would be needed to show that one gives a better fit than the other to any particular study. Both distributions have been employed in many empirical applications.

Since the results are similar, computational ease may be one consideration in choice. For univariate models (a single independent variable) logistic models are simpler to compute. However, in the multivariate case normal models have an advantage because of the useful properties of the multivariate normal distribution. Another factor in choice has been meaningfulness of interpretation. Most economists and some

Figure 1
A Classification of Probit and Logit Models

Values Taken by Dependent Variable:

		2	over 2
Number of Independent Variables	1	Univariate Dichotomous	Univariate Polychotomous
	more than 1	Multivariate Dichotomous	Multivariate Polychotomous

biologists have favored logit because of the direct interpretability of the logistic function (or its differential equation) [for economics see 16; for biology see 5]. To other scientists, the normal distribution has greater theoretical appeal [e.g., 6, 10, 17]. As discussed below, probit provides a theoretically attractive approach to modeling many aspects of consumer behavior.

Figure 1 provides a matrix for classifying the theoretical development of probit and logit. The earliest and basic model is the univariate dichotomous. Finney [10] has fully described the development of this model in the context of biological assay studies. These concerned such problems as estimating the effect of a single independent variable (e.g., an insecticide) on a dichotomous variable (e.g., whether an insect lives or dies). The insect is taken to have a threshold value such that if the dosage exceeds the threshold, the insect dies. In the probit case, this (unobserved) threshold is assumed to be normally distributed across insects, allowing probability of death to be computed for any level of the independent variable. The univariate polychotomous model again considers a single predictor, but here the dependent variable can take on more than two discrete values. Polychotomous models can be classed as ordered (ordinal) or unordered (categorical) responses. For example, in the former, threshold values of the household utility function, which might be a function of income, would determine whether a household was a heavy, light, or non-buyer of a product. Responses would then be a linear function of income. This type of probit model was developed by Aitchison and Bennett [1].

Amemiya [4] has shown how the univariate dichotomous model can be extended to the multivariate case. The ordered form of the multivariate polychotomous case has been developed by McKelvey and Zavoina [17] who used it to study the correlates of the voting behavior of U.S. congressmen. Amemiya [3] has presented the unordered analogue of this model.

Logit has been developed in parallel to probit. Berkson [5] popularized the univariate case. The univariate polychotomous and multivariate dichotomous types have been fully developed by Theil [19, 20]. The last has been extensively used in economics, particularly in travel mode studies [for a review see 16]. Amemiya [4] has formulated the multivariate polychotomous logit model.

A related model, the tobit model, involves dependent variables possessing lower or upper limits. Amemiya [3] has recently provided a full review of the antecedents of tobit in the statistical literature and further developed the properties of the estimator. Finally, Hartley [12], in an important theoretical paper, has shown that tobit, probit, and logit can all be formulated in terms of the linear regression model in the context of incomplete data.

Qualitative Relationships and the Regression Model

An understanding of the rationale for the probit and logit models can be gained from examining the problems arising when regression analysis is used with a nonmetric dependent variable. The data shown in Figure 2 fit a univariate (ordered) polychotomous model: a continuous independent variable x_1 (e.g., income) and a dependent variable y, which can take one of three integer values (e.g., 1 = dislike the brand, 2 = indifferent, 3 = like the brand). The plot illustrates a clear relationship between stated brand preference and the income level of respondents. Linear regression

Figure 2
Linear Regression on a Qualitative Dependent Variable

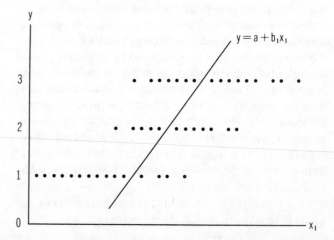

is often used to analyze such relationships.

However, as noted above, the central assumptions of the regression model are violated with a nonmetric dependent variable. First, the constant variance assumption (homoscedasticity) breaks down because here errors vary with the size of the independent variable. As Figure 2 illustrates, the regression line exhibits negative errors for large x_1 and positive errors for small x_1. Second, it follows that the expected value of the error term is nonzero, e.g., at large x_1, the predicted value of y will exceed 3, so that positive errors are impossible. This is also inconsistent with the definition of the dependent variable (i.e., as bounded between 1 and 3) and with the ability to calculate probabilities. Finally, since the dependent variable is discrete, the error term cannot be normally distributed. Clearly what is needed is a model with a different expected error structure.

A Development of Probit Analysis. How may multivariate probit solve these problems and model the consumer decision process more effectively? Probit is chosen because it probably has wider potential in marketing research than logit. However, the logit results are similar and both models can be viewed in the context of a limited information regression model. The multivariate polychotomous case described here is the most general form of probit.

Probit represents both an effective conceptual model of consumer decision processes and a solution to the statistical problems that occur when regression or discriminant analysis is employed. The conceptual issue will be examined first. In the introductory section two reasons were noted for the prevalence of qualitative variables in marketing: the threshold characteristic of many consumer decisions and the problems of measuring consumer attitudes on a continuous scale. Probit can be posited as a response to both these sets of conceptual problems.

First, the threshold concept is central to economic theory and modern theories of buyer behavior [e.g., 9, 16]. According to such theories consumers respond when "utility" or "degree of conviction" exceeds some threshold level. Probit models this concept by having the dependent variable represented as a direct function of the utility construct rather than the observed independent variables. Since the utility threshold will vary over consumers owing to differences in personality, tastes, etc., it can be taken as normally distributed (using the central limit theorem). Utility or conviction is taken to be a linear function of certain observed independent variables (e.g., product and respondent characteristics), so qualitative consumer responses are a normally distributed function of the independent variables through which they are related via utility.

An important implication of this development is that the functional relationship between the dependent and independent variables in probit is no longer linear but in the form of a normal sigmoid (S curve). Consequently, the change in response is not determined simply by the size of the estimated coefficient on the independent variable (as in regression) but also by its level. For example, the effect of a 1% change in income depends on the initial income level of the household. Observed consumer and economic behavior is more consistent with this type of relationship.

McKelvey and Zavoina [17] derive the same results from the second perspective—problems of measuring consumer response. From the viewpoint of marketing research this is a particularly apt approach. The authors assume that the dependent variable actually is continuous, but difficulties of measuring the underlying scale necessitate the use of discrete proxies. Thus multivariate polychotomous probit is an attempt to estimate the true relationship between the independent variables and the underlying scale given the imperfect measure available.

Probit also resolves the statistical difficulties inherent in regression. Since the discrete response probabilities are a function of the independent variables (via the utility or underlying scale concept), maximum likelihood estimates of the variable coefficients can be obtained. It can then be shown that the conditional expectation of any response in the probit model is directly related to the estimated probability that the particular decision in question will be made (for a complete mathematical development see 4). Furthermore, since errors are distributed normally, the statistical significance of the equation coefficients can be tested using the standard t-test or likelihood ratio method.

Thus the desirable properties of probit are that it integrates the threshold concept and an operational statistical technique; errors are normally distributed with a zero mean and constant variance and the expected value of the dependent variable is constrained to lie within the defined range.

Marketing Applications of Probit

That these techniques appear widely applicable given the prevalence of qualitative variables in market research has been emphasized. So far, however, there have only been a handful of examples. But a growing number of applications in other social science areas suggest that this scarcity will be temporary. The applications of probit in marketing so far [6, 14, 22] have all been limited to the multivariate dichotomous case of Figure 1. Bettman [6], for example, used probit to study the binary decision nets illustrated in Figure 3. The dependent variables were subjects' decision on whether a brand was 0 (unsatisfactory) or 1 (satisfac-

Figure 3
Hypothetical Decision Nets for Toothpaste [6].

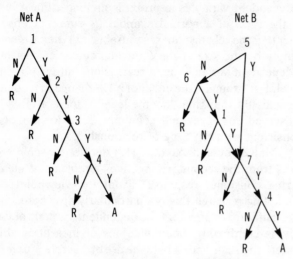

Net A   Net B

Dictionary for Figure 4

N	No
Y	Yes
A	Accept (purchase)
R	Reject (do not purchase)
1	Does it prevent cavities satisfactorily?
2	Is it satisfactorily economical to use?
3	Is it satisfactory to the children?
4	Is it available (in stock) at the store?
5	Is its taste pleasant enough?
6	Does it freshen breath satisfactorily?
7	Does it whiten teeth satisfactorily?

tory) on each of the attributes shown. The independent variables were Fishbein's attribute evaluations and beliefs measured on semantic differentials. These independent variables were hypothesized as affecting decisions via a normally distributed threshold level of "conviction."

The most general case of probit is the multivariate polychotomous model, which is illustrated below. Here we have the results of a product test where 50 respondents rated a new product as 0 (unfavorable), 1 (quite favorable), or 2 (highly favorable). This can be considered an example of the McKelvey and Zavoina formulation above where the underlying "satisfaction" variable is continuous but measurement problems dictate the use of a qualitative scale. The five independent variables thought correlated with response to the product were whether or not the respondent was a regular buyer of the product class (x_1), sex of respondent (x_2), annual income (x_3), family size (x_4), and age (x_5).

Table 1 contrasts the results of five models using first regression and then probit.[1] A number of important differences are now apparent.

Effects of Individual Variables. In both analyses the b_i coefficients indicate the effects of individual predictors. Coefficients are, however, not comparable between analyses. With regression the coefficients vary with the arbitrary scale used to define the dependent variable. With probit, the coefficients depend not on the original codings of the dependent variable but on the units of the estimated underlying scale. To overcome this problem they can be normalized by multiplying each coefficient by the ratio of the standard deviations of the independent variables and the dependent variable. These beta coefficients $(b_i{}^*)$ can be used as qualified indices of the relative strength of the variables within each model [11].

By inspection, it can be seen that the ordering of variables by $b_i{}^*$ is the same across both models. In-

---

[1] Details of the data and program are available from the author.

Table 1
A Comparison between Regression and Probit Results

	Variables	Regression Analysis				Probit Analysis			
		b_i	$b_i{}^*$	t	R^2 (F)	b_i	$b_i{}^*$	t	R^2 (λ^*)
Model 1	Regular buyer	.85	.48	3.84	.24 (14.7)	1.28	.73	3.48	.26 (12.57)
Model 2	Regular buyer	.69	.39	2.74	.26	1.07	.61	2.70	.31
	Sex	−.31	−.18	−1.28	(8.3)	−.55	−.33	−1.50	(14.80)
Model 3	Regular buyer	.61	.35	2.95	.52	1.32	.76	3.00	.72
	Sex	−.41	−.24	−2.06	(16.8)	−1.01	−.60	−2.43	(39.63)
	Income	−.04	−.51	−5.01		−.13	−1.87	−4.04	
Model 4	Regular buyer	.59	.34	2.84	.53	1.43	.82	3.13	.80
	Sex	−.42	−.25	−2.13	(12.68)	−1.26	−.75	−2.80	(43.89)
	Income	−.04	−.50	−4.76		−.16	−2.29	−4.17	
	Family size	.07	.09	.87		.44	.55	1.98	
Model 5	Regular buyer	.59	.34	2.81	.53	1.43	.82	3.12	.80
	Sex	−.42	−.25	−2.07	(9.94)	−1.26	−.75	2.74	(43.88)
	Income	−.04	−.50	−4.67		−.16	2.24	4.17	
	Family size	.07	.09	.83		.44	.55	1.92	
	Age	−.01	−.02	−.19		−.01	.01	.01	

come, followed by purchase regularity and sex of the respondent, appear the three most important correlates. However, a significant difference emerges in model 4 with the introduction of the variable family size. In the regression model this is unimportant and insignificant statistically, whereas in probit it is significant at the 5% level and significantly increases the explained variance (as measured by R^2 and the likelihood test statistic λ^*).

Regression produces a misleading estimate of the effect of this variable because of the correlation between error and regressor, which cannot be handled in this framework. Plotting the data shows that respondents who rated the new brand unfavorably tended to have fewer children than the other two types of respondent. This results in a weak regression relationship but a strong probit one.

Explained Variance. In regression R^2 measures the proportion of variance explained by the model. Table 1 shows that probit leads to a remarkable 50% increase in R^2 — from 53% to 80%. It is obvious that if the true model were discrete, then regression, which makes continuous predictions, will lead to a lower R^2 [e.g., 18]. The closer the data fit the probit model, the poorer will be the fit to the regression model.

However, some caution must be used in interpreting R^2 in probit since the statistic is only an estimate of the true measure. This arises because the deviations about the dependent variable and its mean are not observed — values of the underlying dependent variable are estimated. Since the sampling distribution of $\hat{R}^2$ is not yet known, inferences about the true R^2 are not entirely valid.

To test the significance of $\hat{R}^2$ one can use the likelihood ratio λ, since it can be shown that $\lambda^* = -2 \log \lambda$ has a X^2 distribution [21]. Thus λ^* plays the same role as the F statistic in regression. Both are significant in the models shown.

Scaling and Prediction. Probit also gives information about the underlying scale and the probabilities of respondents with different backgrounds falling into each response category. The model hypothesizes that respondents falling below a particular threshold of satisfaction on the underlying scale respond adversely (0), those falling above a second threshold level respond favorably (2), and those in-between respond indifferently (1). Probit estimates these two thresholds for each model; for example, in model 4, they are 0 and 1.5. Then by substituting into the probit equation we find the expectation of any respondent on the underlying continuum and the estimated probability of his or her falling into any response category; e.g., in model 4, an individual who is a regular buyer ($x_1 = 1$), female ($x_2 = 0$), with an income of £3,000 ($x_3 = 30$), and a family of four (x_4) would have an estimated

value of

$$4.10 + 1.43(1) - 1.26(0) - 0.16(30) + 0.44(4) = 2.49.$$

This is comfortably above the threshold of 1.5, placing the respondent in the favorable response group. Furthermore, we can compute the probabilities of an individual being in each category by assuming that respondents are distributed around their mean with unit variance. In the above case, the probabilities for the individual responding 0, 1, and 2, respectively, are .86, .13, and .01.

Conclusions

In marketing research the analysis of qualitative dependent variables is a common problem. Recent developments have made possible the use of statistical models specifically geared to such problems. By contrast, the standard regression analysis fails to model relevant aspects of consumer decision processes and may lead to serious statistical deficiencies including low explained variance and an underestimation of the effects of certain independent variables.

References

1. Aitchison, J., and Bennett, J., "Polychotomous Quantal Response by Maximum Indicant," *Biometrika* (November, 1970): 253–262.
2. Aitchison, J., and Silvey, S. C., "The Generalization of Probit Analysis to the Case of Multiple Responses," *Biometrika* (April, 1957): 131–140.
3. Amemiya, T., "Regression Analysis when the Dependent Variable is Truncated Normal," *Econometrica* (October, 1973): 977–1016.
4. Amemiya, T., "Qualitative Response Models," *Annals Economic Social Measurement* (October, 1975): 363–372.
5. Berkson, J., "Why I Prefer Logits to Probits," *Biometrika* (April, 1951): 327–339.
6. Bettman, J. R., "A Threshold Model of Attribute Satisfaction Decisions," *J. Consumer Res.* (January, 1974): 30–35.
7. Doyle, P., and Fenwick, I., "Pitfalls of A.I.D. Analysis," *J. Marketing Res.* (October, 1975): 408–413.
8. Doyle, P., and Hutchinson, P., "The Identification of Target Markets," *Decision Sci.* (October, 1976): 152–161.
9. Engel, J. F., Kollat, D. T. and Blackwell, R. D., *Consumer Behaviour*, Holt, Rinehart and Winston, New York, 1973.
10. Finney, D. J., *Probit Analysis*, Cambridge University Press, Cambridge, 1973.
11. Goldberger, A. S., *Econometric Theory*, John Wiley, New York, 1964.
12. Hartley, M. J., "The Tobit and Probit Models: Maximum Likelihood Estimation by Ordinary Least Squares," Discussion Paper No. 374, Department of Economics, State University of New York, Buffalo, 1976.
13. Johnston, J., *Econometric Methods*, McGraw-Hill, New York, 1972.
14. Kau, P., and Hill, L., "A Threshold Model of Purchasing Decisions," *J. Marketing Res.* (March, 1972): 264–270.
15. Kinnear, T. C., and Taylor, J. R., "Multivariate Methods in Marketing Research: A Further Attempt at Classification," *J. Marketing* (January, 1971): 56–58.
16. McFadden, D., "Conditional Logit Analysis of Qualitative Choice Behavior," in *Frontiers of Econometrics*, P. Zarembka, ed., Academic Press, New York, 1974.
17. McKelvey, R. D. and Zavoina, W., "A Statistical Model for the Analysis of Ordinal Level Dependent Variables," *J. Mathematical Sociology* (January, 1975): 1–18.

18. Morrison, D. G., "Regressions with Discrete Dependent Variables: The Effect on R^2," *J. Marketing Res.* (December, 1972): 338–340.

19. Theil, H., "A Multinominal Extension of the Linear Logit Model," *International Economic Rev.* (October, 1969): 251–259.

20. Theil, H., "On the Estimation of Relationships Involving Qualitative Variables," *Am. J. Sociology* (March, 1970): 103–154.

21. Wilks, S. S., *Mathematical Statistics,* John Wiley, New York, 1962.

22. Woodside, A. G., and Pitts, R. E., "Consumer Response to Alternative Selling Strategies: A Field Experiment," in *Advances in Consumer Research,* B. E. Anderson, ed., Proceedings of Association for Consumer Research, Sixth Annual Conference, 1976.

For Discussion

What is the difference between probit and logit analysis and (1) regression analysis, (2) discriminant analysis? Interpret Table 1. When would you prefer probit analysis over regression analysis? What are the advantages of probit over regression?

Section H
CANONICAL ANALYSIS

24

Canonical Analysis: An Exposition & Illustrative Application

Paul E. Green
Michael H. Halbert
Patrick J. Robinson

The purpose of this article is to describe a specific multivariate procedure—canonical analysis—and to illustrate its use in a correlation study which grew out of an attempt to relate information buying behavior to various personality characteristics of subjects who participated in an experimental game. Unlike some other multivariate statistical techniques, such as factor analysis and discriminatory analysis, canonical correlation has received little attention in past reports of marketing research studies. Its potential advantages and limitations, and its relationship to other multivariate techniques, constitute the emphasis of this article.

The reader is no doubt familiar with multiple linear regression analysis, which can be appropriate when one wishes to predict the value of a single criterion variable from a linear function of a set of predictor variables.[1] In some instances, however, interest may not center on a single criterion variable; that is, the analyst may be interested in relationships between *sets* of variables or relationships within a single set. Canonical correlation is a subclass of multivariate analysis which, as defined by Kendall is that "branch of statistical analysis which is concerned with relationships of sets of dependent variates [12]."

In *canonical analysis* [5], the analyst is not concerned with a single criterion, multiple predictor relationship (as in ordinary multiple linear correlation) but, rather, with relationships among sets of criterion variables and predictor variables. His objectives are to:

1. Determine the maximum correlation between a set (of more than one element) of criterion variables and predictor variables.
2. Derive "weights" for each set of criterion and predictor variables, such that the weighted sums are maximally correlated.
3. Derive additional linear functions which maximize the remaining correlation, subject to being independent of the preceding set(s) of linear compounds.
4. Test statistical significance of the correlation measures.

As can be noted from the above description, canonical analysis is a technique for dealing mainly with *composite* association between sets of criterion and predictor variables. Geometrically, it may be viewed as a measure of the extent to which a group of individuals occupies the same relative position in the space spanned by the criterion variables as it does in the space spanned by the predictor variables. The technique, then, does not force the investigator, on an *a priori* basis, to develop a single index to represent the set of criterion variables (in order, say, to run a single, "global," multiple linear correlation), or to compute a set of correlations for each criterion variable taken separately. Canonical analysis can also be used in prediction and, hence, can fill a function that traditional multiple regression serves.

An Illustrative Application of Canonical Analysis

In order to describe canonical analysis more adequately, a numerical illustration seems most appropriate. The data for this application were obtained

---

[1] Strictly speaking, multiple linear regression is to be distinguished from multivariate correlation in terms of assumptions underlying the model-fixed values for the predictor variables in the former, versus multinormal distributions in the latter.

Abridged from *Journal of Marketing Research,* published by the American Marketing Association, Vol. 3 (February 1966), pp. 32–39. The authors are indebted to Professor Donald F. Morrison, University of Pennsylvania, for a critical review of this article, and to the Chemstrand Company for providing financial support for this project. No part of this article may be reproduced in any form without prior written permission from the publisher.

from an experimental game [7]. Essentially, the subjects (36 business graduate students) were given prior information about the likelihood that a set of ten card decks belonged to one of two possible classes. They had the option, on the basis of prior information alone, to guess which class the deck they chose for betting purposes belonged to, or could, for a fixed cost per card, see some or all of the cards before placing their bet. The main purpose of the experiment was to see to what extent subjects' intuitive behavior was consistent with current statistical decision models.

In this article interest centers not on average play, but on *individual* subject behavior and the possible relationship of this behavior to various personality variables; that is, attempting to explain *intersubject* differences in mode of play. Surprisingly, relatively little work has been reported on the relationship of risk taking and uncertainty reduction to personality characteristics. Scodel, Ratoosh, and Minas [15] have reported the results of a set of betting exercises in which subject behavior was related to a set of personality test scores. They concluded that conservative (low payoff-high probability) players were more "other directed, socially assimilated" than less conservative (high payoff-low probability) players. Atkinson, *et al.* [2] and Becker and Siegel [4] have conducted various experiments related to risk taking and personality variables, but as Edwards [6] points out, little experimentation has been undertaken on the relationship of risk taking and personality.

In this study individual subject scores on several personality tests for each game participant were obtained. The relationship between a subject's "personality profile" and two behavioral characteristics which summarized each subject's game performance were of interest.

Characteristic 1: the subject's "sensitivity" attribute is a categorical indicant of whether or not a subject varied the amount of information purchased in the experiment as a function of his prior uncertainty. For example, some subjects, having once decided upon some number of cards to purchase, continued to purchase this fixed number (or close to it) *independently* of the prior information which they received regarding the likelihood that the deck belonged to one of two possible classes. Other subjects *varied* the amount of additional information which they requested as a function of their prior information, buying less when prior uncertainty was low than when it was high.

Characteristic 2: the subject's "bias," is a measured indicant of how much information, in total, a subject bought over the whole tiral sequence. Some subjects, for example, elected to purchase large amounts of information, whether or not purchasing variability about their specific average was related to

prior information. Other subjects, of course, purchased relatively little information before placing their bets.

Thus, two criterion variables, sensitivity and bias, appeared to be describing different things about subject behavior. Moreover, the sample correlation between these two response variables was virtually zero. No strong *a priori* grounds existed for combining these variables into a single criterion measure. That is, no logical basis was available for assigning so much weight to the sensitivity attribute and so much weight to the bias measure. Thus, if the association between these variables (*as a set*) with the set of predictor variables (personality test scores) is studied, a technique would have to be used which would permit description of an *overall* relationship between a set of two criterion variables and a set of several predictor variables. Canonical analysis is just such a technique. Moreover, its use would permit objective discovery of the weights to be assigned to each criterion variable, such that the resulting linear compound would be maximally correlated with the set of predictor variables.

The predictor variables (personality test scores) were represented by the following:

1. The Atwell and Wells Wide Range Vocabulary Test. Reputed to be a good indicator of general intelligence.
2. The Shipley Institute of Living Test. Purports to (conceptual portion) measure a subject's ability to "see patterns" or deal with abstraction and constitutes another type of intelligence measure.
3. The Gough-Sanford Rigidity Test. Attempts to measure the extent of a subject's open-mindedness versus close-mindedness; that is, degree of attitude rigidity.
4. The Rotter Social Reaction Inventory Test. Purports to measure the degree of one's "felt control over his environment;" that is, the extent to which he feels that he can influence events versus viewing uncertainty in a more fatalistic manner.
5. The Hierarchy of Needs Test. Attempts to rate subjects with regard to need level, ranging from "lower-level" physiological needs to "higher-level" needs, such as esteem from others and self-actualization.
6. The Allport, Vernon, and Lindzey Study of Values Test. Purports to classify subjects according to scores in the following classifications: theoretical, economic, aesthetic, social, political, and religious.
7. The Gordon Personal Profile Tests. Attempts to classify subjects according to test scores in personality classifications: ascendancy, responsibility, emotional stability, and sociability.

All of the above tests are of the self-administered type. Subjects required, on the average, about two hours to complete the test battery. Some of the tests, *e.g.,* the Allport-Vernon-Lindzey, have separate scores for various subparts. In total, 20 predictor scores were available for each subject. In combination with the two criterion variables, sensitivity and bias, a 22×22 matrix was required to summarize the intercorrelations. As might be surmised, however, many correlation coefficients were not significant. Those test scores which did not correlate well (alpha risk equal

Table 1
Correlation Matrix of Experimental Game Results

	1	2	3	4	5	6	7
Sensitivity measure	1.00	0.09	−0.27	−0.36	0.19	0.44	−0.23
Bias measure		1.00	−0.29	−0.23	−0.09	0.05	−0.29
Atwell-Wells I. Q.			1.00	0.22	−0.23	−0.23	0.07
Gordon responsibility				1.00	0.18	−0.17	0.07
Gough-Sanford rigidity					1.00	0.24	0.01
Rotter social reaction						1.00	−0.25
Gordon sociability							1.00

to 0.15 for the null hypothesis $\rho = 0$) with at least one predictor were eliminated.

This step resulted in five predictor variables: (a) the Atwell-Wells intelligence measure; (b) the Gordon measure for responsibility; (c) the Gough-Sanford measure of open-mindedness; (d) the Rotter measure of "felt control over one's environment;" and (e) the Gordon measure for sociability, which were used in the canonical analysis. (Subsequent work using all 20 predictor variables indicated, as expected, little improvement over the canonical correlation coefficients based on only these five variables.)

The starting point for the canonical analysis is the correlation matrix in Table 1.

Looking at the sample intercorrelations in Table 1, the following can be seen:

1. The criterion variables, sensitivity and bias, are practically uncorrelated, the sample correlation coefficient being only 0.09.
2. Sensitivity (coded 0) versus nonsensitivity (coded 1) seems to be associated with the predictor variables in the following way: The higher the subject's I.Q., responsibility, and sociability, the greater his tendency to be sensitive to prior information; the higher his attitude rigidity and degree of fatalism with respect to uncontrollable events, the greater his tendency to be nonsensitive to prior information.
3. Bias (total amount of information purchased) seems to be associated with the predictor variables in the following way: The higher the subject's I.Q., responsibility, and sociability, the less the tendency to exhibit high positive biases in information purchasing. (The correlation coefficients relating the bias measure to the Gough-Sanford and Rotter scores are so small as to be insignificant at the 0.15 alpha risk level.)

On an *a priori* basis the observed relationships appear to make sense, but the problem is to determine the overall correlation between the *set* of criterion variables (sensitivity and bias) and the set of predictor variables. This is analogous to finding a coefficient of multiple correlation if each criterion variable was considered separately.

Essentially, two sets of weighting coefficients (a set for the criterion variables and a set for the predictor variables) were sought, such that if linear combinations of each set were formed (thus arriving at a *composite* variable representing each set) and correlated in a *two-variable* linear correlation, a higher correlation *for*

this particular set of composite variables would be obtained than for any other set of combinations which could be formed. As would be surmised, specific numbers satisfying the above criterion are called canonical coefficients. The technique develops these coefficients and also computes the canonical correlation index which would be obtained if the two composite variables were formed and carried through a two-variable linear correlation.

Two other considerations should also be mentioned before presenting the results. First, we were not necessarily limited to finding only one set of canonical coefficients for the criterion and predictor variables. In this problem another set of coefficients could be "extracted" for which the linear compounds would also be maximally correlated, subject to being independent of all previously obtained compounds within the criterion or predictor set, as the case may be. In general, if there are r criterion variables and s predictor variables, as many sets of canonical coefficients can be obtained as are represented by the smaller of the two numbers, r or s. Each new canonical correlation index, however, will be smaller than the preceding value. That is, the highest canonical correlation index will be related to the *first* set of canonical coefficients which are obtained by the technique.

Second, formulas are available for testing the significance of the canonical correlation indexes under the usual assumptions involving multivariate statistical inference. (In this problem both canonical indexes turned out to be significant at the 0.05 alpha level; although, in view of the coded categorical variable, sensitivity, some question arises as to the appropriateness of the test.)

Proceeding now to the results, a canonical analysis was performed on the correlation matrix of Table 1. For illustrative purposes, a description of only the results for the first (maximally correlated) set of canonical coefficients and the associated canonical correlation index is given.[2] The canonical correlation

---

[2] The analyst may wish to extract additional canonical indexes if his interpretation of the resultant relationships is improved in so doing. In this respect the motivation is similar to extracting more than one factor in principal components analysis.

Table 2
Set of Canonical Correlation Coefficients
for Criterion and Predictor Variables

Variable	Canonical Coefficient
Sensitivity measure	0.842
Bias measure	0.465
Atwell-Wells I.Q.	−0.341
Gordon responsibility	−0.516
Gough-Sanford rigidity	0.117
Rotter social reaction	0.358
Gordon sociability	−0.381

index for this problem turned out to be 0.61. This index is interpreted as a measure of the *overall* correlation between the two sets of criterion and predictor variables. (As in the usual case of multiple linear correlation, it has an upper limit of unity.) Notice that this value is higher than the correlation indexes for the original variables taken singly (see Table 1).

The set of canonical coefficients, also found by the technique, is shown in Table 2.

To show how the canonical coefficients in Table 2 are used, the standardized scores (mean equal to zero and standard deviation equal to one) of the first subject in the experiment are shown in Table 3. The linear compounds for the criterion and predictor sets, using the coefficients of Table 2, are also computed, leading to the two composite scores for Subject One:

$$-0.89 \text{ (criterion set)}$$
$$-0.80 \text{ (predictor set)}$$

Similarly, for the remaining 35 subjects, two composite values, $\overset{*}{x}_i$ and $\overset{*}{y}_i (i = 2, 3, \ldots, 36)$, can be computed. Then, if desired, these pairs can be plotted in conventional scatter diagram form. This two-variable plot is in Figure 1.

If the two composite variables were now correlated, the same canonical correlation index (0.61) would be obtained as derived from the original analysis. The figure shows the regression lines for the linear regression of the criterion set Y on the predictor set X, and vice versa.

Table 3
Illustration of Linear Compound Computation for Subject One

	Standard Scores		Linear Compounds
Sensitivity measure	−0.722	$\overset{*}{y}_1$:	0.842(−0.722) = −0.608
Bias measure	−0.605		0.465(−0.605) = −0.281
			$\overset{*}{y}_1 = -0.889$
Atwell-Wells I.Q.	0.741	$\overset{*}{x}_1$:	−0.341(0.741) = −0.253
Gordon responsibility	−0.183		−0.516(−0.183) = −0.094
Gough-Sanford rigidity	−1.124		0.117(−1.124) = −0.132
Rotter social reaction	−0.776		0.358(−0.776) = −0.278
Gordon sociability	0.606		−0.381(0.606) = −0.231
			$\overset{*}{x}_1 = -0.800$

Figure 1
Scatter Plot of Linear Compounds

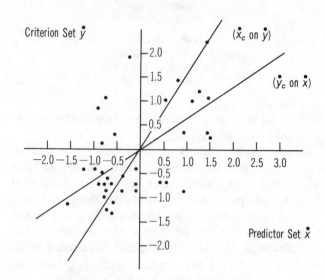

The slope coefficients for the two regression lines plotted in the figure are again:

$$\overset{*}{y}_c = 0.61 \overset{*}{x}$$
$$\overset{*}{x}_c = 0.61 \overset{*}{y}.$$

Since we are dealing with standardized variates, both regression lines will pass through the origin of the coordinate system and the slope coefficients will equal the canonical correlation index, 0.61, by the relationships

$$r_{y \cdot x} = b_{y \cdot x} \frac{\sigma_x}{\sigma_y}$$

$$r_{x \cdot y} = b_{x \cdot y} \frac{\sigma_y}{\sigma_x}.$$

These equations could be used for traditional prediction purposes. That is, if there was a set of personality test scores, say for some *new* individual, the linear compound $\overset{*}{y}_c$ could be estimated in two steps. First, compute the linear compound $\overset{*}{x}$ by substituting the subject's (standardized) test scores in the equation in Table 3. Then substitute this numerical value in the first of the above regression equations and find the appropriate $\overset{*}{y}_c$ value. This predicted value could then be compared with the linear compound obtained by substituting the subject's sensitivity and bias measures (in standardized form) in the linear compound $\overset{*}{y}$.

A few comments should also be made on the canonical coefficients of the predictor and criterion variables in the linear compounds, illustrated in Table 3. With respect to the predictor set note that the highest coefficient (−0.516) is associated with the Gordon responsibility test score, and the next highest coefficient (−0.381) is associated with the Gordon sociability score. With regard to the criterion set of variables, it appears that the sensitivity measure carries the higher coefficient (0.842), which is probably not surprising judging from the correlation coefficients summarized in Table 1. Thus, the appropriate weights to assign to the sensitivity attribute and bias measure are found, which result in maximal correlation with the set of predictor variables.

More important, the canonical coefficients enable one to ascertain the overall relationship between sensitivity-bias and the set of personality variables. It appears as though sensitivity and "unbiasedness" tend to increase with higher scores on I.Q., responsibility and sociability, and decrease with higher scores on attitude rigidity and degree of fatalism with respect to uncontrollable events. This behavior is consistent with the interpretation given to the original correlation matrix in Table 1, but is now applicable to the overall relationship between the two sets of variables.

Additional Considerations in Canonical Correlation

The foregoing illustration hardly exhausts the various aspects of canonical analysis. For example, the technique can be extended to deal with correlations among *more* than two sets of data. That is, if in addition to the present variables, information is known about various socioeconomic variables for each subject, the technique could be extended to handle association among all three sets of data [11].

Furthermore, canonical analysis can be combined with other multivariate techniques for more efficient analysis, should the problem justify it. As an illustration, if one were dealing with a very large set of criterion and predictor variables, one could first conduct a factor analysis on each set and then run a canonical analysis on the principal components. One could also combine all variables into one factor analysis, separating the extracted factors into criterion-predictor versus independent factors for criterion and predictor variables, respectively. The analyst could then run a canonical analysis on the resultant sets.[3] Finally, one might wish to avoid canonical analysis altogether by finding the *first* principal component of the criterion set (by factor analysis) and then correlating scores on this component with the predictor

variables, not unlike an ordinary multiple correlation problem.

Canonical analysis, like other multivariate techniques, is not without limitations. The two major assumptions underlying the model (when canonical correlation indexes are to be tested for statistical significance) are:

1. Both criterion and predictor sets are made up of interval-scaled variables.
2. The observed data represent a random sample of observation vectors drawn from the same multinormal universe.

In the illustrative application covered earlier the sensitivity attribute was a coded variable. As such, tests of significance of the canonical indexes are not strictly appropriate.

The assumption of multinormality (and, hence, linearity) can also be restrictive if statistical significance is to be ascertained. As in traditional multiple correlation, the analyst may be able to make suitable transformations in order to achieve linearity, but in dealing with small samples, the linearity assumption must usually be made by necessity; experimental error is typically large enough to mask the possibility that nonlinearity is present. As the number of variates increases, however, the multivariate extension of the central limit theorem indicates that moderate departures from multinormality probably do not lead to serious errors in the application of significance tests which are based on multinormal distributions.

The computational labor involved in conducting canonical analysis is usually such as to require a computer for handling problems of any realistic size. Fortunately, many "canned" programs are available. The particular program used in the above illustrative problem was part of the "Biomedical Package" of U.C.L.A. Cooley and Lohnes [5] also provide flow charts and FORTRAN programs for canonical analysis.

The use of canonical analysis in marketing research has been virtually nonexistent to date, although other multivariate techniques (discriminatory analysis, factor analysis) are beginning to find increasing application. It would seem that the limitations of canonical analysis are no more or less than those of other multivariate procedures, and that lack of application in marketing research studies to date is principally due to lack of familiarity with the technique. If the analyst is primarily interested in the *overall* relationship between *sets* of dependent variables, canonical analysis is an appropriate method to describe this relationship. Its use can free the investigator from (a) having to pick a single criterion variable from two or more possible criterion variables or (b) arbitrarily weighting the set of criterion variables in order to fit the problem into the standard format of multiple correlation analysis.

---

[3] It should be mentioned that, in general, one would not obtain the same results by using this method. As a matter of fact, dissatisfaction with some aspects of factor analysis gave rise to the development of canonical analysis in the first place. These alternative techniques are merely listed to show some of the possible ways in which a given multivariate problem might be analyzed.

References

1. T. W. Anderson, *Introduction to Multivariate Statistical Analysis,* New York: John Wiley & Sons Inc., 1958.
2. J. W. Atkinson, *et al.,* "The Achievement Motive, Goal Setting, and Probability Preferences," *Journal of Abnormal Social Psychology,* 60 (1960), 27–36.
3. M. S. Bartlett, "The Statistical Significance of Canonical Correlation," *Biometrica,* 32(1941), 29–38.
4. S. W. Becker and Sidney Siegel, "Utility of Grades: Level of Aspiration in a Decision Theory Context," *Journal of Experimental Psychology,* 55(1958), 81–5.
5. W. W. Cooley and P. R. Lohnes, *Multivariate Procedures for the Behavioral Sciences,* New York: John Wiley & Sons Inc., 1962.
6. Ward Edwards, "Behavioral Decision Theory," *Annual Review of Psychology,* 12(1961), 473–98.
7. P. E. Green, M. H. Halbert, and J. S. Minas, "An Experiment in Information Buying," *Journal of Advertising Research,* 4 (September, 1964), 17–23.
8. H. H. Harmon, *Modern Factor Analysis,* Chicago, Ill.: University of Chicago Press, 1960.
9. D. L. Heck, "Charts of Some Upper Percentage Points of the Distribution of the Largest Characteristic Root," *Annals of Mathematical Statistics,* 31 (1960), 625–42.
10. R. N. Howard, "Classifying A Population into Homogeneous Groups," *Proceedings of the Cambridge Conference on Operations Research,* Cambridge, England, September 14–8, 1964.
11. Paul Horst, "Relations Among *m* Sets of Measures," *Psychometrika,* 26 (1961) 129–49.
12. M. G. Kendall, *A Course in Multivariate Analysis,* New York: Hafner, 1957.
13. D. N. Lawley and A. E. Maxwell, *Factor Analysis as a Statistical Method,* London: Butterworths, 1963.
14. W. F. Massy, "On Methods: Discriminant Analysis of Audience Characteristics," *Journal of Advertising Research,* 5 (March, 1965), 39–48.
15. A. P. Scodel, Philburn Ratoosh, and J. S. Minas, "Some Personality Correlates of Decision Making Under Conditions of Risk," in D. Willner, ed., *Decision, Values and Groups,* New York: Pergamon Press, 1960, 37–69.
16. Hilary Seal, *Multivariate Statistical Analysis for Biologists,* New York: John Wiley & Sons Inc., 1964.
17. L. L. Thurstone, *Multiple Factor Analysis,* Chicago, Ill.: University of Chicago Press, 1947.

For Discussion

What is the difference between canonical analysis and regression? Interpret Table 2. What does the low coefficient on the Gough-Sanford rigidity scale imply? Interpret Figure 1. Relate canonical analysis to the MIMIC model described by Aaker and Bagozzi in selection 10.

The Analysis of Interdependence

25

Factor Analysis: An Exposition

David A. Aaker

The Basic Concepts of Factor Analysis

The Function of Factor Analysis. Factor analysis can be used by researchers to do a variety of tasks, including cluster analysis and multidimensional scaling. However, it has two primary functions in data analysis. One function is to identify underlying constructs in the data. Thus, the variables "impersonal" and "large" in a study of colleges may actually be indicators of the same theoretical construct.

A second role of factor analysis is simply to reduce the number of variables to a more manageable set. In reducing the number of variables, factor analysis procedures attempt to retain as much of the information as possible and to make the remaining variables as meaningful and as easy to work with as possible.

A Bank Study. The basic factor analysis concepts will be introduced and illustrated in the context of several examples. The first is a (hypothetical) study conducted by a bank to determine if special marketing programs should be developed for several key segments. One of the study's research questions concerned attitudes toward banking. The respondents were asked their opinion on a 0–9 agree–disagree scale, on the following questions:

1. Small banks charge less than large banks.
2. Large banks are more likely to make mistakes than small banks.
3. Tellers do not need to be extremely courteous and friendly—it's enough for them simply to be civil.
4. I want to be personally known at my bank and to be treated with special courtesy.
5. After being treated in an impersonal or uncaring way by a financial institution, I would never patronize that organization again.

For illustrative purposes, assume that a pilot study was conducted using 15 respondents. An actual pilot study would probably have a sample size of from 100 to 400. The pilot study data are shown in Figure 1. Also shown in Figure 1 are the correlations among

Figure 1
Factor Analysis of Bank Attitudes

Input Data and Factor Scores

	Input Data Variable					Factor Score Factor	
Individual	1	2	3	4	5	1	2
1. Joe E.	9	6	9	2	2	–.97	.79
2. Mary S.	4	6	2	6	7	1.02	–.18
3. Shirley G.	0	0	5	0	0	–.69	–2.20
4. Jan A.	2	2	0	9	9	1.52	–.22
5. Edward B.	6	9	8	3	3	–.80	1.35
6. Joe W.	3	8	5	4	7	.35	.53
7. Tom M.	4	5	6	3	6	.06	.06
8. Heather P.	8	6	8	2	2	–.78	.42
9. Mike T.	4	4	0	8	8	1.54	–.44
10. Bill W.	2	8	4	5	7	.48	.58
11. Gail L.	1	2	6	0	0	–.88	–1.55
12. Alan B.	6	9	7	3	5	–.22	.95
13. Richard Y.	6	7	1	7	8	1.48	–.10
14. Alice D.	2	1	7	1	1	–.98	–.89
15. Susan A.	9	7	9	2	1	–1.13	.92

Correlations

	Variable				
Variable	1	2	3	4	5
1	1.00	.61	.47	–.02	–.10
2		1.00	.73	.19	.32
3			1.00	–.83	–.77
4				1.00	.93
5					1.00

Factor Loadings

	Factor		
Variable	1	2	Communality
1	–.24	.72	.57
2	.06	.87	.75
3	–.94	.33	.99
4	.94	.21	.92
5	.93	.26	.93
Percent Variation Explained	55%	36%	

From David A. Aaker and George S. Day, *Marketing Research*, New York: John W. Wiley & Sons, 1980. Used with permission.

the variables. A factor analysis program will usually start by calculating the variable by variable correlation matrix. In fact, it is quite possible to input directly the correlation matrix instead of the raw data. In any case, the factor analysis program will provide as one of its outputs the correlation matrix. It is a good idea to examine these correlations to see what information and hypotheses can be obtained. Which correlations are the largest? What does this imply?

What is a Factor?

To interpret the balance of Figure 1, it is first necessary to understand the concept of a factor. The input variables will very likely contain a redundancy. Several may, in part, be measuring the same underlying construct. This underlying construct is what is termed a factor. A factor is thus simply a variable or construct that is not directly observable but needs to be inferred from the input variables. The factor might also be viewed as a grouping of those input variables that measure or are indicators of the factor.

Factor Scores.

Although a factor is not observable like the other five variables, it is still a variable. One output of most factor analysis programs is values for each factor for all respondents. These values are termed *factor scores* and are shown in Figure 1 for the two factors which were found to underlie the five input variables. Thus, each respondent has a factor score on each factor in addition to the respondent's rating on the original five variables. The factor is a derived variable in the sense that the factor score is calculated from a knowledge of the variables that are associated with it.

Factor Loadings.

How is the factor interpreted if it is unobservable? Interpretation is based upon *factor loadings* which are the correlations between the factors and the original variables.[1] At the bottom of Figure 1 are shown the factor loadings for our bank study. For example, the correlation between the variable 1 and factor 1 is −0.24. The factor loadings thus provide an indication of which original variables are correlated with each factor and the extent of the

correlation. This information is then used to subjectively identify and label the unobservable factors.

Clearly, variables 3, 4, and 5 combine to define the first factor which might be labeled a "personal" factor. The second factor is correlated most highly with variables 1 and 2. It might be termed a "small-bank" factor.

Communality.

Each of the five original input variables has associated with it a variance reflecting the variation of the 15 respondents. The amount of variable 1 variance that is explained or accounted for by the factors is the *communality* of variable 1 and is shown in Figure 1 to be 57 percent. Communality is the percent of a variable's variance which contributes to the correlation with other variables or is "common" to other variables. In Figure 1 variables 3, 4, and 5 have high communalities and, therefore, their variation is represented fairly completely by the two factors whereas variable 1 has a lower communality. Just over 50 percent of the variance of variable 1 is not due to the two factors.

Variance Explained.

The percent of variance explained is a summary measure indicating how much of the total original variance of all the five variables is represented by the factor.[2] Thus, the first factor explains 55 percent of the total variance of the five variables and the second factor accounts for 36 percent more variance. The percent of variance explained statistic can be useful in evaluating and interpreting a factor as will shortly be illustrated.

Why Perform Factor Analysis on Data?

One reason is to obtain insights from the grouping of variables which emerge. In particular, it is often possible to identify underlying constructs, constructs that might have practical and theoretical significance. Another reason is to reduce the number of questions or scales to a manageable number. This variable reduction can be accomplished in two ways.

1. One mechanism is to select one, two or more of the input variables to represent each factor. The variables would be selected on the basis of their factor loadings and a judgment as to their usefulness and validity. In the example of Figure 1, question 2 might be selected to represent the first factor and questions 4 and 5 might be selected to represent the second factor. If the factor analysis is based upon a pilot study, the larger study to follow will then have fewer ques-

---

[1] Actually the factor loadings will be correlations only when the input variables are standardized (each variable has its mean subtracted and is divided by its standard deviation — $(X - \overline{X})/\sigma_x$) and when the factors are perpendicular or independent (an explanatory comment appears in Footnote 4) two conditions are normally present. As previously noted, most factor analysis programs begin by calculating a correlation matrix, a process which standardizes the variables. If either condition is not present, the factor loadings, although not correlations, still can be interpreted as indicators of the association between the variables and the factors. Further, a matrix of variable-factor correlations, termed a factor structure matrix, is provided as an output of the factor analysis program.

---

[2] The percent of variance explained is proportional to the sum of squared loadings associated with that factor. Thus a factor's percent of explained variance depends in part on the number of variables on which the factor has high loadings. A variable's communality is actually equal to the sum of the squared factor loadings on that variable.

tions to include. A set of 100 questions in a pilot study might be reduced to a group of 20 to 30 in the larger study.

2. A second mechanism is to replace the original input variables with the factor scores. In this, the example represented by Figure 1, the result would be two interpretable factors replacing five variables. In a larger problem 50 input variables might be replaced by eight or nine factors. Subsequent data analysis would become easier, less expensive, and have fewer interpretation difficulties.

Factor Rotation

Factor analysis is complicated somewhat (or made more interesting, depending upon your perspective) by the fact that it is possible to generate several factor analysis solutions (loadings and factor scores) for any data set. Each solution is termed a particular factor rotation and is generated by a factor rotation scheme. Each time the factors are rotated the pattern of loadings changes as does the interpretation of the factors. Geometrically, rotation means simply that the dimensions are rotated. (A geometric interpretation of factor analysis will follow.) Although there are many such rotation programs, varimax rotation is the most common and will here be described.

The basic "unrotated" factor analysis usually employs principal components analysis (also termed principal factor analysis) and will be introduced first. The objective of the principal components is to generate a first factor that will have the maximum explained variance. Then with the first factor and its associated loadings fixed, principal components will locate a second factor maximizing the variance explained in this second factor. The procedure continues until there are as many factors generated as variables or until the analyst concludes that the number of useful factors has been exhausted. Determination of the number of factors to include will be considered shortly.

When principal components are used, the interpretation of the factors can be difficult. The use of varimax rotation can greatly improve the interpretability. A study of the perceptions of 94 consumers of a particular brand of coffee will illustrate.[3] The consumers, after sampling the coffee, rated it on 14 semantic differential scales. The ratings were factor analyzed by the principal components method and the results are shown on the left side of Figure 2. The first factor explained nearly 75 percent of the variance and seems clearly to reflect a general like–dislike dimension. This interpretation is supported by the fact that scale 14 was, in fact, an overall preference rating and had a high loading with the first factor. The remaining three factors really contain no loadings over 0.40 and are difficult to interpret. Such interpretation difficulty is not uncommon and motivates the use of varimax rotation.

Varimax rotation, probably the most widely used rotation scheme, searches for a set of factor loadings such that each factor has some loadings close to zero and some loadings close to −1 or +1. The logic is that interpretation is easiest when the variable-factor correlations are either close to +1 or −1 indicating a clear association between the variable and the factor, or close to zero indicating a clear lack of association.[4]

The right portion of Figure 2 shows a varimax rotated solution. Notice that like the principal com-

---

[3] This example is drawn from Bishwa Nath Mukherjee, "A Factor Analysis of Some Qualitative Attributes of Coffee," *Journal of Advertising Research*, 5 (March 1965), pp. 35–38.

[4] Both principal components and varimax rotation constrain the factors to be uncorrelated or geometrically perpendicular. There are rotation schemes which allow the factors to be correlated or geometrically oblique. They are specialized, create interpretation problems, and will not be discussed here.

Figure 2
Factor Loadings Before and After Rotation

Coffee Attributes	Principal Components				Varimax Rotation				Communalities
	I	II	III	IV	I	II	III	IV	
1. Pleasant Flavor	.86	−.01	−.20	.04	−.63	.38	.36	.34	.78
2. Sparkling Taste	.91	−.01	−.01	−.09	.48	.43	−.53	.38	.83
3. Mellow Taste	.86	−.11	−.28	.002	−.70	.26	.38	.36	.83
4. Expensive Taste	.91	.15	−.001	−.10	.46	−.53	.54	.29	.87
5. Comforting Taste	.87	−.002	−.31	.10	−.74	.38	.30	.32	.87
6. Alive Taste	.93	.03	−.02	−.16	.49	.43	−.59	.35	.90
7. Tastes Like Real Coffee	.90	−.02	.04	−.21	.42	.38	−.64	.37	.86
8. Deep Distinct Taste	.77	.36	.11	.16	.31	−.74	.27	.22	.77
9. Tastes Just Brewed	.79	−.28	.24	−.09	.23	.24	.52	−.62	.76
10. Hearty Flavor	.87	.25	.22	.17	.28	−.75	.33	.39	.89
11. Pure Clean Taste	.89	.11	−.05	.10	.51	−.55	.36	.36	.82
12. Roasted Taste	.76	−.29	.04	.27	.43	.28	.16	−.67	.74
13. Fresh Taste	.84	−.27	.19	.12	.33	.32	.36	−.70	.83
14. Overall Preference	.90	.04	.08	−.23	.38	.43	−.65	.34	.86
% of Variance Explained	74.6	3.4	2.7	2.6	22.9	21.3	20.4	18.7	
Cumulative Variance Explained	74.6	78.0	80.7	83.3	22.9	44.2	64.6	83.3	

ponents solution a total of 83.3 percent of the variance is explained by the four factors. Further, the communalities are the same. However, in the varimax rotation each of the four factors explains a substantial amount of the variance whereas in the principal components solution the first factor explained nearly all of the variance. In this data set the varimax rotation was not successful in pushing some loadings to zero. Thus, the interpretation is still somewhat difficult. However, it is possible to provide an interpretation of the first four factors by considering variables with largest factor loadings. The factors might be labeled:

Factor 1 Mellow-comforting
Factor 2 Heartiness
Factor 3 Genuineness
Factor 4 Freshness.

The varimax rotation thus leads to quite a different perspective which, incidentally, is not necessarily a more correct perspective. A subjective judgment guided by theory is needed to determine which perspective, the principal components or the varimax rotation, is more valid.

The factor solution presented in Figure 1 also was a varimax solution and was actually fairly easy to interpret. Sometimes a varimax solution (or principal components) will generate seemingly interpretable factors even when, in actuality, there is little structure present. To guard against this eventuality it is prudent to split the data in half when possible and run two factor analyses. If the same factors emerge in each then some confidence that the factors actually exist may be warranted.

How Many Factors?

Since factor analysis is designed to reduce many variables to a fewer number of underlying factors or constructs, a central question is: how many factors are involved in the model? It is always possible to keep generating factors until there are as many factors as original variables, but such a practice would defeat at least one of the primary purposes of the technique.

Theoretically, the answer to the question is clear. There are a certain number of constructs that the input variables are measuring. These constructs are identified before the analysis from our theory and knowledge of the situation and then the data are factor analyzed until these constructs emerge as factors. Unfortunately, our theory is rarely that well defined. We, therefore, add some rules of thumb to the theoretical answer.

The rules of thumb most heavily relied upon in factor analysis studies is that all included factors (prior to rotation) must explain at least as much vari-

ance as an "average variable." In Figure 1 the average variable would explain one-fifth or 20 percent of the variance. Actually, the second factor explained 36 percent and the third factor which was not shown explained only 7 percent of the variance. In Figure 2 this rule was violated since with 14 variables the variance explained for an included variable would be one-fourteenth or 7 percent. The logic is that if a factor is meaningful and capable of representing one or more of the variables then it should absorb at least as much variance as an average original input variable.

Just because there is a lot of variance explained, of course, does not mean that a factor is valid or meaningful or useful. If an irrelevant scale or question was basically repeated many times, each with a small modification, a factor underlying those questions would explain much of the variance but not be a very interesting construct because the question on which it was based was not very interesting.

A related rule of thumb is to look for a large drop in the variance explained between two factors (in the principal components solution). For example, if the variance explained by five factors (before rotation) were 40 percent, 30 percent, 20 percent, 6 percent and 4 percent, there is a drop in variance explained in the fourth factor. This drop might signal the introduction of meaningless factors of relative unimportance. Again, in Figure 2 the application of this rule of thumb would result in the consideration of only one factor.

Perhaps the most appropriate rule is to stop factoring when the factors stop making sense. Eventually the smaller factors will represent random variation and should be expected to be uninterpretable. Conversely, if a factor which would be excluded by one of the two rules of thumb was theoretically interpretable of practical interest, or resulted in varimax rotated factors with this quality (i.e., Figure 2), it probably should be retained. Clearly, the determination of the number of factors, like the interpretation of individual factors, contains a large degree of subjectivity.

Additional Perspectives to Factor Analysis

Two additional perspectives may provide additional insight into the somewhat slippery subject of factor analysis. The first is a geometric perspective and the second is an algebraic or "factor model" perspective.

A Geometric Perspective. It is often helpful to consider a geometric interpretation of factor analysis. Principal components, normally the first step in a factor analysis, will be described from a geometric perspective in the context of an example. Suppose a group of prospective students rated, on a −5 to +5 scale, the importance of "good faculty" and "program reputation" in their decision as to which school to attend. Thus a −5 rating would mean that the individual does not really care if the school has a good faculty (rather, he or she might be more concerned about the athletic program). The respondents are plotted with respect to their ratings on the X_1 (good faculty) scale and on the X_2 (program reputation) scale. At this point, two questions arise. First, are there really two dimensions operating, or are both variables really measuring the same thing? If a person values a good faculty, it seems likely that he or she would also value program reputation. Thus, these two dimensions might be measuring the underlying construct of overall quality. Second, there is the practical question of whether the number of variables could be reduced from two to one without sacrificing information.

Principal components provide an approach to these questions. It will generate a new dimension, shown as F_1 in Figure 3, which retains as nearly as possible the interpoint distance information or variance that was contained in the original two dimensions. The new axis is termed F_1 or the first factor. It is also termed the first principal component or the first principal factor. Each person has a "score" or projection on the new dimension just as he or she had on the original X_1 and X_2 dimensions. For example, person 7 has a coordinate factor on 1 which is shown to be $F_{7,1}$ in Figure 3. This projection is termed the factor score for person 7 on factor 1.

An important statistic is the percent of the original variance that is included in the first factor. The original variance is the variance on the X_1 axis plus the variance on the X_2 axis. In this case, the variance of the factor scores on factor 1 might be 90 percent of the total original variance.[5] This statistic provides an indication of how well the factor serves to represent the original data.

In Figure 3, the points do not all lie exactly on the line represented by the first factor. There is variation about the first factor. To capture this variation, a second factor, F_2, is added perpendicularly to F_1. The two factors together will now completely represent the data. They will account for all the variation along the two axes, X_1 and X_2. Just as there were factor scores for the first factor, there will also be factor scores or projections on the second factor. The projection on factor 2 for person 7 is shown in Figure 3.

In Figure 3, since there are only two dimensions, the second factor is automatically positioned. How-

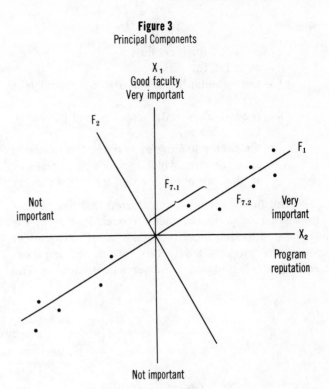

Figure 3
Principal Components

ever, if a third dimension such as "school size" were added to the original analysis (it would be shown coming out of the page), the position of the second factor would have to be determined. It could be a dimension tilted at any angle to the figure and still be perpendicular to the first factor.[6] With three original variables, the second factor is selected so that the variance of the factor scores on the second factor is maximized.

The analysis can continue selecting factors until the process is stopped (using one of the rules of thumb) or until the number of factors equals the number of original variables. Each factor will have associated with it a statistic, the percent of the variance explained by that factor.

After factors have been generated by principal components they can be rotated using one of the many rotation schemes such as varimax rotation.

The Factor Model. The factor analysis model provides another perspective. It shows that a basic assumption of factor analysis is that each input variable is a weighted sum of the factors plus an error term. The weights for each factor are the factor loadings.

$$x_{iv} = a_{v1}F_{i1} + a_{v2}F_{i2} + a_{v3}F_{i3} + \cdots + e_{iv}$$

---

[5] The variance on the X_1 axis is $(1/10)\Sigma(X_{i1} - \overline{X}_1)^2$ where $\overline{X}_1$ is the mean on the X_1 axis and X_{i1} is the value of individual i on the X_1 variable. The sample size here is eleven since there are eleven people in the sample. The variance on the X_2 axis is $(1/10) \times \Sigma(X_{i2} - \overline{X}_2)^2$ and the variance on factor 1 is $(1/10)\Sigma(F_{i1} - \overline{F}_1)^2$ where $\overline{X}_2$ and $\overline{F}_1$ are again the respective means.

[6] Let one pencil represent the third dimension, X_3, coming out of the page and see if possible positions of the second factor can be conceptualized using a second pencil.

where:

i = an index for individual i

v = an index for variable v

x_{iv} = the (standardized) value of individual i on variable v

F_{if} = the (standardized) factor score of individual i upon factor f

a_{vf} = the factor loading of variable v on factor f

e_{iv} = an error term which includes all sources of x_{ir} that are not accounted for by the factors.

The factor model is interpreted just like the regression model. In the factor model, just as in the regression model, there is a small set of independent variables, here termed factors, which are hypothesized to explain or cause the dependent variable. The

regression coefficient, here termed factor loadings, link the factors to the variables and are used to help interpret the factors. In this context the factor loadings are the correlations between the factors and the variables.[7] The error term in both the factor and regression model absorbs measurement error and variation in the dependent variable not caused or explained by the

---

[7] As was noted in Footnote 1, the factor loadings will be equal to the correlations only when the variables are standardized and when the factors are independent (perpendicular). When the variables are standardized, the factor coefficients become "beta coefficients" in the regression context. Unlike regression analysis, where the independent variables are usually correlated, the factors are independent. That is why a factor loading is here a correlation, whereas a beta coefficient in the regression context is not a correlation.

Figure 4
Factor Loadings for a Discount Store
(Varimax Rotation)

Scale	Factor I	II	III	IV	V	Communality
1. Good Service	.79	−.15	.06	.12	.07	.67
2. Helpful Salesmen	.75	−.03	.04	.13	.31	.68
3. Friendly Personnel	.74	−.07	.17	.09	−.14	.61
4. Clean	.59	−.31	.34	.15	−.25	.65
5. Pleasant Store to Shop In	.58	−.15	.48	.26	.10	.67
6. Easy to Return Purchases	.56	−.23	.13	−.03	−.03	.39
7. Too Many Clerks	.53	−.00	.02	.23	.37	.47
8. Attracts Upper Class Customers	.46	−.06	.25	−.00	.17	.31
9. Convenient Location	.36	−.30	−.02	−.19	.03	.26
10. High Quality Products	.34	−.27	.31	.12	.25	.36
11. Good Buys on Products	.02	−.88	.09	.10	.03	.79
12. Low Prices	−.03	−.74	.14	.00	.13	.59
13. Good Specials	.35	−.67	−.05	.10	.14	.60
14. Good Sales on Products	.30	−.67	.01	−.08	.16	.57
15. Reasonable Value for Price	.17	−.52	.11	−.02	−.03	.36
16. Good Store	.41	−.47	.47	.12	.11	.63
17. Low Pressure Salesmen	−.20	−.30	−.28	−.03	−.05	.18
18. Bright Store	−.02	−.10	.75	.26	−.05	.61
19. Attractive Store	.19	.03	.67	.34	.24	.66
20. Good Displays	.33	−.15	.61	.15	−.20	.57
21. Unlimited Selection of Products	.09	.00	.29	−.03	.00	.09
22. Spacious Shopping	.00	.20	.00	.70	.10	.54
23. Easy to Find Items You Want	.36	−.16	.10	.57	.01	.49
24. Well Organized Layout	−.02	−.05	.25	.54	−.17	.39
25. Well Spaced Merchandise	.20	.15	.27	.52	.16	.43
26. Neat	.38	−.12	.45	.49	−.34	.72
27. Big Store	−.20	.15	.06	.07	−.65	.49
28. Ads Frequently Seen by You	.03	−.20	.07	.09	.42	.23
29. Fast Check Out	.30	−.16	.00	.25	−.33	.28
Percent of Variance Explained	16	12	9	8	5	
Cumulative Variance Explained	16	28	37	45	50	

Possible Factor Interpretations:

Factor I	Good Service — Friendly
Factor II	Price Level
Factor III	Attractiveness
Factor IV	Spaciousness
Factor V	Size

factors. It is the source of the unexplained variation in the dependent variable which is an important concept in both factor analysis (percent of variance explained and communality) and regression analysis (r^2).

In regression analysis, the values of the independent variables, the factor scores, were known and were inputs to the analysis. In factor analysis, of course, the factor scores are outputs. Just as an individual has an associated value on each of the original input variables, he or she also has a factor score for each of the factors. In subsequent analysis it may be convenient and appropriate to work with the factor scores instead of the original variables. The factor scores might be preferred because there are simply fewer factors than variables and (if the analyst is lucky) the factors are conceptually meaningful.

Measuring Discount Store Image

Two additional examples will illustrate. The first, based upon a study by Dickson and Albaum, addresses the common research problem of determining how objects such as retail stores are perceived and evaluated.[8]

A list of 29 semantic differential, seven-point scales was generated using 27 depth interviews. In each interview respondents were asked to solicit the first word that they associated with each of four stores—a discount store, a supermarket, a shoe store, and a department store. Among their other tasks was to describe each of the four stores in paragraph form. The interviews were analyzed to obtain a list of 29 words and phrases that were mentioned by more than one respondent.

Among the resulting scales were:

crammed merchandise———well spaced merchandise
low pressure salesmen———high pressure salesmen.

A total of 82 personal interviews were then completed in which respondents were asked to evaluate each of the four stores along each of the 31 bi-polar seven-point scales. The responses involving the discount store were factor analyzed. The input data was the discount store rating on the 29 semantic differential scales by each of the 82 respondents. The output is shown in Figure 4.

To make the interpretation easier, the variables have been grouped in terms of their factor loadings. Thus, the first variable has its highest loading on the first factor and is grouped with other variables having this same characteristic.

The first factor seems to involve both the elements of good service and friendly service and, consequently, has been labeled the "good service-friendly" factor. The second factor, labeled "price level," is remarkably unambiguous. The third factor, labeled "attractive," includes the concept of bright store and good displays and thus is less clear. Note that variable 21 has an extremely low loading and should not contribute much to the interpretation of the third factor. The fourth factor is termed spaciousness because the variable that has the highest correlation with it was "spacious shopping" and because several of the other variables with high correlation have a connotation of spaciousness. However, it would be quite possible to argue that "well organized" might capture the meaning of the first factor better. The final factor, also somewhat unclear, is termed "size" because the only loading over 0.50 relates to the size. There might be some consideration given to excluding the fifth factor because it is ambiguous, it only really reflects one variable, and because the variance explained is only 5 percent.[9]

Note that the variations of a number of variables are not well represented by the five factors. In particular, variables 9, 17, 21, 28, and 29 have communalities below 0.30 and thus their meaning is not really reflected by the five factors. A variable like convenient location (variable 5) may be an important perceptual dimension to consumers but there may be no other variables in this variable set which overlap with it. Therefore, no factor is formed, loading heavily on "convenient location" that explains a substantial percent of the total variance. If theory and management judgment lead to the conclusion that convenient location is a worthwhile variable, then it should be included in subsequent data gathering and analysis even though it did not generate high loadings on any factor. Factor analysis, like many data analysis techniques, needs to be augmented by thought, theory, and common sense.

The Performing Arts

A study of the performing arts in Champaign-Urbana, Illinois, was conducted to learn what types

---

[8] John Dickson and Gerald Albaum, "A Method for Developing Tailor-made Semantic Differentials for Specific Marketing Content Areas," *Journal of Marketing Research*, 8 (February 1977), 87–91.

[9] A variance explained of 5 percent is low relative to the variance explained by the other factors and relative to that expected by one of 29 variables which would be 3.4 percent. However, the reader should note that Figure 3 represents a varimax rotation. The comparable percent of variance explained for the original principal components solution (which, of course, involved different factor loadings and, therefore, different factors) was 25 percent, 10 percent, 6 percent, 5 percent and 4 percent. Thus, before rotation there was a substantial gap between the variance explained by the first two factors and the others. However, given that after rotation at least four factors seem interpretable and useful, the analyst would not be tempted to restrict the number of factors to two.

of people were attending events.[10] Eight hundred respondents were given a questionnaire which asked, among other things, how often in the past year they attended each of nineteen performing arts performances. One goal was to determine what sociodemographic and personality variables would explain attendance. However, it was difficult and inappropriate to work with nineteen different attendance variables. Thus, factor analysis was employed to reduce the nineteen variables to a smaller group of factors.

Figure 5 shows the output of the (varimax) rotated factor analysis. A total of 53 percent of the variance was explained by the three factors. The third factor explained 7 percent of the variance which is more than $\frac{1}{19}$ or 5.2 percent of the variance (there being 19 variables). The communalities indicate that the factors did least well at explaining the variance of variables 9, 12, and 17. Notice that the rotation resulted in most variables loading high on only one factor and a large percentage of relatively low and high loadings.

---

[10] Richard P. Nielsen and Charles McQueen, "Performing Arts Consumer Behavior," *The 1974 Combined Proceedings*, Ronald C. Curhan (ed.), Chicago: American Marketing Association, 1974, p. 393.

Figure 5
Performing Arts: Factor Loadings

	I Modern Music and Dance	II Classical Music and Dance	III Theatre	Communality
1. Jazz music	.62	.02	.23	.44
2. Folk music	.74	.08	.10	.56
3. Ethnic music	.76	.13	.05	.60
4. Symphonic music	.12	.81	.01	.67
5. Oratorio music	.53	.44	.18	.51
6. Chamber music	.07	.65	.19	.46
7. Classical opera	.41	.61	.15	.56
8. Contemporary opera	.61	.35	.17	.52
9. Band concerts	.52	.23	.03	.32
10. Choral recitals	.56	.45	.08	.52
11. Contemporary music	.66	.23	.24	.55
12. Folk/ethnic dance	.45	.16	.22	.28
13. Classical ballet	.46	.57	.11	.55
14. Modern dance	.65	.16	.28	.54
15. Serious theatre	.31	.39	.50	.50
16. Comeda theatre	.32	.31	.57	.52
17. Musical drama theatre	.16	.26	.51	.35
18. Musical comedy theatre	.01	.04	.71	.51
19. Experimental theatre	.25	.01	.68	.53
Percent of Variance Explained	36%	10%	7%	
Cumulative Variance Explained	36%	46%	53%	

Source: Richard P. Nielsen and Charles McQueen, "Performing Arts Consumer Behavior: An Exploratory Study," *The 1974 Combined Proceedings*, (ed.) Ronald C. Curhan (Chicago: American Marketing Association, 1974), p. 393.

The first factor was termed Modern Music and Dance. The variables thought to represent this factor are underlined. The second factor, Classical Music and Dance, had heaviest loadings on variables 4, 6, 7, and 13. A careful look at the loadings for factor 2 will uncover some interpretation judgments. Note that the third factor has generally fewer variables with high loadings and the loadings are not as large. Factors that explain less of the variance have this quality.

Factor Analysis: A Summary

Application. To identify underlying dimensions or constructs in the data; to reduce the number of variables by eliminating redundancy.

Inputs. The input to factor analysis is usually a set of variable values for each individual or object in the sample. It is possible instead to input the matrix of correlations between the variables.[11] Actually, any type of square matrix whose components provide a measure of similarity between variables could be factor analyzed. The similarity measure does not have to be a correlation, although that is the most commonly used one.

Outputs. The most important outputs are the factor loadings, the factor scores, and the variance-explained percentages. The factor loadings, the correlations between the factors and the variables, are used to interpret the factors. Sometimes an analyst will pick one or two variables which load heavily upon a factor to represent that factor in subsequent data collection or analysis. It is also often appropriate and useful to calculate the factor score and use that as a variable in the subsequent data analysis. The "percent-of-variance-explained" terms help to determine the number of factors to include and the quality of their representation of the original variables.

Key Assumptions. The most important assumption is that there are factors underlying the variables and that the variables indeed completely and adequately represent these factors. In practical terms, this assumption means that the list of variables should be complete, in that among them each factor is measured at least once and, hopefully, several times from several different perspectives. If, for some reason, the variables list is deficient from the beginning, it will take a large dose of luck to emerge with anything very useful.

Limitations. The greatest limitation is that the factor analysis is a highly subjective process. The

---

[11] Factor analysis could be conducted on a correlation matrix between people or objects instead of a *between-variable correlation* matrix. The resulting factors would then represent groups of people instead of groups of variables. This approach is called Q-factor analysis. The more common focus upon relationships between variables is termed R-factor analysis.

determination of the number of factors, the interpretation of the factors, and the rotation to select (if one set of factors displeases the analyst, rotation may be continued indefinitely) all involve subjective judgment.

A related limitation is that there are really no statistical tests regularly employed in factor analysis. As a result, it is often difficult to know if the results are merely an accident or do reflect something meaningful. Consequently a standard procedure of factor analysis should be to divide the sample randomly into two or more groups and independently run a factor analysis with each group. If the same factors emerge in each analysis, then confidence that the results do not represent a statistical accident is increased.

For Discussion

How is a factor loading interpreted? What is a communality? What is the implication of low communality for a few of the variables? Why are factors rotated? Do you think that the varimax rotations in Figure 2 are more valid than the principal components factors? Do you agree with the factor labels in Figure 4?

26

Measurement of Corporate Images By the Semantic Differential

Theodore Clevenger, Jr.
Gilbert A. Lazier
Margaret Leitner Clark

The semantic differential was conceived as a device for measuring connotative meanings. Specifically, the process of semantic differentiation locates the connotative meaning of a concept in a multidimensional semantic space.

While an extensive body of theory underlies the use and interpretation of such instruments [4], the development of any particular semantic differential proceeds along empirical lines. The raw materials for this development are: (1) a subject or group of subjects, (2) a concept or set of concepts to be rated and, (3) a series of bipolar adjective scales such as the one below. Any number of bipolar scales may be included and their composition is limited only by the purposes and imagination of the investigator.

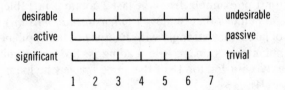

Each subject rates each concept on every scale. In the usual application, a factor analysis of the resulting data is performed across subjects and concepts. The correlations are run between each pairwise combination of scales (where N for the correlation coefficient is equal to the number of subjects times the number of concepts). The resulting matrix of intercorrelations is then subjected to factor analysis, a procedure which identifies clusters of scales which inter-

correlate highly among themselves but relatively poorly with the scales of other factors. For every cluster of scales, or factors, a reference vector is established and each scale is then correlated with the reference vector of each factor. A scale is designated as belonging to a particular factor if the loading of the scale on that factor is relatively high and pure: that is, if the correlation of the scale with the reference vector of the factor in question is relatively high and its correlations with the reference vectors of the other factors are relatively low. Scales with ambiguous factor loadings are discarded. In general only those factors are retained which reduce the residual correlations to a substantial degree.

The result of this analysis is a set of factors (usually from two to four), each of which is measured by several of the scales (usually from two to six). The factors are said to represent dimensions in a semantic space. A score on each factor is obtained for a particular concept usually by averaging the scores of that concept on all of the scales of each factor respectively. The connotative meaning of the concept is then located as a particular point in a multidimensional space defined by the factors of this measuring instrument.

"The connotative meaning of General Motors" is so nearly identical with "the image of General Motors" that the semantic differential has been used to study corporate images. Such a study is usually concerned either with change in the image of a product or corporation over time (perhaps as a result of an advertising campaign); or comparison of the simultaneous images of two persons, products or corporations; or

Reprinted from *Journal of Marketing Research*, published by the American Marketing Association, Vol. 2 (February 1965), pp. 80–82. The research was supported in part by the National Science Foundation. The writers are grateful to the Computation and Data Processing Center, University of Pittsburgh, for technical assistance in computer analysis of these data. No part of this article may be reproduced in any form without prior written permission from the publisher.

comparison of two or more groups of subjects (or consumers), such as a comparison of the late John F. Kennedy's image among a group of university professors with his image among members of a labor union.

All such comparisons involve the assumption that the factor structure of the semantic differential in use is relatively stable from one group of subjects to another, and from one concept to another. Osgood and his colleagues suggest that the semantic differential makes possible the measurement and comparison of various objects by diverse subjects. They imply that the measuring instrument is not grossly affected by the nature of the object being measured, or by the type of person using the scale [5]. If, however, the structure of the semantic space for the image of the Ford Motor Company is quite different from the structure of the semantic space for the Keystone Box Corporation, any effort to compare these two corporations on a semantic differential will lead to serious error. By the same token, if undergraduates at New York University attach a connotative structure to corporations different from that of Tucson housewives, any effort to compare the image of a particular corporation for these two groups of consumers will likewise lead to error. For this reason, there is some interest in the development of semantic differential measuring instruments which are "robust" in the sense that their factor structure remains relatively constant from one subject to another, and from one concept to another.

Recently it has been demonstrated that a semantic differential developed for applications in theatrical research fails to display these characteristics [3]. The purpose of the present research was to determine whether the factor structure of a semantic differential for institutional concepts was subject to a similar limitation.

Methodology

Forty undergraduate students and forty New York housewives were subjects for the experiment at the University of Pittsburgh. Each subject evaluated two corporate images: a nationally known tobacco company and a prominent electrical appliance manufacturer. Each corporation was rated on the bipolar scales: (1) *pleasant-unpleasant*, (2) *strong-weak*, (3) *sharp-dull*, (4) *good-bad*, (5) *heavy-light*, (6) *active-passive*, (7) *clean-dirty*, (8) *large-small*, (9) *fast-slow* and (10) *beautiful-ugly*. Scales 1, 4, 7, and 10 represent an "Evaluative" factor which appears quite commonly in semantic differential research: Scales 2, 5, and 8 are drawn from a "Potency" factor and Scales 3, 6, and 9 from an "Activity" factor which have frequently appeared in previous studies. Occasionally, the "Ac-

tivity" and "Potency" factors have been collapsed into a single factor which is usually called "Dynamism."

In the first phase of the analysis the two groups of subjects were combined and separate factor analyses were performed for the two concepts. In the second phase of the analysis the two concepts were combined and separate factor analyses were performed for the two subject groups. The resulting factor structures were compared and conclusions were drawn concerning the similarity of factor structures for the two concepts and the similarity of semantic space for the two groups of subjects.

Results

Similarity of Factor Structures for the Two Concepts. Both the factor analysis for the electrical appliance manufacturer and that for the tobacco corporation produced two factors with roots greater than 1.0. As shown in Table 1, the factor structures of the two concepts are very similar: that is, the pattern of factor loadings in each image is similar to that in the other.

The first column of each table lists the ten scales in the order mentioned above (Scale #1 is *pleasant-unpleasant*, #2 is *strong-weak*, etc.). In Table 1, the four columns of data list the factor loadings of every scale on each of the two factors for each concept. The first two columns of factor loadings come from the analysis of the tobacco company concept, and the last two columns are from the analysis of the appliance manufacturer concept.

The loading of a scale on a factor represents the correlation of the scale with the reference vector of that factor, and is customarily taken as a measure of the strength of association between the scale and the factor. For example, from the last 2 columns in Table 1, one concludes that Scale #1 (*pleasant-unpleasant*) is associated very strongly with Factor I of the appliance manufacturer's image (the loading is .863), and quite weakly with Factor II of the same image (the loading is −.041).

Table 1
Rotated Factor Structure of Combined Groups for Two Concepts

Scale No.	Tobacco Company		Appliance Manufacturer	
	I	II	I	II
1	.174	−.648	.863	−.041
2	.771	−.182	.131	.853
3	.697	−.208	.344	.732
4	.220	−.524	.822	.253
5	.430	−.059	−.101	.747
6	.568	−.480	.210	.796
7	−.009	.540	.809	.253
8	.749	.045	.415	.315
9	.436	−.522	.345	.445
10	.011	−.737	.859	.086

Factor I for the electrical appliance manufacturer and Factor II for the tobacco company both carry high loadings for the evaluative scales *pleasant-unpleasant, good-bad, clean-dirty,* and *beautiful-ugly.* Factor II for the electrical appliance manufacturer and Factor I for the tobacco corporation carry high loadings on the dynamism scales *strong-weak, sharp-dull,* and *heavy-light.* Thus, each analysis produced a factor similar to the Evaluative factor and each produced a factor similar to the Dynamism factor noted in previous studies.

Using a technique described by Ahmavaara, it is possible to test for the similarities of these factor structures in a more analytic fashion[1] [1]. Ahmavaara's technique calculates from transformation matrices the loadings of each factor from the first analysis upon each factor of the second analysis, and vice versa. The loadings of the Evaluative factor from each analysis upon the Evaluative factor of the other, and of the Dynamism factor of each analysis upon the Dynamism factor of the other all exceeded .99 in absolute magnitude. On the other hand, the loadings of the Evaluative factor from each analysis upon the Dynamism factor of the other, and of the Dynamism factor from each analysis upon the Evaluative factor of the other, were all smaller than .13 in absolute magnitude. This indicates substantial stability in factor structure from one concept to the other.

Stability of Factor Structure between Subject Groups. Both the factor analysis for the New York housewives and that for the Pitt undergraduates produced two factors with roots greater than 1.0. As can be seen from an examination of Table 2, Factor I for the undergraduates and Factor II for the housewives carry heavy loadings on the evaluative scales *pleasant-unpleasant,*

good-bad, clean-dirty, and *beautiful-ugly*; the second factor for the undergraduates, along with the first factor for the housewives, contains heavy loadings on the dynamism scales *strong-weak, sharp-dull, active-passive, light-heavy,* and *fast-slow.*

Application of the Ahmavaara technique in this instance shows factor-to-factor loadings in excess of .97 for similarly-defined factors, and loadings smaller than .20 for oppositely designed factors. The results indicate substantial similarity in the structure of the semantic space from one group of subjects to another.

Discussion

The high degree of factorial similarity displayed by this semantic differential, both from concept to concept and from subject-group to subject-group, indicates that the instrument is quite robust within the range of differences sampled in this experiment. This finding lends support to the contention that the measuring ability of the instrument is not necessarily subverted by the characteristics of the respondents to whom it is administered, or the specific concepts measured.

Certainly the likelihood of obtaining stability in the images and in the semantic space of the subjects was enhanced by selecting scales to represent the factors most commonly obtained from analysis of semantic differential results. It has been argued that these dimensions of connotation are ubiquitous, and represent a substratum of meaning underlying our connotations for most if not all concepts. Nevertheless, there can be no guarantee that these general factors will appear in every instance. While the results of this study do not foreclose the need for pretesting in any marketing research project in which the semantic differential will be used, they do offer encouragement to those who plan to use it for the measurement of certain broad aspects of corporate images.

Advertisers and others interested in corporate images may frequently be concerned with subtler aspects of the image than these, in which case a different set of scales would have to be selected to measure more particular, and presumably less basic, dimensions of the image. Whether these subtle dimensions of meaning are sufficiently stable to allow comparisons between images for different concepts and different subject groups remains to be investigated.

---

[1]The computations were effected by means of the computer program described in A. W. Bendig's "IBM Orthogonal Factor Similarity Program." [2]

Table 2
Rotated Factor Structures of Combined
Concepts for Two Subject-Groups

Scale No.	Housewives		Students	
	I	II	I	II
1	.020	.882	.857	.063
2	.723	.344	.170	.859
3	.561	.512	.172	.757
4	.285	.817	.803	.210
5	.748	.018	−.396	.587
6	.759	.140	.259	.801
7	.439	.754	.758	.114
8	.658	.400	.401	.219
9	.721	.313	.261	.340
10	.237	.713	.842	.075

References

1. Y. Ahmavaara, "Transformation Analysis of Factorial Data," Annales Academia Scientiarum Fennica, SER. B., No. 88 (1954).
2. A. W. Bendig, "IBM 7070 Orthogonal Factor Similarity Program." Unpublished paper, University of Pittsburgh, 1963.
3. G. A. Lazier, Theodore Clevenger, Jr., and M. L. Clark, "Stability of the Factor Structure of Smith's Semantic Differential

for Theatre Concepts." Unpublished paper, Department of Speech and Theatre Arts, University of Pittsburgh, 1964.

4. Charles E. Osgood, George Suci, and Percy Tannenbaum, *The Measurement of Meaning*. Urbana: University of Illinois Press, 1957.

5. Claire Selltiz et al., *Research Methods in Social Relations* (Rev. ed.). New York: Holt, Rinehart and Winston, 1959, 381–3.

For Discussion

How could a researcher develop semantic differential scales to evaluate the image of a set of brands of beer? Generate three such scales. What labels would you give the various factors?

27

A Multidimensional Set of Rating Scales For Television Commercials

Clark Leavitt

In using audience response to select effective television commercials, S's tendency to expertize – to give opinions about the overall quality of the commercial – is often regarded as a nuisance by experienced testers. Yet a careful estimate of the likability of a commercial may help to predict its attention-getting ability. If this is true, then it is desirable to know how many dimensions of commercials can be usefully scaled and what they are. There is no evidence that people can rate even likability of commercials in a unidimensional and meaningful manner, let alone such things as persuasiveness. Therefore, the present study attempts to find out what basic dimensions underlie the viewer's response to commercials when a representative sample of attributes is scaled by self-administered rating scales.

The approach reported here uses factor analysis rather than any of the nonmetric methods of multidimensional scaling. Factor analysis based on attributes seems to be a more appropriate method to use with complex and unique stimulus objects like commercials. Wells (1964) used a similar approach to scaling magazine advertisements. He found three factors: meaningfulness, liking, and newness. The factor scores were used in a multiple-regression equation to predict an independent measure of memorability of the ads. Like Wells, the present study uses attribute ratings and factor analysis as a method of multidimensional scaling, but departs from Wells and from Osgood and Suci (1957), who have used a similar approach to concepts, by using unipolar scales instead of the semantic-differential format.

Method

The study began with a relatively exhaustive list of words and proceeded to winnow out the most useful of these using several different filters. To make up the list, single words and phrases were collected from various sources including advertising studies and also more general studies such as those of Hevner (1935) and Osgood and Suci (1957). This produced 525 words that could be used for scaling commercials.

Four filtering procedures were then used to arrive at a smaller number of words.

1. Eleven commercials were shown individually, each to 30 different respondents. One-third of the total list was given to each respondent, who was asked to check those words that applied to the commercial just seen. Words checked by 2% or more of the respondents were retained. This was about 45% of the original pool.
2. These frequently checked words were now presented to Ss accompanied by a 5-point scale running from "fits extremely well" to "does not fit." Using the rating scale, a different group of 10 Ss rated each of the 11 commercials on all words remaining after Step 1. Thus each word was rated by 110 different Ss divided among 11 commercials. The results for each word were subjected to an analysis of variance using commercials as treatments. Using the .05 level as a cut-off left 206 words out of the original 525, discriminating significantly among commercials.
3. A factor analysis was carried out using the correlations of these 206 words across Ss (pooling commercials). Because of computer capacity, the list was divided randomly into thirds and each was factored separately. There appeared to be sufficient redundancy among the words to produce similar factors in each part-analysis.
4. After eliminating the redundant words within factors, there were 73 words that loaded .50 or higher on some factor. These words were then refactored together. Again choosing high-loading nonredundant words left 45 words as the end product of this four-stage process.

Looking back over the four hurdles that were used to cut down the list to a workable size, it became apparent that there was a possible source of bias: The same 11 commercials were used in all steps. The commercials were a fairly heterogeneous sample except for one thing: They had all been exposed previous to this research. So, in order to provide every chance for emergence of a possible dimension related to newness or to information, the following analysis was carried out.

Eleven new product commercials were selected and each shown to 40 different women. Each woman rated the new product commercial to which she was exposed on one-fourth of the original list of 206 words remaining after Step 1. This gave each word a mean new product rating based on 110 women.

Those words showing the greatest difference from the mean ratings on the old commercials were added to the words to be used in the final analysis. Nine words having a high correlation with novelty were also added. Adding them to the 45 words resulting from the factor analysis gave a total of 71 words.

These 71 words were used in routine testing of commercials over a period of almost a year. This resulted in 76 different commercials each shown to a different group of 30 Ss. The large number of commercials made it possible to use the mean ratings of each commercial (based on 30 Ss) as the data points on which the correlations on each word among the attributes were computed. The resulting matrix was factored using the method of principal components with Varimax rotation as the basis for the final factor analysis discussed in the next section.

Results

The factor analysis of the 71 words produced seven factors. Table 1 shows the six highest loading words on each factor with two exceptions: *amusing* and *familiar*. The six words listed under *amusing* are part of the energetic factor and just missed being among the top six on that factor. They are listed because of their practical utility. The second exception is the familiar factor which produced only three words with significant loadings.

The energetic factor, accounting for 55% of the total variance, was by far the most important. As pointed out, it also contains the *amusing* words (implying that television commercial humor tends to be fast-paced).

Personal relevance is the second largest factor, accounting for 22% of the variance. The words that loaded high on this factor tend to be somewhat subjective in their reference.

The third factor is sensual and it accounts for 9% of the variance. This factor seems to be opposite the energetic in its general meaning.

Familiar is the fourth factor and accounts for 5% of the variance even though there are only three words that load high enough to be useful for scaling.

The remaining three factors are novel, authoritative, and disliked, accounting for 3%, 2%, and 2%, respectively. Since they account for so little variance, their usefulness is mainly for descriptive purposes.

It is interesting to note that the evaluative factor is so minor, at least in its pure form as the disliked scale. Osgood's research shows it to be the most important factor in many of his studies. This inconsistency may be due to the different form of the rating scale — bipolar anchoring versus unipolar anchoring.

Table 1
Highest Loading Words on Each of the Factor Scales

Scale	Loading	Scale	Loading
Energetic		Sensual	
Lively	.95	Lovely	.91
Exhilarated	.94	Beautiful	.90
Vigorous	.91	Gentle	.88
Enthusiastic	.91	Serene	.86
Energetic	.90	Tender	.86
Excited	.87	Sensitive	.81
Amusing		Familiar	
Merry	.86	Familiar	.82
Jolly	.84	Well-known	.82
Playful	.83	Saw before	.69
Joyful	.82	Novel	
Amusing	.70	Original	.71
Humorous	.65	Unique	.62
Personal relevance		Imaginative	.58
Important for me	.83	Novel	.56
Helpful	.83	Ingenious	.50
Valuable	.83	Creative	.50
Meaningful for me	.81	Disliked	
Worth remembering	.68	Phony	.89
Convincing	.63	Terrible	.87
Authoritative		Stupid	.84
Confident	.62	Irritating	.84
Business-like	.62	Unimportant to me	.82
Consistent-in-style	.56	Ridiculous	.81
Responsible	.44		
Frank	.42		
Dependable	.32		

References

1. Hevner, K., "Expression in Music: A Discussion of Experimental Studies and Theories," *Psychological Revue*, 1935, 47, 186–204.
2. Osgood, C., G. Suci, and P. Tannenbaum, *The Measurement of Meaning*. Urbana: University of Illinois Press, 1957.
3. Wells, W. D., "EQ, Son of EQ, and Reactions Profile," *Journal of Marketing*. 1964, 28 (4), 45–52.

For Discussion

Evaluate the labels attached to the factors. Why do you think that the "evaluative" factor was so unimportant? Why were the first two factors so dominant?

28

An Analysis of Catalog Buying Behavior

Fred D. Reynolds

Recent marketing literature reflects an increasing interest in understanding consumer in-home shopping behavior.[1] The current concern can be attributed both to the magnitude of the in-home market and to the tenacity and continuing viability of marketing efforts directed to that segment. Gillett, for example, cited a 1964 estimate that in-home shopping accounted for 9% of total general merchandise sales and would probably capture 10% to 11% of that market by 1975.[2] More recently, an article in *Forbes* heralded the first centennial of catalog marketing by announcing that catalog sales in 1971 exceeded ten billion dollars and continued to grow at a faster rate than total retail sales.[3] The present article examines a relatively unexplored subset of in-home shopping behavior—in-home catalog buying. Specifically, this article explores three factors that affect catalog buying behavior: convenience, offering, and degree of risk.[4]

Convenience is an obvious benefit consumers can anticipate from any form of in-home buying. Accordingly, this behavior is more likely to appeal to persons who can "afford" convenience and to those who "need" it because of some time constraint such as the presence of younger children, social or community involvement, or the subjective value of time. These considerations suggested the following research hypotheses:

H 1: There is a positive relationship between catalog buying and income.

H 2: There is a positive relationship between catalog buying and the presence of younger children in the home.

H 3: There is a positive relationship between catalog buying and time consciousness.

H 4: There is a positive relationship between catalog buying and community involvement.

The *offering* of the large-scale catalog retailer potentially provides additional benefits to shoppers when compared to smaller urban retailing centers. Specifically, the merchandise assortment is greater and may consist of more fashionable styles and unusual items, often at relatively lower prices. This suggests the following research hypotheses:

H 5: Catalog buying is inversely related to attitudes toward local shopping conditions.

H 6: Catalog buying is positively related to attitudes toward larger urban shopping conditions.

H 7: Catalog buying is positively related to price consciousness.

While consumers obtain certain benefits by buying from catalogs, there is an information trade-off when compared to shopping in person. Inherent in the catalog buying process is a greater *degree of risk* regarding the specification of products. To some extent, then, consumers must be willing to take some risk in catalog buying. The notion of risk taking suggests three additional research hypotheses:

H 8: Catalog buying is positively related to venturesomeness—the willingness to take risks in trying new things.

H 9: Catalog buying is inversely related to age, since younger persons tend to be more willing to take risks.

H 10: There is a positive relationship between catalog buying and self-confidence.

[1]Donald F. Cox and Stuart U. Rich, "Perceived Risk and Consumer Decision Making—The Case of Telephone Shopping," *Journal of Marketing Research,* Vol. 1 (November 1964), pp. 32–39; Homer E. Spence, James F. Engel, and Roger D. Blackwell, "Perceived Risk in Mail-Order and Retail Store Buying," *Journal of Marketing Research,* Vol. 7 (August 1970), pp. 364–369; William H. Peters and Neil M. Ford, "A Profile of Urban In-Home Shoppers: The Other Half," *Journal of Marketing,* Vol. 36 (January 1972), pp. 62–64; Laurence P. Feldman and Alvin D. Starr, "Racial Factors in Shopping Behavior," in *A New Measure of Responsibility for Marketing,* Keith Cox and Ben Enis, eds. (Chicago: American Marketing Assn., 1968), pp. 216–226; and Peter L. Gillett, "A Profile of Urban In-Home Shoppers," *Journal of Marketing,* Vol. 34 (July 1970), pp. 40–45.

[2]Gillett, same reference as footnote 1, p. 40.

[3]"Pretty Penny," *Forbes,* March 15, 1972, p. 46.

[4]Cox and Rich, and Gillett, same references as footnote 1.

The Study

Data to examine these hypotheses were derived from a survey of female homemakers in a Georgia community of 18,000 persons. The study was conducted in the fall of 1971. Using a random sampling procedure from a frame defined by the 1971 city directory published by R. L. Polk & Co., 1,099 self-administered questionnaires were mailed to the "Mrs." at each address. Two follow-up mailings were used, each spaced about three weeks after the preceding mailout. The three mailings resulted in 321 returns, of which 302 were usable for this study.

Among the data collected from respondents were several consumer behavior variables, including catalog buying. This dependent variable was measured by a question on the frequency with which goods were ordered from a mail-order catalog over the preceding twelve months. The 41 respondents who reported placing orders twelve or more times in the previous year were defined as *frequent catalog buyers*; the 186 women reporting at least one but fewer than twelve orders were classified as *infrequent catalog buyers*; and the 75 respondents who reported no catalog orders during the past twelve months were classified as *nonbuyers*.

The independent variables selected for this study included several derived from an R-factor analysis of 85 general life style statements and 22 specific trade area statements in response to which respondents indicated their choice on a six-point scale. Specifically, responses to the 107 statements were subjected to principal components analysis and varimax rotation to try to identify a priori conceived underlying themes within the data. Original communality assignments were unity and all components with eigenvalues greater than unity were subjected to rotation. This procedure was repeated with a randomly selected sub-sample (N = 151) to examine the structural stability of the linear combination of the original 107 variables. Of the nineteen factors extracted, fifteen were stable in the subsample analysis and two others were partially stable. None of the unstable factors were germane to the hypotheses of the study. Table 1 lists the factors related to the study, the loadings of items on each factor (only loadings greater than |.40| were used), and the subjective labels of the life style scales. For purposes of analysis, the life style data were scored in the usual Likert fashion. In addition, responses to the demographic and socioeconomic questions were included.

Only those variables that differentiated between catalog buying groups at the < .10 level of statistical significance were used in supporting the research hypotheses.

The Analysis

Table 2 shows the mean profiles of each of the catalog buying groups on the hypothesized variables. The resulting description indicates that catalog buy-

Table 1
Life Style Scales

Scale Titles and Statements	Factor Loading
1. Time Conscious	
• It takes too much time to shop out of town.	.77
• When you consider travel time, it costs too much to shop out of town.	.63
• I always shop where it saves me time.	.61
• I usually buy at the most convenient store.	.61
2. Gregarious Community Worker	
• I am an active member of more then one social or service organization.	.68
• I like to work on community projects.	.70
• I have personally worked on a project to better our town.	.50
• I often visit friends in the evening.	.55
3. Attitude Toward Local Shopping Conditions	
• Local prices are out of line with other towns.	.66
• Local merchants offer good selections.	.59
• Local merchants don't offer the latest styles.	.66
• Local stores try to sell you old stock.	.61
• Local stores offer you good quality for the price.	.69
• Local stores are never open when I want to shop.	.55
• Local stores are attractive places to shop.	.69
• It is hard to get credit in local stores.	.51
• Local salesclerks are poorly trained.	.54
4. Attitude Toward Small City Shopping Conditions	
• Small City merchants really know their jobs.	.74
• The latest styles are always available in Small City.	.73
• Salespeople in Small City are well trained.	.71
5. Attitude Toward Large City Shopping Conditions	
• I like to shop in Large City and frequently do.	.76
• I get more for my money in Large City.	.69
• Parking is a problem in Large City.	.48
• It isn't worth the extra effort to shop in Large City.	.69
• It is more fun to shop in Large City than locally.	.58
6. Shopping Center Oriented	
• I enjoy going to big shopping centers.	.54
• Shopping centers are the best places to shop.	.76
• I prefer shopping centers over downtown shopping areas.	.70
7. Price Conscious	
• I shop a lot for specials.	.83
• I find myself checking the prices in the grocery store even for small items.	.72
• I usually watch the advertisements for announcements of sales.	.81
• A person can save a lot of money by shopping around for bargains.	.55
8. Venturesome	
• When I see a new brand on the shelf, I often buy it just to see what it is like.	.79
• I like to try new and different things.	.61
• I enjoy doing new things.	.52
9. Self-Confidence	
• I think I have more self-confidence than most people.	.74
• I am more independent than most people.	.55
• I think I have a lot of personal ability.	.50
• I like to be considered a leader.	.67

Table 2
Descriptive Profiles of Catalog Buying Groups

Descriptive Variable	Groups		
	Non-buyer (N = 75)	Infrequent Buyer (N = 186)	Frequent Buyer (N = 41)
Family Income Level[a]	4.933	5.565	6.488
No. Children < 12 Years Old[a]	0.547	0.758	1.098
Time Conscious	15.800	15.640	14.781
Gregarious Community Worker	13.227	13.936	14.439
Attitude Toward Local Shopping Conditions[a]	40.360	39.269	34.829
Attitude Toward Small City Shopping[a]	11.667	11.726	12.951
Attitude Toward Large City Shopping[a]	14.160	15.570	16.756
Shopping Center Orientation[a]	12.213	13.339	13.463
Price Conscious	16.120	17.048	17.244
Venturesome[a]	10.827	12.086	12.463
Age Group[a]	4.027	3.543	2.951
Self-Confidence[a]	15.680	16.108	17.805

[a] $P \leq .10$ based on F-tests.

ing may be at least partially explained by several of the research hypotheses.

The idea that the benefit of convenient shopping appeals to those who can afford it and need it is only partly supported by the data. Catalog buyers do report a higher family income [H 1]—a finding consistent with the Feldman and Star study.[5] The need for convenience is suggested in the findings that catalog buying is more pronounced in families with children under twelve years of age [H 2].

Two of the need-for-convenience hypotheses are not supported by the data. Neither time consciousness [H 3] nor community involvement [H 4] are significantly related to the behavior of frequent catalog buyers. Surprisingly, the means on time consciousness decrease in magnitude from the nonbuyer to the frequent buyer. However, this may be accounted for by the composition of the scale and the relationship of catalog buying to another behavior. Several of the items in the time-consciousness scale were specific to outshopping behavior, and outshopping was found to be related to catalog buying—a finding seemingly contrary to that of Hermann and Beik.[6] Their analysis,

however, focused on outshoppers and nonoutshoppers versus catalog buyers and noncatalog buyers without considering the frequency of either type of behavior. The overlap between frequent catalog buying and frequent outshopping suggests that, for a number of catalog buyers for certain types of goods, convenience is not the primary benefit sought.

The comparative strength of the offerings of catalog merchants tends to be supported by the data. Catalog buyers, when compared to their nonbuyer neighbors, report lower opinions of local shopping conditions [H 5]. This finding is highly consistent with the findings of Gillett that merchandise availability, quality, and assortment and lower price were among the most frequent reasons reported for in-store catalog ordering.[7] The consistency of the two studies suggests that catalog buyers in stores may be motivated in a manner similar to catalog buyers in the home. The notion that catalog buyers are biased toward more extensive merchandise assortments is supported by their favorable attitudes toward shopping conditions in the large and small cities and by their higher scores on shopping center orientation [H 6]. While price may be a comparative consideration for specific items, the hypothesis that catalog buyers are more price conscious than nonbuyers [H 7] is not supported by the data.

Each of the hypotheses related to risk taking is supported by the data [H 8-10]. Catalog buyers tend to be younger, more venturesome, and to express greater self-confidence. These findings along with that of higher income all suggest both the ability and the willingness to ignore the inherent risk in ordering from a mail-order catalog.

To summarize, frequent catalog buyers when compared to the other groups seem to be motivated by a desire for convenient shopping in some situations but not in others. Rather, it appears that catalog buying is more a result of the strength of catalog offerings, as revealed in the negative attitudes toward local shopping conditions expressed by the young, affluent risk takers who comprised the frequent buying group.

For Discussion

What labels would you give the various factors? Interpret Table 2. How could a marketer use such a study?

---

[5] Feldman and Star, same reference as footnote 1, p. 218.

[6] Robert O. Hermann, and Leland L. Beik, "Shoppers' Movements Outside Their Local Retail Area," *Journal of Marketing*, Vol. 32 (October 1968), pp. 45–51.

[7] Gillett, same reference as footnote 1, p. 44.

Part 2

The Analysis of Independence

Section B
MULTIDIMENSIONAL SCALING

29

Multidimensional Scaling

David A. Aaker

Multidimensional scaling (MDS) addresses the general problem of positioning objects in a perceptual space. Much of marketing management is concerned with the question of positioning. With whom do we compete? How are we compared to our competitors? On what dimensions? What positioning strategy should be followed? These and other questions are addressed by MDS.

Multidimensional scaling basically involves two problems. First, the dimensions upon which customers perceive or evaluate objects (organizations, products, or brands) must be identified. For example, students must evaluate prospective colleges in terms of their quality, cost, distance from home, and size. It would be convenient to work with only two dimensions, since the objects could then be portrayed graphically. However, it is not always possible to work with two dimensions, since additional dimensions are sometimes needed to represent customers' perceptions and evaluations. Second, objects need to be positioned with respect to these dimensions. The output of MDS is the locations of the objects on the dimensions and is termed a perceptual map.[1]

There are several approaches to multidimensional scaling. They differ in the assumptions they employ, the perspective taken, and the input data used. Figure 1 provides a categorization of the major approaches in terms of the input data. One set of approaches involves object attributes. If the objects are colleges, the attributes could be faculty, prestige, facilities, cost, etc. MDS will then combine these attributes into dimensions such as quality. Another set of approaches bypass attributes and consider similarity or preference

Figure 1
Approaches to Multidimensional Scaling

relationships between objects directly. Thus, two schools could be rated as to how similar they are or how much one is preferred over the other without regard to any underlying attribute. The attribute-based approaches will be described first. A presentation of the nonattribute approaches will follow. Finally, the ideal-object concept will be discussed.

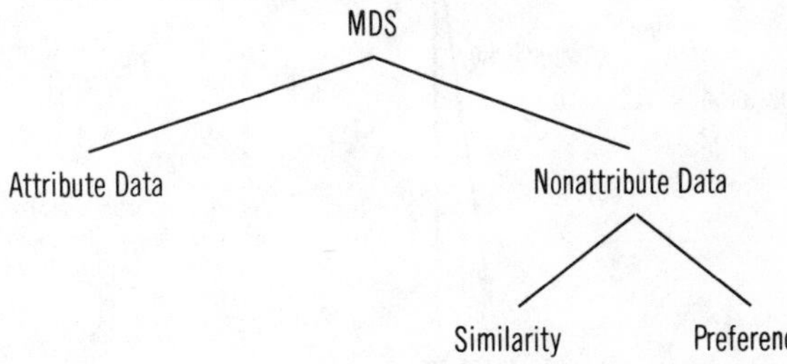

Attribute-Based Approaches

An important assumption of attribute-based approaches is that we can identify attributes upon which individuals' perceptions of objects are based. Let us start with a simple example. Suppose that the goal is to develop a perceptual map of the nonalcoholic beverage market.[2] Suppose further that exploratory research has identified 14 beverages that seem relevant and nine attributes that are used by people to describe and evaluate these beverages. A group of respondents is asked to rate, on a seven-point scale, each of the beverages on the nine attributes. An average rating of the respondent group on each of the nine attributes would be of interest. However, it would

---

[1] There are a variety of programs available to process the various input data and generate a perceptual map. For a summary, see Roger N. Shepard, "A Taxonomy of Some Principal Types of Data and of Multidimensional Methods for Their Analysis," in Roger N. Shepard, A. Kimball Romney, and Sera Beth Nerlove eds., *Multidimensional Scaling* (New York: Seminar Press, 1972), pp. 21–44.

[2] This example is based on research reported in Thomas P. Hustad, Charles S. Mayer, and Thomas W. Whipple, "Consideration of Context Differences in Product Evaluation and Market Segmentation," *Journal of the Academy of Marketing Science*, 3 (Winter 1975): pp. 34–47.

Figure 2
Perceptual Maps of a Beverage Market

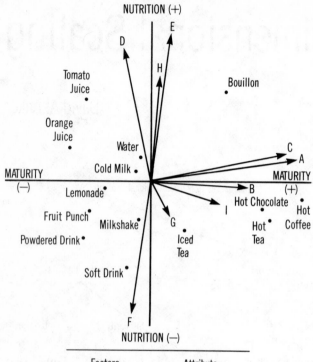

Factors	Attribute
Maturity (27%)[a]	A. Served hot
	B. Adult orientation
	C. Relaxing
Nutrition (26%)	D. Healthful
	E. Consumed with food (vs. best alone)
	F. Sweet
Refreshing (24%)	G. Filling
	H. Energy giving
	I. Thirst quenching

[a]Percent of variance explained.

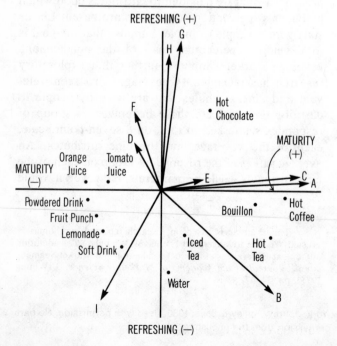

be much more useful if the nine attributes could be combined into two or three dimensions or factors.

Two approaches are commonly used to reduce the attributes to a small number of dimensions. The first is factor analysis, described in the previous section.[3] Since each respondent rates fourteen beverages on nine attributes, he or she will ultimately have fourteen factor scores on each of the emerging factors, one for each of the beverages. The position of each beverage in the perceptual space will then be the average factor score for that beverage. The perceptual map shown in Figure 2 illustrates. Three factors, accounting for 77 percent of the variance, serve to summarize the nine attributes. Each of the beverages is then positioned on the attributes. Since three factors or dimensions are involved, two maps are required to portray the results. The first involves the first two factors, while the second includes the first and third factors. For convenience, the original attributes are also shown in the maps as lines or vectors. The direction of the vectors indicates the factor with which each attribute is associated, and the length of the vector indicates the strength of association. Thus, in the upper map, the "filling" attribute has little association with any factor, whereas in the lower map, the filling attribute is strongly associated with the "refreshing" factor.

A second approach used to reduce the attributes to a smaller number of dimensions is discriminant analysis. The goal of factor analysis is to generate dimensions that maximize interpretability and explain variance. In contrast, the goal of discriminant analysis is to generate dimensions that will discriminate or separate the objects as much as possible.[4] The extent to which an attribute will tend to be an important contributor toward a dimension depends upon the extent to which there is a perceived difference among the objects on that attribute. An advantage of discriminant analysis over factor analysis is that a test of significance is available. The test will determine the probability that a nonzero, between-object distance was simply due to a statistical accident.

Figure 3 shows a MDS solution for the Chicago beer market, based upon discriminant analysis. Each of 500 male beer drinkers described 8 brands of beer

---

[3] There are several ways that factor analysis could be employed. The most common would be to use a respondent's rating of a beverage on the nine attributes as an input. Thus, each respondent would appear fourteen times in the input matrix, once for each time the respondent rated a beverage. An alternative is to generate the factors by factor analyzing importance ratings. Such an approach would, of course, define factors from a different perspective. For a good discussion of this approach, and for a useful conceptual treatment of multidimensional scaling in general, the reader is referred to James H. Myers and Edward Tauber, *Market Structure Analysis* (Chicago: American Marketing Association, 1977).

[4] The dimensions are termed discriminant functions instead of factors.

Figure 3
The Chicago Beer Market

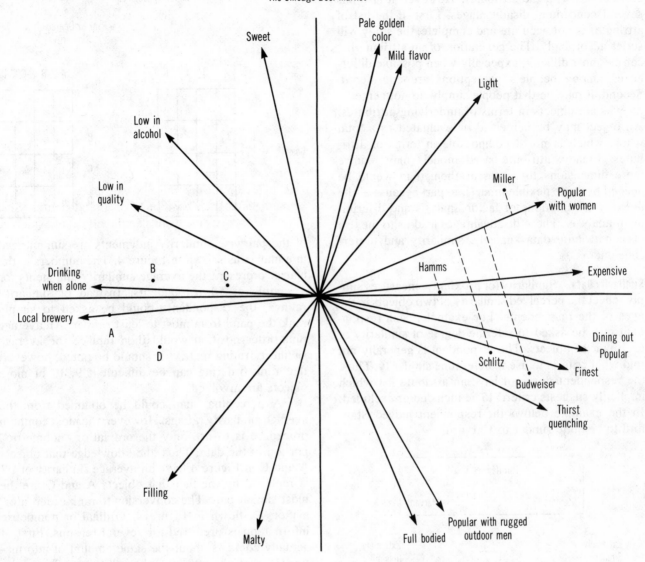

SOURCE: Richard M. Johnson, "Market Segmentation—A Strategic Management Tool," *Journal of Marketing Research* 9 (February 1971), p. 15.

on each of 35 attributes.[5] Each brand is positioned on these two dimensions by averaging over the 500 respondents. Seventeen of the attributes are also shown in the figure. As in Figure 2, their correlations with the two dimensions are reflected by their length and direction. The two dimensions can thus be interpreted by identifying which attribute or cluster of attributes falls closest to them. In this case, the horizontal axis represents a "price-quality" distinction, and the vertical axis represents some notion of "body" (including sweetness, maltiness, etc.). The price-quality axis is

the better of the two in discriminating, since the brands are much more spread out on this axis (horizontal) than on the vertical "body" axis. The brands can be evaluated relative to either the two major discriminant axes or the seventeen attribute vectors by projecting the brand. The dotted lines (drawn perpendicular to the "popular with women" attribute) show that Miller is perceived as being the most popular with women, followed by Budweiser, Schlitz, Hamms, and four popular-priced beers, in that order. Similarly, Budweiser is regarded as being the most expensive beer, and so on.

Nonattribute Data

Attribute-based MDS has the advantage in that attributes can have diagnostic and operational value

---

[5] The two dimensions pictured accounted for about 90 percent of the discrimination among images of these 8 brands. The interpretation is analogous to the percent of variance explained in factor analysis.

and the dimensions can be interpreted in terms of their correlations with the attributes. However, it also has several conceptual disadvantages. First, if the list of attributes is not accurate and complete, the study will suffer accordingly. The generation of an attribute list can be most difficult, expecially when possible differences among people's perceptions are considered. Second, it may be that people simply do not perceive or evaluate objects in terms of underlying attributes. An object may be perceived or evaluated as a total whole which is not decomposable in terms of attributes. Finally, attribute-based models may require more dimensions to represent them than would be needed by more flexible models, in part because of the linearity assumptions of factor analysis and discriminant analysis. These disadvantages lead us to the use of nonattribute data—namely, similarity and preference data.

Similarity Data. Similarity (or proximity) measures simply reflect the perceived similarity of two objects in the eyes of the respondents. For example, each respondent may be asked to rate the degree of similarity of each pair of objects. The respondent is generally not told what criteria to use to determine similarity. Thus, the respondent does not have an attribute list which implicitly suggests criteria to be included or excluded. In the example below, the respondent judged Stanford to be quite similar to Harvard.

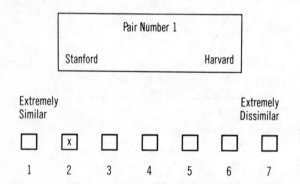

The number of pairs to be judged for degree of similarity can be determined from the formula, $n(n - 1)/2$, where n is the total number of objects. With ten brands, there are 45 pairs of brands to judge. This is a large number of judgments, so it is usually desirable to have a separate card for each pair. The respondent is instructed to place the cards on a "sort board" that has locations corresponding to the similarity of scale categories. When all the cards have been sorted, the respondent should check each pile to ensure that all the pairs in the pile (category) have the same degree of similarity or dissimilarity.

Although it is essential that at least seven or eight objects be judged, the approach is easier to illustrate if only four objects are considered. First, the results

Figure 4
Similarity Judgments

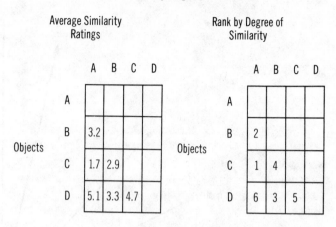

of the pairwise similarity judgments are summarized in a matrix as shown in Figure 4. The numbers in the matrix represent the average similarity judgments for a sample of 50 respondents. Instead of similarity ratings, the respondents could be asked to simply rank the pairs from most to least similar. An average rank-order position would then replace the average similarity rating matrix. It should be noted, however, that rank ordering can be difficult if 9, 10 or more objects are involved.

A perceptual map could be obtained from the average similarity ratings. However, the most common procedure is to use only the ordinal or "nonmetric" portion of the data. Thus, the knowledge that objects A and C in Figure 4 have an average similarity of 1.7 is replaced by the fact that objects A and C are the most similar pair. The conversion to rank-order information is shown in Figure 4. Ordinal or nonmetric information is preferred for several reasons. First, it actually contains about the same amount of information in that the output is usually not affected by replacing interval-scaled or "metric" data with ordinal or nonmetric. Second, the nonmetric data are often thought to be more reliable. Third, programs that operate on nonmetric data have been more readily available than programs that use metric data.

The computer program is then employed to convert the rankings of similarity into distances in a map with a small number of dimensions, so that similar objects are close together and vice versa.[6] The computer program will be instructed to locate the four objects in a space of two, three, or more dimensions, so that the shortest distance is between pair (A, C), the next shortest is pair (A, B), and the longest pair is (C, D). One possible solution that satisfies these constraints in two dimensions is the following:

---

[6] Lester A. Neidell, "The Use of Nonmetric Multi-dimensional Scaling in Market Analyses," *Journal of Marketing* 33 (October 1969): pp. 37–43.

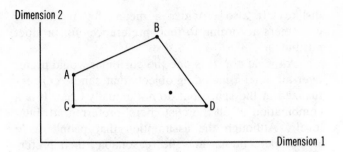

The reader might be able to relocate the points differently and still satisfy the constraints so that the rankings of the distances in the map correspond to the rankings of the pairwise similarity judgments. This is because there are only a few points to move in the space and only six constraints to satisfy. With ten objects and 45 constraints, the task of locating the points in a two-dimensional space is vastly more difficult. In fact, it is only feasible with large-scale computational facilities. Once a solution is found—the points are located in the space—it is unlikely that there will be a significantly different solution that still satisfies the constraints of the similarities matrix. Thus, we can argue that the interval-scaled nature of the distances between points was really hidden in the rank-order input data all the time.

The power of the technique lies in its ability to find the smallest number of dimensions for which there is a reasonably good fit between the input similarity rankings and the rankings of distance between objects in the resulting space. Usually, this means starting with two dimensions and, if this is not satisfactory, continuing to add dimensions until an acceptable fit is achieved. The determination of "acceptable" is a matter of judgment, although most analysts will trade off some degree of fit to stay with a two- or three-dimensional map because of the enormous advantages of visual interpretations. There are situations where more dimensions are necessary. This happened in a study of nine different types of sauces, e.g., mustard, catsup, relish, steak sauce, dressing, etc. Most respondents perceived too many differences to be captured with two or three dimensions, in terms of either the types of foods the sauces would be used with or the physical characteristics of each sauce.[7]

The interpretation of the resulting dimensions takes place "outside" the technique. Additional information must be introduced to decide why objects are located in their relative position. Sometimes the location of the objects themselves can suggest dimensional interpretations. Another approach is to correlate object characteristics, such as attribute ratings, with the object's position on the dimensions.

[7] James H. Myers and Edward Tauber, *Market Structure Analysis* (Chicago: American Marketing Association, 1977).

Table 1
Rank Order of Dissimilarities Between Pairs of Car Models[a,b]

Stimuli	1	2	3	4	5	6	7	8	9	10	11
1	—	8	50	31	12	48	36	2	5	39	10
2		—	38	9	33	37	22	6	4	14	32
3			—	11	55	1	23	46	41	17	52
4				—	44	13	16	19	25	18	42
5					—	54	53	30	28	45	7
6						—	26	47	40	24	51
7							—	29	35	34	49
8								—	3	27	15
9									—	20	21
10										—	43
11											—

Source: Paul E. Green and Frank J. Carmone, "Multidimensional Scaling: An Introduction and Comparison of Nonmetric Unfolding Techniques," *Journal of Marketing Research* 6 (August 1969): p. 331.
   [a] The rank number "1" represents the most similar pair.
   [b] See figure 11 for model descriptions.

An example of rank-order similarity data is shown in Table 1. This could be the ranking of a single respondent or the average of a group of respondents. The resulting perceptual map is shown in Figure 5. In this case, the object locations serve to identify the

Figure 5
Illustration of Joint Space of
Ideal Points and Stimuli

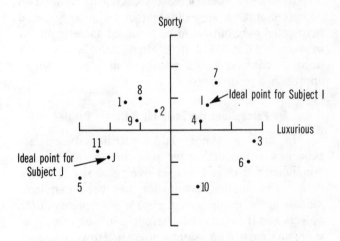

Stimuli — 1968 Car Models

1. Ford Mustang 6
2. Mercury Cougar V8
3. Lincoln Continental V8
4. Ford Thunderbird V8
5. Ford Falcon 6
6. Chrysler Imperial V8
7. Jaguar Sedan
8. AMC Javelin V8
9. Plymouth Barracuda V8
10. Buick Le Sabre V8
11. Chevrolet Corvair

SOURCE: Paul E. Green and Frank J. Carmone, "Multidimensional Scaling: An Introduction and Comparison of Nonmetric Unfolding Techniques." *Journal of Marketing Research* 6 (August 1969) p. 332.

dimensions. For example, objects 3, 6, 5, and 11 provide some insights into the horizontal dimensions labeled "luxurious." Disregard the ideal point notation for now.

Preference Data. Rank-order preference data can also be used as the basis for similarity measures and perceptual maps. Preference data contain similarity information. Objects that are ranked second and sixth in a rank-order preference should be "farther apart" or less similar than objects ranked third and fourth. In general, an individual should be expected to rank close together those objects perceived as being similar. If preference information were obtained not as a rank-order but rather on an interval scale, this information could directly provide a similarity measure between objects. Thus, if an individual rated an object as 7.6 on a 10-point preference scale and another as 4.4, then a reasonable similarity measure would be the difference or 3.2.

The use of preference data to develop perceptual maps introduces a different perspective into the analysis that is quite important. It may be that individuals' perceptions of objects are different in a preference context than in a similarity or attribute-based context. A dimension might be very useful in describing the differences between two objects but it is of no consequence in determining preference. Thus, two objects could be very different in a similarity-based perceptual map but could be regarded as very similar in a preference-based perceptual map. The analyst needs to consider such a possibility in selecting which approach is most appropriate.

Are Perceptions the Same for Different People?

In both attribute and nonattribute-based approaches, it has been suggested that the analysis be conducted for data averaged over groups of respondents. The implicit assumption has been that individuals in the group have the same perceptions of the objects and the observed differences in their responses represent mostly measurement error. However, there may be situations in which there are subgroups that have very different perceptions of the objects. In such cases, it is usually useful to identify those subgroups either by prior knowledge of their characteristics or by clustering them on the basis of their individual responses. Then, separate perceptual maps would be developed for each of the groups with similar perceptions.

Ideal Objects

The concept of an ideal object in the space is an important one in MDS because it allows the analyst to relate object positioning to customer likes and dislikes. It also provides a means for segmenting customers according to their preferences for product attributes.

An ideal object is one the customer would prefer over all others, including objects that can be conceptualized in the space but do not actually exist. It is a combination of all the customers' preferred attribute levels. Although the assumption that people have similar perceptions may be reasonable, their preferences are nearly always heterogeneous—their ideal objects will differ. One reason to locate ideal objects is to identify segments of customers who have similar ideal objects.

There are two types of ideal objects. The first lies within the perceptual map. For example, if a new cookie was rated on attribute scales such as:

Very sweet ——— Not at all sweet
Large, substantial ——— Small, dainty

a respondent may well prefer a mid-position on the scale.

However, if attributes of a proposed new car included:

Inexpensive to buy ——— Expensive to buy
Inexpensive to operate ——— Expensive to operate
Good handling ——— Bad handling

then respondents would very likely prefer an end-point on the scale. For instance, the car should be as inexpensive to buy and operate as possible. In that case, the ideal object would be represented by an ideal vector of direction rather than an ideal point in the space. The direction would depend upon the relative desirability of the various attributes.

There are two approaches to obtaining ideal object locations. The first is simply to ask respondents to consider an ideal object as one of the objects to be rated or compared. The problem with this approach is that the conceptualization of an ideal object may not be natural for a respondent, and the result may therefore be ambiguous and unreliable.

A second approach is indirect. For each individual, a rank order preference among the objects is sought. Then, given a perceptual map, a program will locate the individual's ideal objects such that its distances to the objects have the same (or as close to the same as possible) rank order as the rank-order preference. The preferred object should be closest to the ideal. The second preferred object should be farther from the ideal than the preferred but closer than the third most preferred, and so on. Often it is not possible to determine a location that will perfectly satisfy this requirement and still obtain a small number of dimensions with which an analyst would like to work. In that case, compromises are made and the computer program does as well as possible by maximizing some measure of "goodness-of-fit."

Figure 6
Distribution of Ideal Points in Product Space

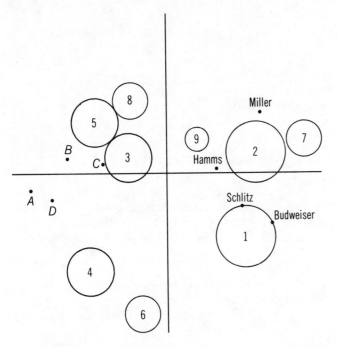

SOURCE: Richard M. Johnson, "Market Segmentation—A Strategic Management Tool," *Journal of Marketing Research* 9 (February 1971), p. 16.

Two individuals' ideal objects have been located in Figure 5. Figure 6 shows a grouping of ideal objects in the perceptual map portrayed in Figure 3.

Multidimensional Scaling—A Summary

Application. MDS is used to identify dimensions by which objects are perceived or evaluated, to position the objects with respect to those dimensions, and to make positioning decisions for new and old products.

Inputs. Attribute-based data involved respondents rating the objects with respect to specified attributes. Similarity-based data involve a rank order of between-object similarity that can be based upon several methods of obtaining similarity information from respondents. Preference data can also provide the basis for similarity measures and generate perceptual maps from quite a different perspective.

Ideal points or directions are based upon either having the respondent conceptualize his or her ideal object or by generating rank-order preference data and using the data in a second stage of analysis to identify ideal points or directions.

Outputs. The output will provide the location of each object on a limited number of dimensions. The selection of the number of dimensions is made on the basis of a "goodness-of-fit" measure (such as the percent of variance explained in factor analysis) and on the basis of the interpretability of the dimensions. In attitude-based MDS, attribute vectors may be included to help interpret the dimensions. Ideal points or directions may be an output in some programs.

Key Assumptions. The overriding assumption is that the underlying data represent valid measures. Thus, we assume that respondents can compare objects with respect to similarity, or preference, or attributes. The meaning of the input data is rather straightforward. The ability and motivation of respondents to provide it is often questionable. A related assumption is that an appropriate context is used by the respondents. For some, a rank-order preference of beer could be based on the assumption it was to be served to guests. Others might assume the beer was to be consumed privately.

With the attribute-based data, the assumption is made that the attribute list is relevant and complete. If individuals are grouped, the assumption that their perceptions are similar is made. The ideal object introduces additional conceptual problems.

Another basic assumption is that the interpoint distances generated by a perceptual map have conceptual meaning that is relevant to choice decisions.

Limitations. A limitation of the attribute-based methods is that the attributes have to be generated. The analyst has the burden of making sure that respondents' perceptions and evaluations are represented by the attributes. With similarity and preference data, this task is eliminated; but the analyst must then interpret dimensions without the aid of such attributes, although attribute data could be independently generated and attribute-dimension correlations still obtained.

For Discussion

How might a perceptual map like that of Figure 2 be used to suggest a new product concept? How would ideal objects be introduced into Figure 2? Suppose, given Figure 3, an advertising objective was to reposition Miller's as being more "full-bodied" and closer to Budweiser. How could MDS be used to test proposed copy? A relevant issue is whether overall similarity judgments are meaningful. Do consumers make overall similarity judgments in their day-to-day life? If not, will such judgments be meaningful?

30

Product Positioning: An Application Of Multidimensional Scaling

Yoram Wind

Patrick J. Robinson

Product positioning, a construct frequently referred to by marketing and advertising practitioners, is rarely, if ever, mentioned in the professional marketing literature. This has resulted in a situation where there seems to be a marginal acceptance of the relevance (and sometimes even importance) of product positioning as a diagnostic device which provides operational guidelines for new product development efforts, redesign of existing products and design of advertising and distribution strategies, while little attention is given to its measurements.

This paper is concerned with just this latter issue—the applicability of one research approach—multidimensional scaling and related techniques—to the measurement of product positioning. While many papers [8, 9, 13] emphasize the methodology of multidimensional scaling, and offer excellent expository discussion of these techniques, this paper offers no discussion of these techniques and emphasizes the *application* of this methodology to one set of marketing problems—product positioning. This will be done by highlighting a number of studies in which various multidimensional scaling techniques have been used to establish product positioning. This is preceded by a brief discussion on the nature and measurement of product positioning. The paper concludes with some comments on the measurement of

product positioning and the relevance of positioning studies as guidelines for marketing strategies.

On the Nature and Measurement of Product Positioning

The term product (brand) positioning refers to the place a product occupies in a given market. Conceptually, the origin of the positioning concept can be related to the economist's work on market structure, competitive position of the firm and the concepts of substitution and competition among products. Marketing also has been concerned with such phenomena as product differentiation [14] and market position analysis, an interest which ranges from simple market share statistics to various approaches (such as Markov processes) for forecasting changes in a firm's market position [1].

More recently, increasing attention has been given to product image. This suggests a new perspective on product positioning, one which focuses on *consumers' perceptions* concerning the place a product occupies in a given market. In this context, the word positioning encompasses most of the common meanings of the word position—position as a place (what place does the specific product occupy in its relevant market?), a rank (how does the given product fare against its competitors on various evaluative dimensions?) and a mental attitude (customer attitudes—the cognitive, affective and action tendencies) toward the given product.

Given this view, the product (brand) positioning should be assessed by measuring consumers' or organizational buyers' *perception* and *preference* for the given product in relation to its realistic competitors

[1] The authors are indebted to Professor Paul E. Green of the University of Pennsylvania who participated in the design and analysis of all the empirical studies reported in this paper, and whose innovative work in the area of multidimensional scaling and its application to marketing problems provided the methodological base for these studies.

(both branded and generic). The necessity to determine product positioning, not only on the basis of its perception (perceived similarity to other products) but also on consumers' preferences for it (overall preference as well as preference under various conditions—scenarios) is a key premise of the "ideal" approach to product positioning.[2] This is based on the premise that customer behavior is a function of *both* their perceptions and preferences and the recognition that buyers may differ with respect to both their perception and the preference for a product.

A somewhat different approach has been taken by Stefflre and his associates in their "Market Structure" analysis [2, 3, 15]. In this new product development procedure, the first few research steps are concerned directly with establishing the market structure, i.e., "determine which items (products and brands) consumers see as constituting a market and the 'position' of each item in the market vis-a-vis the other items."[3] This analysis positions the various brands based on consumers' *perceptions* (similarity) of the various brands and utilizes certain multidimensional scaling procedures. This "positioning" analysis does not utilize preference data in *conjunction with* similarities data but occasionally uses data on patterns of brand-to-brand substitution obtained from large-scale purchase panel data, when these are available.

Whether one uses perceptions, preferences or both as basis for product positioning, it is essential to start with the appropriate set of competing products. This set, which in many cases includes products outside the immediate product class of the product in question, can be generated by marketing experts based on their experience and analysis of existing information or from unstructured depth interviews with consumers. Identifying a broad set of competing items is quite crucial since it constitutes the stimulus set for the positioning study. In designing the stimulus set it is sometimes desirable to include two types of products and brands—brands in the same product class and products and brands outside the product class which may be used by consumers as substitutes for the product in question. For example, in a study of soups, one could include a set of different soup brands, forms, types and flavors as the primary set as well as a set of soup substitutes—sandwich, salad, coffee, various snacks, etc.

Given the stimulus set of brands and products, the next step is to determine consumers' perceived product positioning. This can be done by eliciting (a) consumers' perceptions *via* a variety of available procedures for (overall) similarity measurement, or (b) consumers' preferences—overall and under a variety of usage and purchase conditions[4]—or (c) both consumers' perceptions and preferences.

The data collection procedure employed in each of these cases depends on the number of items in the stimulus set, the total length of the interview, and the researcher's preferences. If one deals with a set of 20 to 40 brands, sorting or rating will be a much more appropriate task than strict ranking which is feasible when a smaller competitive set is included in the study.

Whatever the data collection procedure is, the data should provide, in its original or transformed form, a $P \times P$ matrix of product similarities (or dissimilarity) at the desired level of analysis—individual, segment or total market. This matrix serves as the input data for the appropriate set of multidimensional scaling and clustering programs. The basic idea underlying this analysis is that a market (consumers' perceptions of the various brands) can be conceived as a multidimensional space in which individual brands are positioned. A product's positioning is determined from its position on the relevant dimensions of the similarity space, its position on the various product attribute vectors (if a joint space analysis is undertaken), and its position with respect to other brands, as may be obtained *via* cluster analysis.

A prototypical product positioning procedure is summarized in Figure 1. In designing such a study there are a number of research decisions which have to be made concerning the following topics.

Stimulus Definition. The brands and products selected for inclusion in the stimulus set can be defined in a number of ways and may be presented in terms of the physical objects or services themselves, names of the items, verbalized, profile descriptions of the items, or a mixture of the above. As might be imagined, respondent evaluations may easily differ, depending upon the manner in which the stimuli are described and semantically encoded.

Task Definition. Defining the respondent's task requires an explicit decision. The task could consist of having the respondent react to the stimuli in terms of: overall evaluation of the objects in terms of preference or in

---

[2] In certain empirical studies, because of cost considerations, one may elect to use only preference data as the basis for product positioning.

[3] Barnett [2].

[4] Overall preference cannot reflect the fact that a given product is very preferred for a certain occasion but unacceptable for another relevant occasion (for example, bloody Mary may be the most preferred drink for lunch but totally unacceptable as a before or after dinner drink). This suggests the importance of getting both overall preference and preference under a variety of relevant scenarios. The scenarios included in a positioning study should be based on previous information or generated by some in-depth group sessions with consumers.

Figure 1
Determining Product Positioning

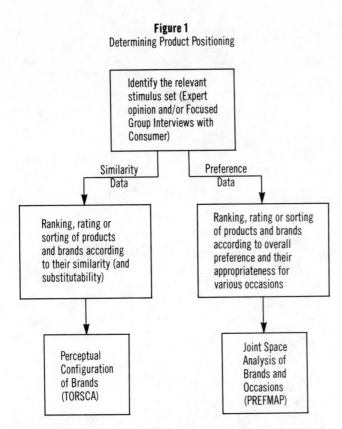

terms of their relative similarity; judgements of objects, similarity or preference (or other types of orderings) according to a set of prespecified scenarios (problem solving conditions) or according to a set of prespecified attributes (other than overall similarity or preference). Alternatively, one can collect objective data on the characteristics of the stimuli in which case an objective performance space rather than a subjective brand space will result.

Response Definition. Assuming that the stimulus set and task have been defined, the researcher must still contend with specifying the nature of the subject's response. Verbal and non-verbal responses may involve ratings judgments, ranking, including strict orderings or weak orderings (those including the possibility of ties) and assignments to prespecified classes.

Even given the restriction of responses to those that represent subjective, verbalized judgments, there are numerous ways for eliciting ratings, rankings and category assignments.

Some Illustrative Studies

To illustrate the applicability of multidimensional scaling to the study of product positioning we will review briefly the results of a number of commercial studies. All of these studies were originally designed for some other purpose such as evaluating a set of new

concepts, evaluating new product designs or promotional programs.[5] They did include, however, as an integral part of the study an examination of product positioning by each of the relevant market segments.

The studies to be reported cover a wide range of products including diet products, medical journals, financial services and retail stores. They also utilize a variety of analytical techniques and develop maps of product positioning based on perceptions, preferences or a combination of the two.

Positioning New Diet Products. A positioning based on contrasting objective and subjective performance evaluations was undertaken in a study of diet food items. In this case one of the objectives of the study was to assess the positioning of some new diet products. The respondents were women who were on a diet and were asked to group food items (some of which were diet products such as Metrecal and some were not, such as pudding, potato chips, milk shakes, etc.) and 13 concepts of new diet products according to their similarity.

In addition they were asked to evaluate the products and concepts according to their overall preference and preference for serving and eating in various eating occasions (scenarios) such as: for lunch, short crash diet to lose weight quickly, to improve appearance, at dinner, when I am by myself, etc. Following this they also rated the products and concepts on a set of 12 attributes including calories, nutrition, taste, convenience of preparation, vitamins, cholesterol and fillingness. This resulted in three sets of subjective data:

1. Product similarity data
2. Product preference rankings (overall and by scenario)
3. Product rankings on various product attributes.

These data were subjected to a variety of multidimensional scaling programs. The 40×40 product similarity data across subjects were submitted to the TORSCA multidimensional scaling program and to the Johnson clustering program. The product evaluative data (both preference for overall usage and usage under certain occasions, and attributes) were submitted to Carroll and Chang's joint space (PREFMAP) program [4].

In addition to these data, a group of food technicians evaluated the various products according to their actual "objective" attributes. These data were also submitted to an appropriate set of multidi-

---

[5] Common to all these studies is the concern with *evaluating* alternative stimuli, and not *generating* them. Occasionally, as a by-product of these studies one can get some ideas for new products. Yet, there are more efficient procedures for generating new product ideas which do not require a positioning analysis.

Figure 2
Two Dimensional Perceptual Configuration of 27 Food Products and 13 New Diet Concepts

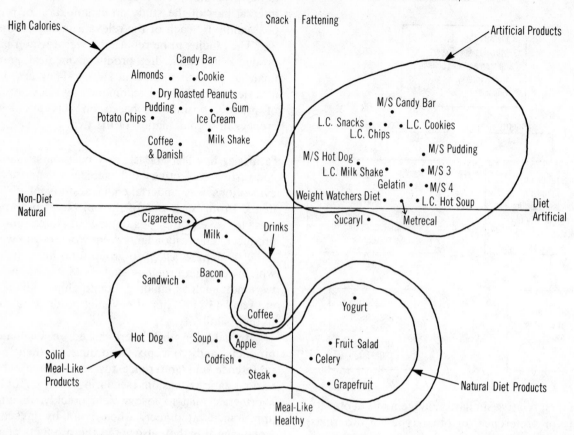

mensional scaling programs enabling a comparison of the subjective-objective maps to be made.

Figure 2 presents the 2 dimensional configuration of the 40 items as derived from the products' similarity data. The product clusters were determined by the Johnson hierarchical clustering program and incorporated into Figure 2. An examination of this figure suggests a number of clusters:

- A cluster of high calorie snack/dessert products such as cookies, candies, milk shakes, etc. (L.C. and M/S stand for low calorie and meal substitute respectively).
- A cluster of "non-natural" diet concepts and products including the new diet concepts and Metrecal.
- A cluster of natural diet foods such as yogurt, fruit salad, celery sticks, etc.
- A cluster of solid, meal-like items.

Examination of any given product or concept reveals its position with respect to other products and concepts as well as its position on the two dimensions. If one is interested in the positioning of the new diet concepts, Figure 2 suggests the following conclusions:

1. The new concepts will compete with other "artificial" diet products such as Metrecal and Weight Watchers Complete Meal.
2. The concepts seem to be positioned opposite their "natural" counterparts. Hence if dimension 2 is viewed as "fattening-healthy" it may suggest that the "fattening" attribute of

the natural products may "rub off" on the diet concepts, leading to overestimation of the fattening attributes of concepts such as a "diet cookie."

Further insight into the position of each concept and product was gained by an examination of the joint space configuration of the products and concepts and their perceived attributes. Figure 3 presents the results of this analysis. Looking at the solid line vectors (subjective evaluations) and the relation of the various products to them suggests:

- "Natural" diet products such as yogurt are perceived as being both nutritious and healthy.
- "Natural" meal items such as steak are perceived as filling and rich in proteins.
- High calorie snacks and desserts such as potato chips and candies are perceived as being "fatty" (fat, cholesterol and carbohydrates), sugary and high in calories. They are, however, convenient for preparation.
- The new diet concepts are perceived as expensive, not tasty, less nutritious than natural diet products and poor on health, protein and fillingness.

A comparison of the "subjective" evaluation configuration with the objective data was done in two stages. First a 2 and 3 dimensions "objective" configuration of the 40 products was derived and compared to the subjective configuration. This suggested that dieters do not perceive diet and non-diet products according to their objective attributes.

Figure 3
Joint Space Configuration
Two Dimensional Perceptual Configuration of 40
Products and Their "Perceived' and Objective Attributes

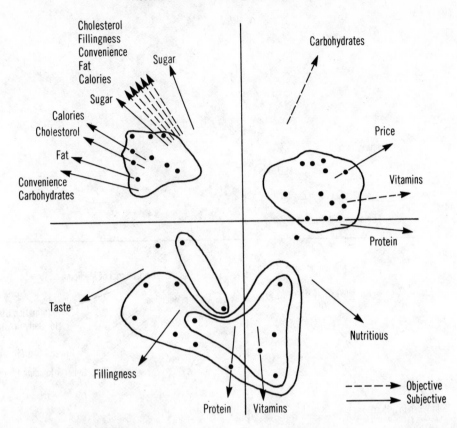

A more direct comparison was undertaken *via* a joint space analysis, the results of which are presented in Figure 3. A comparison of the discrepancies between the objective (broken line) and subjective (solid line) vectors suggests that the greatest discrepancy (50% or greater) exists with regard to fillingness, carbohydrates, proteins and vitamins. Fairly high congruence (less than a 20% discrepancy) is found with respect to calories, sugar, fat, cholesterol and convenience of preparation. This suggests that dieters are more conscious of and interested in—hence knowledgeable with respect to—this latter set of attributes.

Positioning of a Journal.   The concept of positioning can apply not only to industrial and consumer products but also to professional journals. A publisher of a medical journal was concerned with the positioning of his journal. A study was undertaken among a sample of physicians who were presented with a set of 10 medical journals and asked to rank them according to six scenarios such as "general overall preference," "general reading preference," etc. These data provided the input for a journal dissimilarity matrix, across scenarios.

These data were then submitted to the PREFMAP joint space multidimensional scaling program which finds vector directions in the perceptual map (obtained

in an earlier phase *via* INDSCAL multidimensional program [5]). The relationships of the vectors to the journals can be interpreted in terms of preference evaluations. Figure 4 presents the results of this analysis. Interpretation of the dimensionality of this figure shows that the primary attribute by which medical journals are judged are technical versus non technical (horizontal axis) and the specialized versus general (vertical axis). We see for example that *JAMA* is perceived as most technical whereas *Human Sexuality* is seen as the least technical journal.

Observing the six preference vectors illustrates the popularity of *JAMA*, the *New England Journal of Medicine* and *Modern Medicine*. These journals carrying high general preference are those that are viewed as informative as well. The scenarios, "best when in a hurry" and "greatest breadth of appeal" show directions favorable to the news journals such as *Modern World News* and *Medical Tribune*.

The specific position of any of the journals can easily be determined by examining its relations to other journals and its relative position on the two dimensions and the various preference vectors.

In this study one of the objectives was to help the journal in question present itself more effectively to its prospective space-buyers insofar as its relative

Figure 4
Joint Space of Journals and (Vector
Directions of) Evaluative Scenarios — From
PREFMAP Computer Program

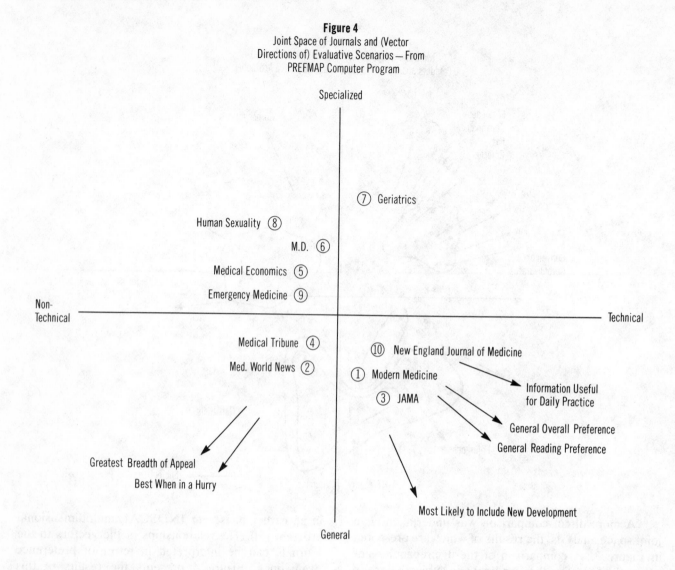

position and strengths versus other vehicles. There
was substantial "surprise value" and yet intuitively
satisfying insights for management in the positioning
and relative strengths and weaknesses of the various
publications. Solicitation policy and various editorial,
format and content changes were clearly identified for
improvement and exploitation.

Positioning of Financial Services. The studies described
so far illustrated a number of direct attempts at positioning a product based on consumers' perceptions
and preferences as well as pointing out the discrepancy
between "objective" and "subjective" product evaluation. Product positioning can also be achieved,
however, by other more indirect methods. One such
procedure is described in the next study. This study
was concerned with the evaluation and positioning of
a number of new financial services. In this case, in
addition to the customary evaluation of new and
existing services on a set of evaluative scales, the
respondents (male heads of households) were also
asked to pick up from a set of 12 occupations the five

occupations whose holders would be most likely to
use the given service. Upon selection of the five occupations, respondents were further asked to rank them
from most to least likely to use the given service.
These data and the similarity configuration of the
various financial services (obtained in an earlier phase,
via the TORSCA program) were submitted to a joint
space program [6]. The results of this analysis are
presented in Figure 5.

An examination of this map suggests a clear
division of the set of financial services based on their
perceived prestige into high prestige services such
as "investment fund" or "special telephone advice"
as opposed to "financial programming" and "monetary
counseling" services which are viewed as low prestige services. In addition a number of services have
a very wide appeal that cuts across all occupations
(as might be the case with income expense reporting
service).

This indirect service positioning was consistent
with the results obtained from the more direct positioning based on perceived similarity of the concepts

Figure 5
Joint Space Configuration of the 8 Concepts
and the 12 Occupations
(MDPREF)

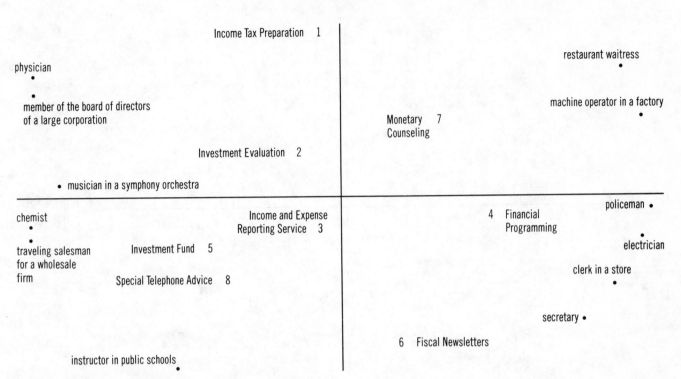

and existing services. It provided further guidelines for promotional strategy than the more common approach, by suggesting the most appropriate type of people (occupations) to be portrayed in promoting the service. For example, the use of testimonials of blue-collar workers for one service and testimonials of professionals such as physician and chemist for another.

Positioning of a Retail Store. Our last illustrative study presents a new dimension in positioning studies. Whereas all of the previous studies focus on a product/service/journal positioning at a point in time, the current study is concerned with the changes in a retail store positioning over time. The study was based on housewives' evaluation of various retail stores in a given metropolitan area over a period of two years. The data for the first three months and last three months were grouped separately and analyzed for the overall market and various *a priori* segments.

Figure 6 presents the results of matching (*via* the Cliff Match procedure [7]) separate TORSCA maps of 9 stores for each of the time periods. The stores in this map have been disguised, but the configuration is the actual configuration that was derived from the actual data. The dimensions of this map could be interpreted as high prestige/relatively expensive versus low prestige/discount (the horizontal axis) and width

of assortment (vertical axis). The change in the perceived position of each store is traced by the dotted line which links the store position in the two time periods. Examination of the magnitude and direction of changes in the stores' positions can provide management with considerable insight into their market position and changes in it as they occurred over the relevant study period.

As in other positioning studies, the time series analysis can be extended to cover changes not only in the stores but also in the stores relative to various evaluative scales (such as good service, easy credit, best value, etc.) and/or various products for which the store may be appropriate (e.g., appliances, clothes, etc.). The analytical procedure is quite similar and the only difference is that instead of developing a "super space" (*via* the Cliff Match program) based on the results of the TORSCA program, the input data to the matching program are the results of the joint space analyses of stores and evaluative scales, or stores and products.

These analyses were of diagnostic significance in revealing relative competing store positions and the extent and direction of movement over a known time interval. As with any time series analysis, certain implications were revealed and of relevance to those concerned with relative standings and trends. More explicit and detailed insights stem from examining

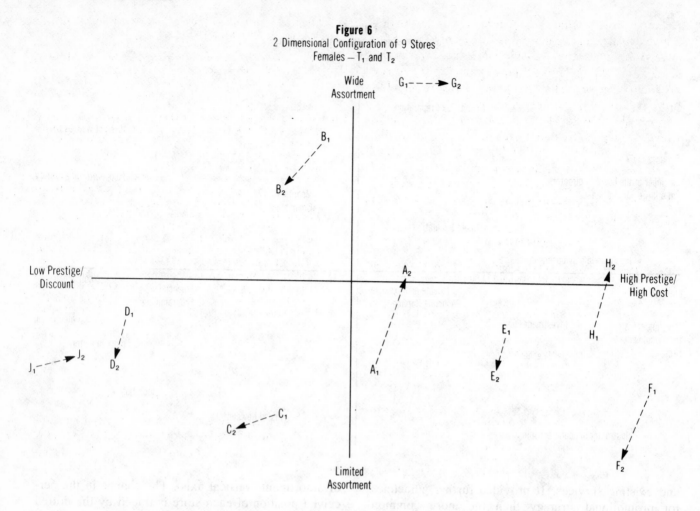

Figure 6
2 Dimensional Configuration of 9 Stores
Females — T_1 and T_2

store policy image positionings and shifts over time. Clearly, significant differences in one's own position may result not only from one's own but one's competitor's policy shifts and positioning and tracing such moves may suggest a number of strategy implications.

Conclusions

The studies which were described briefly in this paper illustrate the wide applicability of the concept of positioning to a variety of products (diet foods and medical journals), services (financial) and retail stores. They further demonstrate the usefulness of utilizing multidimensional scaling and clustering techniques in these types of studies.

Multidimensional scaling techniques include a set of computer algorithms that permit the researcher to develop perceptual and evaluative "maps" (i.e., geometric configurations) that summarize how people perceive various stimulus objects (products, services, stores and the like) as being similar or different, and how such stimulus objects are evaluated on a variety of evaluative scales. As such, this set of techniques is especially suited for the portraying of the perceived position of a product.

Moreover, nonmetric multidimensional scaling

and clustering techniques utilize data that need only be rank ordered (relative similarity or preference for a set of stimuli) which facilitates the respondent's task and places the burden of analysis on the researcher.

In view of the heterogeneous nature of every market the real value of product positioning is revealed, however, only when the positioning is coupled with an appropriate market segmentation analysis. In the studies reported here and in a variety of other studies which included positioning analyses, a segmentation analysis was always included, enabling one to conduct both an overall and segmented positioning analysis. The scope of this paper did not enable us to elaborate on the differences in product positioning by segment. Yet, in all of the studies reported above the findings were quite conclusive in suggesting that such differences do exist and hence justify the value of conducting separate positioning analysis for each market segment.

Product positioning when coupled with market segmentation can provide useful guidelines for the design and coordination of the firm's marketing strategy.

As with segmentation studies the value of a separate positioning study is quite limited. Applying the concept of positioning requires that each marketing research project which is concerned with evaluating a given marketing strategy (e.g., concept evaluation, advertising evaluation and the like) should include a section on the perceived positioning of the given product or service. This should provide a useful addition to almost any marketing study.

Finally, it is hoped that employing multidimensional scaling and related techniques in positioning studies will further the utilization of these and other recently developed techniques in other areas of marketing and image research, hence contributing to improved new directions in the measurement of attitudes and market behavior.

References

1. Alderson, W. and P. E. Green. *Planning and Problem Solving in Marketing* (Homeward, Ill.: Richard D. Irwin, 1964), especially pp. 170–192.
2. Barnett, N. L., "Developing Effective Advertising for New Products," *Journal of Advertising Research*, 8 (December, 1968) pp. 13–20.
3. Barnett, N. L., "Beyond Market Segmentation," *Harvard Business Review*, 27 (Jan.–Feb. 1969) pp. 152–166.
4. Carroll, J. D. and J. J. Chang, "Relating Preference Data to Multidimensional Scaling Solutions via a Generalization of Coombs' Unfolding Model," mimeographed, Bell Telephone Laboratories, Murray Hill, N. J., 1967.
5. Carroll, J. D. and J. J. Chang, "A New Method for Dealing with Individual Differences in Multidimensional Scaling," mimeographed, Bell Telephone Laboratories, Murray Hill, N. J., 1969.
6. Chang, J. J. and J. D. Carroll, "How to Use MDPREF, A Computer Program for Multidimensional Analysis of Preference Data," mimeographed, Bell Telephone Laboratories, Murray Hill, N. J., 1969.
7. Cliff, N., "Orthogonal Rotation to Congruence," *Psychometrika*, 31 (1966) pp. 33–42.
8. Green, P. E. and F. J. Carmone, *Multidimensional Scaling and Related Techniques in Marketing Analysis* (Boston: Allyn and Bacon, 1970).
9. Green, P. E. and V. Rao, *Applied Mutlidimensional Scaling: A Comparison of Approaches and Algorithms*, (N. Y.: Holt Reinhart Inc., 1972).
10. Howard, N. and B. Harris, "A Hierarchical Grouping Routine, IBM 360/65 FORTRAN IV Program," University of Pennsylvania Computer Center, Philadelphia, Pa., 1966.
11. Johnson, S. C., "Hierarchical Clustering Schemes," *Psychometrika*, 32 (1967), pp. 241–54.
12. Kuehn, A. A. and R. L. Day, "Strategy of Product Quality," *Harvard Business Review*, 40 (Nov.–Dec. 1962) pp. 100–110.
13. Silk, A. J., "Preference and Perception Measures in New Product Development: An Exposition and Review," *Industrial Management Review*, 11 (Fall, 1969).
14. Smith, W. R., "Product Differentiation and Market Segmentation as Alternative Marketing Strategies," *Journal of Marketing*, 21 (July, 1956).
15. Stefflre, V., "Market Structure Studies: New Products for Old Markets and New Markets (Foreign) for Old Products," in Bass, King and Pessemier (eds.) *Applications of the Sciences in Marketing*, N. Y.: John Wiley and Sons, 1968, pp. 251–268.
16. Young, F. W. and W. S. Torgerson, "TORSCA – A FORTRAN IV Program for Shepart-Kruskal Multidimensional Scaling Analysis," *Behavioral Science*, 12 (1967), p. 498.

For Discussion

Evaluate the appropriateness of the dimension labels in Figure 2. Interpret Figures 2, 3, 4, 5 and 6. Determine how they might be used to affect marketing strategy.

31

An Application of Multidimensional Scaling & Related Techniques to the Evaluation of a New Product Concept

Larry Percy

Abstract

A new product concept is studied to determine how it will be received in relation to existing alternatives and whom consumers perceive the likeliest user. Various multidimensional scaling techniques are utilized to analyze the new product concept and seven alternatives as well as five homemaker characterizations and five life-cycle stages.

Introduction

One of the realities of marketing is that more likely than not, consumer researchers are asked to determine the viability of some new product idea already developed by a company's research and development section, rather than asked to help determine what will be a viable new product idea. The need for the study reported in this paper arose from the former.

A new concept for a convenience dinner had been originated, then formulated, by a major food manufacturer. As management assessed the potential of the new idea, they were worried by two vexing questions: (1) How will this product be perceived in relation to existing alternatives; and (2) Who is perceived by consumers as the likely user. The first of these questions was doubly confounding, because if the product was perceived to be similar to existing TV-type dinners, the market would be tough to crack; yet there was much in the new product concept that would suggest it was little more than another TV-type dinner.

A study was designed in which one could evaluate the new product concept within the consumer's product-market cognitive domain, and to examine how the new product concept would be evaluated within various usage scenarios. A multidimensional scaling approach is used in order to fully understand the many interrelationships active in consumer positioning of this new product concept. This multidimensional scaling approach is selected over more conventional concept testing procedures (e.g., a straight "concept-to-use" test) because it is felt what is most important is how the "idea" of this new product will be encoded by consumers for evaluation against alternatives within the product market.

Initial exposure to the new product, assuming it is marketed, is in large part due to advertising and promotion. The image conveyed through these communications variables will be compared and evaluated against competing cognitive stimuli, with evaluation of the new product proceeding from this reference. Establishing this point of reference is thus more critical as a first step toward a decision to market the product: not obviating the need for assessing actual product performance through usage testing, but preceding it.

Study Design

Answers to the two questions asked by management are considered the goals of this investigation. A number of dinner alternatives are considered, along with several different perceived usage variables. Personal interviews among thirty female heads-of-household in three geographically diverse cities (Boston, Tampa, Omaha) were conducted: 90 completed ques-

Reprinted from the Proceedings of the 6th Annual Conference of the Association of Consumer Research, 1975, pp. 114–118. No part of this article may be reproduced in any form without prior written permission from the publisher.

tionnaires were used in the analysis. Subjects were selected on an area-wide cluster basis, stratified to ensure representation of a broad demographic base.

Method

Two basic exercises were conducted: (1) a gathering of pairwise proximities data among selected dinner stimuli; and (2) a rank ordering of perceived likelihood of serving the selected dinner stimuli under various usage scenarios. In the first exercise, seven alternative dinner options available from the product-market were selected. These are listed below in Table 1. Each of these alternatives was then reduced to a concept statement: e.g., TV Dinner Plus became "frozen dinner featuring family favorites in a single tray with larger portions of the main dish." Along with the new product concept, 28 cards were prepared, each card containing one of the $n(n - 1)/2$ pairs of dinner concepts.

Table 1
Selected Alternative Dinner Options

Box Dinner
TV Dinner
TV Dinner Plus
Main Dish/Starch Combination
Easy to Prepare Homemade Dinner
Quick Homemade Dinner
Big Homemade Dinner

Subjects were asked to look through all of the cards (which they were told contained the description of two different kinds of dinners), placing all the cards they felt contained descriptions of similar dinners into one pile and all those cards they felt contained descriptions of dinners which were not similar into a second pile. They were then asked to rank the first pile from the card containing the description of the two most similar dinners, and to rank those cards in the second pile from those containing the most dissimilar kinds of dinners. The order of the second pile was then inverted and added to the first, providing a ranking of all 28 pairs from the most to least alike.

In the second exercise, the subjects were presented with a card listing each of the eight concepts used in the first exercise. She was then asked: suppose you were told that a homemaker was described as "modern" i.e., she has a generally contemporary life style without being "hip" or faddish. If this were all you knew about this person, which of these different kinds of dinners do you think she would serve *most* often? All dinners were similarly ranked, the last being the one the subject perceived this scenario homemaker least often serving. All eight dinner concepts were

Table 2
Usage Scenarios

Homemaker Characterizations
1. "Modern" women: a generally contemporary lifestyle without being "hip" or faddish
2. Constantly busy around the house
3. Unwilling to work or take on outside responsibilities which take her away from her home and children
4. "Working" women: a truly active woman who would rather be working than at home all day
5. Homemaking/cooking part of wifely role: sees these activities as part of her feminine, wifely role and duty

Life-cycle Stages
1. Young single student
2. Young single job holder
3. Early marriage (no children)
4. Middle marriage (children)
5. Older adult (no children)

ranked in a similar manner for the four other homemaker characterizations listed in Table 2, as well as for the five life-cycle stages shown. These data then provided rank orderings of the perceived likelihood of each dinner being served often by the person described in each scenario.

Analytic Design. Data collected in the first exercise are considered proximities measurements, and are submitted to Kruskal's (1969) M-D-SCAL 5-M program for non-metric multidimensional scaling.[A] Solutions are sought in three, two, and one dimensions. Data collected in the second phase are considered as two separate data sets for non-metric multidimensional unfolding: the five homemaker characterizations are treated as one set, the five life-cycle stages a second. Spearman rank order correlations are computed for each set in order to determine the "uniqueness" of the rank order profiles. The rank order profiles in each set are then treated as similarity estimates between the eight dinner stimuli and the scenario (cf. Percy, 1975). Utilizing again Kruskal's M-D-SCAL 5-M program, this time exercising the lower corner matrix and split-by-rows options, a non-metric unfolding solution is effected for each set in three, two, and one dimension.

Finally, utilizing the appropriate solution configuration from the multidimensional scaling of the eight dinner stimuli, and the rank order profiles collected for each usage scenario, the perceived usage is integrated with the cognitive evaluation via Chang and Carroll's (1969) PROFIT.

[A] Ed. Note: Non-metric multidimensional scaling refers here to the use of rank-order similarity measures. Thus, respondents in some way provide a ranking as to the similarity of all the object pairs under consideration.

Figure 1
Two Dimensional Multidimensional Scaling
Configuration of Eight Dinner Concepts

Stress = 0.0097

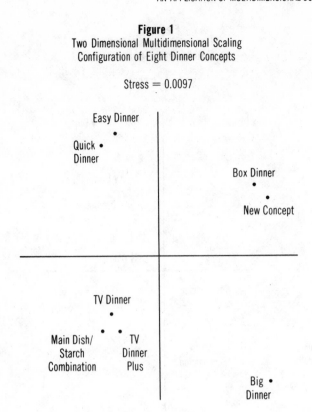

Table 3
Spearman Rank Order Correlations of Homemaker Characterization
Perceived Likelihood of Serving Eight Dinner Concepts

Homemaker Characterization	1.	2.	3.	4.	5.
1. "Modern" women	—	.81	.45	.90	.60
2. Constantly busy around house		—	.12	.83	.26
3. Unwilling to work			—	.24	.90
4. "Working" women				—	.29
5. Homemaking/cooking part of wifely role					—

stimuli within the clusters. But this wasn't important to our purpose: what was important is that we discovered the new concept tended to cluster with box dinners, not TV-type dinners.

Reviewing the resulting multidimensional scaling configuration suggests that four distinct clusters of these stimuli occur within the general consumer cognition, and that these four clusters are considered unlike each other. Looking at the composition of the clusters confirms the logic of the groupings: low versus high involvement "from scratch" dinners and TV-type versus other prepared-type dinners. So, while from a statistical standpoint the degeneracy apparent in the solution may be unappealing, from a practical standpoint the solution positions the new concept within existing perception, responding to the stated goal of the analytic design.

The second step in the analysis is to relate the various usage scenarios to perceived appropriateness of the stimuli. The homemaker characterization and life-cycle stage scenario sets were each submitted to a non-metric multidimensional unfolding analysis. The Spearman rank order correlations shown above in Table 3 for the five homemaker characterizations reveal some strong similarities among the profiles, suggesting that a multidimensional unfolding of these data might be difficult.[1]

And in fact, the two-space solution configuration revealed in Figure 2 does exhibit a rather high stress value of 0.3536. As a result, one must be careful in drawing any conclusions from the configuration. The fact that five of the stimuli cluster together toward the center of the space suggests that substantially more variation probably occurred between those stimuli. Otherwise, one should expect these five stimuli (the Big Dinner, Box Dinner, M/S Combination, TV Dinner, and TV Dinner Plus) to distribute throughout the space just as the homemaker characterization scenarios did.

Study Results

The first step in the analysis is to develop an idea of where the new product concept lies in relation to existing alternatives within consumer cognition. Results of the non-metric multidimensional scaling analysis of the n(n − 1)/2 pair-wise similarities rankings provide a highly acceptable stress in two dimensions of 0.0097. In fact, the remarkable stress value suggests the possibility of a degenerate or quasidegeneracy of the solution.

Looking closely at the solution configuration shown in Figure 1, one does notice the tendency of the various concepts to collapse into vertices of a parallelogram, one of Shepard's (1974) nine forms of two-dimensional degeneracy. Still, the configuration need not be considered too degenerate for our purposes.

The analysis has provided us with a representation of the stimuli in the consumer's mind. What it has perhaps failed to provide is a portion of the actual structural information conveyed by a more non-degenerate solution. It should be noted however that this was an accepted risk in the analytic design, utilizing as it did fewer than ten stimuli for an anticipated two-dimensional solution as well as the inclusion of obviously clusterable stimuli. In fact, one of the principal goals of the analysis was to determine if indeed the new concept conceptually clustered with the more TV-type dinner stimuli. We have learned that the stimuli do cluster together as anticipated, even though we learned nothing about the relationships among the

---

[1] For a more detailed discussion of what to look for in your data to increase the likelihood of a successful multidimensional unfolding, see Moskowitz (1973) and Percy (1975).

Figure 2
Unfolded Homemaker Characterization
Profiles: Two-Space Configuration

Stress = 0.3536

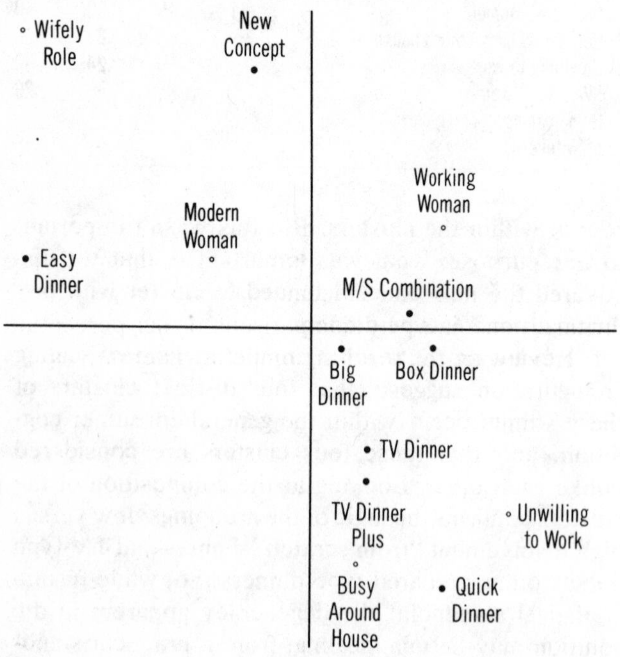

Figure 3
Unfolded Life-Cycle Stage Profiles:
Two-Space Configuration

Stress = 0.0097

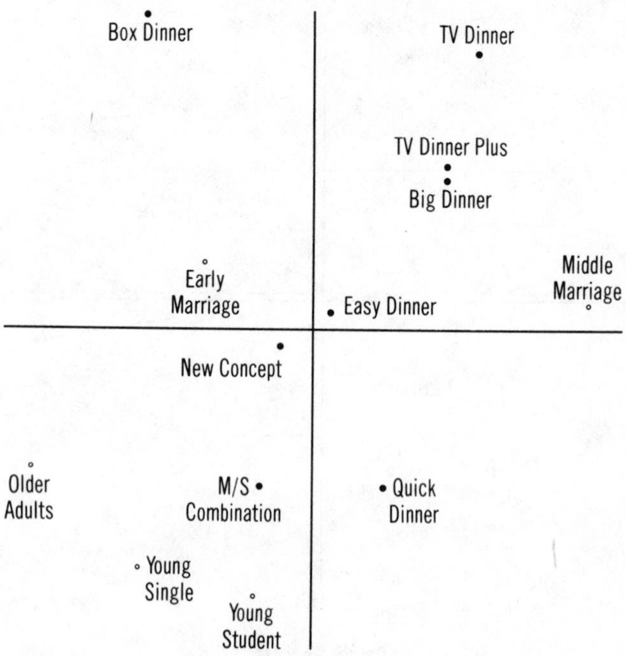

Looking next at the Life-Cycle Stage Scenarios, the Spearman rank order correlation matrix shown in Table 4 indicates very little similarity among the profiles; unfolding of these data should result in a meaningful solution.

Once again, the early look at the profile data predicted the strength of the solution. Looking at Figure 3, one finds a two-space configuration developed with a stress value of 0.0097. One may certainly consider the inter- and intra-relationships among and between the stimuli and scenarios as meaningful. It is interesting to reflect, for example, on the proximity of the new concept to the Easy Dinner and not the Box Dinner (recall that in the multidimensional scaling of pairwise dissimilarities, the new concept and Box Dinner clustered together in solution). What this per-

haps reveals is that in terms of perceived usage, the new concept is rated more constantly like the Easy Dinner than the Box Dinner, even though it is classified in cognition more like the Box Dinner. In other words, different dimensional criteria are involved with each exercise. (This question is addressed in the final step.) Drawing concentric iso-preference curves from each scenario point reflects the perceived likelihood of each dinner stimuli being served. With the exception of Middle Marriage, the new concept enjoys a rather strong likelihood of being served, especially in Early Marriage and by Older Adults—and one notes here a constant of no children.

While the unfolding of the homemaker characterization scenarios did not prove particularly helpful, the unfolding of the life-cycle stage scenarios was revealing of several interesting relationships bearing on a positional evaluation of the new product idea.

The final step in the analysis is the integrating of the perceived usage information with the general cognitive representation. Each of the rank order scenarios was introduced as a property, along with the coordinate values of the eight dinner stimuli as determined by the M-D-SCAL solution in two dimensions, into Chang and Carroll's PROFIT algorithm. The results provide a vector determination, or direction, for each property (or scenario in this case) in the original two dimensional space such that the projections of the eight dinner concepts on that vector correspond optimally to the given

Table 4
Spearman Rank Order Correlations of Life-Cycle Stage
Perceived Likelihood of Serving Eight Dinner Concepts

Life-Cycle Stage	1.	2.	3.	4.	5.
1. Young single student	—	.95	−.57	−.29	−.93
2. Young single job holder		—	−.45	−.48	−.80
3. Early marriage (no children)			—	−.45	.64
4. Middle marriage (children)				—	.17
5. Older Adult (no children)					—

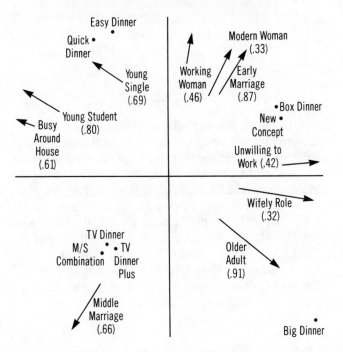

Figure 4
10 Property Vectors Fitted in the Average-Subject
Stimulus Space of 8 Dinner Concepts Using PROFIT

rank order of the perceived likelihood of it being served under that scenario.

Looking now at Figure 4, one finds that life-cycle stage scenarios enjoy good fits to the cognitive representation, while the homemaker characterizations (with the exception of Busy Around House) offer poor fits. This conclusion is drawn by examining the Rho values for each property vector enclosed in parentheses, representing the maximum correlation between each given property and its fitted vector.

If one ignores the homemaker characteristic scenarios, owing to their poor fits, the new concept finds itself associated quite highly with the Early Marriage and Older Adult life-cycle stage scenarios. It would seem that our new product idea tends not to be associated in consumers' minds with the TV-type dinners, which are more oriented in perceived usage to Middle Marriage; rather it is perceived to have a higher likelihood of service among married homemakers with no children, and to cluster with Box Dinners.

Discussion and Conclusion

In this study, attention has been drawn to the application of multidimensional scaling and related techniques in the evaluation of a new product concept. The focus is purposefully narrow, owing to an overriding concern on the part of management that the new product concept may be perceived by consumers as similar to TV-type dinners. The application of multidimensional scaling procedures rather than more

conventional concept testing methods was suggested by this need to determine where the new product concept would be situated within consumer cognition. They are proven particularly useful and sensitive in uncovering certain aspects of cognition, and provide a graphic representation.

Building on past research in the area of food and the meal, a number of made-from-scratch and packaged-convenience dinner alternatives were reduced to simple concept form for comparison with the new product concept. The logic here holds that the introduction of the new product will rely heavily on the consumer's understanding of the "concept" once aware of it, and subsequent trial and usage will be critically mediated by comparisons of her perception of the new product versus competing alternatives. As a further aid in gaining a complete understanding of her cognitive associations, specific homemaker characteristics and life-cycle stage scenarios were considered for all competing dinner alternatives (including the new product concept).

The multidimensional scaling of the pair-wise concept similarities, despite a possible mathematically degenerate configuration, clearly indicated that consumers would *not* encode the new product concept together with TV-type dinner alternatives. This was, of course, welcome news from a marketing standpoint.

Multidimensional unfolding of the concepts and scenarios indicated that women apparently find it difficult to form any consensus regarding possible dinner alternatives and particular homemaker characterizations. The very high resulting stress measure (presaged by high profile correlations) reflected a great deal of similarity in perceived usage attribution. While women may in fact expect little meal serving difference between the homemakers characterized by the scenarios presented, it may also be true that they found the characterizations difficult to relate to this type of behavior.

On the other hand, differences were easily related to life-cycle stages. The multidimensional unfolding in this case revealed meaningful associations between specific life-cycle stages and the likelihood of often serving particular dinner alternatives. The new product concept was related strongly to the Early Married and Older Adult stage (both characterized by no children).

A final exercise combining the cognitive representation with the scenario attribution via PROFIT reinforced the results of the unfoldings. Once again very poor fits generally were found for the homemaker characteristic scenarios, but strong fits for the life-cycle stage scenarios. This embedding of the scenarios in the multidimensional scaling solution represented an external analysis verification of the internal analysis evaluations presented by the multidimensional unfoldings. The consistency of results offers a certain implied level of confidence in the conclusions to be drawn.

We have seen how the utilization of multidimensional scaling and related techniques may be productively applied to new product concept evaluation, particularly when an initial assessment of generalized cognition is important. Having satisfied one's self of the market positioning potential of the general concept, it is possible to proceed comfortably with more detailed analysis (e.g., conjoint measurement of the concept components and possible positionings) evaluating the strength of the concept.

References

1. J. J. Chang and J. D. Carroll, "How to Use PROFIT, A Computer Program for Property Fitting by Optimizing Nonlinear or Linear Correlation," Bell Laboratories, unpublished manuscript, 1969.
2. J. B. Kruskal and F. J. Carmone, "How to Use M-D-SCAL, A Program to do Multidimensional Scaling and Multidimensional Unfolding," (Versions 5M of M-D-SCAL, all in Fortran IV), Murray Hill, N.J.: Mimeo, Bell Telephone Laboratories, 1969.
3. H. R. Moskowitz, "Profile Attributes as Similarities," paper presented at Association for Consumer Research Fall Conference, Boston, 1973.
4. L. H. Percy, "Multidimensional Unfolding of Profile Data: A Discussion and Illustration with Attention to Badness-of-Fit," *Journal of Marketing Research*, 12 (February, 1975), 93–9.
5. R. N. Shepard, "Representation of Structure in Similarity Data: Problems and Prospects," *Psychometrika*, 39 (December, 1974).

For Discussion

Form 21 pairs of dinner options from Table 1. Determine the first, second and third most similar pairs. Rank order the six dinner options from the point of view of the "modern" women (No. 1) and from the viewpoint of the "homemaking" women (No. 5). Such a rank order provides an ideal point for the homemaker types. How do the preferences for the dinner options for the Middle Marriage ideal point differ from the Young Single ideal point in Figure 3? Why do the relative positions of Easy Dinner and Quick Dinner (and the other options) differ in Figures 1, 2, and 3?

32

How Store Image Affects Shopping Habits in Grocery Chains

Peter Doyle

Ian Fenwick

This article describes and provides a pilot illustration of a new methodology for measuring the images of various retail grocery chains. In store image research we are concerned with the question of what draws shoppers to one store rather than another. Early approaches emphasized "gravity" or distance as the determinant of store loyalty. But with urbanization and a more mobile population, convenience is no longer the overwhelming factor in choice (e.g., Thompson [22]). Increasingly, relative prices and such factors as variety of goods sold, reputation for quality, layout, and parking facilities are key determinants. Shoppers' perceptions of these characteristics are often called a store's image.

There are two central problems in measuring such perceptions. The first is to isolate in an unambiguous and parsimonious fashion the salient dimensions shoppers actually use in evaluating alternative outlets selling groceries. This is necessary if we are to compare the relative strengths of competitive shops as consumers see them. The second problem is to meaningfully segment consumers. This is important because it is well known that different socioeconomic groups do not perceive stores in the same way (e.g., Rich and Portis [19]). The common research practice of averaging over respondents throws away some of the most useful information for decision-makers and at the same time tends to produce an "average image" atypical of the perceptions of any group of consumers. It is shown below that conventional survey techniques do not satisfactorily handle these problems. The new approach illustrated—individual difference scaling—appears to offer a more fruitful methodology.

The Place of Image Research

That stores have images is undisputed. Schlackman, for example, found from qualitative research that two British chains had such strong images that their own brands were accepted by shoppers to be of a quality comparable to higher-priced nationally advertised manufacturers' brands. He wrote:

Sainsbury's and Marks and Spencer possess extremely high value-and-quality associations and have established themselves as strong retailers, prepared to stand behind their products; consumers are very willing to accept their brands. In a psychological sense, the Sainsbury and St. Michael labels function very much like the "brand-image" characteristic of the nationally advertised product. The necessary feeling of confidence induced by the nationally advertised product exists here as well. And they are seen to be as acceptable as other brands in product classes which are nationally advertised. [21]

What do we mean by store image? The term is used interchangeably with attitude toward the store to describe the overall impression a consumer has of it. Martineau [18] produced the seminal discussion of store image. While concentrating on personality aspects of the store as "an aura of psychological attitudes" by which shoppers define stores, he went on to describe four elements of image: layout and architecture, symbols and colors, advertising, and sales personnel.

How are store images formed? First, they are not simply a function of advertising and creative promotions. On the contrary, many of the examples of

Reprinted from the *Journal of Retailing*, Vol. 50 (Winter 1974–1975), pp. 39–52. Used by permission. No part of this article may be reproduced in any form without prior written permission from the publisher.

successful image creation cited by Martineau and other studies depend upon *physical*, but nonprice aspects of the store—layout, cleanliness, sales efficiency, etc. Thus rather than classifying image as part of the "non-logical basis of shopping behaviour," as Martineau suggests, it is reasonable to view the customer as rationally evaluating the store on a multi-attribute utility function (*see* Lancaster [16], and Doyle and Fenwick [5]). While psychological appeals may play a part, they are not necessary to rationalize an interest in nonprice factors. Bender [1], for instance, points out the importance of costs other than commodity price—time spent shopping, parking facilities, etc. These, he says, may be termed secondary purchase costs. In making a shopping decision, total costs—secondary *and* primary—are considered. Store image, therefore, rather than being an irrational construct may be regarded as the consumer's evaluation of all salient aspects of the store as individually perceived and weighted.

Management's interest in store image is therefore self-evident. A store's image can be at least partly controlled through decisions about store facilities, layout, and advertising. The resulting image has a significant impact on the store's appeal to shoppers. More particularly, considerable evidence has been amassed to suggest that shoppers seek stores whose image is congruent with their own self-image. As Martineau has pointed out, no store can be all things to all people. As with brands, it makes sense to segment the market and to attempt to develop an image which conforms to the needs of the store's target customers.

A number of empirical studies have used conventional survey techniques to measure store images and test various hypotheses concerning them. Weale, for example, measured store and self-image using semantic differential scales. Dornoff and Tatham [8] also showed that congruence exists between store and customer self-image. Similar studies have been made by Rich and Portis [19] and by Kelly and Stephenson [14]. More recently Lessig [17] employed a Fishbein-type of analysis to evaluate store image and related this to store loyalty.

Multidimensional Scaling

The approach recommended in this article is based upon multidimensional scaling. This title covers a variety of methods of differing complexity. Their fundamental characteristic is that although input data are ordinal-rankings, output is a map showing the relative positions of the stimuli. Instead of rating stimuli on prespecified dimensions (as under both the previous methods), and investing such ratings with interval scale properties, input data is usually collected in the form of rankings of paths of stimuli according to their similarity (*see* e.g., Doyle [4]). This input method has the joint advantage of reducing the level of precision ascribed to the respondent and presenting the subject with the opportunity to make unstructured judgments. This opportunity increases the likelihood that the dimensions most important to consumers will be discovered.

Multidimensional scaling algorithms produce an n-dimensional configuration of stimuli in which distance between pairs of points (d_{jk}) are repeatedly adjusted to the rankings of pairs of stimuli, δ_{jk} (for a complete exposition see Kruskal [15]). A *nonmetric* method specifies $\delta_{jk} = M(d_{jk})$ where M is any monotonic function. A *quasi*-nonmetric method, although using a monotone transformation, imposes a metric criterion for the iteration process. A *metric* method assumes some specific form for the function M, e.g., linear. Thus MDSCAL and TORSCA are popular algorithms which have facilities for metric and nonmetric scaling, but INDSCAL is a metric scaling program with NINDSCAL as a pseudo-nonmetric version (see Green and Rao [13]). It is probably true that the advantages of nonmetric methods have been somewhat overstated. Metric programs such as INDSCAL have facilities not available on nonmetric programs. Further there is increasing evidence that generally final output is robust in the face of violations of assumptions about the form of M (*see* Green and Jain [12]).

INDSCAL is a particularly appropriate algorithm for image studies because it can examine individual differences in perception. Instead of pooling similarities data from all respondents, it is assumed that although all share a common perceptual map, individuals may weight the dimensions of the map differently. Thus a map of stimuli is produced *and* a map of weights showing the relative importance given to dimensions by individuals. Thus we are able to obtain both images and dimension saliences. Furthermore INDSCAL produces configurations which are uniquely oriented (unlike other multidimensional scaling programs). Thus the problems of interpretation are reduced, and the validity of these unique dimensions has been supported in many applications (*see* Wish and Carroll [24]).

The INDSCAL model is given by

$$\delta_{ijk} = M(d_{ijk})$$

and

$$d_{ijk} = \left[\sum_t w_{it} (X_{jt} - X_{kt})^2 \right]^{1/2}$$

where

$\delta_{ijk} = i$th individual's similarity ranking for stimuli j and k

$d_{ijk} = $ weighted distance between j and k on the stimulus map

Table I
Grocery Chains Compared

	Number of branches		
	All	Supermarkets	Self-service
Co-op (Co)	7,000	1,000	3,750
Fine Fare (FF)	1,007	461	371
International Stores (IS)	924	239	639
MacFisheries (MF)	67	67	—
Marks and Spencer (M & S)	251	—	251
Safeway (Sf)	65	65	—
Sainsbury's (Sb)	196	147	21
Tesco (Tso)	774	445	227
Woolworth (W)	1,058	—	251

Supermarkets are defined as self-service units with more than 4,000 square feet of selling space.

x_{jt} = coordinates of stimulus j on dimension t
w_{it} = weight individual i attaches to dimension t

The algorithm uses an iterative least squares method to find X_{jt}, X_{kt}, and w_{it} that give the best fit to the equation.

Data and Aggregate Results

The data are from a small pilot sample of 40 housewives in the London area. The sample was stratified by age and social class in order to obtain a reasonable representation of the population. Each housewife ranked all pairs of nine chains in terms of their similarity as places from which to buy groceries. In addition, they completed a questionnaire on their demographic characteristics and shopping behavior. Then they ranked the chains in order of preference for grocery shopping. Finally stores were rated on a number of conventional semantic differential scales in terms of their value for money, variety, layout, quality, etc. The latter were based on the findings of pre-

Table II
Summary Statistics for INDSCAL in Two and Three Dimensions

	Aggregate R^2	Average Correlation
2 Dimensions	0.30	0.52
3 Dimensions	0.47	0.67

vious studies (Martineau [18], Weale [23], Lessig [17]) and pilot work. Table I shows the chains used in the study and their number and type of branches in the UK.

The first step in the analysis was to input respondents' pairwise similarity rankings into Carroll and Chang's [3] INDSCAL programme. Figure 1 shows the three-dimensional perceptual map which on aggregate best fitted the 40 matrices of similarity rankings. One problem with all multidimensional scaling methods is that the dimensions of the space are not directly identified. Many insights can often be obtained simply from the competitive positions of the stimuli, but there are a variety of methods for using ancillary data to name the axes (*see* Doyle and McGee [7]). Here the dimensions are labeled from the ratings supplied by respondents.

Several intuitively reasonable competitive relationships are clear from the map. Sainsbury's and Marks and Spencer are viewed significantly higher than the others on the vertical dimension (tentatively labeled "quality"). Woolworth's performance was particularly poor. Woolworth's and Marks and Spencer differ from the others significantly on the horizontal axis, probably reflecting the late and smaller commitment to groceries in their stores.

Figure 1, however is not a complete reflection of how consumers view the stores; Table II indicates the overall goodness of fit. Three dimensions account for only 50 percent of the variance over all the similarity matrices, and the average individual correlation (after appropriate differential stretching of the dimensions in proportion to the individual dimension weights) reached only 70 percent. Part of the unexplained variation is due to the incomplete validity of the INDSCAL model where respondents use identical dimensions to evaluate stores. Such error might be expected to be relatively high in this type of study because we are looking not at individual stores but at store chains. Heterogeneity among stores within any chain will accentuate respondent variability.

Disaggregate Results

Previous studies have emphasized the importance of segmenting the market because different groups of consumers do not have identical perceptions of stores. INDSCAL provides a ready approach to studying consumer heterogeneity of perception. Figure 2 shows

Figure 1
Perceptual Space in three Dimensions

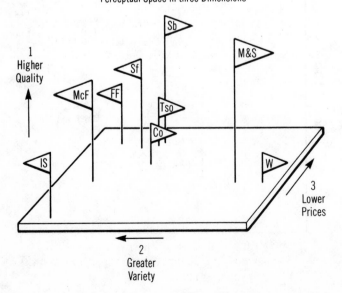

1 Higher Quality

2 Greater Variety

3 Lower Prices

Figure 2
Respondent Space from INDSCAL

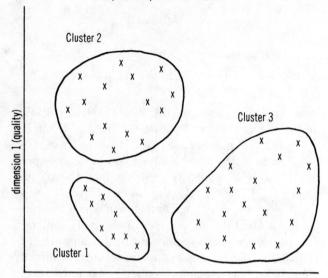

the weights individual housewives attach to the first two dimensions of Figure 1. Two aspects are worth noting in the interpretation of this map. First, distance from the origin is directly proportionate to the amount of variance explained in the individual's rankings. Thus closeness to the origin means that the particular model does not fit the individual's responses effectively. Second, individuals with similar weights perceive the stores in a similar way. Thus application of a conventional hierarchical clustering scheme produces the three groupings shown. Cluster 2, for example, consists of housewives who put a similar heavy weight on dimension 1 ("quality"); housewives in cluster 3 weight relatively more dimension 2 ("variety").

Table III describes the socioeconomic and behavioral background of these clusters. The most homogeneous group is cluster 2. Factors 4 and 5 suggest that cluster 3 contains the least loyal shoppers. Demographically, cluster 2 stands out as young working

Table III
Description of Cluster Characteristics

	Cluster		
	1	2	3
1 Number of members	8	15	17
2 Average distance from centroid	0.20	0.15	0.18
3 Average frequency of shopping (per week)	2.3	2	2
4 Average percent grocery expenditure at favorite store	67	69	46
5 Average frequency of use of favorite store relative to other stores	4.4	4.2	3.3
6 Percent working wives	50	100	40
7 Percent over 35 years old	38	13	82
8 Percent in ABC1 social grades	13	87	47

Table IV
Summary Statistics for INDSCAL Clusters
in Two- (and Three-) Dimensions

	Aggregate R^2	Average Correlation
Cluster One	0.52(0.62)	0.70(0.77)
Cluster Two	0.60(0.70)	0.69(0.86)
Cluster Three	0.38(0.47)	0.64(0.68)

wives with husbands in managerial or professional occupations.*

To isolate the images of the three segments, separate maps were then developed for each cluster. Table IV shows that the resulting representations provided a more meaningful picture of perceptions than did Figure 1. Figure 3 illustrates one of these maps—the two-dimensional perceptual space that represents the views of the young housewives making up cluster 2. The broader images of the competing stores are similar to the aggregate map—the isolation of Woolworth's and the discrimination of Sainsbury's and Marks and Spencer for instance—but the detailed picture does show the expected differences.

---

* In the UK six social grades are used to categorize households: A, B, C1, C2, D, and E. These are defined by the occupation of the head of the household. They vary from A of higher managerial or professional households down to E made up of pensioners and the lowest grade workers. The ABC1 grades are "white collar" households.

Figure 3
Evaluative Space for Cluster Two

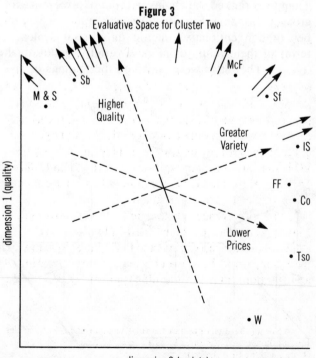

Figure 3 also suggests how dimensions may be interpreted through regressing the average store rankings on the semantic differential scales to store dimensions from the INDSCAL output. The three scales most highly correlated with the dimensions are shown; note how "variety" and "prices" are correlated.

So far we have looked only at how respondents perceive the outlets. In considering the question of evaluation preferences must be brought into the picture. While Sainsbury's and Woolworth's are perceived as polar opposites for grocery shopping, it is not obvious which is most preferred. Indeed it is possible to imagine preference dimensions to be quite different from perceptual ones; as Carroll put it, "While a man may perceive perfectly well the difference between blondes and redheads, this 'dimension' may be irrelevant to his choice of dating partners" ([2], p. 2). Fortunately, of the few empirical studies that have been made (e.g., Doyle and Hutchinson [6]; Green and Rao [13]) perceptual and preference spaces do appear similar in construct.

There are several alternative methods of analyzing preference data. Carroll [3] distinguished between *internal* and *external* analyses: the former develop simultaneously a joint space of stimuli and ideal points from the preference data alone; the latter, on the other hand, use both similarities and preferences in constructing the joint space of stimuli and ideals. Each individual's ideal point or vector is fitted into a stimulus space already obtained from a prior analysis of the similarities data. Green and Rao [13] also distinguish between the type of representation (e.g., point-point models versus point-vector models) and the scaling method employed (e.g., metric versus nonmetric algorithms).

The main method we discuss corresponds to a metric external point-vector model. The stores are represented as points and the preferences of the 15 members of the group as vector directions. The advantage of this type of external analysis is that the sample can first be segmented into relatively homogeneous perception groups before investigating preferences. With the internal analyses, on the other hand, differences in preferences get confounded with perceptions when the latter are heterogeneous.*

The preference vectors are shown surrounding Figure 3. As can be seen, most individuals preferred to move up the vertical or "quality" dimension toward Sainsbury's and Marks and Spencer. Interpretation of ideal regions and the identification of "gaps" in the

market have always been performed cautiously, however. There are at least two pitfalls to watch for. First, in listing preferences individuals are not constrained as they would be in the marketplace. This problem is especially acute if the stimuli cover a wide price range as individuals are not required to consider their budget line before stating their preferences. The second problem is that the ideal region may not be technically feasible. In particular if the stimuli are disparate the preference space may have an ideal region that combines characteristics which although individually favorable are neither technically feasible nor positively evaluated in combination; e.g., hot ice cream or a soft hard-boiled egg. Both these problems appear fortunately to be slight in the present illustration of multidimensional scaling but care is still necessary in reading market opportunities into preference spaces.

Conclusions

There have been various attempts to measure store and corporate images. This article presented a new methodology—individual difference scaling that overcomes several weaknesses inherent in conventional techniques. INDSCAL has two important advantages for store image studies. First, the dimensions are elicited purely from respondent judgments; there is no prespecification by the investigator. Such a procedure makes it more likely that the salient dimensions are parsimoniously represented. Second, the model provides an effective technique for segmenting consumers by homogeneity of perception. This is very important because it is clear that consumers do differ in their perceptions and appear to choose stores with images most congruent with their own self-images. The problem of consumer segmentation bedevils both conventional rating surveys and the Fishbein approach to store image measurement.

Besides facilitating effective disaggregation, the approach also permits preferences to be incorporated. The result is a spatial representation of stores which allows their strengths and weaknesses to be compared along the dimensions regarded as important by consumers and consequently provides a more effective framework for intelligent marketing strategy.

---

* For a fuller discussion of the relative advantages of the different methods see I. Fenwick, *Management Science in Retailing* (London: Doctoral thesis.)

References

1. W. C. Bender "Consumer Purchase Costs—Do Retailers Recognize Them," *Journal of Retailing* (Spring 1964), pp. 68–76.
2. J. D. Carroll, "Individual Differences in Multidimensional Scaling," in R. L. Shepherd, et al., *Multidimensional Scaling* (New York: Academic Press, 1969).
3. J. D. Carroll and J. J. Chang, *Relating Preference Data to Multidimensional Scaling: Solutions via a Generalization of Coombs' Unfolding Model* (Murray Hill, N.J.: Bell Telephone Labs, 1967).

4. P. Doyle, "Nonmetric Multidimensional Scaling: A Users Guide," *European Journal of Marketing*, 7, No. 2 (Spring 1973), 82–88.

5. P. Doyle and I. Fenwick, "Are Goods Goods: Some Empirical Evidence," *Applied Economics*, 1974.

6. P. Doyle and P. Hutchinson, "Individual Differences in Family Decision Making," *Journal of the Market Research Society*, 15, No. 4 (1973), 193–206.

7. P. Doyle and J. McGee, "Perceptions and Preferences for Alternative Convenience Foods," *Journal of the Market Research Society*, 15, No. 1 (1973), 24–34.

8. R. J. Dornoff and R. C. Tatham, "Congruence Between Personal Image and Store Image," *Journal of the Market Research Society*, 14, No. 4 (1972), 45–52.

9. A. S. C. Ehrenberg, "Multivariate Analysis in Marketing," *Annual Conference of the Market Research Society*, Brighton, 1972.

10. M. Fishbein, "An Investigation of the Relationship Between Beliefs About An Object and the Attitude Towards That Object," *Human Relations* (1963), 16.

11. M. Fishbein and B. H. Raven, "The AB-scales: an Operational Definition of Belief and Attitude," *Human Relations* (1962), 15.

12. P. E. Green and A. K. Jain, "A Note on the Robustness of INDSCAL Individual Differences Scaling to Departures from Linearity," *AMA Conference*, 1972.

13. P. E. Green and U. R. Rao, *Applied Multidimensional Scaling* (New York: Holt, Rinehart and Winston, 1972).

14. R. F. Kelly and R. Stephenson, "The Semantic Differential: An Information Source for Designing Retail Patronage Appeals," *Journal of Marketing*, 31 (October 1967), 43–47.

15. J. B. Kruskal, "Nonmetric Multidimensional Scaling: A Numerical Method," *Psychometrika*, 29 (June 1964), 28–42.

16. K. J. Lancaster "A New Approach to Consumer Theory," *Journal of Political Economy*, 74 (1966), 132–64.

17. V. P. Lessig, "Relating Multivariate Measures of Store Loyalty and Store Image," *AMA Conference*, 1972.

18. P. Martineau, "The Personality of the Retail Store," *Harvard Business Review*, 36 (January 1958), 47–55.

19. S. U. Rich and B. D. Portis, "The Imageries of Department Stores," *Journal of Marketing*, 28 (April 1964), 10–15.

20. P. Sampson and P. Harris, "A User's Guide to Fishbein," *Journal of the Market Research Society*, 12, No. 3 (July 1970), 145–66.

21. W. Schlackman, "Psychological Aspects of Dealing," *Annual Conference of the Market Research Society*, Brighton, 1964.

22. B. Thompson, "An Analysis of Supermarket Shopping Habits in Worcester, Massachusetts," *Journal of Retailing*, 43 (Fall 1967), 17–29.

23. W. B. Weale, "Measuring the Customer's Image of a Department Store," *Journal of Retailing*, 37, No. 2 (Summer 1961), 40–48.

24. M. Wish and J. D. Carroll, "Applications of INDSCAL to Studies of Human Perception and Judgment" in E. C. Carterette and M. P. Friedman, *Handbook of Perception* (New York: Academic Press, 1973).

For Discussion

One way to obtain "weights" is to ask respondents directly to indicate on a 1–7 scale how important the attribute's quality, variety and price are to them in selecting stores. How does the data of Figure 1 differ from such an approach? Interpret each of the elements of Figure 3. How does Figure 3 differ from Figure 1?

The Analysis of Interdependence

33

Numerical Taxonomy in Marketing Analysis: A Review Article

Ronald E. Frank
Paul E. Green

Marketing managers and researchers often comment on their difficulty in developing useful ways of classifying customers for formulating marketing policy. The source of the difficulty frequently stems from the abundance of alternative classification methods rather than from a lack of possibilities. Changes in our concepts of customer behavior have more often been associated with the generation of new measures of behavior than with the integration of existing measures. In 50 years, researchers have stopped focusing almost exclusively on customer socioeconomic characteristics as a basis for policy formulation and have begun considering a wide range of measures of sociological and psychological phenomena (such as personality, preferences, buying intentions, perceived risk, interpersonal influence) and an increasing number of measures of actual buying behavior (such as total consumption and brand loyalty).

Much of customer behavior has many factors—it is multidimensional. Researchers often sidestep its complexity by picking some unidimensional attribute assumed to be an indicator of the more complex phenomena to be understood. For example, in studies of household brand loyalty (with respect to frequently purchased, branded food products), the researcher often finds variables used to measure brand loyalty such as the proportion of purchases spent on the most frequently purchased brand or the proportion spent on the brand that is of central interest to the researcher. For many purposes, however, these might be too limited a measure of loyalty since they fail to approximate a full description of a rather complex phenomenon. Customers do not typically buy a single brand or even two brands. Many households purchase three, four, or five brands of a product. In addition, the subset of brands chosen for consumption will vary from household to household.

What procedure could be used to study the clusters of brands that different households consume? All possible combinations of brands could be computed and households sorted into respective classes, but this approach presents a few problems. How many combinations are there in a market with twelve brands? There are over four million if the number of partitions resulting from grouping twelve brands into two or more clusters is added.[1] Even worse, one may want to measure the similarity of brand purchasing behavior not only for the combination of brands but also for the relative proportion of money spent on each brand.

This kind of classification problem is not unique to brand loyalty. How are television programs classified for similarity of audience profiles? Here, too, practitioners often use a single category as the basis for classification, such as the modal audience group (for example, teenagers loyal to "Rat Patrol"). How should market areas for choosing test markets be

---

[1] The general formula [29] for finding all possible partitions of a given set of entities is

$$P(n, m) = [ml^n - \sum_{i-1}^{m-1} m_{(m-i)} P(i)]/m!$$

where

m is number of partitions; $m \geq 2$
n is number of entities in set to be clustered; $n \geq m$
$P(m)$ is number of district partitions containing exactly m clusters
$m_{(m-i)}$ is $m(m-1)(m-2)\cdots(m-i+1)$

Abridged from *Journal of Marketing Research*, published by the American Marketing Association, Vol. 5 (February 1968), pp. 83–98.
No part of this article may be reproduced in any form without prior written permission from the publisher.

grouped? How can a potential purchaser compare the performance specifications of a wide range of computers? How should the readership characteristics of a number of alternative magazines be compared?

Almost every major analytical problem requires the classification of objects by several characteristics — whether customers, products, cities, television programs or magazines. Seldom are explicit classification systems with some combination of attributes, such as those used for measuring a customer's social class or stage in life cycle, found. Such classification systems typically represent self-imposed taxonomies; that is, taxonomies the researcher believes to be relevant because of a theory or prior experience.[2] Although this approach can be useful it has limitations. Regardless of the complexity of reality, it is difficult to classify objects by more than two or three characteristics at a time. If reality requires greater complexity, researchers are severely constrained by their conceptual limitations.

The difficulty of seeing through this often bewildering maze is not unique to marketing (not to mention business problems), as indicated by Sokal, an entymologist:

> Classification is one of the fundamental concerns of science. Facts and objects must be arranged in an orderly fashion before their unifying principles can be discovered and used as a basis for prediction. Many phenomena occur in such variety and profusion that unless some system is created among them, they would be unlikely to provide any useful information [82].

A new technology, numerical taxonomy, has been developed, primarily in biology. It consists of a set of numerical procedures for classifying objects [83]. These taxonomic procedures may be called preclassification techniques since their purpose is to describe the natural groupings that occur in large masses of data. From these natural groupings (or clusters) the researcher can sometimes develop the requisite conceptual framework for classification.

Numerical taxonomy is still new, and to the authors' knowledge, only three articles in marketing have appeared [34, 50, 66]. This article introduces potential marketing applications of this set of techniques, giving some attention to their mathematical bases, current limitations, and assumptions. The following topics are discussed:

1. The nature of taxonomic procedures.
2. Illustrative applications of taxonomic methods to marketing problems.
3. The assumptions and limitations of the procedures.

The authors feel that taxonomic methods will be used increasingly to describe complex marketing data. Hopefully, this article will alert more researchers to the potential of these methods and to some of the cautions associated with use.

The Nature of Taxonomic Procedures

Assume that there is a set of objects, such as people, products, advertisements, and marketing channels, each of which can be characterized by a measurement (or more generally, by an attribute score) on each of a set of characteristics. The researcher has no external criterion for grouping the objects into subsets of similar objects; instead, he wants to identify natural groupings in the data, after which more formal models might be developed.

More formally stated, the problem is: How should objects be assigned to groups so there will be as much likeness within groups and as much difference among groups as possible? From this question four others arise: (1) what proximity measure is to be used to summarize the likeness of profiles, (2) after these likeness measures have been computed, how should the objects be grouped, (3) after the objects have been grouped, what descriptive measures are appropriate for summarizing the characteristics of each group, (4) are the groups formed really different from each other (the inferential problem)?

There are numerous taxonomic procedures for achieving the major objective. The following discussion illustrates the logic of one of them, followed by a brief overview of other kinds of procedures that have been developed. The purpose is to show the relevance of these techniques for establishing multidimensional classification systems, not to provide a definitive methodological statement.

An Example. Suppose that the objects of interest are television programs and the characteristics are (assumed independent) measures of the socioeconomic profile of each program. Let us start with measures of two characteristics, number of teenagers (X_1) and number of adult men (X_2), for each of ten programs. Our problem is to find a way of grouping the programs by the similarity of their audience profiles. Figure 1 plots the programs in two dimensions.

Assume that two clusters of five programs each are desired. A start is to compute Euclidean distances of every point from every other point with the usual formula:

$$\Delta_{jk} = [(X_{1j} - X_{1k})^2 + (X_{2j} - X_{2k})^2]^{1/2}.$$

Points 1 and 2 in Figure 1 appear to be closest together. The first cluster would then be formed by finding the midpoint between Points 1 and 2, the

---

[2]Taxonomies can be distinguished from classifications since they denote interconnections (usually a hierarchy) among characteristics of the objects — a less generic term than classifications. In practice, however, the terms are often used interchangeably.

Figure 1
Illustration of Taxonomic Techniques (Hypothetical)

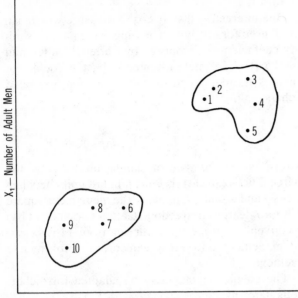

5. The program then proceeds to the next pair of points which are closest together of all unclustered points, and the above process is repeated.
6. If desired, the program can be modified to allow points to be in more than one cluster.
7. The program can be further modified to shift points from cluster to cluster to obtain final clusters which are best in the sense of having the lowest average within-cluster distance summed over all clusters at a given stage in the clustering.

Other Clustering Techniques

Proximity Measure. This program is only one way to cluster points in multidimensional space. Other proximity measures and clustering techniques have been proposed by researchers in the biological and social sciences. With some simplification, the proximity measures can be categorized as:

1. Distance measures.
2. Correlation measures.
3. Similarity measures for attribute data.

The input data—nominal, ordinal, interval, ratio or mixed scales—often determines the proximity measure used to express pairwise relationships among the elements.

Distance Measures. One kind of clustering technique based on Euclidean distance has already been described. Two problems exist with regard to this kind of measure: (1) correlated characteristics and (2) noncomparability of the original units in which the characteristics are measured [69]. The second problem is usually "solved" by standardizing all characteristics to mean zero and unit standard deviation. Thus it is assumed that mean and variance among characteristics is not important in the grouping process.

The first problem can be handled two ways. A principal component analysis may be run on the characteristics and factor scores computed for the objects. Each component score may then be weighted by the square root of the eigenvalue associated with that component before computing the distance measure. A second approach uses the Mahalanobis [60] generalized distance in which the squared distances between objects is measured as a linear combination of the correlated measurements expressed in units of the estimated population dispersion of the composite measure. If the characteristics are uncorrelated and measurements are first standardized (mean zero and unit standard deviation), the square root of the Mahalanobis measure is equivalent to the Euclidean measure discussed.

In practice, distance measures of the kind just described are usually used when data are at least intervally scaled. Kendall [54], however, proposed a distance measure requiring only ordinally scaled measurements. Also, Restle [75] and others have

centroid of the point coordinates. Then the distance of each point from this average would be computed and the point closest to this average would be added (here, Point 3). Similarly, Point 4 and then Point 5 would be added, giving a cluster of five programs as desired.

Generalizing to More than Two Dimensions. In the previous illustration, only two measurements were considered for each point (television program). It is relatively easy to follow the procedure visually.[3] In practice there may be many measurements for each program; hence, the graphical procedure must be supplemented by a computational technique that can deal with several characteristics.

Several computer routines are available for this type of taxonomic analysis often called cluster analysis. For example, one computer routine used involves these steps:

1. Each characteristic is first converted to a standardized variate with zero mean and unit standard deviation.
2. Euclidean distances are then computed for each of all possible pairs of points.
3. The pair with the smallest distance is chosen as the node of the first cluster, and the average of this pair is computed.
4. Additional points are added to this cluster (based on closeness to the last-computed average) until:
   a. Some prespecified number of points has been clustered.
   b. The point to be added to the cluster exceeds some prespecified distance-cutoff or threshold number.

---

[3] The typical Euclidean distance measure can be easily generalized to more than two dimensions as:

$$\Delta_{jk} = [\Sigma_{i=1}^{n} (X_{ij} = X_{ik})^2]^{1/2}.$$

shown that even nominally scaled data may be characterized in distance terms, in the sense of obeying the distance axioms. The resulting metric, however, may not be Euclidean.

Correlation Measures. Probably the most widely used proximity measure in clustering procedures involves the correlation coefficient.[4] Inverse factor analysis, the Q-technique, is a fairly widely used procedure in which objects replace tests in the computation of factor loadings. Clusters may then be formed by grouping subjects with similar factor loadings. Three problems are associated with this class of techniques. First, correlation removes the elevation and scatter of each object, thereby losing information. Second, in grouping objects by factor loadings, the analyst risks obtaining some objects that are split among clusters. Finally, the analyst must usually resort to an R-technique to interpret the clusters' characteristics according to their correlations with underlying factors.

Similarity Measures. Similarity measures are often used in clustering when the characteristics of each object are only nominally scaled, for example, dichotomous or multichotomous. The usual notion of distance seems less applicable here (although it is still possible to use multidimensional scaling techniques to "metricize" such data before clustering). Typically, however, the analyst tries to develop similarity coefficients based on attribute matching.

For example, if two objects are compared on each of eight attributes, the following might result:

Entity	Attribute							
	1	2	3	4	5	6	7	8
1	1	0	0	1	1	0	1	0
2	0	1	0	1	0	1	1	1

The fractional match coefficient would be:

$$S_{12} = \frac{M}{N} = \frac{3}{8}$$

where M denotes the number of attributes held in common (matching 1's or 0's) and N denotes the total number of attributes. If weak matches (nonpossession of the attribute) are to be deemphasized, the Tanimoto [76] coefficient is appropriate:

$$\text{Tanimoto } S_{ij} = \frac{\text{No. of attributes which are 1 for both objects } i \text{ and } j}{\text{No. of attributes which are 1 for either } i \text{ or } j, \text{ or both}}.$$

In this problem the coefficient would be $\frac{2}{7}$. Many other similarity measures have been developed that represent variations of the fractional match coefficient. (See [83].)

One interesting distance-type measure which can also be used for attribute matching is the pattern similarity coefficient, r_p, proposed by Cattell, Coulter and Tsujioka [16]. In interval-scaled data, the coefficient compares the computed distance with that expected by chance alone:

$$r_{p(jk)} = \frac{E_i - \sum_{i=1}^n d_{(jk)}^2}{E_i + \sum_{i=1}^n d_{(jk)}^2}$$

where i is the number of dimensions, $d_{(jk)}^2$ is the squared Euclidean distance in standard units between entities j and k, and E_i is twice the median chi-square value for i degrees of freedom. Cattell's coefficient has the convenient property of varying from $+1$ for complete agreement, 0 for no agreement, to -1 for inverse agreement.

The coefficient may also be adapted for dichotomous items as:

$$r_p' = \frac{E_i - d}{E_i + d}$$

where d represents the number of disagreements on d items.

Finally, some mention should be made of the mixed scale problem in which the characteristics are measured in different modes. One possibility is to degrade interval-scaled data into categories and use similarity coefficients. Another possibility is to upgrade nominally or ordinally scaled data. There seems to be no satisfactory solution to this problem although it is conceivable that some highly general measure of proximity, perhaps one derived from information theory, may be appropriate.

Clustering Routines. After the analyst has decided on some measure of pairwise proximity, he must still contend with the grouping process itself. A variety of approaches are possible. One major class of approaches to the clustering problem consists of hierarchical routines. For example, Edwards and Cavalli-Sforza [24] describe a clustering procedure (based on a least-squares technique) which first clusters the data into two groups. The procedure is repeated sequentially so that progressively smaller clusters are formed sequentially by splitting the original clusters. A hierarchical array is obtained. A variant of this procedure starts with clusters of one object each and builds new clusters hierarchically until one overall cluster results. This approach was described by Ward [93].

Other grouping routines use threshold or cutoff measures similar to the algorithm described earlier.

---

[4] If the characteristics are expressed in standard scores, the Euclidean distance between two objects is a monotone transformation of their correlation [18].

Some procedures, for example, suggest selecting an object closest to the centroid of all the data to serve as a prime node around which other points are clustered until some threshold distance level is reached. An unclustered object farthest from the centroid of the first cluster may then be chosen as a new prime node. The process is continued, the third and subsequent prime nodes being selected on the basis of largest average distance from the centroids of clusters already formed.

Some grouping routines [24, 93] are highly metric since effectiveness measures involve the computation of within-cluster variance around the centroid of the cluster members. Others [83] use only the proximity between an unclustered object and some single member of the clustered set as a criterion for set inclusion.

In Q-technique, objects are often clustered by highest factor loadings, a simple approach; but it does not use all available information.

Finally, there is the possibility of clustering by systematic space-density search routines in which the *n*-dimensional space is cut into hypercubes and the computer program counts the number of cases falling into each region. Relatively little work, however, has been done on this taxonomic routine.

Descriptive Characteristics of the Groups.   Even after objects are grouped, each cluster must be characterized by its representative profile. In some instances the cluster's centroid is used as a description of its members. In others the actual profile of the object closest to the group's centroid may be used. As in choice of proximity measure and choice of grouping routine, however, the criteria for describing each group are usually ad hoc, a main problem being that *cluster* is still not a precisely defined term. Some of these problems and the inferential problem will be reconsidered later in this article.

Illustrative Marketing Applications

Some appreciation for the versatility and unresolved problems of taxonomic methods can be gained from the following short review of studies conducted by the authors in the past two years.

Clustering Analysis in Test Marketing.   One of the earliest pilot applications involved the use of cluster analysis in the grouping of cities (standard metropolitan areas) for test marketing purposes [34]. Data for each of 88 cities were available on 14 measured characteristics, such as population, number of retail stores, percent nonwhite. A clustering program using the Euclidean distance measure grouped the cities into homogeneous

five-point clusters. Centroids of each cluster in 14-space and average distances of each point from the grand centroid and from the centroid of its own cluster were obtained. As an alternative for comparison purposes, the original data matrix was factored, and cluster analysis was performed on the resultant (standardized) factor scores.

The cluster analysis yielded some interesting findings. First, the cluster of five cities closest to the grand mean of all 88 — Dayton, Columbus, Indianapolis, Syracuse, and New Haven — agreed well with various lists of typical cities prepared by such magazines as *Sales Management* and *Printer's Ink* indicating results consistent with industry judgment. This method also provides homogeneous groups of cities with centroids quite distant from the grand origin. Second, the combined procedure of factor analysis (and subsequent clustering of factor scores) indicated that two major dimensions, a city size construct and a demographic construct, explained most of the variance in the data.

This study was only a pilot effort. In practice, the marketing manager would use those city characteristics most relevant to his product line. The clusters could then serve as homogeneous blocks from which individual cities could be chosen to serve as treatment and control units, that is, matched units for various experimental purposes.

Television Program Audience Profile Analysis.   Grouping of television programs into clusters having similar audience profile, which was used to illustrate the nature of taxonomic procedures, comprises still another exploratory investigation currently in progress. American Research Bureau data for both day and evening programs in October, 1965, are the bases for this analysis. For each, program measures of the number of adult men and women in different age categories and the number of children and teenagers viewing the program are available. The primary objective is to group programs by viewer characteristics so that their grouping is a function of viewer reaction to content and casting — not to the effects of time of day, day of week, and lead-in programs.

The analysis is divided into two stages. The first is the adjustment of raw data for the effects of time of day, day of week, and lead-in programs. The adjustment is roughly analogous to making a cyclical adjustment in a time series analysis to ensure a cleaner set of data for studying trend movements. When variations in audience profile from program to program are caused primarily by the effect of program content and casting, the adjusted data are subjected to a taxonomic analysis. The first stage of the study is complete, and the taxonomic work is about to begin. (It will soon appear as a working paper [30].)

Patterns of Customer Brand Loyalty. At the beginning of this article the study of brand loyalty was used to illustrate the tendency for letting unidimensional measures represent customer behavior that may be multidimensional. In this study cluster analysis and Kruskal's algorithm [56] is used to characterize customer brand purchasing behavior. The objective is to develop more comprehensive classification systems for analyzing brand choice.

Chicago Tribune panel data for three product categories (carbonated beverages, regular coffee, and ready-to-eat cereals) for 1961 were used in the analysis. For each product category for each of 480 households, the percentage of units (based on weight) purchased by brand was computed.

Two different approaches were then taken. A Euclidean distance measure was used to group households that had relatively similar percentage distributions of brand purchasing behavior within a product. This is equivalent to studying brand loyalty for the bundle of brands households purchase. The results showed that with only one exception in the regular coffee market each cluster of households bought only one brand at a rate greater than the brand's overall market share. Although other brands were purchased, none was given this degree of favor. The only exceptions are the clusters containing several private brands. Households that purchase one private brand at a greater rate than its overall share are likely to purchase another with a similar degree of concentration. Customers who buy them may be less sensitive to differences in product characteristics, or the products themselves may be more similar.

A second approach organized the data by brand instead of by customer. This part of the analysis started with the transpose of the data matrix used, that is, the data were organized by brand and within brand, by household. For each brand the percentage of purchases devoted to that brand by each of about 100 households was available. Euclidean distance measures characterized brand similarity by pattern of purchase requirements over households.

Results so far have provided few surprises and have raised more questions than can be answered here. For example in the cereal market, evidence appears that old standard brands (Kellogg's Corn Flakes, Cheerios, Wheaties) tend to serve segments which overlap, yet many health-oriented cereals (Special K, All Bran, Grape Nuts) tend to serve a somewhat different group of customers.

Operational Characterization of Inter-brand Competition. In another pilot study, cluster analysis helped to characterize inter-brand competition in the computer field [38]. Performance data were obtained for over 100 different computer models with installation data used to categorize them as first- or second-generation models. For each computer model, data were available on 12 measured characteristics, such as word length, execution time, digital storage, transfer rate, and 10 categorical characteristics, such as whether the computer possessed Boolean operations, table look-up, and indirect addressing.

The data's mixed character (continuous variables and dichotomous features data) required a different approach from that typically used in cluster analysis. First, the attribute data were metricized by a multi-dimensional scaling technique [56]. A two-dimensional representation revealed that each computer model could be characterized by the dimensions of capacity (number of different features) and orientation (scientific versus business), as based on the particular pattern of zeroes and ones.

The resultant clusters, developed by a hierarchical grouping technique, displayed interesting characteristics from the standpoint of intermodel competition. For example, a machine's cluster of features appears to be idiosyncratic to the particular manufacturer, that is, each manufacturer tends to build all his machines with a particular set of features. Each manufacturer's complex, however, may vary from that of his competitors. It is interesting that only IBM has a model in each of the major clusters. However, the time period comparison—first- versus second-generation computers—indicated a trend toward all models having a greater number of features.

The measured variables were then analyzed separately, yielding two main dimensions—speed and size of computers. Finally, the measured data were dichotomized about the median of each characteristic (taken separately) and submitted to a combination multidimensional scaling and cluster analysis.

Figure 2 shows a two-space configuration derived from applying a nonmetric program to proximity measures developed from the above steps. After adjusting for intercorrelation of the characteristics [39], similarity measures were developed by tabulating the number of (weighted) matches for all computer pairs. The higher this number, the more similar each pair was assumed to be with respect to all 22 performance characteristics. For $n = 55$, there are 1,485 interpoint proximities as input to the program; only their rank order is required.

The two-space configuration of Figure 2 shows the boundaries of clusters formed (by another means) on a more precise configuration obtained in four-space. Such compression of results (into two-space) seriously distorts the make-up of Cluster 8; otherwise the clusters are fairly compact. It is interesting to note that Cluster 5 is composed of small, fairly slow, business-oriented machines, but Cluster 7 is characterized by large, relatively fast, scientific machines.

Figure 2
Two-Space Configuration of Computer Models in
"Performance Space"

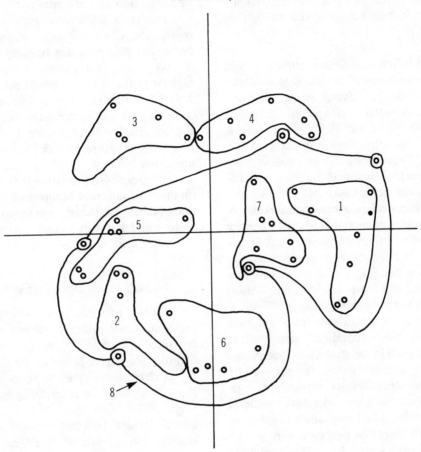

The complete study on which Figure 2 is based revealed that four dimensions—speed, size, number of different features (qualitative characteristics), and orientation (scientific versus business)—appeared to adequately describe the computer market.

The possibilities of such performance-space analyses over time have potential for the study of product innovation and modification—particularly industrial products like electric motors and machine tools. In this approach a whole series of performance spaces could be viewed through time—their dimensions, number of points (models), and interrelationships among points could all be changing, reflecting changes in technology and inter-model competition. Such an approach would seem to indicate the data's fine structure better than the more traditional reliance on S-curves to describe product life cycles.

Physicians' Media Reading Habits.   In another study [41], numerical taxonomy was used to cluster reading profiles of both physicians and medical journals. The basic data consisted of zero-one matrices in which each physician was classified as a light (zero) or heavy (one) reader of each of 19 medical journals. Each

physician was also classified as one who lightly or heavily prescribed each of 29 therapeutic drug classes. Data were also available on the physician's specialty, age, and total weekly patient and prescription loads. The zero-one matrices were again metricized by a multidimensional scaling program. Clusters of journals with similar physician reading habits and clusters of physicians with similar journal profiles were developed.

Findings indicated that, within a given speciality, media reading profiles are not associated with such variables as physician age, total prescribing frequency, and product mix selection. However, the journal clusters provided an interesting output of the analysis by summarizing a diverse set of zero-one data. The marketing manager could use these clusters as a guide to media scheduling. For example, if he wishes to choose journals with high overlap of coverage, he can choose all journals within a given cluster. If, however, he wishes to emphasize diversity, he can choose one journal from each cluster.

From a methodological viewpoint, the interesting concept is the dual use of multidimensional scaling and cluster analysis. The first technique allows the researcher to make a concise description of the data—frequently interpretable in its own right—and the last allows him to organize the data into similar journal profiles that can then be subjected to further analysis.

Taxonomy in Psychometric Studies.

Some mention should also be made of the usefulness of clustering procedures in psychometric studies involving perceptual and preference mapping. A recently completed study [36] involved the analysis of proximities data developed during a study of student perception of six graduate schools of business. Three modes of data collection—similarity triads, direct ratings, and the semantic differential—were used to collect proximity judgments.

In this study a hierarchical grouping method was used to develop clusters of respondents with similar perceptions of the six business schools. That is, although the main objective of this study was the development of perceptual maps, cluster analysis was useful in partitioning the respondents into homogeneous groups with similar perceptions.

The results indicated that a two-space solution adequately portrayed the respondents' perceptions. From other data collected in the study, the dimensions of the space could be characterized as prestige of school and quantitativeness of its curriculum. Not inconsequentially all three data collection methods yielded fairly similar perceptual maps, on an aggregate basis. Moreover, differences in perceptual mappings were not generally explainable by respondent personal data, such as undergraduate major, previous work experience, graduate major. Only one variable, home state of respondent, appeared to influence his perception of the business schools in any significant way.

A similar study [37] involved a multidimensional scaling of professional journals typically read by marketing academics and researchers. Perception and preference data were obtained for eight journals, and respondents were clustered on the basis of similarity of perception and preference.

Figure 3 shows the results of applying a nonmetric clustering routine to the perception data [37]. Note that this program is hierarchical. Respondents 4 and 7 are first clustered because they had the highest proximity measure of the group. Respondents 2 and 11 are next clustered at level two, and so on, until all points are eventually in one large cluster. On the left-hand side of Figure 3 one can see how the proximity measure declines as more disparate points are clustered.

The results of this study indicated that preferences and perception were independent over stimuli, that is, respondents clustered by commonality of perception were unrelated to clusters formed by commonality of preference.

Assumptions and Limitations of Clustering Methods

Cluster analysis is not a single, cohesive set of techniques but rather a variety of procedures, each having a kind of ad hoc flavor and certain advantages and disadvantages. Some of the limitations are shared by all these techniques to some degree, but specific procedures have both advantages and disadvantages.

General Problems in Cluster Analysis.

All clustering techniques have certain general analytical inadequacies because the data are used to generate the groupings. Illustrative questions are:

1. How many clusters should be formed?
2. If, as is usually the case, the characteristics of the objects are measured in different units, how can equivalence among metrics be achieved?
3. If the objects' scores along several dimensions are intercorrelated, how should these interdependencies be handled?
4. Even if the number of clusters can be determined in some satisfactory way, how does the analyst decide on the

Figure 3
Illustration of Hierarchical Clustering Routine

Proximity Measure	Subject Number											
	09	00	11	08	06	02	11	03	04	07	05	12
1.8253	.	.	.	.	.	.	.	.	.	x	x	x
1.7745	.	.	.	.	.	x	x	x	.	.	x	x
1.7111	.	.	.	.	.	x	x	x	.	x	x	x
1.6871	.	.	.	.	.	x	x	x	.	x	x	x
1.5961	.	.	.	.	x	x	x	x	.	x	x	x
1.4724	.	.	.	x	x	x	x	x	.	x	x	x
1.3715	.	.	x	x	x	x	x	x	.	x	x	x
1.2091	.	.	x	x	x	x	x	x	x	x	x	x
1.1388	.	.	x	x	x	x	x	x	x	x	x	x
1.0558	x	x	x	.	x	x	x	x	x	x	x	x
0.8077	x	x	x	x	x	x	x	x	x	x	x	x

appropriate boundaries for clusters, summary measures of the characteristics of each cluster, and their statistical significance?

In some of the illustrative applications described here, the number of clusters was decided in advance. Increasing the number of clusters will tend to reduce the average within-cluster distance but, obviously, one must stop short of ending with each point being a cluster.

In addition, all data including variables originally interval-scaled were standardized to zero mean and unit standard deviation. Although this step enables the analyst to work with common metrics, it is assumed that central tendency and variability among dimensions are not important.

The problem of dealing with intercorrelated characteristics was pointed out in the test marketing illustration. In this study an alternative procedure was used in which the set of characteristics was first reduced to independent constructs by a principal component analysis before the cluster analysis. This procedure can lead to different clusters from those obtained by the first procedure that ignored the inter-correlations among characteristics. Finally, the researcher might wish to use the Mahalanobis generalized distance measure discussed by Morrison [66].

Appropriate boundaries and descriptive statistics of clusters are usually determined by the specific technique used—in many instances by a generalized distance function, the computation of centroids, and the use of a preset number of points or cutoff distances. Even so, it is fair to say that good measures of cluster compactness are not available. In the test marketing illustration each dimension included in the analysis was given (manifest) equal weight in determining similarity. In a given situation one might choose to give a single dimension or some subset of dimensions more weight than others in defining proximity measures. Cluster analysis can be easily modified to take into account unequal weights, but this approach still largely varies with circumstances.

Still less is known about the inferential characteristics of clustering techniques. Unlike other multivariate techniques, such as discriminant analysis and principal component analysis, clustering techniques are much less structured, and little investigation has been made to date of their statistical properties.

Limitations of Specific Proximity Measures. In earlier sections of this article, the characteristics of specific proximity measures—distance measures, correlation techniques, similarity coefficients—were briefly described. Each measure suffers from certain specific limitations.

Distance measures are usually restricted to instances in which the objects' characteristics to be measured can be expressed as interval-scaled variables. This represents a limitation on the kind of variable meaningfully handled although Kendall's nonparametric measure (mentioned earlier) could be used to handle data that are scaled only ordinally and the researcher could develop non-Euclidean metrics.

In addition, the Euclidean measure suffers from the disadvantage that two objects may be viewed as different solely because their values on one variable differ markedly. Finally, it should be reiterated that the researcher would, in general, obtain different results by using original versus standardized data for the characteristics of the objects being clustered by this method.

Correlative techniques, such as Q-factor analysis, have an even more serious limitation because one must standardize over objects, thus losing mean and scatter information. That is, in this technique, each object is given the same mean and variance.

A second disadvantage is that rotation of factor axes (to get purer loadings) lends a certain arbitrariness to the procedure. Finally, also mentioned earlier, in this procedure objects may be split on factors, leading to uncertainty of the placement of an object into a specific group.

Similarity measures are flexible since they can be adapted to handle nominal, ordinal, and interval-scaled data. Furthermore, it can be shown that similarity measures can be metricized by multidimensional-scaling procedures. Morover, similarity measures are generally less sensitive to the impact of a single characteristic on the resultant dissimilarity of two objects than are the Euclidean distance measures.

However, similarity measures have their set of limitations. First, if a group is to be formed on the basis of overall matches, two objects may not be grouped even if they match well on some subset of characteristics. Conversely, an object may be in a group because it is similar to different members of the group on different subsets of characteristics.

Second, if a large number of characteristics are involved, objects which match may do so for accidental reasons, reflecting the noise in the data; and third, if some variables are dichotomous and others are multichotomous, the two-state attributes will tend to be more heavily weighted in the similarity measures. For example, if one attribute were broken down into 100 states, we would rarely find matches. Hence this attribute would receive little importance in the overall similarity measure.

Finally, if continuous data are discretized in order to use similarity measures, valuable information can be lost. The analyst is thus plagued with the problem of deciding both the kinds of attributes to include in the analysis and the number of states to be associated with each.

Choosing Appropriate Techniques. Numerical taxonomy invites some ambivalence by the analyst wanting to use the techniques. On one hand, the procedures are designed to cope with a relevant aspect of marketing description—the orderly classification of multivariate phenomena. On the other hand, the varying character of various proximity measures and clustering techniques—and the basic lack of structure at either the descriptive statistic or inferential statistic level—suggests that the analyst be cautious in applying them.

Until more structure is introduced, it seems prudent to conduct analyses in parallel where alternative proximity measures and grouping procedures are used [40]. Moreover, sensitivity analyses on synthetic data might by helpful in exploring the various idiosyncrasies of alternative techniques. If the data are well clustered to begin with, similar results over alternative techniques will usually be obtained—but how often will these pleasant states of affairs exist? Though the authors believe numerical taxonomy can be useful in marketing analysis, they would urge prudence in its application and the systematic study of similarities and differences among alternative procedures. (The references may help to facilitate this study.)

References

1. G. H. Ball, "Data Analysis in the Social Sciences: What About the Details?" *Proceedings Fall Joint Computer Conference,* 1965, 533–59.
2. B. M. Bass, "Iterative Inverse Factor Analysis: A Rapid Method for Clustering Persons," *Psychometrika,* 22 (March 1957), 105.
3. J. F. Bennett and W. L. Hays, "Multidimensional Unfolding: Determining the Dimensionality of Ranked Preference Data," *Psychometrika,* 25 (March 1960), 27–43.
4. A. Birnbaum and A. E. Maxwell, "Classification Procedures Based on Bayes' Formula," *Applied Statistics,* 9 (November 1961), 152–68.
5. Jack Block, "The Difference Between Q and R," *Psychological Review,* 62, (1955), 356–8.
6. ——, Louis Levine and Quinn McNemar, "Testing for the Existence of Psychometric Patterns," *Journal of Abnormal Social Psychology,* 46 (July 1951), 356–9.
7. R. E. Bonner, "Some Clustering Techniques," *IBM Journal of Research and Development,* 8 (January 1964), 22–33.
8. A. D. Booth, "An Application of the Method of Steepest Descent to the Solution of Simultaneous Non-linear Equations," *Quarterly Journal of Mech. Applied Mathematics,* 2 (December 1949), 460–8.
9. G. E. P. Box, "The Exploration and Exploitation of Response Surfaces: Some General Considerations and Examples," *Biometrics,* 10 (March 1954), 16–60.
10. S. H. Brooks, "A Discussion of Random Methods of Seeking Maxima," *Journal of Operations Research Society,* 6 (1958), 244–51.
11. ——, "A Comparison of Maximum Seeking Methods," *Journal of Operations Research Society,* 7 (1959), 430–57.
12. Cyril L. Burt, "Correlations between Persons," *British Journal of Psychology,* 28 (July 1937), 59–96.
13. H. Cartwright, *Structural Models: An Introduction to the Theory of Directed Graphs,* New York: John Wiley & Sons, Inc., 1963.
14. Raymond B. Cattell, "r_p and Other Coefficients of Pattern Similarity," *Psychometrika,* 14 (December 1949), 279–98.
15. ——, "On the Disuse and Misuse of R, P, Q, and O Techniques in Clinical Psychology," *Journal of Clinical Psychology,* 7 (1951), 203–14.
16. ——, M. A. Coulter and B. Tsujioka, "The Taxonometric Recognition of Types and Functional Emergents," in R. B. Cattell, ed., *Handbook of Multivariate Experimental Psychology,* Chicago: Rand McNally and Co., 1966, 288–329.
17. W. W. Cooley and Paul R. Lohnes, *Multivariate Procedures for the Behavioral Sciences,* New York: John Wiley & Sons, Inc., 1963.
18. C. H. Coombs, *A Theory of Data,* New York: John Wiley & Sons, Inc., 1964.
19. ——, "A Method for the Study of Interstimulus Similarity," *Psychometrika,* 19 (September 1954), 183–94.
20. Douglas R. Cox, "Note on Grouping," *Journal of American Statistical Association,* 52 (December 1957), 543–47.
21. Lee J. Cronbach and Goldine C. Gleser, "Assessing Similarity between Profiles," *Psychological Bulletin,* 50 (November 1953), 456–73.
22. Frank M. duMas, "A Quick Method of Analyzing the Similarity of Profiles," *Journal of Clinical Psychology,* 2 (January 1946), 80–3.
23. ——, "On the Interpretation of Personality Profiles," *Journal of Clinical Psychology,* 3 (1947), 57–65.
24. A. W. F. Edwards and L. L. Cavalli-Sforza, "A Method for Cluster Analysis," *Biometrics,* 52 (June 1965), 362–75.
25. G. A. Ferguson, "The Factorial Interpretation of Test Difficulty," *Psychometrika,* 6 (October 1941), 323–29.
26. R. A. Fisher, "The Use of Multiple Measurements in Taxonomic Problems," *American Eugenics,* 7 (1963), 179–88.
27. W. D. Fisher, "On Grouping for Maximum Homogeneity," *Journal of American Statistical Association,* 53 (December 1958), 789–98.
28. Claude Flament, *Applications of Graph Theory to Group Structure,* Englewood Cliffs, N.J.: Prentice-Hall, Inc., 1963.
29. J. J. Fortier and H. Solomon, "Clustering Procedures," Unpublished paper, International Symposium on Multivariate Analysis, University of Dayton, June 1965.
30. Ronald E. Frank, "Television Program Audience Similarities: A Taxonomic Analysis," University of Pennsylvania, December 1967, mimeographed.
31. Eugene L. Gaier and Marilyn C. Lee, "Pattern Analysis: The Configural Approach to Predictive Measurement," *Psychological Bulletin,* 50 (March 1953), 140–8.
32. J. A. Gengerelli, "A Method for Detecting Subgroups in a Population and Specifying their Membership," *Journal of Psychology,* 55 (1953), 140–48.
33. L. A. Goodman and W. H. Kruskal, "Measures of Association for Cross Classifications," *Journal of American Statistical Association,* 59 (September 1964), 732–64.
34. Paul E. Green, Ronald E. Frank, and Patrick J. Robinson, "Cluster Analysis in Test Market Selection," *Management Science,* 13 (April 1967), 387–400.
35. ——, "A Behavioral Experiment in Risk Taking and Information Seeking," Working paper, University of Pennsylvania, January 1967.
36. Paul E. Green and P. J. Robinson, "Perceptual Structure of Graduate Business Schools—An Application of Multidimensional Scaling," Working paper, June 1967.
37. ——, "Perceptual and Preference Mapping of Professional Journals," Working paper, May 1967.
38. —— and F. J. Carmone, "Structural Characteristics of the Computer Market—An Application of Cluster and Reduced Space Analysis," Working paper, May 1967.
39. ——, "WAGS: An IBM 7040 Computer Program for Obtaining Weighted Agreement Scores for Multidimensional Scaling," Working paper, May 1967.
40. ——, "Cross Techniques Study—Computer Model Clustering," Working paper, August 1967.

41. ———, "A Reduced Space and Cluster Analysis of Physicians' Media Reading Habits," Working paper, September 1967.

42. H. H. Harman, *Modern Factor Analysis,* Chicago: University of Chicago Press, 1960.

43. C. W. Harris, "Characteristics of Two Measures of Profile Similarity," *Psychometrika,* 20 (1955), 289–97.

44. G. C. Helmstadter, "An Empirical Comparison of Methods for Estimating Profile Similarity," *Educational and Psychological Measurement,* 17 (1957), 71–82.

45. J. L. Hodges, Jr., "Discriminatory Analysis I: Survey of Discriminatory Analysis," USAF School of Aviation Medicine, Randolph, Texas, 1950.

46. Karl J. Holzinger, "Factoring Test Scores and Implications for the Method of Averages," *Psychometrika,* 9 (December 1944), 257–62.

47. Paul Horst, *Matrix Algebra for Social Scientists,* New York: Holt, Rinehart and Winston, 1963.

48. ———, "Pattern Analysis and Configural Scoring," *Journal of Clinical Psychology,* 10 (January 1954), 1–11.

49. K. J. Jones, *The Multivariate Statistical Analyzer,* Cambridge, Mass.: Harvard Cooperative Society, 1964.

50. J. Joyce and C. Channon, "Classifying Market Survey Respondents," *Applied Statistics,* 15 (November 1966), 191–215.

51. H. F. Kaiser, "Formulas for Component Scores," *Psychometrika,* 27 (March 1962), 83–7.

52. M. G. Kendall, *The Advanced Theory of Statistics,* Vol. 1, New York: Hafner Publishing Company, 1958.

53. ———, *Rank Correlation Methods,* London: Griffin Publishing Company, 1948.

54. ———, "Discrimination and Classification," London: CEIR Ltd. 1965.

55. J. B. Kruskal, "Nonmetric Multidimensional Scaling: A Numerical Scaling Method," *Psychometrika,* 29 (June 1964), 115–30.

56. ———, "Multidimensional Scaling by Optimizing Goodness of Fit to a Nonmetric Hypothesis," *Psychometrika,* 29 (March 1964), 1–28.

57. E. O. Laumann and L. Guttman, "The Relative Association Contiguity of Occupations in an Urban Setting," *American Sociological Review,* 31 (April 1966), 169–78.

58. J. C. Lingoes, "A Taxonometric Optimization Procedure: An IBM 7090 Classification Program," *Behavioral Science,* 8 (October 1963), 370.

59. ———, "An IBM 7090 Program for Guttman-Lingoes Smallest Space Analysis," Computer Center, University of Michigan, 1965.

60. P. C. Mahalanobis, "On the Generalized Distance in Statistics," *Proceedings National Institute of Science,* Vol. 12, India, 1936, 49–58.

61. F. Massarik and P. Ratoosh, *Mathematical Explorations in Behavioral Science,* Homewood, Ill.: Richard D. Irwin, Inc., 1965.

62. P. McNaughton-Smith, *et al.,* "Dissimilarity Analysis: A New Technique of Hierarchical Subdivision," *Nature,* 202 (June 1964), 1033–4.

63. Louis L. McQuitty, "Hierarchical Syndrome Analysis," *Educational and Psychological Measurement,* 20 (1960), 293–304.

64. ———, "Typal Analysis," *Educational and Psychological Measurement,* 20 (1960), 293–304.

65. ———, "Best Classifying Every Individual at Every Level," *Educational and Psychological Measurement,* 23 (July 1963), 337–46.

66. Donald G. Morrison, "Measurement Problems in Cluster Analysis," *Management Science,* 13 (August 1967), B-775–80.

67. Jim Nunnally, "The Analysis of Profile Data," *Psychological Bulletin,* 59 (July 1962), 311–19.

68. Charles E. Osgood and George J. Suci, "A Measure of Relation Determined by Both Mean Difference and Profile Information," *Psychological Bulletin,* 49 (May 1952), 251–62.

69. J. E. Overall, "Note on Multivariate Methods of Profile Analysis," *Psychological Bulletin,* 61 (March 1964), 195–8.

70. K. Pearson, "On the Dissection of Asymmetrical Frequency Curves," *Contributions to the Mathematical Theory of Evolution,* Phil. Trans. of Royal Society 1894.

71. ———, "On the Coefficient of Racial Likeness," *Biometrika,* 18 (July 1926), 105–17.

72. R. G. Pettit, "Clustering Program: Continuous Variables," Advanced Systems Development Division, IBM, Yorktown Heights, New York, 1964.

73. C. R. Rao, "Tests of Significance in Multivariate Analysis," *Biometrika,* 35 (May 1948), 58–79.

74. ———, "The Utilization of Multiple Measurements in Problems of Biological Classification," *Journal of Royal Statistical Society,* Series B, 10 (1948), 159–203.

75. F. Restle, *Psychology of Judgment and Choice,* New York: John Wiley & Sons, Inc., 1961.

76. D. J. Rogers and T. T. Tanimoto, "A Computer Program for Classifying Plants," *Science,* 132 (October 1960), 1115–22.

77. P. J. Rulon, "Distinctions Between Discriminant and Regression Analysis and a Geometric Interpretation of the Discriminant Function," *Harvard Educational Review,* 21 (June 1951), 80–90.

78. R. N. Shepard, "The Analysis of Proximities: Multidimensional Scaling With an Unknown Distance Function: I and II," *Psychometrika,* 27 (June 1962, September 1962), 125–40, 219–46.

79. ———, "Analysis of Proximities as a Technique for the Study of Information Processing in Man," *Human Factors,* 5 (February 1963), 33–48.

80. G. G. Simpson, "Numerical Taxonomy and Biological Classification," *Science,* 144 (May 1964), 712–13.

81. P. H. A. Sneath, "The Application of Computers to Taxonomy," *Journal of General Micro-Biology,* 17 (August 1957), 201–27.

82. R. R. Sokal, "Numerical Taxonomy," *Scientific American,* 215 (December 1966), 106–16.

83. ———, and P. H. A. Sneath, *Principles of Numerical Taxonomy,* San Francisco: Freeman & Company, 1963.

84. William Stephenson, "Some Observations on Q Technique," *Psychological Bulletin,* 49 (September 1952), 483–98.

85. S. A. Stouffer, *et al., Measurement and Prediction,* Princeton, N.J.: Princeton University Press, 1950.

86. Robert L. Thorndike, "Who Belongs in the Family?", *Psychometrika,* 18 (December 1953), 267–76.

87. Warren S. Torgerson, "Multidimensional Scaling: Theory and Method," *Psychometrika,* 17 (December 1952), 401–19.

88. ———, "Multidimensional Scaling of Similarity," *Psychometrika,* 30 (December 1965), 379–93.

89. Fred T. Tyler, "Some Examples of Multivariate Analysis in Educational and Psychological Research," *Psychometrika,* 17 (September 1952), 289–96.

90. Robert C. Tyron, *Cluster Analysis,* Edwards Bros. 1939.

91. ———, "Cumulative Communality Cluster Analysis," *Educational and Psychological Measurement,* 18 (March 1958), 3–35.

92. J. W. Tukey, "The Future of Data Analysis," *Annals of Mathematical Statistics,* 33 (March 1962), 1–67.

93. J. H. Ward, "Hierarchical Grouping to Optimize an Objective Function," *Journal of American Statistical Association,* 58 (March 1963), 236–44.

94. Joe E. Ward, Jr., and Marion E. Hook, "Application of an Hierarchical Grouping Procedure to a Problem of Grouping Profiles," *Educational and Psychological Measurement,* 23 (1963), 69–82.

95. Harold Webster, "A Note on Profile Similarity," *Psychological Bulletin,* 49 (September 1952), 538–9.

96. Joseph Zubin, "A Technique for Measuring Like-Mindedness," *Journal of Abnormal Social Psychology,* 33 (October 1938), 508–16.

For Discussion

How might factor analysis be used to cluster variables or objects? What are the differences between proximity measures? Under what circumstances would each be preferred? What are the differences between hierarchical routines and non-hierarchical routines?

34

Visual Clustering from a Perceptual Map

David A. Aaker

Cluster analysis or numerical taxonomy, which has been introduced into the marketing literature only recently [5, 7], has shown promise of being a useful tool. The marketing applications of cluster analysis are pervasive and numerous. Brands can be clustered to obtain a feel for market structure. Customers can be cluster analyzed to determine market segments. TV programs can be clustered to answer questions of audience composition more analytically. We could easily extend this list.

Literally hundreds of computer programs are available for performing cluster analysis. Several have been described in some detail in the marketing literature [1, 2, 5, 6, 7, 10]. Each systematically searches through different combinations of objects to try to get "similar" (with respect to a criterion or objective function) objects in the same clusters and "different" objects in different clusters. The number of clusters and the level of clustering will depend upon the data and the objective of the analysis. One can always specify a criterion that would imply only one cluster and another which would place each object in its own cluster. Thus, the researcher is required to specify in some manner the level of clustering desired. With the level specified, the cluster program can be applied to data, and a set of clusters will emerge that is optimal as far as that program is concerned. The user will obtain numerical values associated with the resulting clusters and their objects that provide additional insights into the cluster structure. Although powerful tools, nearly all cluster programs share some rather undesirable attributes. They are relatively difficult to use and interpret, and they are often expensive to set up and to run.

Recognizing these problems with large-scale cluster programs, Kamen [8] recently suggested a "simple but usable technique" for obtaining clusters from a data set. As Kamen observed, his technique, "quick clustering," is crude and its power is limited. However. he correctly notes that, for some researchers in some situations, it can have considerable value.

The purpose of this paper is to describe Kamen's approach and to present a compromise between it and a formal cluster program. The compromise, termed visual clustering, involves obtaining a lower space representation of the objects and visually determining the clusters. Although requiring more effort, such an approach avoids several of the limitations of "quick clustering." It also has several advantages over cluster programs even though it lacks their power and is not presented as a substitute. In the following, visual clustering will be described and then compared with quick clustering in the context of an example.

Visual Clustering

Suppose that consumers' perceptions of brands of coffee were measured along two dimensions, taste (bitter-sweet) and color (dark-light). The brands could then be displayed in a "perceptual map" as in Figure 1. Clearly, three "clusters" of brands can be identified.

Visual clustering shares several problems with other clustering approaches. First, it is usually not so easy to determine which objects should be assigned to which clusters. A cluster program will have a very specific quantitative objective function and a search routine. In visual clustering there is no such aid. In crude terms, one simply stares at the result until clusters emerge. More scientifically, it means that the analyst develops his own heuristic or search procedure compatible with his project objective, to discern clusters from the graphical representation. Such a technique is certainly crude and subjective, but at least the heuristic is exposed. Too often, the objective

Figure 1
Perceptual Map of Coffee Brands

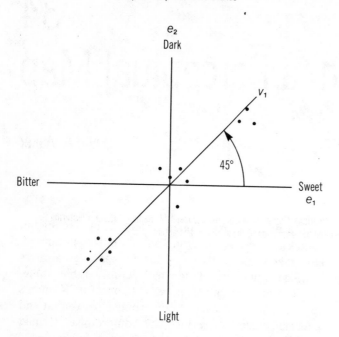

The Perceptual Map

The perceptual map can be obtained in several ways as the section on multidimensional scaling made clear. In particular, similarity or preference data could be used or the perceptual map could be based upon attribute data. If attribute data are used the appropriate techniques are discriminant analysis, factor analysis or principal components. In the example which follows principal components is used.

Principal components, unlike factor analysis, is not a statistical or conceptual model, but is only a set of geometric operations. The objective is to reduce the number of dimensions involved to a small number while retaining, as much as possible, the interpoint distance information contained in the original data set. A simple example will illustrate the axis rotation that is principal components.

Suppose, in Figure 1, it became desirable to work with one dimension instead of two. What single axis could be drawn that would retain as much of the two-dimensional interpoint distance as possible? Clearly, v_1, which can be viewed as e_1, rotated 45°, is the logical candidate. The v_1 component of the interobject distance is shorter than the true distance, but for most object pairs it is not a bad approximation.

More precisely, the object is to project the points from a two-dimensional space to a one-dimensional space so as to retain as much of the squared interpoint distance as possible. The v_1 is that one-dimensional space. When projecting to a two-dimensional space from a higher dimension, the axis v_1 is first found in the same manner. We then ask what axis perpendicular to v_1 should be included. The answer is the axis that will permit us to obtain the maximum amount of squared interpoint distance not contained in v_1. The process is continued until the desired number of dimensions is reached.

function is not deliberately selected by the researcher but is simply the one used in a convenient cluster program and may not really be suitable. More important, a lack of structure is often easier to detect, since the user is not presented with an output listing each cluster member. Such an output can create an illusion of exactness even though one intimate with the program could readily discern the true state of affairs from other measures.

A second problem is how to select the appropriate number of clusters. Here, again, the determination of the number of clusters in visual clustering is entirely subjective, but the visual presentation does admit a good feel for the structure. Such a feel is much more difficult to achieve when working with a cluster program without a great deal of experience with it.

The selection of the original dimensions is a third problem. In the example, it must be determined that taste and color are somehow relevant for purposes of the investigation. In addition, it may be useful to make the resulting display independent of the choice of units. If the dimensions are standardized by dividing all the variables by their respective standard deviations, such independence will be achieved. After standardization, the measures will be the same whether the original units were in feet, yards, or miles. Further, the relative importance of the dimensions must be considered. It is quite appropriate to adjust one dimension (by multiplying its components by a positive constant) to reflect a subjective judgment about its importance (see Morrison [9]).

An Example

To illustrate visual clustering and principal components analysis, the 11 by 11 matrix of correlations shown in Table 1 which was used by Kamen to present quick clustering will be used. The eleven objects are gasoline brands which respondents were asked to rate along a scale from 7 (very favorable) to 1 (unfavorable). The matrix is actually the brand correlations which appeared in one market during a 1965 test.

In quick clustering, the highest entry in each column is underlined. Then the highest such number is noted (0.640), and the brands involved form a cluster (Martin-Owens). If another brand in either the Martin row or the Owens row has an underlined coefficient,

Table 1
Correlations Among Gasoline Brands in Rockford. Illinois, in Terms of General Attitude

		Standard 1	Martin* 2	Shell 3	Texaco 4	Phillips 5	Mobil 6	D-X 7	Owens* 8	Skelly 9	Clark* 10	Gulf 11
Standard	1	—	.006	.358	.382	.325	.289	.262	.108	.368	.178	.404
Martin	2	.006	—	.157	.088	.134	.161	.130	.640	.184	.360	.200
Shell	3	.358	.157	—	.337	.375	.343	.340	.057	.322	.256	.336
Texaco	4	.382	.088	.337	—	.430	.452	.326	.053	.357	.325	.281
Phillips	5	.325	.134	.375	.430	—	.445	.484	.170	.432	.177	.322
Mobil	6	.289	.161	.343	.452	.445	—	.358	.119	.454	.300	.230
D-X	7	.262	.130	.340	.326	.484	.358	—	.110	.393	.301	.180
Owens	8	.108	.640	.057	.053	.170	.119	.110	—	.349	.238	.307
Skelly	9	.368	.184	.322	.357	.432	.454	.393	.349	—	.238	.208
Clark	10	.178	.360	.256	.266	.325	.177	.300	.301	.238	—	.208
Gulf	11	.404	.200	.336	.337	.281	.322	.230	.180	.307	.208	—

* Independent brands. All others are majors.
Reprinted from *Journal of Marketing Research,* published by the American Marketing Association. Joseph M. Kamen, "Quick Clustering," *Journal of Marketing Research,* VII, July 1970, pp. 199–204. Reprinted by permission of the publisher and author.

it is added to the cluster with a link to the appropriate brand—a link that is weaker than that joining Martin and Owens. Clark is thus included in the Martin-Owens cluster with a link to Martin. The procedure then repeats itself on the matrix with brands already clustered deleted. By this method four clusters were found in the data set of Table 1: Owens-Martin-Clark, D-X–Phillips–Shell, Skelly-Mobil-Texaco, and Standard-Gulf. Quick clustering, of course, requires only a pencil and paper. The problem is that it doesn't take into consideration intercorrelations. Further. it provides little feel for the tightness of the clusters, the distance between clusters, and the relative positioning of clusters in the total market structure. Visual clustering overcomes many of these limitations.

Principal components analysis was applied to the correlation matrix. The first five components (as described by "factor loadings"—correlations between the component and the brand) are presented in Table 2.

They provide the coordinates for the first five dimensions in the spatial representation of the eleven objects. Also presented is the percent of total (squared) interpoint distance that is contained in each dimension. The first two dimensions, which are plotted in Figure 2, contain 37 percent of the interpoint distance information. All five dimensions together contain 68 percent.

From Figure 2, it seems clear that Owens and Martin belong in the same cluster. The balance of the figure is less obvious, but the following clusters seem plausible:

1. Owens-Martin
2. Phillips–D-X
3. Clark
4. Texaco–Mobil–Skelly–Shell
5. Standard–Gulf.

Table 2
Output of Principal Components Analysis

Brand	Components				
	1	2	3	4	5
Standard	−.33	.44	.04	.43	−.21
Martin	.76	.05	.02	−.18	.18
Shell	−.24	.06	.32	.10	.62
Texaco	−.35	.09	.05	−.41	−.29
Phillips	−.24	−.35	−.04	.01	−.09
Mobil	−.26	−.10	−.36	−.40	.15
D-X	−.20	−.48	.05	.20	.03
Owens	.74	.10	−.25	.13	−.05
Skelly	−.07	−.07	−.47	.25	−.05
Clark	.29	−.24	.55	−.03	−.31
Gulf	−.12	.55	.10	−.17	−.01
Percent of variation	23	14	11	10	10
Cumulative percent of variation	23	37	48	59	68

Figure 2
Components 1 and 2

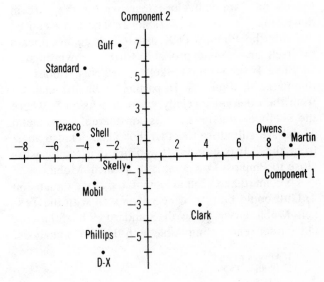

Figure 3
Components 3 and 4

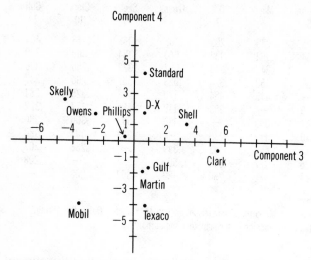

If a high percent of the variation (ideally, 80 to 90 percent) were contained in the first two components or dimensions, the analysis would be complete. However, in this example, such is not the case.

To pursue the analysis further, components 3 and 4 are plotted in Figure 3. Of course, Figures 2 and 3 are not comparable with a four-dimensional graph, and thus the actual "quantity of information" presented is something less than 58 percent. However, this approach does permit one to obtain considerable information on the effect of higher dimensions.

Figure 3 indicates that the structure is not really very well defined and that an unambiguous set of clusters does not exist. This observation, it should be noted, is not insignificant. Often an output which lists several clusters fails to convey this type of conclusion to those not intimate with the program. With the above qualification several judgments emerge. The Owens-Martin pair are still close together (as they are in dimension 5 recorded in Table 2). The same can be said for the Phillips–D-X pair. Clark again appears by itself and should probably form its own cluster.

The Texaco–Mobil–Skelly–Shell cluster does not re-emerge in Figure 3. In particular. Shell seems far from the others, especially when dimension 5, where the Shell coordinate is .62, is considered. Texaco and Mobil are still close together. but Skelly is also apart from these two brands. It appears that Skelly is as close to Phillips–D-X as it is to Texaco–Mobil.

Standard and Gulf are separated along dimension 4. Gulf could be placed nearly as well with the Texaco–Mobil group as with Standard. The following cluster set seems compatible with the above analysis:

1. Owens-Martin
2. Phillips–D-X–(Skelly)
3. Clark
4. Texaco–Mobil–(Skelly)–(Gulf)
5. Shell
6. Standard–(Gulf)

This analysis differs from the quick clustering conclusion in that there are six clusters instead of four and in that two objects are considered to have attachments to two clusters. More important, it provides a different and more intuitive feel for the market structure.[1]

The analysis could continue. We could present the data differently by using a three-dimensional portrayal or by plotting the objects on a space with dimensions 1 and 3 or with dimensions 2 and 4. Dimensions 5 and 6 could be introduced more formally. It would be undoubtedly possible to improve the heuristic itself. However, one reason for visual clustering (as opposed to using a formal clustering program) is to economize on the time and money of the analyst. One does not want to sacrifice this advantage without a worthwhile compensating gain.

Conclusion

There is great heterogeneity in problem situations and in the background of researchers. With this in mind it seems reasonable to suggest alternatives or complements to formal cluster programs. Visual clustering is presented in this spirit. It should provide a compromise in sophistication and cost between cluster programs and Kamen's quick clustering approach.

References

1. Frank, Ronald E., and Paul E. Green. "Numerical Taxonomy in Marketing Analysis: A Review Article," *Journal of Marketing Research*, 5 (February 1968), 83–98.
2. Frost, W. A. K. "The Development of a Technique for TV Programme Assessment," *Journal of the Market Research Society*, 11 (January 1969), 25–44.
3. Gower, J. C. "Some Distance Properties of Latent Root and Vector Methods Used in Multivariate Analysis," *Biometrika*, 53 (1966), 325–337.
4. Green, Paul E., and Frank J. Carmone. "Multidimensional Scaling: An Introduction and Comparison of Nonmetric Unfolding Techniques," *Journal of Marketing Research*, 6 (August 1969), 330–341.

[1] In correspondence with the author. Professor Kamen made the following comment upon this analysis: "I believe that your conclusion is fully justified by your analysis. The method you presented does make sense and overcomes a weakness in the method I presented. For example, Clark, which markets a premium grade only at a price between Majors and conventional Independents, is really in a class by itself, but quick clustering doesn't adequately take this matter into account. In Rockford, we know from other studies that Skelly is psychologically divided as you indicate, that Shell does possess uniqueness, and that Gulf, while most closely linked to Standard, also is related to brands in the two clusters you indicated."

5. Green, Paul E., Ronald E. Frank, and Patrick J. Robinson. "Cluster Analysis in Test Market Selection," *Management Science*, 13 (April 1967), 387–400.

6. Inglis, Jim, and Douglas Johnson. "Some Observations on, and Developments in, the Analysis of Multivariate Survey Data," *Journal of the Market Research Society*, 12 (April 1970), 75–98.

7. Joyce, T., and C. Channon. "Classifying Market Survey Respondents," *Applied Statistics*, 15 (November 1966), 191–215.

8. Kamen, Joseph M. "Quick Clustering," *Journal of Market Research*, 7 (May 1970), 199–204.

9. Morrison, Donald G. "Measurement Problems in Cluster Analysis," *Management Science*, 13 (August 1967), B775–780.

10. Myers, John G., and Francesco M. Nicosia. "On the Study of Consumer Typologies," *Journal of Marketing Research*, 5 (May 1968), 182–193.

11. Neidell, Lester A. "The Use of Nonmetric Multidimensional Scaling in Marketing Analysis," *Journal of Marketing*, 33 (October 1969), 37–43.

12. Sokal, R. R., and P. H. Sneath. *Principles of Numerical Taxonomy.* San Francisco: W. H. Freeman and Company, 1963.

For Discussion

Can you extend the quick clustering approach so that the four clusters can be combined into two or three clusters? Visually cluster the objects in Figure 2 in the Wind and Robinson article in selection 28. Do your clusters differ from those of the cluster program (the circled objects)? Why? What clusters do you see in Figures 2 and 3?

35

The Development of a Technique for TV Programme Assessment

W. A. K. Frost

Introduction and Background

In the past, the information concerning audience reaction that has been available to television programme planners in the independent companies has been largely limited to viewing figures. Such behavioural data is, of course, of vital importance and does contribute to major planning decisions, but it also gives rise to a host of questions concerning the reasons underlying a particular programme's success or failure in attracting an audience.

From time to time sporadic "diagnostic" research has been carried out but this has usually been qualitative and the bulk of it remains unpublished.

The Independent Television Authority, conscious of its obligations under the 1964 Television Act, asked us to consider the feasibility of systematically researching the television audience's attitudinal reactions to the whole spectrum of television programmes on an individual programme basis.

In doing so we were concerned with two broad problem areas, the first of which involved the mechanics of data collection, i.e., panel recruitment, control and maintenance, whilst the second comprised questionnaire design and data processing/analysis. Whilst the two problems are not entirely unrelated it is the second area with which this paper is primarily concerned.

Early Considerations and Rationale

It was decided that some attempt should be made to categorise the various TV programmes in terms of a viewer-based classificatory system and thence to develop specific attitude measuring instruments for each programme category.

A number of alternative methods of arriving at a programme classification were considered and it was decided to attempt to employ a combination of semantic differential and cluster analysis. This lacked some of the disadvantages of alternative techniques and as it was intended to construct specific semantic differentials for any programme types which we might identify there appeared to be a clear advantage in having the information that a generalized semantic differential would yield.

An overall research concept was conceived which involved:

Stage 1. The construction of a semantic differential which would be generally appropriate to all TV programmes.
Stage 2. The use of this semantic differential to collect attitude ratings (programme profiles) of all TV programmes.
Stage 3. The use of cluster analysis to group the obtained programme profiles into categories of "similar" programmes.
Stage 4. The construction of specific semantic differentials—one for each programme type revealed by the cluster analysis.
Stage 5. The use of the specific semantic differentials to obtain programme profiles.

The Research Programme

Stage 1—The Development of the General Semantic Differential. Initially a series of 20 Repertory Grid interviews were carried out and whilst it is not intended to dwell at length on the details of the basic technique or the reasons for using it as a precursor to the construction of a semantic differential as these have been described elsewhere, a few points of rationale and procedure may be worth emphasising.

1. The stimuli employed comprised virtually the whole of the then current ITV and BBC weekly schedules—61 programmes in all. These were, of course, randomly rotated between respondents, with each interview involving 18 programmes.

2. As the scales obtained from these interviews were to be factor analysed it was important that they be as linear as possible, i.e., that the universe of programmes be Normally distributed along them. To this end, and so as to ensure that each of the derived constructs was generally relevant to all TV programmes, respondents were required to divide the programmes into equal groups at the sorting stages. If at these times, respondents found themselves unable to sort into equal groups, they were required to adjust the extremity of the adjectival phrases until equal sorting was possible.

3. After analysis the interviews yielded 58 constructs which were transposed into seven-point semantic differential scales which were felt to be:

   a. Exhaustive.
   b. Relevant to all TV programmes.
   c. Meaningful to the majority of viewers.

The list of scales involved items such as those shown below.

Enjoyable   Unenjoyable

Simple   Lavish

Fictional   Factual

etc.

Next, a random sample of approximately 750 television viewers were asked to provide ratings via the 58 scales of two programmes each. The 61 programmes were rotated randomly between the respondents and a substitution procedure was employed so that no one was required to rate a programme with which they were unfamiliar.

In all approximately 1,500 programme ratings were obtained and this data, being found to be largely devoid of irregularities, was then subjected to a series of Principal Component Analyses, the correlation-coefficients being computed across all respondents and all programmes.

This analysis indicated the presence of nine factors and these are summarised in Table 1.

It should be noted that whilst names have been attached to these factors, this has been done simply

Table 1
Nine General Factors Relating to All TV Programs

Factor
loading

Factor 1 "General Evaluation"
0.85 Enjoyable	Unenjoyable
0.84 Pleasing	Irritating
0.83 Absorbing	Boring
0.79 Grips the attention	Loses the attention
0.69 Well presented	Poorly presented
0.67 Fast	Slow

Factor 2 "Information"
0.89 Little scientific interest	Much scientific interest
0.80 Makes the viewer relax	Makes the viewer think
0.79 Has little information	Has much information
0.75 Pure entertainment	Has educational value
0.73 Has no effect on people	Influences people
0.63 Superficial	Deep/penetrating

Factor 3 "Romance"
0.77 Less of a woman's programme	More of a woman's programme
0.74 More of a man's programme	Less of a man's programme
0.44 Unromantic	Romantic
0.43 Tough	Tender

Factor 4 "Violence"
0.80 Involves crime	Has little to do with crime
0.68 American type	British type
0.54 Fictional	Factual
0.44 Unbelievable	Believable

Factor 5 "Conventionality"
0.73 Unconventional	Conventional
0.54 Informal	Formal
0.52 Unique type of programme	Average type of programme
0.44 Liked by younger people/teenagers	Liked by older people

Factor 6 "Scale of production"
0.69 Lavish	Simple
0.64 Big production	Small production
0.46 Spectacular	Unspectacular
0.44 Much artistic interest	Little artistic interest

Factor 7 "Noise/activity"
0.83 Noisy	Quiet
0.83 Loud	Soft
0.50 Tough	Tender
0.45 Violent	Gentle

Factor 8 "Acceptability"
0.85 Suitable for children	Unsuitable for children
0.44 Much scientific interest	Little scientific interest
0.43 Unsuitable for adults	Suitable for adults
0.38 Family entertainment	Specialist viewing

Factor 9 "Humour"
0.68 Unamusing	Funny
0.65 Little or no humour	Much humourous content
0.55 Serious	Lighthearted
0.44 Does not depend on the personality	Built around the personality

for ease of reference and that the proper interpretation of a factor is to be found amongst the individual attitude scales which have substantial loadings upon it. Thus, for example, Factor 2 called "information" in fact describes a dimension of viewer differentiation which has at one end programmes which tend to have much scientific interest, which make the viewer think and which convey educational information, and which has at the other end programmes which contain little scientific interest which encourage the viewer to relax, being of a less informative and generally more entertaining type.

The nine factors which the analysis yielded were regarded as the basic dimensions of viewer discrimination which are generally appropriate to all TV programmes and to the majority of TV viewers. As such,

they comprise generally valid bases for comparison between any TV programmes.

Stage 2 — General Programme Profiles. Having identified the nine factors used by viewers to discriminate, in a general way, between TV programmes it was possible to compute programme attitude ratings for all of the 61 programmes covered in the survey on each of the nine factors.

There is not room in this paper to show all the results, but an extract of the data is shown in Figure 1.

In Figure 1 the "information" ratings of 14 of the 61 programmes are shown. These are not specially selected cases, but are very typical results and serve to illustrate and confirm our original interpretation of this factor as being a dimension which differentiated primarily between educational programmes and entertainment programmes. Similar results were, in fact, obtained for the other eight factors.

The general semantic differential was therefore producing meaningful results at least. As a check on its potential reliability and ability to discriminate, the differences between the mean programme ratings were tested for statistical significance and it was found that, although the sample sizes for each programme averaged in the region of 25 viewers, factors were discriminating at very satisfactory levels of statistical significance. In fact, all factors discriminated in excess of the 5% level and the majority in excess of the 1% level.

Stage 3 — The Establishment of a Programme Typology by Cluster Analysis. An alternative presentation of the programme ratings to that given in Figure 1 is to examine the programme profiles, i.e., to examine the ratings obtained by a programme on all nine factors simultaneously. Some programme profiles are shown in Figure 2.

It will be seen that the profiles given in Figure 2 appear to fall into two distinct groups in which any of the members of one group are more "similar" to each other than they are to members of the other group. This pattern illustrates the type of result which we were seeking in undertaking a cluster analysis operation.

The programme clusters shown in Figure 2 were derived, along with 18 others, by means of a fairly complex computer analysis which operates on the following broad lines:

1. The frame of reference for the analysis is an *n*-dimensional hyperspace; in this case the hyperspace had 9 dimensions which were the 9 factors in terms of which the programme profiles were computed.
2. The computer, on being supplied with the 61 programme profiles, each of which may be represented by a point in the hyperspace, generated 20 random points within the hyperspace and allocated each programme to the nearest random point. This produced an initial set of 20 clusters of programmes.

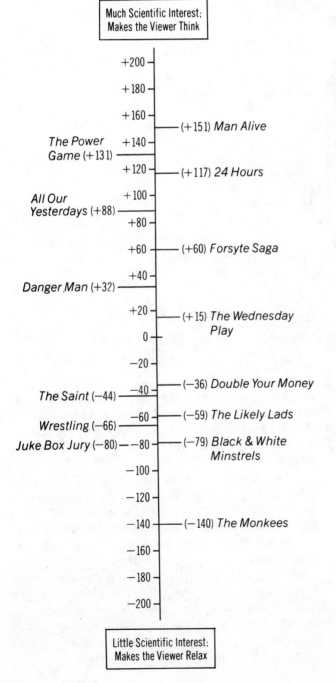

Figure 1
Programme Rating

Factor 2 'Information'

Much Scientific Interest;
Makes the Viewer Think

+200
+180
+160
        (+151) *Man Alive*
The Power +140
Game (+131)
        +120
        (+117) *24 Hours*
        +100
All Our
Yesterdays (+88)
        +80
        +60   (+60) *Forsyte Saga*
        +40
Danger Man (+32)
        +20
        (+15) *The Wednesday Play*
        0
        −20
        −40   (−36) *Double Your Money*
The Saint (−44)
        −60   (−59) *The Likely Lads*
Wrestling (−66)
Juke Box Jury (−80) −80 (−79) *Black & White Minstrels*
        −100
        −120
        −140   (−140) *The Monkees*
        −160
        −180
        −200

Little Scientific Interest;
Makes the Viewer Relax

Figure 2
Profiles of Two Clusters from the 20 Cluster Level

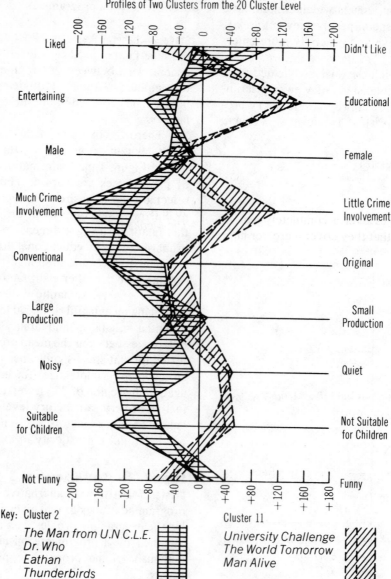

Key: Cluster 2

The Man from U.N C.L.E.
Dr. Who
Eathan
Thunderbirds

Cluster 11

University Challenge
The World Tomorrow
Man Alive

3. Next the original random points were abandoned and the real "centres of gravity" of each of the 20 clusters were computed. Each point was then considered in turn to see if moving the point from its original cluster to its next nearest cluster would effect a reduction in the total residual sum of squares. A point to be borne in mind here is that such a re-allocation will affect the centres of gravity of both the clusters concerned.

4. The analysis proceeded in this way, re-computing the locations of the cluster centres and re-allocating programmes to the closest one, until no further improvements in the clustering were obtained at which time the initial analysis was considered complete.[1]

Following the initial cluster analysis described above, further solutions were obtained by progres-

sively "compressing" the data through 19, 18, 17 clusters and so on down to 2 clusters. At each level of clustering optimisation was achieved iteratively by re-computing cluster centres and re-allocating programmes.

The reason for requiring a range of alternative solutions from which to choose is that there is no very satisfactory way of deciding how many "real" types exist within a particular population. In fact it is important to note that we were not looking for a single "correct" answer. In a sense all of the alternatives which were produced may well have been equally correct. What was required was the identification of a reasonably small number of relatively homogeneous programme types so that any particular programme could be assessed in terms of the ways in which its ratings compared with those of similar programmes.

[1]*Note:* It should be emphasized that provided there is a sufficient degree of clustering within the data, then the precise location of the original 20 random points does not affect the final outcome of the analysis.

In examining the alternative solutions therefore and the selection of one, the main criteria employed were those of interpretability, practicality and general expediency. Of course, it was also possible to examine, in a statistical way, the homogeneity of the programme groups at various levels of clustering and this information was included in our deliberations, but it would be misleading to suggest that the typology with which we eventually proceeded has an absolute basis in reality. In fact, the typology simply represents a convenient way of thinking about television programmes and a useful system for providing bench marks. In addition, of course, it lays the foundations for developing specialised semantic differentials which have two important advantages over a completely general semantic differential in that they cover a greater number of programme attributes and they permit more sensitive measurements.

As was intended the 20 cluster solution provided some interesting insights into the reasons underlying broader programme typologies. It may, therefore, be useful to examine the results of the 20 cluster analyses in some detail before moving on to consider the solution which was eventually adopted.

The 20 clusters that emerged are shown in Table 2. Some of the groupings that occurred are along lines that might have been anticipated. *Cluster No. 4*, for instance, groups the romantic women's programmes together. *Cluster No. 5* groups the pop music programmes together and so on. Some of the groups seem, however particularly strange. *Cluster No. 1*, for instance, which groups *Wrestling* and *Till Death Us Do Part* seems, at first sight, to represent a curious proximity. The factors on which this clustering largely takes place are factors 6, 7, and 9. Both *Wrestling* and *Till Death Us Do Part* are seen as "simple," "noisy" and "funny" and both are also seen as having little scientific interest!

In *Cluster No. 2* which contains the *Man from UNCLE, Dr Who, Batman* and *Thunderbirds*, a number of exciting children's programmes seem to be grouped together. *Man from UNCLE* which is screened comparatively late in the evening would seem to be an exception to this rule; it is, however. the most typical member of the cluster and is actually seen as more suitable for children than is *Dr Who*.

Cluster No. 3 contains some serious programmes which more than anything are seen as suitable for men and also funny. The humour seems to be of a more subtle kind because the programmes are also regarded as being quiet and soft.

Cluster No. 6 contains only one programme, *Bewitched*. This is an example of a programme with extreme scores on a number of factors. It is seen as highly uninformative, highly American, unconventional, funny and suitable for children. A characteristic

Table 2
The 61 TV Programmes Divided into 20 Clusters

Cluster one
Wrestling
Till Death Us Do Part

Cluster two
The Man from UNCLE
Dr Who
Batman
Thunderbirds

Cluster three
The Walrus & the Carpenter
On the Braden Beat
The Frost Programme
Points of View
Late Night Line Up

Cluster four
The Sunday Film
Dr Kildare
Peyton Place
The Love Affair

Cluster five
Top of the Pops
Juke Box Jury
The Monkees

Cluster six
Bewitched

Cluster seven
Emergency Ward 10
The Wednesday Play
Dr. Finlay's Casebook
The Newcomers

Cluster eight
Motor Racing

Cluster nine
World of Sport
Sportsview
Football

Cluster ten
Horse Racing
Boxing

Cluster eleven
University Challenge
The World Tomorrow
Man Alive

Cluster twelve
The Levin Interview
The Epilogue
The Sky at Night
Cricket

Cluster thirteen
The London Palladium Show
The Morecambe & Wise Show
The Andy Stewart Show
The Black and White Minstrel Show
Crackerjack

Cluster fourteen
Coronation Street

Cluster fifteen
Blue Peter

Cluster sixteen
Take Your Pick
Double Your Money
The Likely Lads
The Eamonn Andrews Show

Cluster seventeen
Perry Mason
The Saint
Danger Man
The Virginian

Cluster eighteen
This Week
All Our Yesterdays
The News
24 Hours
Panorama

Cluster nineteen
No Hiding Place
Z Cars
Seaway

Cluster twenty
The Power Game
The Forsyte Saga

of this type of programme profile is that it will only cluster with other programmes at a later stage of the analysis.

Cluster No. 7 is another example of the programmes that are suitable for women. This factor seems to be a particularly important one in discriminating between programmes.

Having examined the 20 cluster solution and all the other levels of clustering the 6 cluster solution was chosen for use in the subsequent stages of the research.

In Table 3 (a)–(f) are given the identity of the programmes in each cluster together with two measurements which assist in the interpretation of the clusters. These are:

1. Distance of programme from the cluster centre.
2. Distance of programme from the centre of the next closest cluster.

In examining these tables it should be borne in mind that the closer a programme is to its cluster centre, the more typical it is of that cluster. Also programmes which are only marginally nearer to their "own" cluster than to the next cluster should really be regarded as fringe items and their current classification treated with some reserve.

Table 3 (a)
The Programmes Comprising Cluster 1 at the 6 Cluster Level

Name of Programme	Distance from Centre of Own Cluster	Distance from Centre of Next Nearest Cluster
Likely Lads	0.791	2.079
Take Your Pick	0.824	1.789
Double Your Money	0.844	1.738
Newcomers	1.083	1.349
Andy Stewart Show	1.089	1.874
Eamonn Andrews Show	1.139	1.357
The Morecambe & Wise Show	1.150	2.233
London Palladium Show	1.199	2.134
Crackerjack	1.482	2.375
The Walrus & the Carpenter	1.484	2.078
Points of View	1.539	1.992
Juke Box Jury	1.672	2.121
The Black and White Minstrel Show	1.752	2.286
Coronation Street	2.005	2.428
Till Death Us Do Part	2.064	2.483
Blue Peter	2.072	2.755

The particular aspects which characterise programmes within Cluster 1 (Table 3a) and therefore the cluster as a whole, are those concerned with relaxation and entertainment (rather than being informative), little or no crime content, suitability for children and general family viewing and, finally, a fairly strong element of humour and light-heartedness. For easy reference, it would be useful to apply a composite label to each cluster and Cluster 1 can be most conveniently labelled "Family entertainment programmes."

The peculiar characteristics of Cluster 2 (Table 3b) are that programmes within it are seen as being particularly uninformative, highly unconventional/informal, noisy and suitable for children. We feel that the most suitable general label to apply to this cluster would be "pop programmes."

Table 3 (b)
The Programmes Comprising Cluster 2 at the 6 Cluster Level

Name of Programme	Distance from Centre of Own Cluster	Distance from Centre of Next Nearest Cluster
The Monkees	1.140	2.580
Dr Who	1.156	2.446
The Man from UNCLE	1.249	2.027
Thunderbirds	1.282	2.347
Batman	1.359	3.158
Top of the Pops	1.507	1.826
Bewitched	1.935	2.509

Table 3 (c)
The Programmes Comprising Cluster 3 at the 6 Cluster Level

Name of Programme	Distance from Centre of Own Cluster	Distance from Centre of Next Nearest Cluster
Seaway	0.693	1.926
Danger Man	0.882	2.094
Z Cars	0.946	1.408
The Virginian	0.999	1.876
No Hiding Place	1.133	1.587
Perry Mason	1.215	1.843
The Saint	1.352	1.811
Wrestling	1.436	1.772
The Frost Report	1.796	1.977

Cluster 3 (Table 3c) is characterised by a "violence" content (as indeed was Cluster 2), but it differs markedly from our so-called "pop programmes" in being much more suitable for adult viewing. Cluster 3 may therefore best be referred to as the "Adult crime/violence" cluster.

Table 3 (d)
The Programmes Comprising Cluster 4 at the 6 Cluster Level

Name of Programme	Distance from Centre of Own Cluster	Distance from Centre of Next Nearest Cluster
The Sunday Film	0.869	1.448
Emergency Ward 10	0.965	1.531
Love Affair	0.993	1.938
The Wednesday Play	0.996	1.297
Dr. Kildare	1.069	2.166
Dr. Finlay's Casebook	1.315	1.740
Peyton Place	1.417	2.512
The Forsyte Saga	1.933	2.474

Apart from consisting of "quiet" programmes, Cluster 4 (Table 3d) is particularly characterised by its feminine appeal and clearly justifies the title of "Women's romance" programmes.

The particular characteristics common to programmes in Cluster 5 (Table 3e) are that they are seen as being highly informative, unromantic and more suitable for men, very quiet and very much for adult viewing. It therefore seems reasonable to label this the "Intellectual" cluster of programmes.

Table 3 (e)
The Programmes Comprising Cluster 5 at the 6 Cluster Level

Name of Programme	Distance from Centre of Own Cluster	Distance from Centre of Next Nearest Cluster
24 Hours	0.622	1.591
This Week	0.668	1.507
World Tomorrow	0.796	2.036
Late Night Line Up	0.836	1.585
All Our Yesterdays	0.957	1.255
Panorama	0.994	1.641
University Challenge	1.151	1.762
The Sky at Night	1.195	2.717
On the Braden Beat	1.355	1.511
Man Alive	1.376	2.196
The Levin Interview	1.696	2.894
Cricket	1.776	2.436
The Power Game	1.890	2.842
The Epilogue	1.949	2.492

Table 3 (f)
The Programmes Comprising Cluster 6 at the 6 Cluster Level

Name of Programme	Distance from Centre of Own Cluster	Distance from Centre of Next Nearest Cluster
World of Sport	0.723	2.129
Football	0.753	1.962
Sportsview	0.973	2.009
Horse Racing	1.114	2.203
Motor Racing	1.174	1.901
Boxing	1.393	2.246
News	1.500	1.680

Two programmes are conspicuous by their absence from Cluster 6 (Table 3f), *Cricket* and *Wrestling*. Subjectively, one might easily have included them under a general "sports" heading. In *viewers'* terms, however, watching cricket is more of an intellectual exercise (hence its inclusion in Cluster 5), whilst *Wrestling*, quite unlike the sports programmes, is considered to have a high humorous content as well as undertones of crime, violence and Americanism and, indeed an element of fiction and unbelievability. This places *Wrestling* firmly in Cluster 3.

In order to summarize the characteristics of the six programme clusters, mean profiles for each cluster are given in Figure 3. These profiles are very different from one another and this observation together with a statistical examination of the data supports the view that each of the clusters is dramatically more homogeneous than the parent population of all TV programmes.

Stage 4 — The Development of Specific Semantic Differentials.
Having established a working programme typology it was necessary to examine each of the programme types in order to see whether there was any truth in our earlier belief that different programme types would be construed by viewers in different attitudinal frameworks and would, therefore, require measurements along different dimensions.

As a first check six separate factor analyses were carried out on the data from each of the six clusters. The factor structures which emerged were quite different and whilst some of the factors emerged relatively unchanged in other cases factors disappeared altogether and totally new factors emerged. Some of the changes were, of course, due to changes in the properties of the scales which, having been derived for the whole universe of programmes, had distributions which were severely skewed when they were applied to a single programme cluster. Despite this effect, however, there was clear evidence that the actual meanings of many of the scales were changing from context to context.

At this point the problem of developing six specific semantic differential batteries had to be faced and, as the whole project was essentially a pilot operation, it was not possible to carry out quite such a thoroughgoing preparation in all six areas.

In fact, an examination of the data already to hand, together with a few additional Repertory Grid interviews in each of the clusters, led to the somewhat subjective development of six separate batteries of semantic differentials scales.

A survey was then carried out in which each of these semantic differential batteries was used to collect approximately 350 ratings of appropriate TV programmes. The six sets of data so obtained were factor analyzed and the factor structures for the six programme types provided some interesting comparisons.

Table 4 shows the number of factors which emerged in each of the clusters.

Table 4

Cluster 1	15 Factors
Cluster 2	10 Factors
Cluster 3	12 Factors
Cluster 4	11 Factors
Cluster 5	12 Factors
Cluster 6	6 Factors

It will be seen from this result alone that viewers used more elaborate conceptual frameworks to construe some types of programme than they used for others.

Furthermore, a close inspection of the emergent factors showed that no factor was entirely appropriate for all programme types. Some factors appeared to express the same basic notion from cluster to cluster and might, therefore, be given the same general label in each case. However, the content of these factors (i.e., constituent scales and their loadings) usually changed quite markedly from one cluster to another. Even the General Evaluative factor which would have been expected, on theoretical grounds, to be more or

Figure 3
Mean Profiles for Each Cluster at the 6 Cluster Level

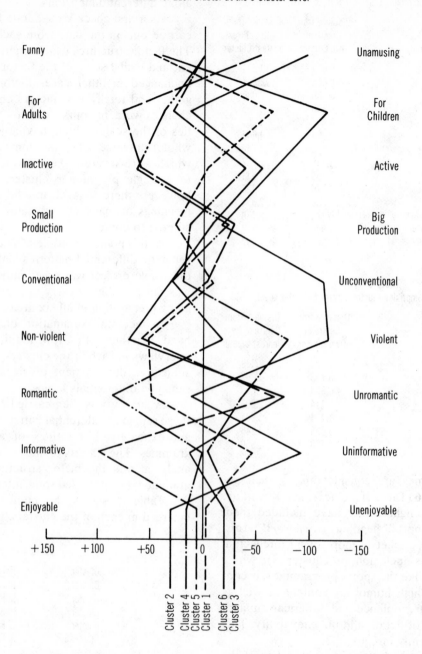

less the same for all programme types showed some degree of inconsistency for. although some words such as "enjoyable" tended to load highly on the evaluative factors in all the clusters, in the case of the "pop" programmes the highest loading words were "trendy," "fast," and "much action," whilst in Cluster 5 which contained the more intellectual programmes the highest loading evaluative words were "lasting interest" and "absorbing."

The information in Table 5 is an attempt to represent, in summary, the results of the six factor analyses. As has been already mentioned no single factor was common in a precise way to all programme clusters.

However, it was possible in a subjective way to recognize certain basic notions which were frequently common to several of the clusters. The table shows that approximately 23 such basic notions were identified in all, and in addition it gives the distribution of these notions throughout the six programme clusters.

Stage 5—The Specific Semantic Differentials in Use. The final stage of the pilot consists of a panel operation extending over five weekly reporting periods. During this time panelists were required to rate the television programmes which they had seen on appropriate sets of semantic scales. In those cases where respondents

Table 5
The Distribution of Various Factors throughout the 6 Programme Clusters

	Cluster 1 Family Entertainment	Cluster 2 Pop	Cluster 3 Adult Crime/Violence	Cluster 4 Women's Romance	Cluster 5 Intellectual	Cluster 6 Sports
"Evaluation"	•	•	•		•	•
"Age appropriateness"	•	•	•	•	•	—
"Noise" ⎫	•	⎧ •	•	—	•	•
"Activity" ⎬		⎨ •				
"Violence" ⎭		⎩ •				
"Sex appropriateness"	•	—	•	•	•	—
"Suitability for children"	•	—	•	•	•	—
"Reality/credibility"	•	•	•	—	•	—
"Formality"	•	—	•	•	•	•
"Profundity" ⎫ "Heaviness"	⎧ •	—	•	•	•	—
"Information" ⎭	⎩ •					
"Dependence on a personality"/ ("Individualism")	•	—	•	•	•	•
"Scale of production"	•	•	•	—	•	•
"Conventionality"	•	—	•	•	•	•
"Addictiveness"	•	•	•	•	—	•
"Romance"	—	•	•	•	—	—
"Humour"	—	—	•	•	—	—
"Intelligibility"	—	•	•	•	•	—
"Star content"	—	—	•	•	•	—
"Impartiality"	—	—	•	•	•	—
"Importance of event"	—	—	—	—	—	•
"Presentation/commentary"	—	—	—	—	—	•
"Visibility"	—	—	—	—	—	•

• Indicates that a factor is operative in the cluster

were giving ratings of programmes which had already been classified they were directed to employ the sets of scales which were specifically relevant to the cluster of programmes concerned. In some cases, however, respondents had been exposed to television programmes which were not being screened when the programme typology was established, and in these cases they were instructed to use an abbreviated set of the general (all programmes) semantic differential, the intention being to attempt to allocate new programmes to clusters within the established typology if possible.

In examining the data obtained from the pilot panel operation we were particularly concerned with the following three questions:

1. Were the specific semantic differentials sufficiently sensitive given the sample sizes obtained?
2. To what extent was it possible to allocate new programmes to categories within the existing typology?
3. Were the results obtained meaningful to the people who were required to use them, that is to say, did the findings contribute to their understanding of viewers' behavioral reactions towards the programmes?

1. The Sensitivity of the Instrument. In all, the semantic differentials were extremely successful in differentiating between programmes. Not only did they succeed in distinguishing between programmes from the same cluster but, in many cases, significant discrimination was obtained between consecutive programmes of the same series.

2. Allocating New Programmes to the Existing Typology. In all 26 new programmes were studied and of these 21 were easy to classify within the existing programme categories. For the five remaining programmes it was possible to see in each case precisely why they were difficult to classify. This result suggests that because of the continual development of new programmes and new programme concepts it is unlikely that a completely permanent and stable typology can be arrived at.

On the other hand a classificatory system which caters for the majority of programmes is likely to prove viable for a useful period of time, i.e., one or two years. It seems probable, therefore, that such a system may be used provided it is up-dated at regular intervals.

3. The Meaningfulness of the Results. The detailed results obtained have been considered in the light of programme content and whilst in many cases they appear to have been somewhat predictable, in others they do appear to have been genuinely informative.

It is, of course, extremely difficult to measure success in this area but an encouraging number of favorable reactions have been received from people within the programme companies and the Independent Television Authority.

In summary, therefore, we would conclude that the pilot panel operation has been successful and has confirmed the viability of the basic research concept. It must, however, be emphasised that the study, although fairly elaborate, was in fact only a pilot and consequently a great many questions of detail remain unanswered and much work has yet to be done.

References

1. Bannister, D. (1962) "Personal construct theory: a summary and experimental paradigm." *Acta Psychol.* XX. 2.
2. ——— (1966) *A new theory of personality — New horizons in psychology.* Penguin Books Ltd.
3. Emmett, B. P. (1968) "The exploration of inter-relationships in survey data," *J. Market Research Soc.,* 10, pp. 65–77.
4. Frost, W. A. K. and Braine, R. L. (1967) "The application of the repertory grid technique to problems in market research," *J. Market Research Soc.,* 9, pp. 161–175.
5. Gatty, R. (1965) *Factor analysis for market research — usefulness and limitations.* (Paper to American Marketing Association Marketing Research Group, New York City.)
6. ——— (1966) "Multivariate analysis for marketing research: an evaluation." *Appl. Statist.,* XV. 3.
7. ——— and Allais, C. (1961) *The semantic differential applied to image research.* New Brunswick, N.J.: Rutgers University, Technical A.E. No. 5.
8. ——— and Heim, R. (1961) *The application of factor analysis to marketing research.* New Brunswick, N.J.: Rutgers University, Technical A.E. No. 2.
9. Harman, H. (1960) *Modern factor analysis.* Chicago University Press.
10. Joyce, T. and Channon, C. (1966) "Classifying market survey respondents," *Appl. Statist.,* XV, 3.
11. Kelly, G. A. *Psychology of personal constructs.* Volumes I and II. New York: Norton.
12. Kendall, M. G. (1957) *A course in multivariate analysis.* New York: Hafner.
13. Osgood, C. E., Suci, G. J., and Tannenbaum, P. H. (1957) *The measurement of meaning.* University of Illinois Press.

For Discussion

Explain how Figures 1 and 2 were generated. What is the significance of the "distance from the centre of own cluster" and the "distance . . . of next nearest cluster" information in Table 3? How is it used? Interpret Figure 3.